RUSSIA'S ROSWELL INCIDENT

And Other Amazing UFO C(
Soviet Un

By
Paul Stonehill and Ph.... Mantle

Noe Torres, Editor

RUSSIA'S ROSWELL INCIDENT
First edition published in 2012 By Roswell Books and in 2017 by FLYING DISK PRESS
FLYING DISK PRESS
4 St Michaels Avenue
Pontefract
West Yorkshire
England
WF8 4QX

Published by
FLYING DISK PRESS

1

CONTENTS

INTRODUCTION

"According to Aleksand Krivenyshev, a Russian-American scientist, an interesting mathematical correlation exists between the world's three majoralleged UFO crashes – the suspected crash in Tunguska, Russia, in 1908, the1947 crash near Roswell, New Mexico, and the Dalnegorsk, Russia, crash of1986. These three events are separated by an interval of 39 years, which is 13times 3 -- a very significant number in numerology." -- Noe Torres, UFO researcher and author.

Unidentified objects have been seen both on land and in the sea throughout Russia's history. In addition to an in-depth analysis of two reported UFO crashes, each of which has been called "Russia's Roswell Incident," our book also gives you an overview of the most important cases, observations, and sightings in the lands formerly known as the Soviet Union. Russia is a huge country. Many of its areas, especially in Siberia, Far Eastern provinces and the Arctic regions, have not been completely explored even today, in the early 21st century. During the last one hundred years Russia has gone through bloody revolutions, wars, transformations of its economy, purges, famine, invasions, and other life-shattering events. Millions of Russians perished in concentration camps created by Soviet Marxist Leninists and German National Socialists. Hundreds of thousands, if not millions, died from famine and starvation. Others were exiled, banished, maimed, their lives torn apart by terrible events of the 20th century, by totalitarian onslaught on humanity. And yet, even in the darkest of times, there were those in the USSR who had observed strange and perplexing unidentified flying or submersible objects and found ways to preserve their observations. Such anomalous phenomena had been of great interest to Soviet Union's rivals throughout the nation's existence, as readers find out in our book. Such anomalous phenomena had never escaped attention of the Soviet rulers and the nation's Armed Forces. Since UFOs were a forbidden subject for citizens of the Soviet Union, this book mostly contains UFO reports by scientists, pilots, military personnel, cosmonauts, and other Soviet "officials" with a high enough standing to risk telling their stories. As a result, the reader will not find accounts from random, run-of-the-mill citizens who, after their encounter, ran to the local newspaper to "tell all." Instead, the UFO sightings in this book are mostly from sources generally considered to be "highly reliable," including many highly-trained observers such as astronomers, cosmonauts, and aircraft pilots. We express our sincere appreciation to those who have helped us in our endeavour -- Mikhail Gershtein, Vadim Chernobrov, Anatoly Kutovoy, Genrikh Silanov, Nikolay Subbotin, and many other former Soviet and contemporary UFO researchers -- kind, decent, intelligent, and open-hearted people dedicated to the pursuit of knowledge.

Paul Stonehill and Philip Mantle

CHAPTER 1:

RUSSIA'S ROSWELL INCIDENT

THE DALNEGORSK CRASH

Early in 2012, media headlines throughout the United States announced, "Russian Roswell UFO Artefact Featured at National Atomic Testing Museum in Las Vegas." For most Americans, it was their first exposure to one of the world's most intriguing UFO stories since the reported crash of a UFO near Roswell, New Mexico, in July 1947. The mysterious 1986 crash-landing of a spherical flying object on a hill in the town of Dalnegorsk in South-eastern Russia was finally getting the attention it has long deserved. At the National Atomic Testing Museum, an affiliate of the Smithsonian Institution, a clear glass case displays glassy spheres and bits of metal in vials recovered from a red orb that streaked over the Russian mining town of Dalnegorsk and crashed into Mount Izvestkovayaon January 29 1986. The exhibit's description reads: "Three Soviet academic centres and 11 research institutes analyzed the objects from this UFO crash. The distance between atoms is different from ordinary iron. Radar cannot be reflected from the material.

"Elements in the material may disappear and new ones appear after heating. One piece disappeared completely in front of four witnesses. The core of the material is composed of a substance with anti-gravitational properties." The case is notable because of this extremely strange trace evidence, which continues to puzzle scientists today. It is also noteworthy because of recently released Central Intelligence Agency (CIA) documents, obtained through the Freedom of Information Act (FOIA), which indicate that the U.S. intelligence community apparently took a great interest in the Dalnegorsk UFO crash. *Document in CIA Files about Dalnegorsk UFO Crash*

 Some of the scientists have concluded that the object that crashed into Hill 611 was an "extraterrestrial" space vehicle constructed by highly intelligent beings. Doctor of Chemical Sciences V. Vysotskiy stated that "without doubt, this is evidence of a high technology, and it is not anything of a natural or terrestrial origin." He cited the fact that the remnants of fine mesh included bits of thin threads with a diameter of only 17 microns and that these threads, in turn, were composed of even thinner strands twisted into braids. Extremely thin gold wires were discovered intertwined in the finest threads—evidence of an intricate technology beyond the present capabilities of terrestrial science, according to Vysotskiy.

Document in CIA Files about Dalnegorsk UFO Crash

In *Document Release 42346*, the CIA received a brief from the Foreign Broadcast Information Service Group (FBIS) that talks of "an amazing event that took place on Hill 611 near the village of Dalnegorsk in Primorskiy

Kray." According to the brief, "Many observers saw a flying sphere crash into one of the hill's twin peaks. Scientists examining the crash site later found 'fine mesh,' 'small spherical objects,' and 'pieces of glass' that are considered to be small remnants left behind by the sphere. According to the article, the alleged spacecraft

was nearly obliterated in the crash, but there appears to be enough material at the site for the scientists … to eventually 'penetrate this mystery.'"

Photo of Dalnegorsk with Impact Site Marked

The brief goes on to state that a scientist, A. Makeyev, reported finding gold, silver, nickel, alpha-titanium, molybdenum, and compounds of beryllium. The brief then makes a shocking statement, "Some of the scientists have concluded that the object that crashed into Hill 611 was an 'extraterrestrial' space vehicle constructed by highly intelligent beings. Doctor of Chemical Sciences V. Vysotskiy stated that 'without doubt, this is evidence of a high technology, and it is not anything of a natural or terrestrial origin.' He cited the fact that the remnants of fine mesh included bits of thin threads with a diameter of only 17 microns and that these threads, in turn, were composed of even thinner strands twisted into braids. Extremely thin gold wires were discovered intertwined in the finest threads – evidence of an intricate technology beyond the present capabilities of terrestrial science, according to Vysotskiy." The same document goes on to deliver another shocker, stating that Russian physical scientist, Vladimir Azhazha was convinced of striking similarities between the Dalnegork UFO crash and the 1947 Roswell, New Mexico, UFO crash. "He [Azhazha] believes there is sufficient evidence to support the claims of UFO crashes in both cases – in Dalnegorsk and in Roswell."

The POISK article contrasted Platov's view with that of another physical scientist, Vladimir Azhazha, who was recently elected chairman of the new All-Union Commission for the Study of Unidentified Flying Objects of the Union of Scientific and Engineering Societies. Azhazha compared reports of a UFO crash in the USSR with a claim by UFO enthusiasts in the United States that a UFO had crashed in the desert near Rosvell, New Mexico, in 1947. He believes there is sufficient evidence to support the claims of UFO crashes in both cases--in Dalnegorsk and in Rosvell. In the latter case, he cited the testimony of eyewitnesses who maintained that they had seen the bodies of four extraterrestrials lying near the smashed spacecraft.

One additional mention of Dalnegorsk occurs in *CIA Document Release 43370*, which reports that a meeting of UFO researchers from both Russia and China was held in Dalnegorsk in 1990 to "exchange video and photographic materials" regarding UFOs. According to the brief, Dalnegorsk was not chosen "by chance" for this UFO summit. "In the last few years the number of cases of visual observation of UFOs has noticeably increased there (in Dalnegorsk). In just the last four years alone, no less than 10 UFOs have been recorded. Specialists link their [UFOs'] heightened interest i

in places here with the variety and wealth of useful minerals in maritime Kray." The mystery of Dalnegorsk continues to grow, although admittedly many scientists believe that what crashed on Hill 611 was not extraterrestrial, with explanations ranging from a fallen, secret Russian space probe to fragments of NASA's space shuttle Challenger, which broke apart on lift off the day before the Dalnegorsk event. These explanations sound rational if one ignores the hundreds of other UFO sightings that have taken place in and around Dalnegorsk both before and after the alleged UFO crash on January 29, 1986. Also strange is the fact that the object that crashed on Hill 611 was described by witnesses as a solid metal sphere, rather than something jagged or already starting to break apart.

SOURCE: MOSCOW DOMESTIC SERVICE IN RUSSIAN 2100 GMT 21 MAY 90
TEXT:

((TEXT)) A REPORT FROM VLADIVOSTOK -- SCIENTISTS OF THE PRC AND THE SOVIET FAR EAST HAVE BEGUN JOINT STUDY OF UFO'S. THE FIRST MEETING OF UFOLOGISTS OF THE TWO COUNTRIES HAS ENDED IN THE SMALL MARITIME TOWNLET OF DALNEGORSK. THE SOVIET AND CHINESE SPECIALISTS ON ANOMALOUS PHENOMENA HAVE MAPPED OUT A PROGRAM FOR INVESTIGATING INCIDENTS THAT ARE ALREADY KNOWN AND HAVE ALSO ARRANGED TO DIRECTLY EXCHANGE VIDEO AND PHOTOGRAPHIC MATERIALS ON NEW SIMILAR PHENOMENA. DALNEGORSK HAS NOT BEEN CHOSEN BY CHANCE AS THE PLACE FOR SUCH ACQUAINTANCE. IN THE LAST FEW YEARS THE NUMBER OF CASES OF VISUAL OBSERVATION OF UFO'S HAS NOTICEABLY INCREASED THERE. IN JUST THE

UNCLASSIFIED

Approved for Release
JUN 1994

LAST FOUR YEARS ALONE NO LESS THAN 10 UFO'S HAVE BEEN RECORDED. SPECIALISTS LINK THEIR HEIGHTENED INTEREST IN PLACES HERE WITH THE VARIETY AND WEALTH OF USEFUL MINERALS IN MARITIME KRAY. SIMILAR INCIDENTS HAVE ALSO OCCURED IN MOUNTAINOUS REGIONS IN CHINA WHOSE CLIMATIC CONDITIONS AND NATURAL LANDSCAPE RESEMBLE OUR OWN.
ADMIN
(ENDALL) 212100 ⬛⬛⬛ 23/0830Z MAY
BT

#5072

NNNN

Document in CIA Files about Dalnegorsk UFO Crash

The Russian news agency Pravda had this to say about what happened at Dalnegorsk: "An unidentified flying object has crashed in the Far East. Hundreds of people witnessed the event. The UFO crashed into the rocky mountains located in the town of Dalnegorsk. A strange spherical object has slightly brushed upon the mount at approximately 8:00 p.m., January 29th, 1986. Witnesses claim they saw a bright flash but did not hear anything. The glow from the fire appeared rather strange: blue aureole lasted for about an hour and a half."

The late Leonard Stringfield, an American UFO investigator who was the first to focus primarily on UFO crashes, commented about the Dalnegorsk crash in his 1991 publication *Status Report VI, UFO Crash/Retrievals: The Inner Sanctum* (pages 74-82): "The latest UFO crash in the USSR happened on January 29, 1986. Shortly before 8:00 p.m., dozens of witnesses in the city of Dalnegorsk in eastern Siberia near Vladivostok observed a ball-shaped object, flying parallel to the ground before crashing with an angle of 60-70 degrees in the 611 meter (2,004 foot) high 'Hill 611' or 'Izvestkovaya Mountain' in the center of the city. The reddish glowing object had a speed of 45 feet/second before it crashed. According to the eyewitnesses, it jumped up and down for some time before it finally crashed into the mountain,

exploded soundlessly and burned for nearly an hour. "On February 3, 1986, an expedition of the Far East Department of the Investigation Committee for Anomalous Aerial Phenomena of the Academy of Science led by Dr. Valery Dvuzhilny arrived in Dalnegorsk, starting the investigation.

Photo with Diagram Showing Approximate Path of Falling Object
(Courtesy of Kosmopoisk - Vadim Chernobroiv)

"The scientists discovered many fragments, including lead and iron balls, bits of glass, traces of high temperature activity, magnetic anomalies, damage to nearby trees and the most mysterious discovery - a fine mesh of netting woven out of inert metal threads out of an alloy of gold, silver, nickel, alpha-titanium, molybdenum and beryllium. One of the scientists who analyzed the material, V. Vysotky, Doctor of Chemistry at Vladivostok University, came to the conclusion in his man-paged investigation report that, 'This fine metallic webbing is undoubtedly a high-technology product and not a thing of natural or terrestrial origin.' He supposed the object in question was an automatic scout probe of alien origin. Some of the threads, Dr. Vysotky pronounced, were only 17 microns thick and even woven with even finer material - impossible for terrestrial technology (of the time)." Stringfield goes on to summarize the initial sighting and crash of the Dalnegorsk object: "The UFO which made a crash landing on January 29, 1986, was spotted at 7:55 p.m. Its speed was 15 m/s. The unidentified object seen over Dalnegorsk (Soviet Union) on January 29,

1986, at 7:55 p.m., had a solid cover that was ball-like and was stainless steel color. It did crash land at the altitude of 611 meters (2,004 feet), leaving behind samples of

steel alloys, ferrous balls, and the so-called 'netting' type samples. It also had strange effects on the humans, animals and radio sets. The samples of ferrous balls have a very high degree of solidity. It could not be cut by steel instruments, but only by diamond. These have very complex composition. They contain almost all the elements in the Mandeleyev table, such as Fe (iron), Mn (Manganese), Ni (Nickel), Mo (Molybdenum), W (Tungsten), and SiO2 (Silica dioxide, or quartz sand), Co (Cobalt), Cr (Chromium). Whence melted in the vacuum, strange glass-like structures appear. The carbides of the metal elements are absent.

Leonard Stringfield

"As mentioned before, the sample of the 'netting' element is made of amorphous carbonaceous materials with metal atoms standing separately. The basic elements ¬ carbon basis, Zn (Zinc), Ag, Au, La, Pr, Si, Na, K, Co, Ni, Y and many others. It is almost impossible to interpret its structure. It resists the acids. When a temperature of 2800 Centigrade is applied to it in the air, some elements would disappear and new elements appear instead. In vacuum heating, gold, silver and nickel disappeared and molybdenum and beryllium sulphide appeared. The latter disappeared after five months. This does prove, however, that we are dealing with artificial materials. The great quantity of organic matter might be the sign of a type of life still unknown to us. "Before the heat application, the 'netting' is a dielectric substance. During the course of the heating, it becomes a semi-conductor and in vacuum heating, it is a conductor. After three years, the site of this incident still has some effect on the humans. It affects the blood and causes reduction in leukocyte and bacilli increase. It also causes high blood pressure, fast pulse and sense of unknown fear. The site still affects the film imprint and simply erases it. "The flint samples collected from the site are magnetized. But to magnetize a flint is as impossible as magnetizing a brick!

The site suffered a temperature of 4,000 C. during the crash, and the radiation of an unknown nature. Vegetation is still affected by this radiation. The chemical composition of the steel alloy and the iron corresponds with the high content in peat after the Tunguska so-called meteorite aerial explosion (June 30, 1908): Pr (Praseodymium), La (Lanthanum), Y (Yttrium), Pb (Lead), Zn (Zinc), Fe (Iron). The type of the radiation is identical." Stringfield concluded his report on the Dalnegorsk UFO crash by stating, "It is obvious that we are dealing with a spacecraft of an unknown civilization."

UNITED STATES SPACE COMMAND
PETERSON AIR FORCE BASE, COLORADO 80914-5003

Dr Armen Victorian   2 6 MAR 1991
P.O. Box 99
West PDO
Nottingham NG8 3NT
England

Dear Dr Victorian

This replies to your 13 February 1991 Freedom of Information Act
(FOIA) request for any records concerning a satellite reentry on
28, 29, or 30 January 1986 in Dalengorsk, Primorsky region of USSR
(Far Eastern part of USSR).

A search was accomplished of applicable records and all reentries
in the 28-30 January 1986 window found no large objects with
ground paths crossing eastern USSR near Dalengorsk, Primorsky.

Portion of Letter from Leonard Stringfield's Files on Dalnegorsk

Additional important evidence for those who think the Dalnegorsk object was just a piece of space junk is a letter that was published by Stringfield along with his article about the Dalnegorsk case. The letter, dated March 26, 1991 is from Colonel Jerry W. Felder of the United States Space Command at Peterson Air Force Base in Colorado and is addressed to UFO researcher Dr. Armen Victorian. In the letter, the colonel states "This replies to your 13 February 1991 Freedom of Information Act request for any records concerning a satellite re-entry on 28, 29, or 30 January 1986 in Dalnegorsk, Primorsky region of USSR (Far Eastern part of USSR. A search was accomplished of applicable records and all re-entries in the 28-30 January 1986 window found no large objects with ground paths crossing eastern USSR near Dalnegorsk, Primorsky." The letter goes on to state that "the search found two objects that decayed on 27 January 1986 with a ground path passing over the far eastern part of the USSR. The first, object 16506, International Designator 1986-001D, was a piece of debris from Cosmos 1715 which was launched on 8 January 1986. It decayed on 27 January 1986 at 0145Z at 30.0S/275.1E. "The second piece, object 16430, International Designator 1985-120B, was a rocket body from Cosmos 1713 which was launched on 27 December 1985. It decayed on 27 January 1986 at 2313Z at 35.3S/266.2E. Although the predicted decay time for both these objects did not fall over Dalnegorsk, Primorsky area, it is possible that a piece from one of these two objects, especially the rocket body, remained in orbit half a revolution longer and then decayed over Eastern USSR."In addition, several small pieces of debris decayed over the 28 through 30 January time-frame. No decay and impact predictions were made on these objects. They are all significantly smaller than the two objects mentioned above and it is highly unlikely that any of these four pieces of debris survived re-entry."

Now, we shall backtrack and look carefully at how the Dalnegorsk even unfolded. As previously noted, this most unusual of UFO cases took place on January 29, 1986 at 7:55 p.m. Some people still refer to it as the Roswell Incident of the Soviet Union.

The information about it was sent to the Russian Ufology Research Center by several Russian ufologists. Alexander Rempel also provided us with the actual report of Dr. Dvuzhilni.

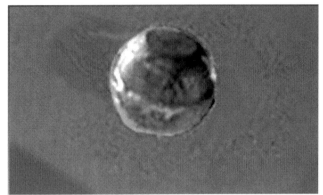

Artist's Conception of Dalnegorsk Object (Courtesy Noe Torres)

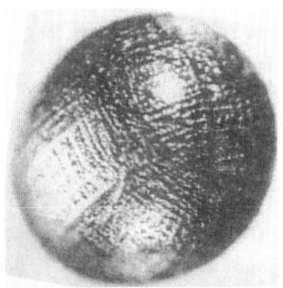

One of the original silver balls

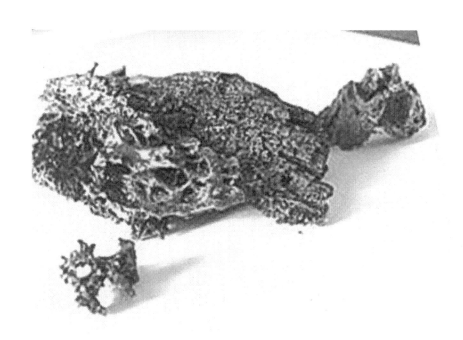

Mesh-like fragment found on Height 611

Hill 611 showing location of crash site

In 1897 a small mining settlement was established in the Russian Fareast; it carried a name that in Chinese means Valley of Wild Boars, or Tetyukh. American movie star Yul Brynner's grandfather, emigrated from Switzerland to Russia at the end of the 19th century and developed mining in the area. In 1972, the settlement received a new name, Dalnegorsk, during a campaign by the Soviets to eradicate Chinese-sounding place names. At that time, China and Russia were engaged in a deadly competition that included occasional armed skirmishes. Dalnegorsk did not become a full-fledged town until 1989. This picturesque town is located in a narrow valley alongside the

Rudnaya River, surrounded on all sides by forests and hills. A number of deep caves dot the area.

The internationally famous Dalnegorsk UFO incident took place in 1986, on January 29, at 7:55 p.m. Some have called it the Roswell Incident of the Soviet Union. Data and photographs about the case were sent to the Russian Ufology Research Center by several Russian ufologists. Alexander Rempel also provided us with the initial actual report by the main investigator, Dr. Dvuzhilni. On that cold January day in 1986, a reddish sphere flew into Dalnegorsk from the southeast, overflying a section of the town, before crashing at the Izvestkovaya Mountain, also known as Height or Hill 611, because of its height (611 meters or 2,004 foot). The object flew parallel to the ground, without making any sound at all. Its shape was a near-perfect sphere approximately three meters (9 feet) in diameter, with no projections or cavities. The object's color was described as similar to that of burning stainless steel. An eyewitness, V. Kandakov, said that the speed of the UFO was close to 15 meters per hour (about 50 feet per hour). The object slowly ascended and descended, and its glow would become more intense every time the UFO would rise. On its approach to Hill 611, the object "jerked," and fell down like a rock.

All witnesses reported that the object "jerked" or "jumped." Most of them recall two "jumps." Two girls remember that the object actually "jumped" four times. The witnesses heard a weak, muted thump. A fire was visible at the edge of a cliff on Hill 611 for about an hour after the crash. Some researchers believe the object that crash landed on Hill 611 suffered damage and shed debris on the hill but later managed to regain flight and escape, mostly still intact, in a north-easterly direction, only to crash later -- probably in the surrounding, dense boreal forest known as *taiga*. A geological expedition to Hill 611, led by V. Skavinsky of the Institute of Geology and Geophysics of the Siberian Branch of the Soviet Academy of Sciences (1988), confirmed the object's movements through a series of chemical and physical tests of the rocks collected from the site. Valery Dvuzhilni, head of the Far Eastern Committee for Anomalous Phenomena, was the first to investigate the crash. The case was also investigated by Soviet scientist and ufologist Anatoly Listratov, who was later involved in the government's secret UFO research group SETKA, and several other ufologists. Although some Western researchers wrote about the case, no one has heretofore presented the accurate account of all that has happened.

Dr. Valery Dvuzhilny in Dalnegorsk

Prior to his involvement in the Dalnegorsk case, Dr. Dvuzhilni, a trained biologist, had witnessed a UFO during a 1980 expedition to Kamchatka, a peninsula in the Russian Far East. He became frightened when he observed a strange disc landing near a 290-foot-deep lake. Dr. Dvuzhilni arrived at the site two days after the crash. Deep snow covered the area, as is typical in January. However, the site of the crash, located on a rocky ledge, was totally devoid of snow. Dvuzhilni found, all around the site, remnants of silica, which was "smoky" looking and had been splintered due to high heat. Many of the silica pieces, and a nearby rock, contained traces of a silvery metal, some of which was in the form of solidified balls and some of which looked like it had been "sprayed" on. At the edge of the site a tree-stump was found, which Listratov allegedly still has in his possession, which emitted a strong chemical smell.
The objects collected at the site were later described as "tiny nets" (or mesh), "little balls," "lead balls," and "glass pieces," based on their appearance. Closer examination revealed very unusual properties. One of the "tiny nets" contained torn and very thin (17 micrometers) threads. Each of the threads consisted of even thinner fibers, tied up in plaits. Intertwined with the fibres were very thin gold wires. Soviet scientists, at such facilities as the Omsk branch of the Academy of Sciences, analyzed the collected pieces. The results of the analysis, while highly technical, yielded an extraordinary general conclusion: that the technology to produce such materials was not yet available on Earth in 1986.

To give an idea of the complexity of the composition of the pieces, let us look at the "iron balls." Each of them had its own chemical composition: iron and a large mixture of aluminium, manganese, nickel, chromium, tungsten, and cobalt. This analysis suggests that the Dalnegorsk Object was not just a piece of lead and iron, but was of heterogeneous construction, having been "made" from various alloys with differing characteristics.

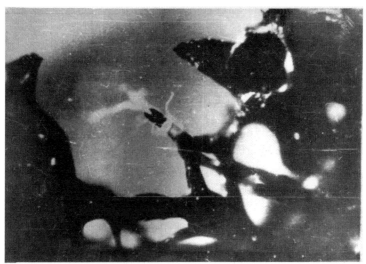

Close-up of Wire Mesh (Courtesy Mikhail Gershtein)

When melted in a vacuum, some pieces would spread over a base, while at another base they would form into balls. Half of the balls were covered with convex, glass-like structures. Neither the physicists nor metallurgists can say what these structures are or what their composition is. Also, the "tiny nets" (or "mesh") have confused many researchers. It seems impossible to understand their structure and nature of the formation. A. Kulikov, an expert on carbon at the Chemistry Institute of the Far Eastern Department of the Academy of Sciences, USSR, wrote that the nature of the mesh is also a great unknown. It resembles glass carbon, but exactly how it was formed is unknown. Conventional methods involving the use of fire could not produce such glass carbon.

The most amazing aspect of the Dalnegorsk crash debris was discovered when pieces containing gold, silver, and nickel were melted in a vacuum. To the astonishment of scientists, the elements "disappeared" and were replaced, seemingly out of nowhere, by molybdenum, which was not present in the chamber at the start of the experiment. Molybdenum does not occur as a free metal on Earth. Traces of it have been found on both iron and stone meteorites.

Остатки обугленного пня (Далёни горах)
Tree Stump from Hill 611

In summarizing their exhibit of debris from the Dalnegorsk crash, the National Atomic Testing Museum in Las Vega, Nevada, noted, "Three Soviet academic centres and 11 research institutes analyzed the objects from this UFO crash. The distance between atoms is different from ordinary iron. Radar cannot be reflected from the

material. Elements in the material may disappear and new ones appear after heating. One piece disappeared completely in front of four witnesses. The core of the material is composed of a substance with anti-gravitational properties." The only material found at the Dalnegorsk crash site that seemed to have "normal" characteristics was the ash found on Hill 611. It was clear that something biological was burned during the crash. Perhaps the ash came from some unfortunate wildlife caught in the blast, or might it be possible that one or more living beings were burned to death inside the crashed object?

Photo of Debris at Crash Site (Courtesy Mikhail Gershtein)

Photo of Dalnegorsk (Wikipedia.org)

Much of what we know about Dalnegorsk comes from the work of the main investigator in the case, Dr. Valery Dvuzhilni, who published an article titled "Dalnegorski Phenomena" in the Soviet Uzbekistan Magazine *NLO: Chto, Gde, Kogda?* In his article, Dvuzhilni gave many details about the Dalnegorsk event that had never previously been released.

The south-western trajectory of the object coincides roughly with the Xichang Cosmodrome of People's Republic of China, where satellites are launched into geosynchronous orbit with the help of the Great March-2 carrier rockets. However, there is no data of any rocket launches occurring at the PRC at the end of January 1986. Meanwhile, China's Xinhua Press Agency reported that, two years after Dalnegorsk, in January 1988, a glowing red sphere was sighted near the Chinese Cosmodrome. The object, which almost exactly matched the description of the Dalnegorsk Object, hovered for 30 minutes. Is it possible that UFOs were conducting some form of surveillance on the activities of Chinese rocket launches in the years 1989 and 1988?

Проведение геофизических работ на высоте 611.

Scientists Investigating Dalgenorsk Crash

In another curious detail about Dalnegorsk, what appeared to be volcanic ash (tuff) of a light grey color was discovered on Hill 611, but only in the area directly contacted by the mysterious object. This tuff did not match any of the local varieties of soil. Even more amazing is that spectroscopic analysis of these tuff specimens matched them to the Yaroslavl tuffs of the polymetalic deposits. In other words, the specimens

resembled tuffs from the Yaroslavl area, located 160 miles northeast of Moscow – nearly 6,000 miles from Dalnegorsk! The samples did not match the characteristics of tuffs found in the Dalnegorsk area. Some researchers have theorized that the Dalnegorsk Object "collected" samples of tuff in the Yaroslavl area prior to arriving in Dalnegorsk. Tuffs experience metamorphosis when exposed to high temperatures.

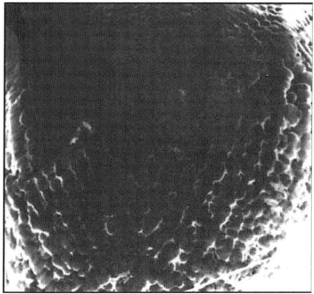

Close-up of Dalnegorsk Fragment

In addition to the amazing trace evidence found on Hill 611, the site itself soon gained a reputation as an "anomalous zone," characterized by the presence of strange forces that seemed to affect both plants and animals in the area. These strange effects seemed to remain "active" for about three years after the crash. Insects avoid the place. Humans entering this anomalous zone experienced sudden and unexplained changes in blood chemistry, pulse rate, and heart rate. They also suffered loss of coordination and loss of sensation in various parts of the body. Some people, including a local chemist, actually got very ill. The zone also affected mechanical and electronic equipment. Additional mysterious effects were noted in an article in the Soviet digest *Tainy XX Veka* (Moscow, 1990). According to the article, photographs taken at the site, when developed, failed to show the hill, although they did clearly show surrounding terrain. Also, members of an expedition to Hill 611 reported that their flashlights stopped working upon arrival at the site. When they checked the flashlights upon returning home, they discovered burned wires.

On February 8, 1986, eight days after the Dalnegorsk UFO crash, at 8:30 p.m., witnesses observed two yellowish spheres flying from the north and heading south over the town. When the UFOs reached the site of the Dalnegorsk crash, they circled it four times, as if searching for something. The objects then turned back to the north and flew away. The following year, on Saturday, November 28, 1987, the skies over

the Dalnegorsk area suddenly lit up at 11:24 p.m., as 32 flying objects appeared, seemingly out of nowhere. Flying in formation, the objects were witnessed by hundreds of local residents, including members of the military. The objects flew over 12 different settlements around Dalnegorsk. Thirteen of the objects flew directly over Dalnegorsk and Hill 611. During this mass sighting, witnesses observed that at one point, while three of the UFOs hovered over Dalnegorsk, five others flew over Hill

611 and seemed to be illuminating the site of the 1986 crash. The objects moved noiselessly, at altitudes varying between 500 and 2,600 feet. Most of the eyewitnesses thought they were seeing aircraft involved in some kind of search and rescue mission, looking for a downed aircraft. Other witnesses thought they were seeing falling meteorites. As the objects flew over the town, they caused interference with the local television signals and telegraph functions. Ministry of Internal Affairs officers, who were present, testified later that they observed the objects at precisely 11:30 p.m. while standing on a street in Dalgenorsk. They noted one fiery object, flying in from the direction of Gorely settlement. In front of the fiery "flame" was a lustreless sphere, and in the middle of the object was a red sphere. Other eyewitnesses included workers at the Bor rock quarry. At 11 p.m., they observed a giant cylindrical object flying straight at the quarry. The workers estimated the object's length at between 600 and 1,000 feet! UFO researchers usually refer to objects of such a massive size as "mother ships." The front part of the object was lit up, like burning metal, and the quarry workers were afraid that the object would crash down upon them. One of the managers at the quarry, a Mr. Levakov, made his own UFO observation, independent of the workers, at 11:30 pm. What he saw was a huge, cigar-shaped object moving very slowly across the sky at an altitude of about 1,000 feet. The witness stated that he was well acquainted with aerodynamics, knew the theory and practice of flight, and did not believe that such a massive object could fly noiselessly through the air without wings or engines. Another eyewitness, a kindergarten teacher named Markina, saw a different type of craft. She observed a blindingly-bright, spherical craft moving through the sky without sound at an altitude of between 90 to 135 feet. In front of the sphere, Markina observed a dark, metallic-looking elongated object 30 to 40 feet long. As the object hovered over a local school building, it emitted a "beam" or ray that was violet-blue in color and about two feet in diameter. The beam illuminated the ground below, but witnesses said that the hovering object itself did not cast a shadow on the ground. The strange object and hovered over them. While over a mountain, it emitted a red light beam that shone down as if it were a powerful searchlight. The object seemed to be searching for something in the general area of the 1986 Dalgenorsk UFO crash. After some time, the "search beam" flicked off, and the object departed, flying over the mountain. Research on these Dalgenorsk sightings indicated that no rocket launches took place at any of the Soviet Cosmodrome either on January 29, 1986, the date of the Dalgenorsk crash, or on November 28, 1987, when the mass sighting of 32 objects took place.

Площадка взаимодействия объекта с горными породами

Hill 611

Is it possible that the Soviet military staged fake "UFO" flights to confuse and mislead ufologists and Western intelligence services? To recap, the objects observed on November 28, 1987 consisted of different shapes: cigar-like, cylindrical, and spherical. Their flight was noiseless, smooth, at various altitudes. Most witnesses thought they had observed some type of aircraft. While in flight, the objects affected power lines throughout the area. Lieutenant Zhivayev of the Interior Ministry troops described the object he observed as a flame with a lustreless sphere in the front and a reddish ball in the rear. And three workers from the Bor quarry--Bistryancev, Anokhin, and Grigoriyev -- saw a giant cylindrical object at an altitude of about 1,000 feet. Its front part was illuminated, like melting metal.

Regarding the Dalnegorsk UFO crash, Dr. Dvuzhilni, the principal investigator in the case, reached the conclusion that a malfunctioning space probe of extraterrestrial origin crashed into Hill 611. Perhaps the additional sightings in February 1986 and November 1987 were of UFOs that had come to survey the original crash site? There remain today many differing opinions on what exactly crash-landed on Hill 611 in 1986. Journalist V. Psalomschikov, an expert on aircraft crashes, has stated that the object was most likely manufactured in the USSR and was probably a Soviet-built spy vehicle of some kind. Psalomschikov believes that the debris found at Hill 611 represents technology that was available as far back as the 1970s. He has stated that he has found ultra thin filaments, such as those found at the crash site, which were

21

manufactured in the USSR in the 1970s. The problem with his theory, however, is that Soviet space probes of the era were all rigged to immediately self-destruct upon crash-landing, whereas the Dalnegorsk Object reportedly tried to lift-off again several times and may have actually succeeded.

In 1993, Russian ufologist, scientist, and author Gennady Belimov also proposed that what crashed on Hill 611 was a Soviet military probe. As support for his theory, he offered documentation on other crashes of highly classified Soviet probes. He concluded that ufologists misinterpreted the evidence from the Dalnegorsk crash, and that what crashed there was actually a secret probe. As for the lead collected at the site, Belimov believes it was extracted from the Kholodnensky deposit in the Northern Baikal region. New generations of Russian UFO researchers, expressing their views on various Internet forums, have proposed that the probe may have been an aerostat (balloon) reconnaissance vehicle that was possibly equipped to take infrared photographs. Proponents of the aerostat theory point to the very slow speed of the Dalnegorsk Object as evidence that it did not have a sophisticated means of propulsion. But even among the new breed of UFO researchers, there is no consistent belief as to the origin of the probe. Vladimir Smoly, for example, does not think the object was a Soviet probe, due to the apparent lack of a thermite self-destruction device aboard. If it had been a Soviet probe, it would have self-destructed immediately, which is not what happened at Height 611. Could it have been a NATO probe? V. Psalomschikov pointed out that even NATO reconnaissance balloons were rigged for self destruction, at one time utilizing TNT and later thermite. A TNT-equipped probe fell on a house in the USSR and then destroyed itself and the house; fortunately, the home was not occupied at the time of the explosion. The Soviet government filed a protest against NATO over the mishap, and the incident was even debated at the United Nations. After that, NATO probes were equipped with thermite, which does not explode, to minimize potential fatalities in the event of a crash.

Another researcher, Vladimir Smoly, believes the Dalnegorsk Object was an aerostat created for entertainment or advertising purposes. This theory, however, does not take into account that the object left a clearly defined "trail" as it moved across the sky, according to researcher M. Gershtein. The trail suggests that the object was not a balloon moved only by the wind holding it aloft. Something else, heretofore unknown in the West, took place in the town of Khabarovsk that could shed some light on what happened in Dalnegorsk. Khabarovsk is located approximately 400 miles south-southeast of Dalnegorsk. According to Alexander Rempel, in a report published in the Vladivostok newspaper *Priroda* in July 1991, a fiery object was observed over the Khabarovsk on the night of August 24, 1978. The object was about a four feet in diameter, and at one point in its flight, it emitted a hissing or "whooshing" sound, like a jet engine does. The area around it became illuminated, as bright as if were daylight. As the object descended slowly, it lit up very brightly. An explosion ensued, causing the soil all around the area to be burned, despite the presence of much water. After the incident, pieces were found throughout the area of a coal-like substance containing holes and glasslike structures.

For ten years after the Khabarovsk event, the soil remained burned and barren. No vegetation of any kind grew at the site of the explosion. Eyewitnesses reported that a dark object flew away just before the explosion, but no trace of it was ever found. Ten years later, Rempel and his colleagues received numerous reports about an "anomalous zone" near Khabarovsk. Some investigators claimed that the Khabarovsk object did indeed fall to the ground and that it caused many strange anomalies in the area for years afterward. Yet, at the time, Rempel could not confirm these reports, because the military had sealed off the area. Later, following the Dalgenorsk incident, Remple and his group investigated an area where the Dalnegorsk Object allegedly fell after it flew off the Hill 611, and they discovered some similarities to the Khabarovsk explosion site. Among other anomalies, Remple and his group found unusual mutations among the local wildlife.

A new angle to the Dalnegorsk UFO crash was introduced in December 2000, when the Russian newspaper *Komsomol'skaya Pravda* published an article about the case ("NLO svili v Primorye gnezdo") by Andrey Pavlov. The article stated that, in the early 1990s, Russian Air Force generals grew so alarmed over the frequent UFO sightings in the Dalnegorsk area that they actually offered to work with local UFO researchers and exchange information on UFO sightings with them! It is extremely rare for a mainstream Russian newspaper to ever mention anything about government involvement in UFO investigations. The author of this particular article actually quoted Dr. Dvuzhilni, the chief investigator of the Dalnegorsk UFO crash. In another article about the crash, published in the Soviet newspaper *Ribak Primorya* (Issue 14, 1991), author Y. Vasilyev sought to discredit Dvuzhilni's "extraterrestrial" hypothesis by claiming that Dvuzhilni's original visit to the crash site did not disclose anything other than traces of a meteor impact. According to Vasilyev, Dvuzhilni and a group of his students arrived at the site, searched the area thoroughly three times, and found tiny metallic drops. All required measurements were taken, and photographs were taken. Then Dvuzhilni's group initiated physical and chemical analyses of the findings. The temperature at which the metallic debris melted was 390 degrees Celsius. At that temperature, the silvery metal became very soft and could be easily broken with a pair of tweezers.

According to the article, about a week after the crash, on February 8, 1986, Dvuzhilni and V. Berliozov, a geologist who had studied the Sikhote- Alin' meteorite again ascended the hill. It was during this second trip that geologist Berliozov proposed that the crashed body was "cosmic" in origin and that the trace evidence affirmed this. Its luminescence was similar to that of usual meteorites. According to Vasilyev's article, Dvuzhilini did not start making claims of an extraterrestrial origin until five years later. Vasilyev refers to the ET hypothesis as "fantastic." According to Alexander Rempel (*NLO Magazine*, 1999), over time, fewer and fewer Russian ufologists seemed interested in investigating the 1986 Dalnegorsk event. However, interest in the case has actually been growing outside of Russian ufology circles. Rempel pointed out that fragments of the crashed object have been examined in Vladivostok, Khabarovsk, Munich, Liege, and other places. In 2000, four Japanese and Korean expeditions examined the crash site at Hill 611.

Ufologists from Korea and Japan have made offers to purchase the "balls." Recent, the going rate for one gram of any Dalnegorsk fragment was $500, and the price has been going up. Although there have been offers of up to $1,500 per gram, demand continues to exceed supply. The Dalnegorsk debris has been studied at numerous institutes and laboratories in Russia and abroad, with widely differing results. Scientists have yet to definitively prove that the Dalnegorsk object was manufactured on Earth. Neither can they definitely prove that it was of extraterrestrial origin. The only thing that can be definitely stated is that there remain some peculiarities about the fragments that still cannot be adequately explained. Since the year 2000, no further reports have been received of any "anomalous" events at Hill 611. Although interest in the case seems to have dwindled among many Russian ufologists, that is certainly not true of ufologists in Vladivostok, which is a major Russian port city located about 300 miles southwest of Dalnegorsk.

Vladivostok's UFO Museum boasts an exhibit related to the Dalnegorsk incident, featuring debris collected at the crash site. An exhibit about the crash can also be viewed at a museum in Dalnegorsk. And, as previously noted, fragments from the Dalnegorsk crash have been exhibited abroad, including a major exhibit that opened in April 2012 at the National Atomic Testing Museum in Las Vegas, Nevada. In retrospect, the evidence available in the Dalnegorsk incident consists mostly of eyewitness testimony and sketches drawn by witnesses. There were dozens of actual eyewitnesses and many drawings, but no photographs exist of the UFO. The only other "proof" is the trace evidence found at the crash site, including the aforementioned "spheres" and wire "mesh."

Artist impression of the HEIGHT 661 crash: Copyright Daniel Ramirez

Numerous individuals known as *kontaktyori*, who claim to be in contact with extraterrestrial civilizations, have written books and created paintings about the Dalnegorsk crash. Some years ago, they predicted that a UFO would land at the Dalnegorsk stadium on a certain date. Attracted by the prediction, thousands of Russian citizens arrived in Dalnegorsk at the appointed time, but nothing happened. Some of those hoping to meet the "aliens" remain in Dalnegorsk today … in the local mental asylum. The RUFORS Round Table members, including Anatoly Kutovoy, as well as Vladimir Smoly's UFO Forum participants, have discussed the case and actively exchanged scientific information about it. As interest in the case has grown overseas, the Russian media has lately also paid some attention to the event, too.

Another possible explanation has been proposed. On January 28, 1986, American shuttle Challenger disintegrated at an altitude of 46,000 feet above the Atlantic Ocean. The catastrophe scattered fragments all over the Atlantic.

Some researchers wonder if it might be possible that one of the fragments, flying from the southwest, travelled 7,000 air miles and landed in Dalnegorsk on the following day. This seems unlikely, however, because none of the pieces of the shuttle reached an altitude higher than 65,000 feet, which is well below sub-orbital flight, before they rained down on the ocean. In addition, it seems improbable that pieces from the Challenger could have travelled in the air without propulsion to finally land in southeast Russia. Also, the initial sighting of the Dalnegorsk object mentions a smooth, metallic sphere, rather than something jagged or deformed, as wreckage from the shuttle would be.

Hill 508

In 2010, the Dalnegorsk official site (*http://www.dalnegorsk.ru*) published Valdimir Popov's article about Dr. Dvuzhilni's latest research. According to the article, Dvuzhilni may have found evidence of very ancient UFO visitations in the Dalnegorsk area. He researched and performed detailed analyses of rocks excavated during drilling of a borehole for one of the supports of the bridge to connect Cape Nazimov with Russkiy Island. The Russian scientist claims to have found alloys of rare earth metals in sedimentary rocks -- sandstones from the Permian Period, 299 to 251 million years ago. Dvuzhilni is currently the head of the Far East division of Kosmopoisk (international Russian paranormal research organization) and is also a researcher for the Meteorites and Space Dust Commission of the Siberian Branch of Russia's Academy of Sciences.

Dvuzhilni took probes of the soil seeking traces of ancient meteorites. As a result of his research, he collected metallic fragments of different configurations. Initially, he thought he had found remnants of an ancient meteorite. Scientists have found evidence of huge meteorites having fallen about twenty million years ago at the site of modern Seoul and the Sea of Japan. These impacts left craters about 7-12 miles in diameter. Hence, some fragments of the meteorites might have fallen on the territory of modern Primorye Province. However, Dvuzhilni's samples had a distinctive metallic shine that suggested they were something other than meteorites. Dvuzhilni immediately sent the fragments to a senior Russian nuclear scientist, Igor Okunyev. He asked that special attention be paid to a small pyramid with five-millimetre facets.

Okunyev took the fragments, and used the most precise equipment to analyze them. He found out that the pyramid consisted of iron (60%), cobalt (20%), and tungsten (20%). This was 100% alloy, yet there are no meteorites that contain such alloys; and no such alloy exists on this planet. Other fragments collected by Dvuzhilni were equally as unusual.

Okunyev offered as a possible explanation that a torpedo exploded in the area. Some torpedoes do have tungsten skin. But Dvuzhilni's pyramid was excavated from the 29-foot deep layer of sedimentary quartzite, which is a depth to which torpedoes could not penetrate. If we take into the account that many thousands of tons of meteorites have fallen on Earth and none of them contains tungsten-containing alloys, then according to Valeri Dvuzhilni, there is only one explanation -- this pyramid was part of some flying extraterrestrial apparatus that had visited the area about 250 million years ago.

Valdimir Popov's article insisted that Dvuzhilni forces no one to accept his sensational explanation. Using tables received from Okunyev's institute in Gatchina, Dvuzhilni points to spectral analysis for each of the fragments sent to Saint Petersburg, focusing on the high percentage of the rare earth metals in the excavated alloys. Popov's article disclosed another important finding. On December 17, 2009, Dvuzhilni held a press-conference in the Dalnegorsk Administration Center. He reported findings from the Cape Nazimov, as well as summarized results of his latest research in the Terneyski area of the Primorsky Krai. Primorsky Krai, informally known in Russia as Primorye, is a federal subject of Russia (a krai). Primorsky means "maritime" in Russian, and in this book, we sometimes refer to the area as Maritime Province.

For seven years Dvuzhilni had worked in the forested area of Hill 508, next to Sobolevka Village. A site was found at Hill 508 that indicated the surrounding terrain had been exposed to extremely high temperatures. According to Dvuzhilni, this was caused by the near approach of a UFO. On one of the slopes of Hill 508, Dvuzhilni found a very strange, small crater, measuring 65 feet deep and 147 feet in diameter. Okunyev, who received samples of charcoal from Dvuzhilni, determined that the crater is 750 years old. That's important, because it puts to rest the notion that the crater was caused by Japanese bombs during World War II. Volcanic activity was also ruled out as an explanation for the crater. An examination of the surround soil failed to uncover any evidence of a meteorite.

2009 when he discovered various metal fragments at the site. Recovered from a depth of ten centimetres was a 3.5-centimeters-long tetrahedral rod that contained a sharp point of a raven (black) hue. He immediately sent the rod to Okunyev for scientific investigation, and the Russian physicist was shocked by what his analysis showed. Although it was mostly iron (86%), it also contained a very unusual mix of elements - - a half percent each of manganese, strontium, and samarium; 0.7 percent of barium; and one and a half percent each of Lanthanum and Gadolinium. Okunyev informed his Far eastern colleagues that no such alloys were produced in the USSR or abroad. Dvuzhilni and his colleagues are certain that their discovery was an alloy -- not a meteorite. Okunyev concluded that the rod found at Hill 508, and another found at another site in Terneyski, were composed of ferrite alloys of artificial origin that could not be produced on Earth. Humankind is not as yet capable of producing such alloys, according to Dvuzhilni. Russian Far Eastern ufologists are convinced that Hill 508 contains traces of extraterrestrial activities, or perhaps remnants of a crashed UFO.

Our research indicates that the Russian nuclear scientist who conducted the analyses of Dvuzhilni's latest finds, Igor Okunyev, is affiliated with the Petersburg Nuclear Physics Institute (PNPI), which is an official State Research Center of Russia. More information about the institute can be found at
http://www.pnpi.spb.ru.

Although the claims of finding extraterrestrial artefacts may seem outlandish to some, Dvuzhilni is not overly surprised by the results, because he has never doubted his assertion that the region been visited by extraterrestrial beings on numerous occasions. Dr, Dvuzhilni told reporter Larisa Rekova, of the *Utro Vostoka* newspaper (March 26, 2011), that he dreams of establishing a UFO museum in Dalnegorsk. He has the support of former Soviet cosmonaut Viktor Petrovich Savinykh [more about him in chapter four]. Dvuzhilni told Rekova that he gave an artefact from the Hill 611 crash to Savinikh.

Ufologists from a number of countries have visited the Dalnegorsk area. Some have gathered in Dalnegorsk on World UFO Day in July. In January of 2012 researchers from Kosmopoisk, Dalnegorsk-Kosmopoisk, and Granat organizations visited the Maritime Province to study anomalous sites, including Hill 611 and the Nikolayevskaya Cave, which is located about 310 miles from Vladivostok. At Hill 611, they collected several more burned rocks and Dvuzhilni gave his Kosmopoisk colleagues several artefacts recovered in the area, as well as results of his latest research. Kosmopoisk has shared some of the artefacts with those who are interested in their research.

Many researchers think that the Hill 611 crash may have a conventional explanation, but exactly what remains to be seen. It does have its parallels in the West -- the Roswell case being one of them. It remains a fascinating case that is sure to divulge more information and more theories in years to come.

CHAPTER 2:

RUSSIA'S "OTHER" ROSWELL

THE 1908 TUNGUSKA CRASH

JUNE 30, 1908, 7:17 AM

This case has also been labelled as "Russia's Roswell Incident," and it was perhaps the most famous Russian UFO case of the early 20th century. "Something" burst in the air over Siberia on June 30, 1908, flattening more than 1,300 square miles of forest but leaving no crater and no evidence of what caused the event. Over 100 years after the Tunguska incident, scientists are still not sure what struck Siberia. Some investigators have claimed it was an unidentified flying object that exploded perhaps due to a malfunction of its onboard power plant. The question of what actually happened over Tunguska has been on the minds of Russian scientists, researchers, and ufologists since at least the 1920s. Some of those who studied the phenomenon died in concentration camps; some perished while conducting research; others were ostracized, forgotten, or crushed underfoot during Russia's bloody 20th century. There remain conflicting viewpoints about the Tunguska event, even regarding the direction from which the object(s) came. Some researchers question whether what struck Tunguska was an actual, physical "object" or something else altogether. In our search for an answer, we have looked at numerous reports from eyewitnesses. We have studied reports of animal mutations in the affected area, as well as looking at the overall ecological impact of the explosion. Although many theories have been proposed, Russia's most important UFO event remains no closer to being solved. This chapter presents the many varying points of view on the Tunguska event and will look at the ongoing quest to solve its mystery. The Tunguska, a vast area, remains a wilderness, full of mosquito-infested swamps and marshes. While the surrounding taiga [boreal forest] is spectacularly beautiful, the journey required to reach this remote and desolate wilderness has been described as sheer hell. The native people of the area are the Evenk, indigenous nomads whose lineage results from a mix of ancient Eastern Siberian populations with Tungus tribes arriving from the Baikal Lake area in about 1000 C.E. At one point in Russia's history, the Evenks were the most numerous people in Siberia. Evenks lived in the taiga which extends from the River Irtysh to the Sea of Okhotsk, including the territories of the River Lena, the River Angara and Lake Baikal. They were hunters, reindeer herders, and fishermen. Currently, the Evenk population numbers only about 2,000 people.

THE STRANGE YEAR OF 1908

The year 1908 was marked by a number of astronomical and atmospheric anomalies. According to Pesach Amnuel, an Israeli astrophysicist and writer of Soviet Jewish origin, solar activity was higher than normal in 1908. Y. Koptev, in an article published in *NLO Magazine* (Issue 2, 1997) described strange phenomena in the skies over Russia prior to the Tunguska event and which possibly were related to it

According to Koptev, on a clear morning on February 22, residents of the Russian town of Brest observed a bright, V-shaped object in the north-eastern sky, moving in a northerly direction. Oddly, as the object's size grew larger, its brightness diminished. Within half an hour, the strange object was barely visible off to the northeast. In April, a huge, and rather odd-looking, meteorite fell to Earth in the Kovelskaya Province, in the Novoaleksandrovsky district. According to local newspaper accounts, the space rock slammed into the ground near some railroad tracks, causing a nearby train to slam on its brakes. After the train came to a stop, its passengers got off to look at the strange meteorite, which was mostly buried in the soil, with only its very top section visible. Very strange in appearance, the rocky mass was white in color. In the autumn of that year, yet another meteorite exploded over the Teletsky Lake, scattering its fragments all over the surrounding landscape. In September, a meteorite was observed flying over the city of Melitopol.

In the summer and autumn of 1908, it literally rained meteorites throughout the East, as revealed by archival documents from that period. Many areas experienced an extraordinary increase in the number of observed bolides (small meteorites). Estimates suggest that three times the number of meteorites were reported in 1908 as in any previous year. Newspapers throughout the world published reports about these meteorites, as strikes were reported in European Russia, the Baltics, Siberia, Central Asia, China, and England. There were observations of additional phenomena. From June 17 through 19, in the area of the Middle Volga in Russia, local residents were astonished to see a sight that does not normally appear at their latitude -- the Aurora Borealis (northern lights). Meanwhile, residents of the Orlovskaya Province were at loss to explain the sudden appearance of strange, silvery clouds in the sky. Several days later, people in the suburbs of Yuryev city (now known as Tartu) and other areas were amazed to see purple-colored skies at sunrise, something which they had never seen before.

It seemed as if nature was preparing itself for something highly unusual to occur. Beginning on June 21, people in a number of European areas as well as some in the Western Siberia observed very bright multi-colored skies at sunrise. Also, during sunset, the unusual, silvery clouds again made an appearance, stretching across the sky from east to west. After June 27, the number of reported sightings of such clouds increased drastically. Crews of sailing ships in the Atlantic reported seeing dense clouds of dust or ash, moving high in the atmosphere. Reporters commented that not since the 1883 Krakatoa volcanic explosion in the Pacific did mankind witness such exotic atmospheric manifestations. At the same time, many areas were also experiencing abnormal weather conditions and other terrestrial phenomena. In the spring of 1908, unusually heavy snowfalls blanketed Switzerland, followed by catastrophic flooding. Then there were the earthquakes. In the Siberian city of Irkutsk, scientists at the local observatory registered over 1,500 earthquakes of varying intensities. When the observatory sent questionnaires out to local observers all around the region, the responses were extremely strange. None of the observers logged down any earth tremors, but they did report what sounded like unusually loud thunder, despite the fact that the sky was clear and cloudless! Observatory director A. V. Voznesensky, after studying about 60 of the reports, concluded that the "earthquakes" were somehow related to the Tunguska event.

On June 30, the day of the event, the observatory at Irkutsk registered an earthquake early in the morning, according to Pesach Amnuel. The ground started moving at 7:19 a.m., and the observatory's equipment measured three waves, each lasting over two minutes. The observatory director and his assistants quickly pinpointed the epicenter of the earthquake as being between the rivers Nizhnyaya and Podkamennaya Tunguska, to the north of the Vanavara indicated that the last earthquake took place at 7:46 a.m., about half an hour after the Tunguska explosion occurred over the taiga. A. V. Voznesensky, the observatory director, believed that the final seismograph reading detected not an earth tremor at all, but rather a dramatic burst of air currents.

A sonic wave, caused by the explosion, reached Irkutsk 45 minutes after the event and continued moving around the planet. When the authors of this book researched materials about the Tunguska Explosion, they were struck by the fact that the event itself was barely noticed by Russia's science establishment at the time. Later, of course, the event generated hypotheses, discussions, and expeditions that still continue today. There certainly were individuals and groups who reacted to the event almost immediately, but we have very scant information about them. We will discuss them later in the chapter.

THE "EXPLOSION"

The object approached from an azimuth of 115 degrees, and descended at an entry angle of 30 to 35 degrees above the horizon. It continued along a north-westward trajectory until it seemingly disappeared over the horizon. When the object reached an altitude of 1-5 miles over the area, an air burst occurred, engulfing the forest below in flames and destroying an area of over 600 square miles. Ash was throughout the planet by upper air currents. The mass of the object is estimated at 100,000 tons, and the force of the explosion at 40 megatons of TNT – 2,000 times the force of the atomic bomb exploded over Hiroshima (Japan) in 1945.

Fallen trees in the area of Tunguska

Perhaps, the Tunguska event would not have created worldwide attention (Kulik, Kazantsev, Zigel, Korolyov and others notwithstanding) had it not been for one glaring inconsistency in the observed behaviour of the object. Ballistics experts, who researched the event, deduced that, before the explosion, the Tunguska object had flown slowly from east to west. This trajectory was confirmed by eyewitnesses who resided to the east of the Lake Baikal. But, amazingly enough, witnesses observing the object from west of the lake swore that the body flew from south to north! In 1969 Feliks Zigel, a famous Soviet scientist and UFO researcher, suggested in an article in *Tekhnika-Molodezhi* magazine (Issue 12, 1969) that the Tunguska object was a UFO that flew over the forest, made a few steep turns in the skies above Siberia, and then exploded due to unknown causes. Some of those who had observed the flight of the body over the taiga later said that at one point, the object changed its trajectory and turned over Baikal. There were other inconsistencies in the witness testimony. The "southern object," seen in the early morning hours, was described as "star-like" and its colours "a mix of white and blue." However, the "eastern object" was seen much later during the day, and it was described as a fast-moving reddish flying object.

Aleksey V. Zolotov, Russian scientist and researcher of the paranormal, suggested that the Tunguska event involved two completely different objects that flew in from different directions and converged over Tunguska. Zolotov theorized that two UFOs, one from the south, and the other from the east, flew to the same point over the taiga, before exploding possibly due to a collision. Was it a case of one object intercepting the other over the impenetrable Siberian taiga, in 1908? Could it have been some sort of alien missile defence system? This idea has been discussed by Russian investigators since 1991. And yet, if there was an explosion or disintegration of the flying object, no fragments (despite claims to the contrary) of it have ever been found. Another Russian scientist explains the discrepancy between witness testimonies by arguing that the observers saw two different meteorites on two different days, thus accounting for the two entirely different descriptions. Some researchers believe that the so-called "Vashka Object," found in 1985 some 1,864 miles away from Tunguska, could possibly be a fragment from the 1908 event.

Map showing where the Tunguska event took place in Siberia

THE AFTERMATH

In the aftermath of the Tunguska event, tens of millions of people throughout Western Siberia and Europe witnessed an extremely unusual phenomenon – a strange illumination that lit up the night and lasted 72 hours. For those 72 hours, night time did not come to any of the areas located to the west of the Tunguska event. In northern Europe, for several nights, an eerie glow illuminated the night. The glow was sufficient to light the streets of London during the night time hours. Also, the Irkutsk Observatory reported disturbances in the Earth's magnetic fields 559 miles southeast of the Tunguska epicentre. The local geomagnetic disturbance shared some similarities to the after-effects of an airburst of a nuclear weapon in the atmosphere, but unlike the latter, Tunguska exhibited a kind of delay, as the geomagnetic disturbance occurred well after the initial explosion.

Other anomalies caused by the "explosion" included strange mesospheric clouds, bright "volcanic" twilights, disturbances of atmospheric polarization, and intense solar halos. Trees were felled in an outward direction, forming a radial pattern. In the center of the affected area, a large section of trees remained standing, although all their bark and branches had been destroyed. It is noteworthy that the forest recovered very rapidly following the Tunguska event, and there were clear signs of accelerated growth in the trees. Accelerated growth is a phenomenon that has been observed at the site of many other UFO encounters in forested areas. The observed ecological effects of the Tunguska explosion included genetic impact on humans and wildlife in the area, a remarkably quick revival of the taiga, and accelerated growth of young trees. Not much is known about the genetic aftermath of the Tunguska explosion. There has been serious discussion of the genetic consequences by N.V. Vasilyev, MD, a member of the Russian Academy of Medical Sciences, in the Ukrainian *RIAP Bulletin* (January-March 1995). He mentions a rare mutation in Rh-antigen that reportedly arose among the natives of the region, the Evenks, in the 1910s. That mutation originated in Strelka-Chunya, one of the settlements closest to the site of the Tunguska explosion. There are also morphometric peculiarities of certain ant species found in the area of the epicentre.

Russian paranormal researchers A. B. Petukhov and L. A. Pankratov looked at an interesting angle to the Tunguska event in the *Anomaliya* newspaper in 1997. They noted that the year following Tunguska saw the births of an unusually high number of very intellectual and highly influential people, many of them born in Russia. Their research found 207 notable people were born around the world, nearly twice the number as in previous years (1900-1907) and in later years (1909-1915). Of the 207 important people born following Tunguska, 117 of them were born in Russia, which was far above the norm. The list of important Russians born in 1908 and 1909 reads like a who's who in many fields of study – and includes noted mathematician Sergei Lvovich Sobolev, as well as several Russians that excelled in science and the fine arts. Was this a coincidence? Is it possible that the Tunguska blast, which seemed to invigorate the forest and cause dramatic tree growth for decades afterward, may have also somehow "boosted" human civilization at a molecular or psychic level? Perhaps our planet gained much more than we realize from Tunguska.

THE EYEWITNESSES

A number of eyewitnesses came forth or were found in the years following the 1908 event. Their recollections help us to objectively evaluate the incident. Many of the witnesses spoke of seeing an oval-shaped mass moving across the sky, as well as seeing the object change course, and of having a very low speed. A traveller on the Trans-Siberian Railway set up his camera to get a picture of the train during a relief stop at Kansk, Russia. The date was June 30, 1908. Suddenly, he saw a brilliantly radiant object in the sky. He was able to get but a poor picture on tintype before the object vanished. It zoomed away in the easterly direction, moving right and left, leaving a bright tail behind it. Eyewitness Okhchin, a local hunter, always warned those who went into the taiga after 1908 to beware of a certain brook. He told them that its water was like fire and that it burned people and trees. "I will pray to Agdi to see you back alive," he would say. Twenty years after the Tunguska event, the rivers over which the object exploded were devoid of fish. There were many reports, accounts, and stories in the aftermath of the explosion. Soviet and Russian researchers were able to collect and keep much of the information so that future generations of scientists could continue the study of the incredible event that occurred on our planet in 1908.

LEONID KULIK

Tunguska investigator Pesach Amnuel noted one odd fact about the event – that the scientists of the time period seemed to pay little attention at all to the event for more than ten years after its occurrence. A notable exception to this were the group of scientists that comprised a very secretive expedition of the Russian Geographic Society and several other even more secretive expeditions that followed shortly thereafter.

Professor Kulik

A report about a gigantic meteorite falling down in Siberia was printed on the backside of a page in a calendar – behind the calendar entry for June 15, 1910. Although many people probably saw the report, few seemed to pay much attention to it. But ten years later, Leonid Alekseyevich Kulik, a scientist at the St. Petersburg Mineralogical Museum, happened to see the report in the calendar, and he took serious notice. Kulik had been working as the chief curator for the meteorite collection in the museum since 1913, when Academician V. I. Vernadsky hired him. By sheer chance, D. O. Svyatsky, editor of the Soviet magazine *Mirovedeniye*, paid a visit to the museum, and showed Kulik the calendar page in question. The report on that page described a meteorite's crash near Filimonovo, some eleven "verstas" from Kansk [one versta equaled 1.06 kilometres in Old Russia]. Kulik had a great interest in meteorites and was always eager to lead an expedition into the wilds of Russia to search for celestial rocks. In this very difficult period, Russia was suffering the consequences of its Civil War. Famine reigned in its cities. The infrastructure of the Old Empire was falling apart, and terrors of the new rule were felt all throughout the land. And yet the Academy of Sciences authorized the expedition.

Valdimir Ivanovich Vernadsky

It seemed like fate had intervened when Kulik discovered the calendar and read about the Tunguska event. A man of action, he led his first expedition to Siberia in September of 1921. He talked to numerous people, questioned eyewitnesses, and soon realized that Tunguska was an event of enormous proportions. During this first expedition, he did not quite reach the center of the Tunguska explosion before returning to Petrograd, as Saint Petersburg was called at the time. The second expedition to the area, funded by Soviet Academy of Sciences, was dispatched in 1927. Kulik, who later came to be regarded as the founder of Russian meteorite science, again led the expedition. Kulik intended to locate and research the actual impact site of what he still suspected was a very large meteorite that had fallen in Tunguska. Kulik and his assistant Gulikh arrived in the tiny Russian hamlet of Vanavara in March 1927. In April, both scientists and their Evenk guide Lyuchetkan left Vanavara and pushed to the north. On April 13, they began observing huge areas of fallen trees, a sight that amazed all the members of the expedition. The expedition did not locate any fragments of a meteorite. Neither did several other expeditions to the area, conducted by Kulik over the next 14 years. As his pursuit continued, he developed a number of highly placed enemies among Soviet scientists, but he also had a strong ally, too, the Academician V. I. Vernadsky.

The Ukrainian Vladimir Ivanovich Vernadsky, a Soviet mineralogist and geochemist, is considered to be one of the founders of geochemistry, biogeochemistry, and of radio-geology. His research ranged from meteorites and cosmic dust to microbiology and migration of microelements via living organisms in ecosystems. His ideas preceded and influenced later global ecology movements. Regarding Tunguska, he understood Kulik's zeal. As for Kulik, his life could actually have been the basis for an action adventure movie, a la Indiana Jones. In a life full of twists and turns, Kulik was a tough, resourceful "everyman" who occasionally used questionable means to obtain an objective. As his travels through the taiga were harsh and difficult, he often resorted to strong-arm tactics, involving the use of his trusty revolver, to get what he needed. Many Siberian old-timers, who found themselves looking up the barrel of Kulik's weapon, no doubt remembered their encounter with the scientist for many years afterward. Kulik usually ended up getting whatever he needed, including supplies, guides, boats, carts, and reindeer.

The hut where Kulik stayed during his time in Siberia

It was also Kulik's philosophy not to tolerate any dissenting opinions during the harsh treks through the mosquito-infested, hellishly hot Siberian taiga in the summer. The taiga forests of eastern Siberia cover more than a quarter of Russia's territory. The summer is short and very hot, with temperatures soaring up to 105°F, and winter is bitterly cold, with temperatures dipping down to between -70° and -80° F, but the snow cover over the permafrost is only moderate or thin. The average temperature during the year is below freezing.

Kulik insisted on strict discipline throughout his numerous expeditions. He single-mindedly pressed on in search of the elusive meteorite that he believed caused the Tunguska event. But those who wanted to see tangible results from his expeditions became restless, and finally, Kulik's enemies took their complaints to Moscow. As a result, Kulik was denounced as an enemy of the people who, according to his detractors, wasted the money and resources of the working people of Russia. There were no meteorites in Tunguska, they argued, and the felled trees were probably merely the result of a hurricane or other natural disaster. Although, as a dedicated scientist, Kulik wanted to continue his search for the meteorite, Moscow delayed his funding, and when they finally did fund him, what they sent was not enough. Kulik did his best to convince the authorities that he was certain the meteorite, when he found it, would likely consist of pure nickel, a metal that Russia's leaders were very interested in obtaining due to rumours of a coming war. It was 1939, and Stalin's Russia was preparing for war, while devouring Eastern Europe with its Nazi allies. Kulik assured them the meteorite he was seeking was, most certainly, pure nickel in its content. The last time Kulik visited the area of the epicentre was on August 6, 1939. The next year, his funding totally dried up. In 1941, Hitler's forces invaded his Russia, and Kulik volunteered to go to the front line to defend his country. He was captured and died in 1942, in a German prisoner of war camp. As he lay dying, in a state of delirium, Kulik raved to fellow prisoners about the Tunguska object, to which he had dedicated so much of his life.

Old Moscow University

In the autumn of 1944 a Soviet Yak aircraft was flying over the epicentre of the Tunguska explosion when suddenly all of its electronics failed, causing it to spiral down to the forest below. The plane crashed in the River Chamba area, about 20 miles south of the epicentre. No official explanation was ever given for the failure of the airplane's instruments. Many years later, in 1996, the crash site was visited and photographed by Russian scientist Vadim Chernobrov, a noted researcher of the paranormal. No officially sanctioned expeditions returned to Tunguska until 1958. However, there were "unsanctioned" expeditions, which we will mention later.

The 1958 expedition, sent to Tunguska by the Soviet Academy of Sciences concluded that there was an explosion of a celestial body over the taiga. The altitude of the explosion was actually higher than the one suggested by A. Kazantsev, a war veteran, engineer, and science-fiction writer [more about him later].

Young Russian scientists Viktor Zhuravlyov and Gennady Plekhanov, who led other expeditions to the taiga, found that discovering the cause of Tunguska was more complicated than they previously thought. They found neither radiation nor meteorite fragments. For years, Soviet scientists went to Tunguska, collected a huge amount of data, and yet got no closer to the truth. After the end of the Cold War, Western scientists joined their Russian colleagues in trying to find answers. And such prominent UFO researchers as Vadim Chernobrov, of whom we will speak often, have also joined the quest. Chernobrov and his colleagues conducted an expedition in 1996, and they continue their research in the new millennium. After all, according to an old legend among those who have gone to the Tunguska taiga in search of the answers to the mystery of the phenomenon, "those who enter the area leave there a piece of themselves." However, they also acquire a certain spiritual energy, a special essence that accompanies them for the rest of their life. This spirit forces them to go back, time after time.

MAKARENKO'S EXPEDITION

Ukrainian scientist Alexander Leonidovich Kul'sky published a truly fascinating book in 1997 titled *Na perekrestkah vselennoy* (*At the Crossroads of Universe*). He was able to collect a great deal of interesting, and usually previously unavailable, information about paranormal phenomena in the Czarist Russia, USSR, Eastern and Western Europe. Among such materials there is a brochure written by A. Voytsekhovsky in which a previously unknown Tunguska expedition is revealed. The expedition took place at the end of June of 1908, when a Russian scientific team, led by A. Makarenko, worked in the area of the Katonga (the local Evenki name for Podkamennaya Tunguska River or "open water"). A brief report about the expedition's work was prepared by A. Makarenko, a member of the Geographic Society, and was discovered later.

According to the report, scientists took photographs of the Katonga and measured its depths and the depths of the navigating channel. The report mentions no traces of any evidence that could be associated with the fall of a meteorite, which is extremely strange. Russian scientists of the pre-Revolutionary Russia were educated to no lesser degree than their European neighbours, and the Geographic Society was a prestigious group of science luminaries, which means it is doubtful that the members of this expedition would fail to see evidence that a meteorite or other object had struck Tunguska. It seems inconceivable that, having observed such evidence, the scientists would fail to give even a brief account in their report. A. Kul'sky offers us two explanations: either the report was later changed for unknown reasons, or the members of the expedition did not see that which they were not specifically looking for – in other words, their minds were "turned off" to the possibility. Whatever faults could be attributed to Czarist Russia, totalitarian secrecy was certainly not one of them. The press reported anomalous phenomena quite openly. What might the expedition have observed in the taiga that day that would have caused authorities to confiscate its diaries and change A. Makarenko's report to remove all references to the after-effects of the Tunguska phenomenon? A. Kul'sky favours the second explanation - that the expedition's members were simply not focused on the Tunguska mystery and therefore did not seek evidence about it. The first expedition that was sent to Tunguska specifically to investigate the Tunguska event, according to A. Voytsekhovsky, took place three years after the incident, in 1911. Unfortunately, little is known about the results of this expedition. Commissioned by the Omsk Department of Highways and Waterways, the mission was headed by Vyacheslav Shishkov, an engineer who later became an acclaimed novelist, author of *Ugryum Reka* (*Gloomy River*). The book, a bestseller in the 1960s in the USSR, contained very detailed descriptions of daily life in the taiga and its colourful inhabitants. The book, which was adapted into a Soviet motion picture in 1969, also contains some paranormal themes related to life in the taiga.

In addition to the 1911 Shishkov expedition, additional archival evidence points to the existence of one exploratory journey to Tunguska that supposedly took place sometime in 1909 or 1910. The little information known about it has been gathered from a few obscure articles in the newspapers of the time, the testimony of taiga dwellers in that period, and the dim recollections of pre-revolutionary Saint-Petersburg scientists. The only thing known is that a group of people with unusual equipment visited the alleged Tunguska crash site and reportedly observed very strange phenomena. The identities of the members of the expedition are not known. What their "strange" equipment consisted of is also totally unknown. Perhaps they found some of the same types of evidence that was discovered in 1991 by Far Eastern UFO researchers from Vladivostok during their search find the "Devil's Cemetery," the alleged impact site. The 1991 team received many reports of strange, possibly genetically-altered animals and humans living in the area after 1908.

AND ANOTHER SECRET EXPEDITION

Valentin Psalomschikov, noted Russian scientist and journalist, published an article in *NLO Magazine* in 1999 about a secret Soviet military expedition to Tunguska, sanctioned by Lavrenty Beria, Soviet statesman and at the time and Politburo member. Beria was the chief of the dreaded Soviet secret police and was put in charge of the Soviet atomic weapons project in the late 1940s. In the summer of 1949, Beria, during a high-level secret meeting, announced his interest in sending a research team to the area of the Tunguska phenomenon. Unlike previous expeditions, Beria's group had no interest at all in looking for fallen meteorites. Beria suspected that a nuclear-powered spaceship might have exploded over the Siberian taiga in 1908, and if that were true, he wanted complete information about the incident for its possible military applications. Beria's Tunguska expedition was to take place one year after the testing of the first Soviet atomic bomb. Alexander Petrovitch Kazantsev, a retired Soviet army colonel who later became a leading ufologist and popular science fiction writer, first proposed the theory that the Tunguska event may have involved an ET spacecraft. Kazantsev was not mentioned as being involved in Beria's expedition, although he clearly may have been the inspiration for it. Meanwhile, Beria refused to invite any civilian scientists to be a part of his expedition, and instead, selected military experts in the fields of atomic weapons and ballistics. Before the expedition left, Beria demanded that his assistants to collect all information about the geophysical effects of the explosion on the surrounding areas. Thus it was that, with great care, readings of devices of Russian and German meteorological stations from June 30, 1908, were analyzed and researched. This project confirmed that the "wave" of air, caused by the explosion, circled the Earth several times. Research showed that the energy produced by the explosion was the equivalent of several dozen megatons. Also, the air burst occurred at the altitude of 12 miles. Information received from the Irkutsk Geophysical Observatory was also confirmed -- that intensive disturbances of the

Earth's magnetic field, recorded several minutes after the event, were like the effects of a nuclear detonation in the atmosphere and included increased ionization. It was noted that this increased ionation allowed the Irkutsk scientists to receive radio waves from Europe, something that had never occurred before. Before Beria expedition left for the taiga, a reconnaissance airplane twice flew over the area of the Tunguska event, and took photographs of the forest, at different altitudes. Each member of the team carefully studied Kulik's reports and photographs from his expeditions. Then, in the summer of 1949, members of Beria's secret expedition, posing as geologists on a routine mission, were flown to the Vanavara settlement, where they boarded a hydroplane and flew them to the Cheko Lake, a small, freshwater lake in Siberia, near the Podkamennaya Tunguska River. They were forbidden to ask local residents questions about the Tunguska event, but they were permitted to log down any information they might happen to overhear.

The scientific findings of Beria's expedition were never published, but enough details about them have leaked out to suggest that the findings were quite different from data gathered by expeditions sent later by the Soviet Science Academy and the Committee for the Study of Meteorites. Beria's military scientists established that the trees were felled by a percussion wave resulting from the energy of the object itself, and not by a ballistic wave, such as is created by the passing of a high-speed flying object. They also confirmed that the air burst occurred at a high altitude and that its force was over one megaton. However, they also reported that no traces of radiation of any significance were found in the area. After an atomic bomb explodes, there is substantial radioactive present in the atmosphere. Beria's military scientists concluded that the explosion had to be thermonuclear in nature (fusion rather than fission).

Upon their return to Moscow, the scientists in charge of the different fields -- ballistics, radioactivity, etc. -- prepared their reports, working in isolation from each other and supplied only with typewriters and paper. No group discussions or brainstorming sessions were allowed. When the groups finished their work, Beria's officials collected the completed reports, and nobody ever heard a word about what happened to the final report or what it was used for.

DR. ALEXEY V. ZOLOTOV

When Dr. Alexey V. Zolotov was murdered in October of 1995, Russia lost a fearless researcher, and a daring scientist. Born in 1919, Zolotov developed an early interest in radio physics, and became a noted geophysicist. Zolotov worked in Soviet Bashkiria and later in the city of Kalinin (now, Tver), doggedly pursuing the hypothesis that Tunguska was caused by the explosion of an ET spacecraft.

Dr Alexey Zolotov

His objective was to provide scientific background for Kazantsev's ideas. Eventually his name became inseparable from the history of the Tunguska event, but not without cost. Zolotov's work earned him many opponents, and on occasions, the wrath of the "official" scientific community. Highly ethical and a true intellectual, Zolotov was also a man of action. He was not content to be an armchair researcher of the Tunguska event and actually visited the area of the incident to conduct research. His monograph *Tungusskaya Katastrofa 1908 goda* was published in 1970, in Minsk, despite powerful opposition to the book from Soviet astronomy officials, who tried to block publication. However, the Vice-President of the Soviet Academy of Sciences, V. P. Konstantinov, supported Dr. Zolotov and helped him publish his important treatise on Tunguska.

Tunguska Today

BELIEFS, IDEAS, THEORIES, HYPOTHESES

Many of the Evenks, natives of the Tunguka area, believe that on that fateful day in 1908, a deity named Agdi descended from the Heavens down into the taiga. They say that Agdi spoke to their people, and that the deity was actually seen by many. For many years, their shamans kept the area sealed off from the rest of the world, fearful of enraging the deities whose anger had caused the 1908 Tunguska explosion. As previously noted, Russian scientific officials did not really become interested in the Tunguska event until 1920s. Outside the fields of science, however, there were many theories as to the origin of the Tunguska blast, ranging from it being a "Sodom and Gomorrah"-type event to the start of the second Russo-Japanese war. Others blamed the event on various catastrophes such as an explosion of ball lightning, an aerolite explosion, an unusual earthquake, or the eruption of an ancient volcano. Beginning in 1927 scientists focused in on the meteorite hypothesis and began looking for evidence in the area. They investigated the possibility that, after striking, the meteorite turned into streams of fragments and gas. In 1929, scientists considered the possibility that the Tunguska blast was caused by the near fly-by of a meteorite. In 1930, they entertained the theory that Tunguska had been struck by the central core of a comet. In 1932, the notion arose that it might have been a cosmic dust cloud. And in 1934, scientists suggested that Tunguska was hit by a comet's tail.

In 1945, the extraterrestrial spacecraft explosion theory surfaced, leading to the Beria expedition mentioned earlier. In 1946, researchers suggested that an extraterrestrial spaceship, possibly from Mars, had crashed due to a catastrophic failure of one of its onboard systems. Then, in 1947, another group championed the theory that Tunguska was caused by a meteorite composed of antimatter.

More theories arose in the 50s and 60s. In 1958, some suggested that the culprit was a meteorite made of ice while, in 1959, others hypothesized that it was a fragment of the hypothetical planet Phaeton. Perhaps the most bizarre explanation surfaced in 1960, suggesting the explosion was caused by a cloud made up entirely of mosquitoes -- over 3 cubic miles in density! Talk of an exploded flying saucer gained prominence in 1961, although attempts at more conventional explanations continued. In 1962, it was suggested that a meteor caused a "hole" in the ionosphere. The following year, some researchers proposed that an electrostatic meteor had discharged in Tunguska. In 1964, there was talk of a laser ray from outer space hitting the taiga. In 1965, the jaw-dropping theory was advanced of an alien invasion attempt by a race of abominable snowmen aboard a malfunctioning spaceship. In 1966, some claimed Tunguska was caused by a fragment of a super dense white dwarf star. In 1967, researchers considered the possibility of an explosion of swamp gases resulting from a lightning strike.

In 1984, scientists Aleksey Dmitriyev and Viktor Zhuravlyov from Novosibirsk theorized that plasma was involved in the Tunguska event. And, in1996, it was suggested that Nicola Tesla caused the Tunguska explosion by launching a wireless energy torpedo, during a long-distance test of the unconventional weapon. Russian scientist Boris I. Ignatov proposed that the Tunguska explosion was caused by the impact and detonation of three bursts of ball lightning – each burst being over three feet in diameter.

Siberian scientists Viktor Zhuravlyov and Aleksey Dmitriyev recently proposed an interesting hypothesis. Using a computer, they analyzed numerous archived accounts from various eyewitnesses and also documents and reports from newspapers of the period. The computer analysis suggested that there may have been three bodies involved, flying in different directions -- one from south, another from southeast, and the last one from southwest. The three objects converged at Tunguska, resulting in the massive explosion. The epicentre of the explosion corresponds to the site of an ancient volcano, which was active two hundred million years ago. The East-Siberian magnetic field, also located in the same area, is one of the fourth greatest magnetic anomalies of our planet. This magnetic field, reaching from the bowels of the earth into the space, is something like a gigantic trap. It could have "sucked in" the explosion and resulting debris.

Zhuravlyov and Dmitriyev also revealed some new facts about the Tunguska phenomenon. They determined that six minutes after the explosion, the Irkutsk Observatory's devices recorded a magnetic storm that had lasted almost five hours. They have made available to other researchers the Irkutsk magnetogram that registered the magnetic storm. Many researchers believed a comet caused the Tunguska event, and yet, they have been unable prove it. The view is opposed by Feliks Zigel, who taught aerodynamics at the Moscow Institute of Aviation and whose quest to explain the UFO phenomena greatly irritated the official Soviet scientific establishment and attracted the attention of the Central Intelligence Agency. Zigel explained that the comet hypothesis is groundless in the article "Mif o Tungusskoy komete," in the Soviet magazine *Tekhnika-Molodezhi*, Issue 3, 1979).

In conclusion, below is a list of some of the more interesting proposed causes of Tunguska:
• Airburst of an asteroid
• Comet that detonated in the atmosphere
• Black hole
• Antimatter particles
• Nuclear-powered spaceship(s)
• Solar energophore (another hypothesis from Dmitriyev and Zhuravlyov)
• Spacecraft travelling faster than light and experiencing time dilation
• Super conductive meteorite
• Powerful electrical charges of a meteorite interacting with Earth surface, causing the destruction of the Tunguska object
• Explosion of natural gas. Note: If there happened to be deposits of natural gas in the taiga, then due to tectonic processes, the gas would be released into the atmosphere. About 2.5 million cubic meters of it to cause an explosion the Tunguska-type force. The gas would have been dissipated and carried away by winds. Once in the upper reaches of the atmosphere, the gas would interact with the ozone, and oxidize. There would be luminescence in the sky. Within a 24-hour period, a huge trail of over 200 miles would cover the sky. Once mixed with the air, the natural gas would become a huge cloud, ready to explode. The spark would be caused by a thunderstorm many

miles away from the Tunguska epicentre; and like a gigantic bolide this fiery trail would race through the sky, to the epicentre. There, in a hollow, the natural would be highly concentrated, and it is there that a tremendous explosion would result in a fireball. The explosion would shake the mighty Russian taiga. The force of the explosion would move the ground below, close the tectonic splits below, and natural gas would cease its movement to the atmosphere. The author of this hypothesis, D. Timofeyev of Krasnoyarsk, reminded readers of *Komsomolskaya Pravda* newspaper (November 11, 1984 issue) that the Evenks said they saw water "burning like fire" in local swamps. There is hydrogen sulphide in the composition of natural gas. When burning, it forms sulphurous anhydride; and the latter, when mixing with water, becomes an acid. Incidentally, some scientists believe that the atmospheric nitrous oxide created by the 1908 Tunguska phenomenon in all probability caused the 30% depletion in the northern hemisphere ozone shield that was observed in the year following the Tunguska explosion.

Few people know of another episode related to the Tunguska phenomenon. Soviet astronavigation specialist A. Shternfeld calculated something very interesting, but it has rarely appeared in publication. At the beginning of the 20th century, scientists expected two great oppositions -- an opposition being the position of two heavenly bodies when their celestial longitudes differ by 180 degrees. Opposition especially refers to the position of a planet or the moon when either is on the opposite side of the earth from the sun. Shternfeld knew about the expectations, and decided to calculate when a spaceship would have to leave Venus, and through the use of the Earth-Venus opposition, get to our planet using the least energy output. The result was quite fantastic. Were such spaceship to blast off from Venus at the most favourable time, it would have arrived on Earth on June 30, 1908 – the date of the Tunguska event! Is it a coincidence? Additionally, if a spaceship blasted off from Mars, during its opposition to Earth, it too would have arrived on the same date.

In 1991, Russian engineer E. Krutelev published his analysis of the Tunguska phenomenon, in the *Rabochaya Tribuna* newspaper. He is convinced that what happened in the taiga that day was not the explosion of an alien ship, but rather its take-off. His conclusion was reached after he considered reports from the locals, the lack of any material traces of an explosion, and the fact that what the locals heard was the sound of a mighty thunderous roar, moving away in the northern direction. Are Krutelev's views credible? S. Privalikhin, an eyewitness from the Kova Village reported that he first heard a "shot from cannon." The next moment he saw a long, flying object, thick in its forepart. The object flew horizontally over the ground, leaving behind a fiery trail. I. Starichev observed the object from the Kama River. When he and other observers looked up they saw "moving fire" in the sky, and inside it was a body whose size was that of half-moon. V. Okhchin, a hunter, was in a hut 21 miles from the epicentre. He witnessed the instant uprooting of century- old Siberian trees. He saw that the upper parts of trees were ablaze, and the next moment, people saw a giant mushroom-like cloud, rising into the sky at the horizon. Professor A. Zolotov, who continued where L. Kulik left off, also believed the Tunguska phenomenon was caused by an object of artificial origin. However, in his opinion, the object was a "UFO bomb," with a release of energy equal to 40 megatons. This alien bombing of our planet was a sort of signal from another world, meant to get our attention. Kind of like a slap on the cheek. In order to minimize the bomb's impact on the planet's life forms, the device was deliberately exploded in one of the most remote and least populated places on Earth.

The comet hypothesis received a boost in the 1980's. Researchers pointed to the presence of iridium as proof that a comet exploded over the Siberian taiga in 1908. Iridium is a rare element on Earth but is common in meteorites, comets and asteroids. Iridium anomalies in Siberian peat deposits seem to support a cometary impact hypothesis in the minds of a number of Western and Russian scientists. Soviet expeditions of the late 1950s and early 1960s discovered microscopic spheres of metal and glass in the soil of the taiga. Ramachandran Ganapathy, an American scientist, analyzed trace elements in several spheres and discovered enrichments of iridium. He believes the spheres are extraterrestrial in origin. But his data is not sufficient to determine whether comets or asteroids were the cause of the Tunguska Phenomenon.

In 1984, Ramachandran Ganapathy uncovered a clue to Tunguska buried deep in the ice of Antarctica. While looking at ice formed during the first twenty years of the 20th century, he found that a sample from 1909, once melted, left microscopic residues rich in meteoritic material. He found on the ice sub-micron-size debris sticking to dust grains. If it resulted from the Tunguska Phenomenon, the discovery could mean the Tunguska object was much larger than previously believed. Ganapathy estimates the object was a seven million-ton, 524-foot-diameter monster – given the South Pole, Antarctica, data as evidence to the total amount of atmospheric fallout from the event.

There is another interesting hypothesis. The plasma origin theory of the Tunguska phenomenon may be explained today by contemporary military research in Russia. Russian scientist Boris Belitsky, during a 1996 interview in a *Voice of Russia World Service* segment, was asked about microwave generator development in Russia. His responses were of great interest to proponents of the plasmoid theory for the Tunguska event.

In a scenario of interest to weapons developers, powerful microwave generators can be used to fire a plasmoid "blob." Plasma, a mixture of electrons and ions, is observed, for example, in electric air discharges and in sparks. Plasma is also a characteristic of thermonuclear reactions, as occur within the sun. Space scientists in Russia have a long record of experimenting with plasma and attempted to build plasma engines for early Soviet Mars probes in the 1970s. Extensive studies of plasma have been carried out as part of research into controlled nuclear fusion. Research into the military applications has been conducted at some of the leading research institutes of the military industrial complex, including at the Research Institute of Radio Instruments.

If perfected, microwave generators could fire a blob of plasma into the path of an incoming missile or aircraft. The plasmoid would effectively ionize the region of impact and severely disrupt the incoming object, causing it to fail. During the 1993 Russian American summit in Vancouver, the Russians proposed a joint experiment to test such microwave generators or plasma weapons (as they are called in Russia) as an alternative to the Strategic Defence Initiative (SDI).

THE BRITISH DEFECTOR'S TALE

Lieutenant Colonel Anthony Godley, a British defence expert and an official at the Royal Military College of Science, disappeared from England in April 1983, at the age of 49. Despite the fact that he was due to receive an inheritance of over $60,000 simply by showing up to claim it, he never did and thus was presumed dead. What does his disappearance have to do with the Tunguska phenomenon? Though complex and convoluted, there is a definite link.

Godley is one of 22 British scientists that have died or disappeared under mysterious circumstances since 1982. All of them were highly trained and skilled in computer use and all of them were working on highly classified projects related to the U.S. Strategic Defence Initiative (the Star Wars program). The U.K. government has said that the deaths and disappearances are strictly coincidental. In the case of Godley, he suddenly surfaced in Moscow in April of 1985. The Soviets claimed he was a colonel in British Intelligence, and they said he revealed to the KGB that the British were involved in the alleged development of a "guided comet" weapon. According to the KGB, the Brits planned to send a guided comet to annihilate Leningrad. The comet was to approach the Earth from the direction of the sun. Astronomers would see it at the last moment, but countermeasures would be futile. A comet strike cannot be defended against without a period of long and complex preparation. According to Godley, the British and their American counterparts argued over the comet's target, with Americans preferring that Moscow be targeted. Destruction of both targets at the same time would arouse suspicions. Since Leningrad was the largest Soviet Naval base, it was the more attractive target for the United Kingdom.

Supposedly, a scientist involved in the British SDI research whose last name was Brockway, presented a secret lecture for the military leaders regarding the use of comets as weapons. He claimed that guided comets had previously been used by an extraterrestrial intelligence. Following his presentation, British SDI military officials allegedly decided to concentrate on the development of the comet weapons, thus curtailing other, more promising programs. Brockway supposedly committed suicide, and afterward, the fledgling British "comet weapons" group was disbanded. Another British scientist, who Russians refer to as "Drankwater," suggested that Brockway was killed by the ETs for revealing the comet guidance technology. Godley, on the other hand, did not believe Brockway's death was a suicide, and neither did he blame ETs; rather, he was convinced that Brockway was executed by MI5, the British intelligence agency. Godley, himself an MI5 officer, knew that the agency then headed by Dame Stella Remington was not pleased at his analysis of Brockway's death.

Godley decided that his only escape from MI5 was behind the Iron Curtain. While ETs could get their hands on him anywhere on Earth, Godley's more immediate concern was his former colleagues in the MI5. Godley told the KGB that the British requested a "limited impact" of a comet on a Soviet target. NATO strategists reportedly based their plans on published research by Soviet scientists regarding the "cometary hypothesis" of the Tunguska event. Although the findings were published in the USSR, they soon became widely available to scholars throughout the world.

One paper proposed that if the Tunguska event was caused by a comet, as some believed, then comets could potentially be used as weapons. A comet like the one believed to have hit Tunguska could deliver explosive power of between 20 and 40 megatons. After studying these Russian reports, the British apparently became convinced the body that exploded over the Siberian taiga had been a comet.

The source for the story of British defector Godley is *Entsiklopedia Nepoznannogo* (*Encyclopedia of the Unknown*), compiled by Vadim Chernobrov, and published in Moscow in 1998. Chernobrov's compilation appears to also include information from an article by Yevgeny Merkulov, published in *Znaniye-Sila* magazine (Issue 5, 1995). Perhaps the Godley story was nothing but the ravings of a "nut" that needed to find a reason to leave the U.K. and hide in the USSR? Or is there something more to it? Was there a connection between Godley and other British scientists involved in the SDI program who died in mysterious ways after 1982? Chernobrov asks another question: could those involved in the British SDI "comet weapons" program have based their information on Valery Burdakov and Yuri Danilov's popular book, published in the USSR in 1980, *Raketi Buduschego* or *Rockets of the Future*? Chernobrov thinks it is highly possible that Burdakov's book, in which he speculates about exotic weapons of the future, may have inspired the secret British "guided comet" program. The idea of comets as weapons apparently started with studies conducted in April 1957 on a comet called "Arend-Roland." A very unusual comet that some claim contradicted many laws of astronomy was observed and studied at the Oslo Solar Observatory at Harestua. During the latter half of April 1957, it was seen from the northern hemisphere as an extraordinary object in the north-western sky as night was falling. On April 15th, the comet's head exhibited zero magnitude, trailing a 25-30 degree tail. Between April 20th and May 3rd, the comet displayed a bright, antitail (the tail that points toward the sun) up to 15 degrees long. At the conclusion of April brightness, it had fallen to the 3rd magnitude. The comet traversed Triangulum, Perseus, and entered Camelopardalus during this period. After the middle of May, when the comet had become a circumpolar object, it was finally lost to the unaided eye. The unexpected long and narrow antitail showed up quite clearly. In most other images this antitail is shorter and points to the side. The tail pointed at the sun disappeared as inexplicably as it appeared. Also, astronomers discovered a strange radio source in the comet. The most powerful signals, which still have not been deciphered, were registered between the 16th and 19th of March, just prior to the appearance of the tail. The comet behaved like an artificially created and guided object – or perhaps it contained an artificial object inside it. Burdakov and Danilov speculated that the comet's many instances of anomalous behaviour might indicate that it was somehow linked to an extraterrestrial civilization. The strange behaviour included unexpected orbital changes; the appearance and disappearance of comet tails; and emission of unknown radio signals.

Apparently, Godley told his KGB handlers that the British scientists chose the "comet weapons" program as their contribution to the U.S. SDI program. Although they disregarded the theory that ETs were involved with comets such as Arend-Roland, the Brits reportedly liked the idea of artificially manipulating a comet's course through technology. By sending a space probe to a chosen comet and fixing it on the comet's body, they felt they could change its trajectory and guide it toward a specific target.

Researcher Vadim Chernobrov has compiled much data regarding the technical aspects of how such guided comets are supposed to work, and he has also proposed another theory about Tunguska regarding a shift in space-time, based on the findings of A. Zolotov in the 1960s. Those topics, however, are far beyond the scope of this book.

KAZANTSEV

Sergey Korolyov, father of Soviet space science, became quite interested in the Tunguska phenomenon after reading a story written by the previously mentioned Alexander Kazantsev, who later became part of the Kosmopoisk UFO research organization. In 1946, Kazantsev, a former colonel in the Soviet army, wrote a short story in which he suggested that only a nuclear explosion could have caused the destruction at Tunguska, and since no such weapons existed on Earth in 1908, the event must have been the result of an extraterrestrial spaceship that exploded over the taiga. Hence, Tunguska must have been caused by a disastrous explosion on board a nuclear-powered ET spacecraft.

Tunguska

The story became quite popular in the Soviet Union, reprinted several times. In 1958 it was published in book form and titled *Guest from Space*, which become a bestseller. Kazantsev's concept of a distressed ET spacecraft came to him after hearing a radio broadcast about the atomic bombs dropped on Japan by the U.S. Having himself experienced the horrors of World War II as a soldier, Kazantsev was returning home from Europe in August 1945, when he heard an English-language radio broadcast about the devastation at Hiroshima and Nagasaki. Kazantsev immediately made the connection in his mind to the Tunguska event, which bore so many similarities to a nuclear detonation. Kazantsev knew a lot about Tunguska, having read extensively about Kulik's expeditions and having known at least one person involved in them. After making the connection between the bombs dropped in Japan and the Tunguska blast, Kazantsev discussed his ideas with close friend Victor A. Sitin, in Moscow, and Kazantsev also studied the Evenk legends about Tunguska. It was at this time that Kazantsev sought details about nuclear technology, which was very hard to come by in the Soviet Union in 1945.

Eventually, he made contact with prominent Soviet physicist Lev Landau, who later won the Nobel Prize in physics. Landau revealed to Kazantsev the fundamental principles of the atomic bomb, which led Kazantsev to write a science fiction story, published in 1946, titled "THE Explosion," which appeared in the leading Soviet magazine of popular science, *Vokrug Sveta*. The story was later adapted into play disguised as a scientific lecture, staged at the Moscow Planetarium. Many spectators arrived at the planetarium expecting a lecture, only to find themselves in the midst of a cleverly conceived stage play – which was probably a first in the annals of science. The assistant director of the planetarium and one of the "actors" in the play was none other than Feliks Yuryevich Zigel, a Soviet researcher, Doctor of Science and docent of Cosmology at the Moscow Aviation Institute. Zigel, considered one of the founders of Russian ufology, went on to author more than 40 popular books on astronomy and space exploration.

During the play, Zigel would discuss the Tunguska event and various anomalous phenomena discovered by Kulik. Suddenly, an "audience member," who was really an actor wearing the uniform of a Soviet colonel, would stand and ask him questions regarding atomic explosions. Other "guests" would rise up and discussions ensued, with the real guests eventually joining in. The staged lecture became a sensation in Moscow and tickets to the performances were extremely difficult to obtain. Also, it re-opened dialogue regarding the Tunguska phenomenon. Suddenly, discussions about Tunguska became both fashionable and relevant again. This event at the Moscow Planetarium in 1946 was basically the beginning of Soviet inquiry into the UFO phenomena – the origin of Soviet ufology.

Not everyone was pleased, though. Some Soviet astronomers expressed outrage at what they viewed as pseudoscientific nonsense. They published articles in scientific magazines critical of Kazantsev and Zigel. Despite the fact that the play at the planetarium was a staged production based on a work of fiction, the critics treated it as if it were an authentic scientific lecture. Major Soviet newspapers began publishing articles arguing against the ET hypothesis for Tunguska. Still, the younger Russians were irreversibly mesmerized by the concept, and interest in UFOs grew tremendously. Inspired by the ET idea, in 1960, Sergey Korolyov, the father of the Soviet space program [More about him in our next chapter.], organized an expedition, which included two helicopters, to the taiga to discover what the "aliens" used as materials for their spacecraft. Under a veil of secrecy, the members of the expedition, which included highly-trained space program scientists, were officially merely "on vacation" in Tunguska. Their "vacation" consisted of scouring the hostile landscape of Tunguska for anything resembling fragments of an alien craft and other tell-tale signs of the explosion. Among the engineers in the group was Georgy Mikhailovich Grechko, a future Soviet cosmonaut, who was also well-trained as a diver but did not have a chance to explore underwater before being called back to Moscow. When the Korolyov expedition completed its work, it too had found absolutely no evidence of any substance.

Another curious note about the Tunguska area has to do with the local beliefs and legends. We already mentioned that the Evenks, who reside there, worship Agdi. According to their legends, Agdi ("Thunder") is the lord of thunder and lighting, and he arrives to its spouse, Water, in the warm summer months. The Evenks, Oroks, Orochi, and some other taiga tribes believe that the arrival of Agdi in 1908 caused the powerful explosion in the taiga. And, as we mentioned, the locals were forbidden to visit the area of the explosion, for it was the residence of Agdi on Earth. The unique Tunguska State Nature Reserve was founded in 1995 and allows tourists to visit the area associated with the Tunguska phenomenon and take a close look at the exotic life of the Evenk people. The eastern Siberian taiga still preserves vast pristine habitats, probably one of the most extensive in the world.

URI LAVBIN

On August 10, 2004, the Russian newspaper *Pravda* published an article about a new scientific expedition in search of the supposed Tunguska "meteorite." According to *Pravda*, members of the scientific expedition, which was organized by a group called the Tunguska Spatial Phenomenon Foundation of Krasnoyarsk (Siberia), said they had managed to recover from Tunguska fragments in the shape of "blocks" that represent extraterrestrial technology. The press service of the Evenkiya republic administration reported that the expedition had worked in the western part of the region in the summer of the 2004. The mission's itinerary was based on an analysis of photography from space of the Tunguska region. Team members believed they discovered chunks of an extraterrestrial machine that crashed in 1908. In addition, they claimed that they found the elusive stone that had been mentioned by Tunguska eyewitnesses in their reports. The mysterious stone, weighing 110 pounds (50 kilograms), was delivered to the city of Krasnoyarsk for study and analysis. Called the "Reindeer Stone" by locals, the strange stone is made up entirely of a crystalline material. The researcher in charge of the expedition, Yuri Lavbin, who has spent years trying to solve the mystery of Tunguska Phenomenon, is the president of the Tunguska Spatial Phenomenon Foundation, which has been involved in mounting expeditions to the area since 1994. Among the explorers have been chemists, physicists, geologists and mineralogists. Lavbin believes that a comet and an artificial flying machine collided six miles above the planet, resulting in the Tunguska explosion.

Lavbin claimed his group found two strange black stones, shaped like cubes and measuring about four feet on each side, in the area of the Podkamennaya Tunguska. The stones, according to Lavbin, are not of a natural origin and are "manufactured" from a material that resembles alloys that humans use to make space rockets. As of this writing, more tests had been scheduled to find out the exact composition of these mysterious stones. Yuri Lavbin told MosNews agency that his researchers had traced the possible trajectory of the 1908 object, and they contend that it moved eastward, not westward as has always been believed. To solve the mystery of Tunguska once and for all, Lavbin plans further expeditions to the area. In May 2009, Lavbin unveiled a new theory about Tunguska -- that an alien spacecraft sacrificed itself to prevent a gigantic meteor from slamming into the Earth. Lavbin told the Macedonian International News Agency that he thinks quartz slabs with strange markings found at the site are remnants of an alien control panel, which fell to the ground after the alien spacecraft was smashed by the meteor. According to Lavbin, no Earth technology exists capable of creating such intricate etchings on a crystal surface. He also found samples of ferrum silicate, which can only be produced in space. It is clear that no matter how many scientists visit the site of the blast, even with today's modern sophisticated equipment, all attempts to identify what exactly did explode that day in 1908 have failed so far.

To this point, we have examined two major UFO cases that have each, at one time, been labelled "Russia's Roswell Incident." Interestingly, the world's "top three" suspected UFO crashes – Tunguska (1908), Roswell (1947) and Dalnegorsk (1986) – are each separated by exactly 39 years. This numerical anomaly was first pointed out by Aleksand Krivenyshev, a Russian-American scientist. The number 39, which is 13 times 3, is of special significance in the field of numerology. Now, to fully understand Tunguska and Dalnegorsk within the context of other Russian UFO sightings, we will look at some of the region's other important UFO events of the past. Most of the UFO reports that follow were filed by very credible witnesses, such as pilots, soldiers, sailors, astronomers, and cosmonauts. As previously noted, during the era of the Soviet Union (1922-1991), common citizens were forbidden to talk about most paranormal subjects, including UFOs. Those who talked about UFOs faced ridicule, shame, confinement in mental institutions, or even worse. On the other hand, reports from "reliable" witnesses could not be dismissed so easily. The Soviet government was, secretly, as eager (if not more so) than most of its citizens to find out the mystery behind the UFOs, which appeared to mock the Soviets' attempts to control access to secret bases and military facilities throughout the country. The UFOs seemed to thumb their nose at the Soviets and their military secrets, while remaining impervious to all attempts by Soviet jets, bombs, and missiles to bring them down. In our next chapter, we examine some of the most amazing of the numerous UFO sightings reported by members of the Soviet armed forces.

CHAPTER 3.

SOVIET MILITARY ENCOUNTERS WITH UFOs FROM THE CIVIL WAR THROUGH THE 1930s

History is mostly silent about sightings and encounters between the Red Army and UFOs that took place prior to the 1940s. Occasionally, long-lost accounts are found. Most reports are probably still locked away in the impenetrable archives left behind after the fall of the USSR. N.I. Khrenov, director of the Donetzk Center of Air Travel and an airline captain, recalls a story told him by his grandmother, a nurse in the Red Army during the bloody Russian Civil War. Nurse Khrenova was a courageous woman who, if needed, would shoot to protect her patients. The incident she revealed took place in the Crimea. Many of the wagons that comprised the military unit's transport were lost in the battle and left behind. Wounded soldiers were being transported on the few remaining wagons, and not many guards were available to protect them. Any attack by the enemy would mean a massacre of the Red Army soldiers. The members of the convoy moved ahead very slowly, refrained from smoking, and used very little light. A machine-gun cart (*tachanka*) pressed forward, while members of the convoy including Nurse Khrenova, scoured the area, looking for enemies. It was then that she and the others with her noticed a very strange spectacle.

In the darkness ahead of them they observed a radiant object described as a "marquee" [large tent or canopy], and around it moved figures clad in "armour," as if covered with "scales." The Red Guards felt something sinister and alien coming from the strangers. After a brief deliberation, the Red Guards decided to approach the object and open fire on the "counter-revolutionaries" dressed in "armour." When they did so, their horses became suddenly uncontrollably frightened and bolted, pulling the machine-gun cart away into the darkness (*Almanac NLO-Svyazniye vselennoy*, Issue 22, 1995). In the following years, Soviet soldiers and officers would use other, more advanced weapons against similar strange entities and their unidentified flying objects. The results were almost always the same -- disastrous. We know almost nothing about UFOs in Russia in the 1920s and 1930s, except that the KGB had a deep interest in the paranormal, spearheaded by Gleb Bokiy, the head of one of the NKVD/KGB's most powerful departments. Stalinist terror and its purges of political opponents took their toll. People were afraid to discuss anything outside the normal range of existence. This changed, however, after Nazi Germany's bloody invasion of the Soviet Union.

Soviet World War II Tu-2 Aircraft

UFOs OVER SOVIET BATTLEFIELDS

Just as their allies did, the Soviet military observed strange flying object over their troops and battlefields in World War II. Sightings of UFOs had also been reported by the Germans, perhaps as early as 1940. A report on file at the Russian Ufology Research Center describes a UFO sighting over Poland in 1944. The principal eyewitness was Lev Petrovich Ovsischer, a decorated Soviet pilot-navigator of bomber aircraft, who had fought against Hitler's armies throughout the war. He later graduated from the Military Air Academy of the Soviet Army and served for many years in the fighter aviation division of the Soviet Air Force. A former colonel of the Soviet Air Force, later in his life he resided in Israel, where he was an honorary colonel of Israel's Defence Forces. In November of 1944, Ovsischer and other Soviet aviators observed a strange, bright object in the sky over a frontline airfield in the Warsaw area. The brightly-illuminated UFO hovered at high altitude, in a stationary position, for about fifteen minutes. Suddenly, it ascended at great velocity and own phenomenon, Ovsischer and the other observers had no idea what they had just seen. As a result of this sighting disappeared from view. Since "flying saucers" were not yet a widely-known, Ovsischer began to collect reports about UFO sightings by military personnel in the Soviet Union.

Another significant sighting took place on August 26, 1943, at the Kursk Bulge, site of a crucial tank battle between the Soviet Army and the Nazi panzers. Senior Lieutenant Gennady Zhelaginov was watching Soviet artillery shells flying into the sky, headed toward the German defence lines when he noticed an odd, sickle-shaped object. The strange object was generally dark blue in color but had a bright orange middle. It moved to the southwest at great velocity and soon disappeared from Zhelaginov's view. Zhelaginov was left with the impression that he had seen a living organism, because the midsection of the UFO continually expanded and contracted as if it were "breathing." The object stood out distinctly against a background of explosions from the Soviet artillery. The report about this strange sighting was signed by a number of other military personnel who witnessed it. There was also a report of a huge UFO that hovered over the neutral Kursk Bulge area just before the start of a battle between the USSR and Germany. The Soviet high command feared that the object was a secret Hitler super weapon. A drawing of the UFO was made and was signed by several Soviet colonels, who asserted that it was authentic. The drawing found its way into in ufologist Feliks Zigel's archives, but then disappeared. Professor Burdakov, a friend of the late ufologist, knew the contents of his archives, but said he never saw the actual report.

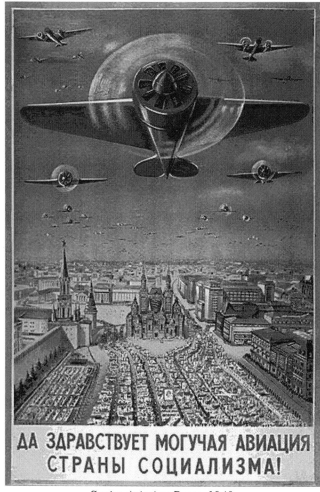

Soviet Aviation Poster1940s

Retired Soviet Colonel Gherman Kolchin published an article in *NLO Magazine* (2000), in which he gave the recollections of A. Kovalchuk, a Lieutenant Colonel during the World War II. A huge, dirigible-like object between 300 and 500 feet in length, visited the military airfield where Kovalchuk was stationed. Although it seemed to be a dirigible, it had no gondola and hovered at an altitude of 1,600 feet. Perceiving a possible threat to the airfield, air defence units fired on the "dirigible" with cannons and machine guns, but the weapons did not affect the object at all. Seemingly oblivious to the attack against it, the UFO continued flying at a leisurely pace over the airfield and disappeared into the distance.

Poster Depicting Soviet Military Leaders

Regarding alleged Nazi experimentation on flying discs, Sergey Korolyov, and M.K. Tikhonravov, prominent Soviet scientists, reportedly mentioned "German discs" in at least one of their reports, but did not give many details. They visited Germany after the Nazis were defeated. Tikhonravov went through Pomerania with a group of scientists in the ranks of Marshal Konev's armies. He was the first Russian to see the bases, factories, and barracks of the SS forces that guarded and maintained the V-1 and V-2 projects. S.P. Korolyov was later sent to Germany on an official mission to study and select materials directly related to the V-2 program. Professor Burdakov maintains in his possession many interesting reports about the V-1 and V-2 programs from those Soviet experts who had worked in Germany during the last months of the war, and in 1945-46. He has materials on the jet-propelled aircraft tested in the Third Reich prior to such tests having been undertaken in either the United States or the USSR. However, he has no reliable data on the testing of any "flying discs." The Germans, he stated, did have diagrams. They had prepared plans, had done some testing using models, and had done many calculations, but there was no evidence of any actual flights. The professor thinks that the Germans encountered difficulties turning their ideas into a viable aircraft. The Nazis did test strange-looking aircraft at Prague's Khbely airfield in 1944. Czech journalists representing *Signal* magazine reported in 1990 that the Nazis tested an aircraft that, according to eyewitnesses was spherical, and had a diameter of about 22 feet. It had a small, dropped cockpit, four tall "legs" (supports) with tiny wheels. The aircraft's hull was made from metal or possibly was covered with a silver-colored fabric. There was something like a jet engine. The craft commenced its flight by gaining an altitude of 250 feet and then flew for a few hundred feet before serious instability forced it to land. When the Red Army liberated Prague, the NKVD removed everything from the airfield. Another report, by a Russian prisoner of war, who survived Nazi concentration camps, tells a similar story of German test flights of experimental aircraft in the vicinity of Pennemunde in September of 1943. One primitive machine, equipped with a Messerschmitt 262 engine, crashed and burned. Given all these difficulties encountered by German engineers, it is probably safe to say that the UFOs sighted in wartime Europe were not of German origin.

ENCOUNTERS AFTER THE WAR

Two of the better-known Soviet UFO cases of the 1940s involved a test pilot named Apraksin. On June 16, 1948, he was conducting flights over Baskunchak Lake, a salt lake in the Astrakhan Region of Russia, when he encountered a cigar-shaped UFO. Baskunchak Lake is the largest salt lake in Russia and is flanked by Bolshoye Bogdo Mountain, a hill that rises nearly 600 feet above the surrounding grassland. The lake is located about 170 miles north of the Caspian Sea and about 30 miles east of the Volga River. After spotting the UFO, Apraksin gave chase, approaching the object at an altitude of about 6.5 miles. The UFO's response was quick and pitiless, emitting a ray that temporarily blinded Apraksin and damaged his engine and other equipment. One year later, on May 6, 1949, Apraksin had another encounter with a UFO. In the area of Vol'sk, while flying at the altitude of 9 miles, Apraksin sighted a cigar-shaped craft. The UFO would not allow his aircraft to approach closer than 6 to 7 miles before moving farther away. Finally, the UFO turned on a beam that damaged the airplane's onboard electrical hardware, turned off radio communications, and damaged the protective glass of the cockpit, affecting the structural integrity of the cockpit. Apraksin was barely able to land his aircraft on Volga's shore before passing out. He spent the next two and a half months in a hospital. The encounters were first mentioned in the underground "samizdat" publications of the 1980s and in Vadim Chernobrov's 1997 book *Nad propastyu neraskritikh tayn (Over the Abyss of Unsolved Mysteries)*.

Interestingly, the hill located just south of the lake is a very unusual and dynamic geological landmark. A fault line that runs directly through the area continues to push Bolshoye Bogdo Mountain upward as Lake Baskunchak decreases at a rate of about one millimetre per year. The hill is home to many unexplored caves and narrow shafts. The caves that have been explored (about 30 in total) are fascinating. The Baskunchakskaya Cave, the largest in the Caspian region, was discovered in 1939. The Crystal Cave is 328 feet long and 100 feet deep. Three entrances are gateways to mysterious mazes, passages, and unexplored rock formations. In the days of the nomads, the hill was called Bogdo-ona (Sacred Mountain). A long time ago, a Kalmyk temple existed at the apex of the hill. The Kalmyks believed that on the eastern, rocky slope of the sacred mountain lives the spirit of the fallen giant Tsagan Ebugay. He chased away those who were not initiated, scaring them with terrifying sounds.

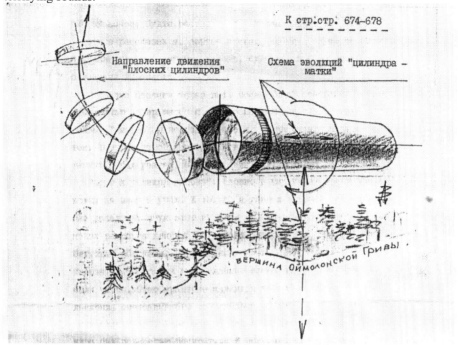

1953, Drawing of Object Sighted Over Siberia

SINISTER SIGHTING OF 1953

In 1953, a bizarre and frightening UFO incident took place in the area known as Krasnoyarsk Kray, not very far away from the site of the Tunguska Explosion. The eyewitness to the incident was a highly reliable source, a writer, scientist, and lecturer named Veniamin Dodin. He had authored 26 books and for 20 years had taught Soviet military engineers, but after running afoul of the government, he was arrested in 1940 and spent the next 14 years in prisons, concentration camps, and exile throughout the USSR. On a clear night in June of 1953, Dodin walked back to his hut at the Ishimba River. The taiga [forest] was quiet, light winds chased away all clouds. All of a sudden, Dodin heard a high-pitched noise, seemingly inside his head. Looking up, he saw a long cylindrical craft, which seemed to be gleaming as it hovered over the clouds at a distance of about two miles from Dodin. Dodin could see that the UFO had a rotating, drum-shaped body. The hull was girded with something that resembled a moving staircase with many steps. Completely opened and half-turned toward Dodin was the aft end of the cylinder. Dodin immediately assumed that the object was a dirigible, but the absence of cabins or cockpit confused the scientist. The object, slowly rotating, moved in Dodin's direction. He noticed that the cylinder had something like a narrow aft-end protruding from its otherwise ellipsoid body. The design of the "dirigible" appeared to be technologically incorrect to Dodin. He had no doubts that the object was a dirigible. What worried the exiled scientist was what payload the object could be carrying. There was a top-secret Soviet research center in the area, the so-called "Box 26." New types of super-powerful weapons were being developed behind the walls of "Box 26," and Dodin assumed that he had inadvertently entered the testing area. Then he noticed that the "aft end" was actually a flat, drum-shaped body. It separated itself from the cylinder and ascended rapidly. The noise Dodin felt in his ears diminished somewhat but became even less pleasant, sounding something like a painful squeak. Several more of these "flat drums" exited from the dirigible and ascended. Then the open end of the mysterious object closed, and the cylinder flew away. Dodin's earache was gone, too. He looked for the "flat drums" that had come out of the cylinder, but they had all zoomed out of sight into the night. The sky was brighter now, as the morning was approaching. Dodin kept observing the sky from his hut, but there was nothing left to see.

The "dirigible" returned the following night. As a scientist, Dodin knew perfectly well that no man-made object could travel at such velocities as to be able to instantly disappear from view. Was this object some kind of super aircraft? Dodin was quite worried that those who ran the sinister "Box 26" would come to the area. Even exiles like him and inmates of local concentration camps heard horrible rumours about the projects of the secret research center. And yet, Dodin was a scientist and a researcher; hence, he decided to investigate. He took photographs of the object with his camera. Should authorities catch him, his fate would be sealed; an exile taking photographs in the forbidden Oimolon area would be sent back to the GULAG camps, or worse. But Dodin was a brave person, and he observed the UFOs for over 40 hours. The objects continued to "pour out" the smaller flat drums. In turn, the "drums" vanished almost instantly. Dodin estimated that each "drum" was approximately 80 feet in diameter. The mother ship ("dirigible") was approximately 650 feet in diameter. Each mother ship "threw out" eight perfectly and smoothly polished "flat drums." Dodin used a Zeiss theodolite to observe the strange objects, for he had no other tools. The eyepiece he looked through enabled him to discern slight luminescence emanating from the panels of the "drums." The mother ship did not emit any radiance. Dodin tried, in vain, to reach the site of the nearest cylinder. He failed every time. Moreover, he became ill whenever he approached the site. Prior to the incident Dodin had experienced no major ailments. Now, he experienced sharp pains in his joints. The same sharp, painful noises as on the first day he observed the cylinder returned. It was an unbearable pain, and it forced Dodin to turn back. As soon as he got home, Dodin fell asleep for a long time.

The MVD troops (KGB of the period) arrived in the area in early July, accompanied by Soviet military pilots. The secret police noticed Dodin's camera, and confiscated it and the film. He was questioned extensively, and after they took away his camera, Dodin was certain that he photographed some kind of top secret Soviet project. The scientist found out later that he was wrong. As it turned out, the objects Dodin had seen were also greatly troubling to the Soviet military commanders in the area, too. They also had apparently seen the objects. Even worse, the "mother ship" gave off some form of radiation at super high frequencies that interfered with local radar and other electronics. The radiation became so intense that the MVD and pilots decided to "evacuate." Before fleeing the site, however, they ordered Dodin to continue his observations. The entire incident is still classified in Russia, but Mark I. Shevelyov, who later headed the Arctic Aviation Agency, knew the reason for the secrecy. It turns out that the Soviet leadership was very concerned about the UFOs of the Oimolon area but originally held back from mounting an assault against the objects. Stalin had died just months prior to these sightings, and the political situation in the USSR was unstable. Nonetheless, on August 7, 1953, the Soviets decided to try to evict the UFOs from their airspace over Ishimba. Two interceptor aircraft, each carrying a two-man crew, were launched against the strange objects. When the Soviet aircraft fired air-to-air missiles at the UFOs, the missiles inexplicably turned away from their targets and plunged down to the forest below, starting a massive forest fire. During the engagement, all radar equipment within a 120-mile radius of the brief air battle ceased to function. When the dust of battle had settled, the two Soviet aircraft and all four men aboard had vanished into thin air and were never seen again.

Dodin never forgot the evening of the doomed air attack. His radio made a piercing noise and powered down. Then an ear-piercing noise hit Dodin, causing him to black out. He awoke hours later and, when he went outside his hut, he discovered a world painted in a strange greenish hue. The eerie green luminosity in the area persisted for over a month, before fading slowly, like radiation after a nuclear explosion. Four years later, on July 24, 1957, Soviet aircraft engaged another UFO that had appeared suddenly over Soviet anti-aircraft installations on the Kuril Islands. Not a single shot fired by the Soviets struck the target, and it left the area unaffected by the engagement.

ALTAI, 1950-1957

The Altai Kray and Mountainous Altai are located near the Pamir, Himalayan and Tien-Shen mountainous systems. Mountainous Altai is a sparsely populated area, and the Soviet government had used it for weapons testing - and abused it repeatedly. The Baikonur Cosmodrome is in the area, as well as the Semipalatinsk nuclear test range and the Katunski power station. Because the Soviets conducted nuclear explosions in Kazakhstan between 1950 and 1957, the Altai was contaminated no less than eight times. It was around this time that Soviet military commanders began reporting to Moscow that UFOs frequently visited the Mountainous Altai. A. Plaksin, an important military UFO researcher, mentioned the area in an interview with the Russian newspaper *Komsomol'skaya Pravda* on May 31, 2002. The Soviet military ufologists consider the area one of the most important anomalous zones in the former USSR Sergei Skvortzov, researcher of paranormal phenomena in the Altai, writing in *NLO Magazine* (1999), revealed an amazing UFO encounter that occurred in the area. It happened on August 17, 1954, at 8:12 a.m., according to a log entry of an anti-aircraft unit guarding a missile battalion very close to the Chinese border. Radar registered strange interference, and a few moments later, soldiers observed an object that resembled a rocket but had no stabilizers and moved horizontally at a very low speed. The movement of the UFO somewhat resembled that of a dirigible. Three missiles were fired at it, but all three exploded before reaching the target. The object ascended rapidly and soon thereafter disappeared. A commission from the Ministry of Defence, sent to investigate, arrived the day after the sighting. The commission members determined that there was no "justifiable" reason for firing missiles, and the commanding officer of the missile battalion was removed from his position.

THE LOTOS GROUP, ALTAI

Rumours about this military group circulated back in the 1980s. Sergey Skvortzov confirmed the existence of Lotos in his article in *NLO Magazine* (1999). If true, the Lotos Group was formed in the middle of 1960s. It was created in the Main Intelligence Directorate of the Defence Ministry, USSR. The duties of the secret group included collection of reports and data about all paranormal activities taking place in the Armed Forces of the USSR. The group had a special laboratory where experiments were conducted aimed at creating cutting-edge weapons, based on use of gravitational and electromagnetic fields. Those unit commanders who sent reports to the Lotos Group signed secrecy oaths. According to researcher Skvortzov, the officers from Lotos were frequent visitors to the Altai Mountains area, presumably to study the paranormal events there.

Soviet Photo from Unknown Souce Depicting UFO Behind Soviet Fighter

UFO ENCOUNTER IN 1967: SOLID RAYS

In March of 1993, *AURA-Z* magazine (Moscow) published an account of a UFO sighting and ensuing encounter. The principal eyewitness was Lev Vaytkin, Fighter Pilot of the 1st Class and a Lieutenant Colonel. He was an experienced aviator and a graduate of the Yeisk Top Naval Aviation College. On August 13, 1967, he flew his interceptor jet on a training flight. The night was calm, and the visibility unobstructed. A few minutes after 11 p.m., Vyatkin climbed to 32,000 feet. Below him, the lights of Yalta, a city on the shores of Black Sea, flickered. Readings from his instruments were normal, and everything was proceeding without incident. Suddenly, looking up from the instrument panel, Vyatkin noticed a large, oval-shaped UFO very close along his port side (left). A strange object so close to a military airplane worried the pilot, and he asked the flight commander, Major Musatov, "Who is in the zone?" Musatov checked the instruments and reported that all other planes had landed, and no one else was in the zone.

Vyatkin banked the plane to the right, trying not to lose sight of the UFO. Careful not to approach too close, the pilot tried to determine the direction in which it was moving. Several seconds later, the strange object's lights gradually dimmed, as if someone inside it were using a rheostat switch. Meanwhile the plane made a complete right turn and came back to its starting point. Vyatkin considered his next move and then decided to make the left turn he had planned. Banking to the left and adjusting the speed and thrust, Vyatkin noticed a flash of bright light from above straight ahead of his airplane. A slanting, milky-white, "solid" ray appeared in front of his airplane and closed in on him rapidly. Levelling his plane out at the last minute, Vyatkin was able to avoid running into the ray with the main part of his plane. However, the ray did make contact with his left wing. As soon as the ray touched the wing, there was a burst of tiny "sparkles" like those of a spent firework. The plane shook violently and the instruments registered readings that were off the scale. Vyatkin thought the ray appeared to be "solid." The strange "sparkling" effect seemed like a pillar stretching downward. Soon the light above and the ray below disappeared. Flying back to the airfield, Vyatkin kept searching the sky for the object, but it was gone. After landing safely, he noticed a slight glow emanating from the surface of the plane's wing that was struck by the strange ray. For many days afterwards, the wing's strange glow could be seen at night. Vyatkin was puzzled by the concept of a "solid ray" – that is, a ray that was not transparent or translucent but seemed to have taken a definite three dimensional solidity. He wondered if that's what he had really witnessed. Then he read an article in *Komsomolskaya Pravda* newspaper (October 17, 1989) titled "Cosmic Ghosts," which stated that "solid rays" do really exist, and that others have come in contact with them. The police chief of Voronezh, V. Selyavkin, described an experience where a bright, powerful ray of light suddenly descended upon him from above. It seemed "solid," pinning him to the ground with its "weight." Later it moved away and vanished.

Vyatkin collected other accounts of similar rays and discovered instances of where witnesses saw "solid" rays being projected from UFOs like telescope supports or probes. Vyatkin is of the opinion that the ray was a column of highly-magnetized, fluorescent gas, which was focused into a "pillar." Interestingly, Vyatkin had another UFO sighting six days prior to the solid ray sighting. Vyatkin's account was published in Vadim Chernobrov's book *Nad propastyu neraskritikh tayn*, Moscow, 1997. On August 7, 1967 at 6:30 a.m., Vyatkin was sitting inside the cockpit, checking the onboard indicators of his interceptor jet at a military airfield near Sevastopol. Suddenly, a jet maintenance technician, Nikolay Yemelyanenko, tapped on his glass and pointed to a huge, luminescent sphere hovering in the sky about one the airfield. The UFO, which moved north to south at about 40 miles per hour, had the color and appearance of a burning match, and its diameter was over 250 feet. The sun was not up, yet, and the Soviet airmen were able to see the object very clearly against the cloudless background. They noticed that the UFO had a blue, spherical center with bright-green edges. The strange sphere moved noiselessly across the sky at an altitude of about 1,000 feet, as more and more witnesses gathered down below to view its passing. It was later determined that radar had not detected the object. Vyatkin was eager to power up his jet and chase the object, in order to investigate further. He repeatedly asked his control center for permission to pursue the UFO, but his requests were denied. He was told that a chase of the object could not be authorized. Vyatkin determined later that his superiors were fearful of the consequences of taking any aggressive action against what was clearly a UFO possessed of superior technology. They feared that any attempt to pursue the object could be interpreted as the initiation of an attack. Apparently, the Soviet air force commanders were prompted by earlier episodes of UFOs attacking or destroying Soviet planes when threatened. Vyatkin and five technicians continued their observation of the UFO, which until now had been moving at the same speed and altitude, and maintaining a uniform luminosity. Suddenly, the object stopped, and from its center, a small ray appeared and shot down toward the ground. Moments later, the sphere "turned off this ray" and vanished instantly. Some witnesses stated that the UFO disappeared into thin air. Vyatkin disagrees; he is sure that the sphere zoomed up into the atmosphere at a high rate of speed. He heard loud noises in his earphones, resembling mechanical "hissing" sounds.

1974, BOROSOGLEBSK AREA

The Borosoglebsk area is described by researcher A. Plaksin as one of the most important anomalous zones of the former USSR. In 1974, a very interesting case took place there, at the Povorino airfield. A motionless black cloud, about one mile long, appeared over the field, hovering at the altitude of four miles. Radar indicated that it was an aircraft, and a Soviet fighter jet with a two-man crew was scrambled to intercept. As soon as the jet entered the cloud, a sharp siren pierced the both men's helmet earpieces. The sound was intense, far above the "pain threshold." At the same time, their instrument panel illuminated the "dangerous altitude" reading, and the aircraft began shaking violently. With great difficulty, the fliers powered down their onboard systems and barely managed to guide the aircraft out of the cloud. After the harrowing encounter, the mysterious cloud remained over the airfield for four hours, before finally disappearing. SETKA researchers were never able to determine what that "cloud" was or what it consisted of.

ENCOUNTERS IN THE YEARS 1976 THROUGH 1978

Colonel Lev Ovscischer (From SETKA Program Document)

Apparently as a result of the dire consequences suffered by Soviet aviators when engaging UFOs, a number of important UFO-related policies were reportedly put into place sometime around 1976. The Soviet Air Force high command absolutely prohibited pilots from having any contact with unidentified flying aircraft. Furthermore, pilots were prohibiting from getting any closer than six miles from a UFO. Clearly, the Soviets had sustained loses at the hands of these strange craft and feared further retribution.

STILL CLASSIFIED

Among the tragic encounters between Soviet aviators and UFOs was a remarkable incident that occurred in the late 1960s, reported by Colonel Ovsischer and Veniamin Dodin. It happened along the Soviet border with both Iran and Afghanistan. Six Soviet jet aircraft and all twelve airmen perished in an incident involving unidentified flying objects. Apparently it was a UFO attack, but who attacked first? A directive issued in 1965 by the Supreme Commander of the Soviet Air Defence Forces absolutely prohibited aviators from firing on or taking any military action against UFOs. Nonetheless, the Soviets were often faced with the conundrum resulting from the frequent presence of UFOs in top secret areas, such as sites for the testing of nuclear bombs, missiles, rockets, new technologies and weapons systems. UFOs were often seen hovered over missile silos and other secret facilities. To the great irritation of aviation, civil, and military officials, the UFOs also frequently appeared over forbidden Arctic territories. Legendary Soviet Arctic pilot Akkuratov once told E. Loginov, civil aviation minister, about four UFO encounters that he himself experienced. In addition, Akkuratov mentioned that other pilots had many more encounters but were hesitant to report them. Because the Soviet press had declared that UFOs did not exist, the pilots felt they would be ridiculed.

The highly militarized Soviet Arctic often attracted these mysterious, uninvited guests. In 1972, reddish, noiseless discs hovered over a radar installation. Panicked soldiers, including the principal eyewitness named Stieglitz, contacted the regiment's headquarters requesting orders and were told, "Do not report anymore. UFOs do not exist." Stieglitz and his comrades spent the next six hours observing the "non-existent" UFOs and tracking them on radar. Like all armies in the world, the Soviet Armed Forces had its share of bureaucrats, daredevils, political functionaries, brilliant strategists, and dull, bored commanders dreaming of retirement. The UFO phenomenon was more or less a priority, but just as their Western colleagues, the Soviet military were at loss as to how to classify UFOs and how to deal with them. 1976 was a wake-up year. In the summer, something occurred in the sensitive area along the Chinese border, in the Chita region. The border guards, air defence unit, and civilians reported a very unusual object in the sky that looked like an elongated cylinder with portholes. It moved horizontally around the area for three hours. At one time, it emitted three rays, directed downwards. Then suddenly, it vanished. Although seen by numerous eyewitnesses, the UFO did not register on any of the three different types of military radar that were in use in the area.

URKAN, SIBERIAN TAIGA

In the early1970s, both the USSR and China reported numerous UFO sightings and possible UFO landings in an anomalous area around the River Urkan, between Tinda and Zeya in Siberia, according to *Entsiklopedia Nepoznannogo* or *Encyclopedia of the Unknown*, compiled by Vadim Chernobrov, and published in Moscow in 1998. It was a time when tensions were dangerously high between the Soviets and Chinese, as warfare had recently broken out over the possession of the tiny Damansky Island. Into the middle of this boiling pot, frequent UFO sightings were reported by both sides. The Soviet Air Force dispatched units to search for UFO landing sites. And, when the UFOs appeared over Mongolia, Chinese border guards tried in vain to shoot them down, in vain. In fact, it was the Mongolians who first publicly revealed the UFO presence in the area. The Mongolians said that typical UFO flight routes went over Soviet territory, approximately 1,000 miles to the northeast of Ulan-Bator. Soviet radar operators scanned the area, trying to pinpoint more precisely where the UFO activity was occurring, but all attempts to locate the UFOs ended in failure. The only thing the Soviets could establish was that the UFOs appeared and then disappeared over the same area of the remote Siberian taiga, not far from Urkan. Feliks Zigel's book *UFO Landings in the USSR and Other Countries* (Volume 5, 1979) contains an amazing story of a UFO landing in Mongolia. Back in 1951, Soviet veterinarian V. D. Petrenko witnessed a UFO landing in the Gobi-Altai Almak area. One evening at about 7:00 p.m., he and a companion observed blinding flash on the slope of a mountain. About a mile away, they saw a curved object shaped like the "cap" of a mushroom cap over 300 feet in diameter. Moving up and down between the UFO and the ground directly below it were a number of humanoid beings. The beings seemed to be projecting light from both their "eyes" and their "abdomens." The eyewitnesses tried to approach the object, but encountered an invisible "energy field" about 1,600 feet before reaching the site. They stood and watched helpless for another twenty minutes, when suddenly the UFO began "flashing" and departed rapidly. The landing site contained scorched ground of 100 feet in diameter. Years later, at this very site, prospectors discovered rich veins of uranium ore.

"DO NOT FIRE!"

An astonishing UFO incident in Kazakhstan in 1976 shook up the Soviet military high command. At the Emba 11 air defence and anti-missile weapons test range near the Mugojar Hills, in the middle of a missile test, a huge UFO, measuring approximately 1,600 feet in diameter, suddenly appeared overhead. In the confusion that followed, the Soviet government's directive not to attack UFOs was disregarded, and the commanding general of the test range gave the "open fire" order and directed that an antiballistic missile be launched at the unidentified object hovering above them. The missile ascended toward the object, riding a plume of smoke, when suddenly the UFO emitted a beam that struck the missile, causing it to explode. No further aggressive action was taken, and the UFO later departed unmolested. According to an article by Mark Shteynbert in *Anomaliya* magazine (April 1992), the general was later punished by Soviet military officials for his aggression against the UFO. The Soviet Minister of Defence reminded his troops of the previous ban against attacking UFOs. The incident is also mentioned in Vadim Chernobrov's book *Nad propastyu neraskritikh tayn* (Moscow, 1997).

The order not to shoot was disobeyed at least once more, that we know about, this time in summer 1981, during the Afghan War. Mark Shteynberg, a Russian-American journalist and former veteran of the Soviet armed forces, reported that in August of that year a large, cigar-shaped UFO appeared near the USSR border with Iran, in the Turkmen town of Kizil-Arvat or Gyzylarbat [now called Serdar]. It was a time of tension along the Iranian border, because Saddam Hussein's Iraqui forces were fighting Ayatolla Khomeni's Iranian armies. The strange elliptical object, estimated at between 300 and 600 feet in diameter, hovered at an altitude of four miles over the air defence regiment of the Soviet 12th Army of the Air Defence Forces. It lit up the military radars in the area, verifying that it was a tangible, physical aerial object. As it moved toward the north in a noiseless and leisurely manner, two MIG-27 jets were scrambled to intercept it. The captain who flew the leading interceptor told his ground control that he had the target acquired. There was a tense pause as he awaited the command to fire from his ground controllers. Moments later, he was ordered to launch two missiles against the target. Pressing the release button, the two missiles slipped away toward the UFO. What happened next is beyond belief. The unidentified ship suddenly zoomed away at an incredible speed. The Soviet MIG and the two missiles it had fired just "winked" out of existence. No debris from the plane or its missiles was ever found, despite an extensive ground search following this incident.

According to Vadim Chernobrov's book *Nad propastyu neraskritikh tayn*, (Moscow, 1997), a special commission investigated the incident and confirmed all facts in the report prepared by the regiment's commander. As a result of his decision to attack the UFO without clearing it first with his superiors, he was demoted in rank (*Vestnik*, Issue 3, 1992). The commission did not accept his argument that his actions were justifiable because the sighting took place so close to the volatile Iranian border (within 60 miles). The Soviets had settled on a policy of not engaging UFOs, as had been previously advised by SETKA.

LENINGRAD AREA, 1977

Another curious airborne UFO encounter was revealed by ufologist A. Plaksin. On June 22, 1977, during training flights of the Soviet Tu-16 jet, one of the pilots saw something that he was destined never to forget. The jet was equipped with a so-called "cone" (target for shooting). At the moment that the pilot initialized the "cone," he observed a gigantic fiery sphere in front of the aircraft. Simultaneously, he heard a popping sound, the "cone" lost power, and the jet's engine stopped functioning. The pilot tried unsuccessfully to restart it, but after a few seconds it started working by itself.

BALKHASH, 1978

Did technology from a crashed UFO enable the Soviet Union to bolster its missile defence systems in the 1970s and 80s? That was the assertion of Alexey Valentinovich Smirnov, an engineer and former Soviet military officer, in an interview with Ukrainian newspaper *Nasha Gazeta* (December 18, 1999). Smirnov stated that at least ten people who resided in Ukraine, had served with him, and could confirm his account. In the 1980s the Soviets knew that U.S. Pershing missiles would take just eight minutes to reach Soviet borders. Smirnov and his colleagues worked to create a missile that would be able to shoot down the Pershings during the eight minute window. The problem Soviets faced was that while operating at the supersonic speed, their missile became engulfed by a plasma "hat" when flying in the thick layers of the atmosphere. The missile's manoeuvrability was lost, and it could not be controlled. Thousands of Soviet researchers had tried to improve their missile's design.

1990 Sighting at Dorozhkino Village

Smirnov had access to the Tupolev Design Bureau albums, which contained photographs and technical descriptions of UFOs. Those in charge of the project apparently believed that such photos and drawings might help inspire the design creativity of Soviet missile design engineers. Smirnov heard a story from fellow engineers about the shooting down and recovery of a flying saucer in 1978. The UFO was reportedly felled by a missile designed by rocket engineer Pyotr Grushin, the man responsible for the V-750 rocket that brought down the American U-2 spy plane piloted by Francis Gary Powers.

Late in 1978, a UFO was observed hovering about 18 miles above the vast Soviet Sary Shagan anti-ballistic test range on the steppe by the Lake Balkhash (Kazakhstan). The Sary-Shagan ("Golden Bay" in Kazakh) test site was engaged in testing strategic anti-aircraft defence, anti-ballistic missile defence, and anti-satellite systems. Grushin is said to have ordered the launch of one of his missiles at the strange object, and the missile reportedly scored a direct hit. The UFO burst into many fragments. For an entire week, large numbers of Soviet soldiers scoured the ground where the UFO crashed, picking up every fragment, no matter how small, of the unearthly object. Soldiers who found fragments were rewarded with vacation leave.

The wreckage from the UFO proved to be a gold mine of technological information for the Soviets. Fragments showed that the UFO consisted of unusual elements that resembled manmade electronic circuit boards, except that their elements consisted of atoms and molecules skilfully "mounted" on a silica (silicon) base. Grushin noted that human technology did not yet have the ability to mount elementary particles; however, he was able to extrapolate certain principles and apply them to his missile designs. As a result, the nose and rudder controls of Soviet anti-aircraft missiles were redesigned to include a silicon coating, which is applied using a plasma-spray technique. This innovation, supposedly derived from studying the crashed UFO's technology, enabled Soviet designers to create a missile able to cross the supersonic barrier in the atmosphere and shoot down incoming ICBMs.

1981: A SECOND SUN

Engineer Smirnov was also witness to another startling UFO event that occurred on July 26, 1981 at a test range of the Soviet anti-air defence forces. That morning, a little after 5 o'clock, Smirnov woke up, filled with a sense of dread. He was scheduled to observe several test missile launches later the same morning. As he went through his routine of waking up, he glanced out an open window of his apartment and received the shock of his life. In the predawn sky, he could see two suns. In addition to the sun we all see every day, there was another - a sinister, red sphere. The engineer dismissed what he saw was an optical phenomenon due to atmospheric conditions and went on about his business. Soon thereafter, while he and fifty more officers were in a meeting area before leaving for the test range, they all saw the same crimson "sun," flying at an incredible speed, approaching their position from the south. The bizarre sphere hovered over their heads for about five seconds and then turned around, disappearing off to the east.

Soviet engineers were shocked. They knew perfectly well that such a manoeuvre, at the given velocity and altitude was impossible, according to their understanding of physics. No human being could survive such turns and the stresses involved. No terrestrial flying craft could maintain its structural integrity while flying in such manner. Later, while discussing the incident, Soviet officers recalled the overwhelming fear they all experienced at the time. Smirnov lived in Kiev at the time of the interview, and another witness, Yelena Grigoryevna Zaslavskaya, resided nearby, and could attest to his story, according to the former engineer. The wife of an officer at the test range, she required hospitalization because of the distress associated with the UFO sighting. The townspeople quietly discussed the incident. Unit commanders were under orders from their superiors to collect all information about UFO sightings, document it on special forms, and send it to a designated military unit in Moscow. Smirnov and his colleagues were eager to report what they had seen to the SETKA program. The airspace over the test range was divided into sectors. Each sector was observed by special radio telescopes that registered all flight details of launched missiles. Thus, visiting UFOs were photographed frequently. Reports about UFOs were then sent to the appropriate place; Smirnov recalled at least twenty such reports.

1981, MUKACHEVO, SOUTHWEST UKRAINE

In early 1970s, building of the new Soviet *Dnepr* above-the-horizon radar system began near Mukachevo, Ukraine. According to ufologist A. Plaksin, on September 14, 1981, a MIG-23 jet encountered a UFO while conducting a training flight. The *Dnepr* had a large airdrome with a small interceptor base As the MIG flew over the area, a fiery sphere appeared from nowhere, right in front of the aircraft. Fire or radiation from the object destroyed the front end of the jet, forcing the pilot to eject from the burning cockpit. Plaksin claimed that this incident and other similar UFO encounters were never explained.

1981: STANISLAV MOSKALENKO'S TALE

The Naval Historical Center in Washington, D.C. has a copy of an article published in *Soviet Soldier* (August 1991) about a striking UFO encounter reported by Soviet pilot Stanislav Moskalenko. The USSR Ministry of Defence published the magazine in English and German, and the author of the article, V. Vasilyev, went to great lengths to confirm the episodes told him by Moskalenko. According to Vasilyev, the pilot is a well-balanced, clear thinking man, not prone to fantasies. In the early 1980s, Moskalenko served in Central Asia and was the youngest pilot in his regiment. On weekdays he flew missions, and on weekends, he was on standby. The political situation was tense and a neighbouring state continuously resorted to muscle flexing. Its bombers often skirted the Soviet border, and Soviet planes had to escort them out.

As Moskalenko relaxed at the flight headquarters, the code to scramble came over the loudspeaker. Moskalenko ran to his supersonic fighter and was airborne moments later, climbing rapidly into a bright, cloudless sky. He made a corrective half-turn and noted that in front of him lay the expanse of foreign territory. Moskalenko and another pilot were both being guided by ground controllers to a target that was visible on radar but was not visible to the naked eye. The other fighter pilot, dispatched ahead of Moskalenko, had attempted to fire at the coordinates given to him but was unable to find a target. His second and third attacks also failed. There simply was no target that he could see. The mystified pilot could not detect the UFO either visually or on his radar sight. The jet fighter was ordered back to the base, and Moskalenko was ordered to give it a try.

Moskalenko's attacks also failed. However, the controller ordered him to maintain his direction of flight straight at the object on the radar screens. The pilot understood that he was supposed to ram his aircraft into the target. But, what was it that he was about to ram? When the fighter plane pierced the air at the spot where the target supposedly was, a light fog enveloped the canopy for a split second. There were no clouds, and yet there was fog. The ground controllers were shouted at Moskalenko that the target was right below his plane. The pilot made a sharp downward turn but could see nothing at first. Then, far below him, hovering very near the ground, he saw an object moving left to right. The aircraft controller, Captain Oleg Kazyunin, later stated that the target blip on the radar scope had turned into a "thick dot." It flashed suddenly, turned green, and began moving quickly towards the scope's upper rim. Its movement was so swift that Oleg exclaimed that the target was leaving the area at a vertical velocity much faster than a missile.

Meanwhile, in his cockpit, strange sensations were sweeping over Moskalenko. His vision became blurred, and then he seemed to start hallucinating. He saw strange visions of fires and "masks" that seemed very blurry. When he came to, Moskalenko levelled out his plane and reported to ground control that he had been unable to find the target. His altimeter showed that instead of descending in an inverted flight, he was actually ascending. For three days Moskalenko's entire regiment sought out the ghostly target. They flew hundreds of sorties, tried using several different types of radar sights, and even requested that Moscow allow them to test secret equipment. When it became clear that what they sought was something incomprehensible and inexplicable, it was decided to terminate the missions. In 1990, Moskalenko related the incident to a friend, Major Oleg Belomestnov. During the telling of the story, Moskalenko suddenly felt a powerful blow to the back as if delivered by an invisible fist. He was then suddenly lifted up off the ground a few feet and then flung down violently. That this happened was confirmed by Belomestnov and corroborated by *Soviet Soldier* editors. Belomestnov helped Moskalenko back to his feet, taken aback by what he saw.

Walking home, assisted by Major Belomestnov, Moskalenko was in pain and confused. He had visions, vague and hazy, of strange landscapes. Suddenly he and Belomestnov were ordered to stop. A short lean man, clad in black, warned him that he might suffer another "energized strike." The stranger paid no attention to Belomestnov, who verbally assaulted him. He told Moskalenko that this was a warning only. The stranger leaned down and touched Moskalenko's swollen leg with the palm of his hand. At the touch of the man's hand, sudden heat was generated and all pain vanished. Not only did the touch seem to heal Moskalenko's body of all pain, it also cleared away all the troubling "visions" that had haunted him since the attack on the UFO.

The stranger asked Moskalenko questions that convinced the Soviet pilot that the man was telepathic. He told Moskalenko that the visions he experienced for years had been part of an information package stored in his subconscious by the UFO occupants, whom he described as "evil." This information had been transmitted to Moskalenko in the form of visions by the UFO he had been ordered to shoot down that day. The transfer of information had not been entirely successful, because Moskalenko resisted it, and the result was distorted information that led to visions and hallucinations. The stranger also told Moskalenko that the UFO beings had psychically "assaulted" him while he was talking to Belomestnov, because he was disclosing too much information about his UFO encounter. The stranger described the UFO occupants as "forces of evil." Then, suddenly, the man in black "disappeared" before the startled eyes of both Moskalenko and Belomestnov.

IRANIAN BORDER, 1985

The previously mentioned Soviet engineer, Alexey Valentinovich Smirnov, disclosed another major UFO encounter along the Soviet border with Iran, in an interview with Ukrainian newspaper *Nasha Gazeta* (December 18, 1999). Early on August 17, 1985, at about 3 a.m., reports came in to the military headquarters about strange objects appearing in the sky over weapons testing areas. Eyewitnesses saw numerous objects of different shapes, including crosses, rings, and bright dots. The officer on duty, Lieutenant Colonel Valentin to photograph the objects and an estimated six miles of film was shot. Photographers were ordered to develop the film and use the photos in writing Ivanovich Kan, issued orders a report about the incident. The report also contained 30 illustrations of the various objects observed in the sky over the test range. The main UFO seen was a huge white cross against the dark sky, with each of the two crossing bars being about 2,600 feet long. It hovered in the sky for a long time and then disappeared, as if into thin air. Lieutenant Colonel Pyotr Sergeyevich Meleschuk was in charge of the putting together the report, and Lieutenant Colonel Alim Antonovich Ustimenko, was responsible for the technical portion of the project. Both men were residing in the Ukraine in 1999 when their story was disclosed. Also seen on the night of the event were seven white rings visible against the dark sky. The rings all moved the time. Two of the rings flew on a parallel course and then the smaller was absorbed into the larger, and there remained only one ring.

From Russian UFO Archives

A third group of objects consisted of bright dots. Strong light shone from a bright dot in the sky and became diffused in a cone-like manner. The light was very intense and

70

did not abate anywhere along the luminescence. The report on these unusual sightings was sent to Moscow. Smirnov and his colleagues made no further inquiries. The Cold War was in full swing, and they were trying to create new missile technology. Nobody knew what hovered over Soviet test ranges and facilities on that day. Some people believe they were UFOs; others think they were enemy spy equipment of some unknown type. The Soviets were concerned that so many strange objects appeared right before tests of new missiles. When Smirnov was asked about his opinion as to the nature of UFOs, the Ukrainian replied that he is an engineer and a pragmatist and does not really believe in mystical events. He said he does believe that intelligent extraterrestrials exist but does not think we are knowledgeable enough to communicate with "them." Smirnow said, "One can fantasize as much as possible, but that is how things are now." Smirnov often observed rockets piercing the ozone layer of the atmosphere and harsh cosmic radiation entering the air. It was a stunning spectacle. Half of the sky was filled with waves of blinding white color. "We feel pride, but do we really understand what happens at the moment? Maybe our experiments cause pain to an alien intelligence that co-exists with us in some other dimension. Similar to how a human being would feel pain, if a nail pierced his skin. So, they send objects to us in order to understand who we are, what we want, and why we do what we do," Smirnov said.

THE MONCHEGORSK OBJECT

In one of the most highly classified Soviet UFO incidents, the Soviet military reportedly captured a flying saucer and sent it to Monchegorsk for study and possibly reverse engineering. According to ufologists Konstantin Volf and Valentin Psalomschikov, former Soviet military pilot, Captain N.V. Fedotov, was ordered to a military post at the city of Monchegorsk. Once there, he was told that a UFO had been captured by the Soviet military and transported to the Monchegorsk area.

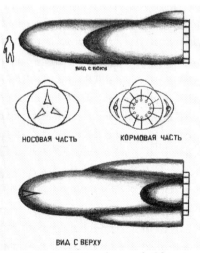

Sketch of Monchegorsk Object

Fellow officer told Fedotov the story, but they did not know the exact details, nor did they know of the location where the UFO was captured. They had no knowledge of the object's shape and size, but they did know that an explosion destroyed the UFO. Fedorov could not determine the precise date of the object's delivery to Monchegorsk, but in the approximate period when it happened, Mikhail Gorbachev, who was then the USSR president, had visited the region rather unrepentantly. Although his itinerary indicated he was to visit Severomorsk, for some reason, he visited Monchegorsk instead. Nobody seemed to be able to explain Gorbachev's sudden decision to go there, and some researchers believe he may have gone to view the captured UFO.

Soviet leader Mikhail Gorbachev

Noted Russian ufologist Yuri Stroganov, interviewed a former Soviet military man who claimed to have seen the Monchegorsk Object. Because the man signed a written statement of non-disclosure of the highly classified information, he did not want his real name released. He will be referred to as "B." The anonymous former soldier provided diagrams of the Monchegorsk object to Stroganov, who passed them along to the Russian Ufology Research Center.

The witness waited for five years after leaving military service before agreeing to tell his amazing story. Here is what he says he saw: In early August of 1987, B and four other servicemen from the Leningrad military region (*okrug*) were sent on an unusual mission to a military base in Northern Karelia to guard an "object" of unknown origin and purpose. The object had been recently discovered near Viborg. It was delivered to the vicinity of Monchegorsk by a military transport airplane, placed in the former fuel depot and put under heavy guard.

The guard detail was given strict orders not to let anyone come near, but the guards had an opportunity to look under the cover more than once. Their commanding officers gave the soldiers no explanations as to what they were guarding, but one of the Leningrad servicemen who, according to B, worked in the Leningrad HQ confided to them that the object was a UFO. Externally, the object resembled an American "space shuttle." Initially, the object's front part was mistaken for an aircraft's hull (fuselage). The object was estimated to be 45 feet in length, 14 feet wide and 8 feet high. The body appeared to possess a smooth, seamless, tan-grey finish. When touched, the surface seemed to be somewhat rough, as if ceramic. B claims that when the guards initially approached the object, each experienced pain. Three triangles in the front part were perceived only by the faint hue of their color. No exits or entry doors were visible.

In the rear (aft), the object looked somewhat chopped off, and there were neither wheeled undercarriages nor any supports. The bottom part of the body was completely smooth. Since the floor of the room was sloped, the object was placed on logs and railroad ties to prevent it from rolling away. About one week after the object's arrival, a special commission comprised of senior officers also arrived on location and at once began to study the object. Although B did not take any direct part in the investigation and research, he was able to observe from a distance. The commission tried to enter the object using autogenous welding techniques, but failed. After that unsuccessful attempt, the object was moved inside an aircraft hangar, which was essentially an artificial mound with metal gates. Once the object was inside, the gates were immediately welded shut and all the servicemen from Leningrad, except one, were dismissed from further duty at the site.

In early September of the same year, the Leningrad officer who had stayed behind -- the only one from the Leningrad group to take part in the actual study of the object – returned to Leningrad. He told the others that the commission had finally been able to penetrate part of the fuselage. The triangles, visible on the outside only because of their color tint, were transparent from inside of the object. Most likely, the area entered was a cockpit, or a control room. It definitely was not made for adult humans because two officers could barely stand inside it. Inside the cockpit they found two armchairs. What seemed like two steering wheels and a control panel, were located nearby. The control panel looked like a smoothly polished plate with no buttons, switches or devices of any type.

According to the officer, it took him half an hour to figure out how to put his hands on the "steering wheel." No one risked sitting in the armchairs. The officers then attempted to break something off. They were able to extract some shiny rods, which varied in size from about twenty centimetres to a meter, and were about 6 centimetres thick. The officers who had extracted the rods had worn gloves; yet traces of thermal burns were found on their unit from the *okrug*'s HQ. He told B and others that at the end of September the object, still sealed securely inside the hangar, had suddenly "just disappeared." The disappearancnce occurred in the midst of a sudden episode of intense and prolonged interference that affected radio transmissions and other electrical equipment at the base.

Stroganov cautions us to be prudent. The lieutenant's mission might have been to plant *dezinformatsia* (disinformation) and confuse members of the former special guard unit. One thing that seems hard to explain is how a 45-foot-long object could just suddenly "vanish" from a guarded shelter. Some researchers believe that the object did not disappear, but rather was moved to a top secret laboratory associated with the SETKA-MO program. Stroganov also thinks that is what happened. Ufologist A. Anfalov later reported that the Monchegorsk object had actually been recovered near the Veschevo Air Force base.

SOVIET TOP MILITARY BRASS AND UFOs

Gorbachev's platform for the new Soviet Union was founded on two now quite famous terms: *glasnost* (openness) and *perestroika* (restructuring). *Glasnost* set the stage for the Soviet military revelations about UFOs over the Soviet Union. The first report, about a sighting dated March 21, 1990, was published in the *Stalker-UFO* (Issue number 1, 1990) newspaper (Leningrad), and other media. The report was made by Colonel-General Igor Maltsev, who at the time was the Chief of the Main Staff of the Soviet Air Defence forces. The UFO he mentioned was a disk about 650 feet in diameter with pulsating lights forming a line along both sides. When the object flew horizontally, the line of lights was parallel to the horizon. When the UFO moved vertically, the lights were perpendicular to the horizon. The object moved around its axis, and travelled along a zigzag-like trajectory. The UFO was seen in the areas of Zagorsk, Pereyaslavl-Zalessky, Fryazin and Kirzhach. Radar confirmed the reports of eyewitnesses. Two fighter planes, one flown by Lieutenant Colonel A. Semenchenko, were dispatched to look at the object. The UFO hovered over a certain area and then resumed its movements. Its speed was three times greater than that of any manmade aircraft. The higher was its velocity, the brighter became its lateral lights. It was a noiseless craft, and it reached the altitude of 23,000 feet. The UFO clearly impressed Soviet generals. They refrained from attacking it, because it could have possessed formidable capacity for retaliation, according to General Ivan Tretyak, who was Commander in Chief of the Soviet Air Defence Forces and Deputy Minister of Defence at the time.

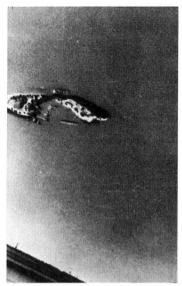

Norilsk, 1961

He confirmed Maltsev's statements during his own interview with the *LiteraturnayaGazeta* newspaper (November 9, 1990). What is curious, and supports other UFO military reports, is that the onboard radar of the fighter planes did not detect the UFO. At the same time, Tretyak refused to acknowledge the existence of UFOs and refused to speculate on the nature of the object. Colonel-General A. Maximov, Hero of the Socialist Labor and expert of Soviet Space program, stated that the Soviet Armed Forces had received special instructions to inform certain, special "institutes" about UFO in Each institute had "working groups" to study the incoming information. (*Stalker-UFO*, November 1990). In 1993 the existence of these special institutes was confirmed by Colonel-General V. Ivanov, Commander of the Military Space Forces. During an interview by the famous and highly respected Russian newspaper *Argumenti I Fakti* (Issue 16, 1993), Ivanov mentioned the existence of a military institute for UFO studies.

Former Soviet colonel and one of Russia's top UFO experts, Gherman K. Kolchin, discussed his military's interest in UFOs in an interview published in *Anomaliya* newspaper (Issue 2, 1995). He recalled the conversation with Colonel General Sapkov, who informed Kolchin about the bright green, elliptical UFO that hovered over the Kapustin Yar test range during secret tests of new military technology. The same Colonel-General gave more details in his memoirs.

The episode, reported in *Stalker-UFO* (Issue number 3, 1990), was dated November 1979. As Sapkov and other officers observed the UFO, it changed colours and hovered for thirty minutes over the secret rocket test range. Seven years later, Colonel General Sapkov observed what he believed was the very same UFO over Kapustin Yar, one of the most important military missile testing grounds in the USSR. It was Russia's first missile test range and was also used for satellite launches of the smaller Kosmos space vehicles. V-2 rockets were launched from there in 1946, becoming the very first ballistic missiles fired on Soviet territory. The officers assured Sapkov that UFOs were observed frequently over the testing area. According to General Yevgeniy Tarosev, the existence of UFOs is beyond doubt. He states it in a one-page article published in the popular Russian newspaper *Trud* on August 22, 1992. Tarosev at the time was the Chairman of the Scientific and Technical Committee of the "Commonwealth of Independent States," the political successor of sorts to the USSR. While he did not doubt the reality of UFOs and admitted that Soviet military aircraft had given chase, Tarosev stated that the "physical nature" of the phenomenon was unknown.

There has not been overt hostility from UFOs, as far as he knew, but the pilots had been warned to treat UFOs in a "peace-loving" way. Additional encounters between Soviet pilots and UFOs were disclosed in 1996 by Colonel-General Gennady Reshetnikov, Chief of the top Command Academy of the Air Defence Forces and a former Commander of the Air Defence Forces of the Soviet Far East. In an interview with noted ufologist Valery Uvarov, published in *Anomaliya* (January 30, 1996), Reshetnikov confirmed that he knew of several incidents where aircraft were scrambled to chase UFOs. He also investigated a UFO sighting in the late 1970's over the Arctic area of Norilsk. The UFO, a cigar-shaped craft with portholes, visited the area several times, alarming the local military units. A group of Soviet soldiers reportedly found a way to communicate with the UFOs, according to V. Alexeyev, Major General of the Russian Air Force, and official at the Space Communications Center. In comments made in the *Anomaliya* newspaper (Issue 8, 1997), Alexeyev said that at some "unnamed" weapons test ranges of the Soviet Armed Forces, when UFOs appeared, soldiers tried using a series of signals. Mostly they were physical signals, like spreading one's arms to one side or another. These signals would cause the UFOs, which were mostly spherical, to "compress" their shape in the direction that the signal was given. For example, if arms were raised upwards three times, the sphere would compress itself vertically three times in response.

In later years, ufologist Mikahil Gershtein acquired several SETKA documents, one of which listed the site of the contact and those involved with it. In the early 1980s, the Soviet leadership allowed conducting UFO-related experiments using various technologies, such as theodolites, radar, and so forth. These technologies did succeed in registering the presence of unidentified flying objects. Alexeyev, in his capacity with the military, received information about UFOs from military units throughout the former USSR. He was aware of the existence of the secret UFO research group that conducted the actual research, but due to secrecy, his tasks were limited to sending the collected data and information to his superiors. Military people do not press for explanations when none are offered. The question was put forth in this manner: we are interested in this and that. Then a chart containing images of UFOs that have been registered would be demonstrated. There were approximately fifty of such images, elliptical, spherical, spaceship-like UFOs, and so on.

THE SETKA INSTRUCTIONS

Information about the SETKA instructions issued to the Soviet Armed Forces comes from many sources, including noted ufologists Yuri Stroganov, Anatoly Listratov, and their colleagues. Of course Colonel-General A. Maximov was instrumental as well.

We will discuss the main instruction throughout this book, uncovering more sources and information. Suffice it to say that Vladimir Ajaja provided the exact language of the instruction; rather, according to many sources, he actually wrote it for the Soviet Armed Forces. A sharp increase in UFO activity in 1977-1978 (especially, the Petrozavodsk Case) had forced appropriate departments within the USSR Academy of Sciences to agree to a research program for anomalous atmospheric phenomena. The code name for this program was SETKA-AN (Akademii Nauk Set'--Academy of Sciences Net, or AS-NET.) This was the "academic" group. Simultaneously, the Soviet Ministry of Defence embarked on a similar program, dubbed SETKA-MO (Ministerstva Oboroni Set'). This was the "military" group. Reportedly, it was the Military-Industrial Commission that had ordered this research and decided on two separate UFO research centres, one within the USSR Academy of Sciences, the other within the USSR Defence Ministry. The two entities aided each other's research and exchanged information.

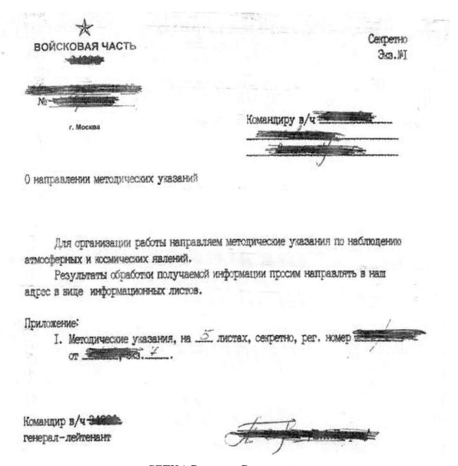

SETKA Program Document

Eyewitnesses would be asked what the object looked like and where the sighting occurred, etc. Then the reports would be sent elsewhere. When asked to comment on the KGB's research of UFOs, Alexeyev said that interest in UFOs among the military and special services was founded on the desire to determine what the new phenomenon was and what its nature was. Possibly also involved in the creation of these centres was Yuri Andropov, the chairman of the KGB from 1967 to 1982, and General Secretary of the Communist Party of the Soviet Union from 1982 to 1984. Andropov was extremely interested in the UFO phenomenon (specifically, in one case investigated by SETKA researchers). He had enough power to give impetus to the creation of the secret programs.

And so, at the end of 1978, anomalous phenomena research in the USSR Academy of Sciences came under the umbrella of SETKA-AN. Its functions were distributed among different departments, and a number of Soviet research institutes of the USSR Academy of Sciences received tasks to research various, specific aspects of the anomalous phenomenon issue. The first act of the SETKA-AN was to sanction use of "anomalous atmospheric phenomena" as the descriptive term, instead of the forbidden acronym "UFO." The prohibition against use of the term UFO was finally removed in 1989. The well-coordinated activities of the SETKAs had a terrifyingly effective impact on UFO research in the USSR. The "Academic Commission" did its best to prove there are no UFOs, only misidentification of rocket launches and of natural phenomena such as ball lightning.

SETKA-AN served as a powerful cover, diverting attention away from the work of its counterpart, the Ministry of Defence's SETKA-MO, which is said to have been more serious in its pursuit of UFO truth than the academic group. SETKA-MO was very interested in occasions when "anomalous phenomena" led to the unauthorized launches of mobile missiles and when the appearance of UFOs during military training exercises had resulted in the breakdown of radio communications and equipment malfunctions. In 1981, the SETKA research program was given another name, GALAKTIKA-AN and GALAKTIKA-MO. In 1986, the name changed again – this time to GORIZONT-AN and GORIZONT-MO. After the programs ended either in 1990 or 1991, a group of UFO experts remained at work in the Department of General Physics and Astronomy of the Russian Academy of Sciences where they analyzed incoming reports until 1996. Scientific arguments regarding the nature of UFOs had been the least of the military researchers' concerns. They did, however, pay close attention to the hypothesis that UFOs are manifestations originating from an extraterrestrial civilization. Most of all, they have been concerned with UFOs' impact on military technology and on personnel. Such impact could be quite unpredictable. They definitely wanted to know how they could use UFO technologies for their own pragmatic, military needs. The Russian Ufology Research Center obtained several excerpts from the Systematic Guidelines of the Ministry of Defence, implemented in 1980, which apply to UFOs. The Guidelines (Instruction) for the Soviet Navy had been dated March 7, 1980, and signed by Deputy Commander of the Main HQ of the Navy, Vice Admiral Saakyan.

Each and every serviceman who had observed UFOs had to immediately turn over the information to authorized officials. That particular "step" had resulted in a marked increase of reports of sightings by servicemen. The success of this effort proved to be contagious. In 1984, four years later, the State attempted to increase the ranks of informants through the creation of so-called "anomalous phenomena commissions."

The Instruction signed by Saakyan mentioned two military units where the most serious UFO data collected was to be telegraphed to immediately: Unit 67947 (Mitischi city, Moscow region), and Unit 62728 (Leningrad). "Serious" data concerned the following: physical traces of anomalous phenomena, death of military personnel (as a result of contacts with the anomalous phenomena) and breakdown of technology.

Between the end of 1988 and March of 1989, all Soviet military units, including the one stationed in Yeisk, had destroyed the Instructions of Ministry of Defence, USSR (UFO-related). Units 67947 and 62728 became more classified than before. While *glasnost* still intoxicated Soviet people, Stalinist secrecy shrouded military collection of UFO data. A military institute empowered to study such data is mentioned later.

THE LABORATORY

Korolyov and Termen mentioned the "flying saucers research laboratory," and we became curious. Even during the *perestroika* years, it was not possible to find out its location. Russian UFO researchers knew it existed. Finally, the search brought them to the city of Akhtubinsk (not to be confused with Aktuybinsk). The laboratory for "saucer" research has been under the territorial authority of the Kapustin Yar test range and the Cosmodrome. Although the location of the laboratory had been a State secret, UFOs were not affected by the Soviet secrecy. "They" have been observed over the lab since immediately after its creation.

Stroganov and his colleagues were able to collect interesting and relevant information about the lab. Its main research has to do with antigravity and propulsion assisted by electric and magnetic fields. Numerous Soviet directors of research institutes would be quite surprised if they had found out that the projects, financed and managed by the military-industrial complex, were actually part of the research into the "flying saucer" mystery. V. Pupkov, a Lieutenant Colonel (Retired) added more information about Akhtubinsk. His article, published in 1995 in *Chetvertoye Izmereniye i NLO* newspaper, confirms the existence of such a lab in the city. Akhtubinsk is also home to the famous V.P. Chkalov Institute and the flight and testing center of the Air Force. Among Russian "top guns," the center is better known as Vladimirovka. Vladimirovka is the place where most advanced Russian jet fighters are tested, as well as other aircraft. The same place is the center of pilot and pilot-navigator training. One could compare Vladimirovka to the American Area 51. Instead of the Nevada desert, the endless Kalmik and Kazakh deserts separate the Vladimirovka from the rest of the former Soviet states. A few dozen miles from the Vladimirovka, one finds Russian Cosmodrome and missile test range Kapustin Yar. In 1978 Nilolai Semirek was sent to serve at the Center, after having graduated from the Tambov Military Aviation Technical College. In spring 1979 (before the SETKA Instruction was in force), he was operating his radar and noticed several targets moving at impossible speeds. They flew more than 200 miles in 50 seconds. Over all, that night hundreds of UFOs moved through the sky at these incredible speeds. Neither Semirek nor the officer on duty wanted to report the incident to the commanding officer (*NLO Magazine*, Issue 46, 1997).

WHAT HAPPENED IN 1982?

Details about this remarkable and frightful case are found in the chapter about KGB and UFO files. We want to elaborate on this case because of former Colonel Sokolov. Reports received from Russia indicate that Soviet Colonel Boris Sokolov investigated the case, and on October 5, 1982, he was sent to Ukraine. Sokolov knew quite a lot about UFOs, as he was involved in the information collection Ukraine was an urgent report from an ICBM base, sent to the Chief of General Staff. On October 4th, a UFO was observed in the area, at Usovo; it remained there for about four hours. But the control panel indicated that an order came in to prepare launch of the bases missiles. Lights actually lit up on the panel, and launch codes enabled the missiles. There were many officers present that witnessed the incident that could have started a nuclear war. Apparently Boris Sokolov's team came to the conclusion that it was the UFO that bears responsibility for arming the Soviet missiles. In the year 2000, Sokolov changed his views, perhaps under direct pressure, and came out against UFO hypothesis in this and other cases.

SOVIET CENTRAL ASIA

A very interesting meeting took place between civilian UFO researchers / lecturers and Soviet military officials, in the town of Temga in 1990. The lecturers were from SAKKUFON, a UFO study organization. Those present included patients of the Temga military hospital. The town is located in a strategic area. Not all of the officers present had been aware of the Instruction of the Ministry of Defence USSR, which seems to confirm Stroganov's arguments. However, not the entire Soviet military stationed in the Asian republics (today's sovereign states) had been uninformed. The area of special interest to SAKKUFON was the former Soviet-Chinese border along the Tien-Shien Mountains. The area, on the border with China, has had its share of UFO sightings, and SAKKUFON had collected data on many of them. Its expeditions to the mountains included participation from Soviet military and KGB personnel. Among what was discussed at the meeting was a UFO sighting with multiple witnesses. Between May 15 and 18, 1990, near the top-rated Alma-Ata Military All-Branches Command College, cadets and officers saw a large, cigar-shaped object that appeared to be emitting some kind of light beam. The incident occurred during military tactical exercises for second-year cadets at the Avoku firing range. Lieutenant Colonel Chernov and his assistant were riding in their automobile to the designated area when they saw the huge UFO right above the firing range. As they watched in amazement, the UFO separated into four parts, and each flew in a different direction. Ten minutes later the same "parts" re-combined to form a sphere, which then entered into a larger UFO that the witnesses described as a "mother ship." All students at the exercises observed the incident, as well as their instructors and superior officers. It all took place 29 miles to the north of Alma-Ata.

From Russian UFO Archives

HELICOPTER ENCOUNTER

On March 25, 1990, according to *Izvestiya* newspaper, air traffic controllers at the Nalchik Air Detachment observed a UFO for 23 minutes on their radar screens. The crew of a Mi-2 helicopter also observed the same object. The commanding officer of the detachment, as well as a flight controller named in the newspaper article, stated that the object appearing on their radar screens was not a weather-related or natural occurrence.

Because the object flew at low altitude at a low speed (between 60 and 120 miles per hour), some observers of the radar image thought it might be a helicopter. But, inquiries revealed that no helicopters were present in the area, except for the previously mentioned Mi-2 helicopter, whose crew reported that they visually observed the UFO in question. Radar screens indicated that Mi-2 approached the UFO. When the distance between them was narrowed to three miles, both objects disappeared from the screen for about 20 seconds. Yet the two-way communications continued between the helicopter and the air traffic controllers. When both objects "reappeared," ground control noticed that the UFO was flying parallel to the Mi-2. A short time later the object changed its course, and headed toward the helicopter. The Mi-2 immediately changed its course and headed back to the base. The same UFO was sighted by a number of other local air defence units. According to the commanding officer of the Mi-2 helicopter, the pilots noticed a brightly lit object and flew towards it. As they approached the object, they noticed that it seemed to be surrounded by a "haze." The UFO was spherical and had an estimated width of only 9 feet. The object then headed straight toward the helicopter, as if trying to ram it. The UFO won this unusual game of "chicken, "as the helicopter crew swerved their craft out of the way and headed back to base. This case was bolstered by the radar data, which clearly showed that an unidentified object was present in the sky. Also, the conversations between the helicopter crew and the ground were recorded, according A. Kazikhanov, reporter for *Izvestiya*.

STRANGE AIRCRAFT

Another retired Soviet colonel, I. Tikhonov, wrote about an unusual sighting he had in the *Agitator Armii I Flota* newspaper (Issue 17, 1990). Tikhonov said that the sighting occurred shortly before the newspaper article was published, while he was looking up at the sky one morning. He saw an aircraft that had no wings and flew totally without noise. The object's inversion trail was as large as five such airplanes and disappeared immediately, unlike the ones made by regular aircraft.

RUSSIAN MILITARY AND UFOs

In a story that is beyond amazing, a UFO measuring about 75 feet in diameter made a soft landing on three landing support legs in front of the main building at a missile base that is part of Russia's air defence system. The landing reportedly took place on March 15, 1994, at 2 p.m., according to ufologist Yuri Stroganov. The report states that "something" resembling a flying saucer landed in the plaza in front of the main building. Five minutes later all soldiers not on combat duty formed a perimeter around the UFO, their machine guns at the ready. Observing the object from a distance of 300-500 feet, the soldiers said it was a classic "saucer" – a silver disk with a dome on the top, three semi spheres on the bottom, and three landing supports. As noted, the object's diameter was about 75 feet, and the dome's diameter was about 20 feet. The three semi-spheres on the bottom were about 15 feet in diameter. The object's silver color was accentuated by a slight hint of blue, and it gleamed very brightly in the sunlight of mid afternoon.

Within 10 minutes of the landing, as per the SETKA Instruction of 1980, the unit's watch officer reported the UFO to superiors. They were ordered not to approach the UFO and to cease all activities that might be viewed as aggressive and might initiate a retaliatory response from the object. The orders also instructed the base to get ready to receive an airplane containing a "mobile laboratory" of UFO researchers, presumably from SETKA. The plane carrying 15 military research specialists arrived about three hours later. After filming the object on their approach to the site, the researchers split up into three groups. Dressed in shiny, hermetically-sealed, biohazard suits, and waving various instruments, the rapid response team approached the UFO. When they got within about 20 feet, the object or the surrounding air suddenly "rippled" as if struck by some type of distortion wave. A strange sizzling noise was heard, and the soil shook a little underneath the observers' feet. Then the UFO began a slow ascent, and as it lifted off, it "pulled" the asphalt-covered surface of the plaza towards it. That "pull" extended from the edges to the center of the plaza.

When the UFO reached the altitude of about 50 feet, it stopped ascending, and its support legs disappeared into its lower hull. Then, it made a spiral-like turn and vanished with a blast of bright light. After the object's departure, the UFO research team remained in the area for another day, presumably to collate its data and write reports. When this incident occurred, the head of Russia's military UFO research program was Major-General A. Savin, commander of one of the units of the General Staff of Russia's Armed Forces. It became obvious during this UFO landing that Russia maintained rapid response teams that could be mobilized fairly quickly to the site of a UFO encounter. Then, there was the rumour that the Russian military had in their possession a captured UFO or parts from a downed UFO. Among the Russian ufologists who tried to confirm this were Gherman Kolchin and his colleagues in 1992. Kotenkov, the deputy chief of the legal department of the President of Russia, in charge of the defence and security matters, gave a vague answer, stating that he personally did not hear of any unidentified objects kept anywhere for some research and study. Colonel Sokolov, who revealed several aspects of the Soviet and Russian military research to visiting American journalists in 1993, stated that he never saw any physical traces that would verify the existence of UFOs. But Sokolov, according to Kolchin (*NLO Magazine*, 2000), also mentioned that three Soviet jet fighters crashed, when they tried to chase a UFO and that one pilot perished.

Listratov stated that the Soviets did capture remnants of a UFO in the Omsk area and that some of the technology they found helped inspire their "Star Wars" program. Ufologist A. Anfalov later claimed the Omsk retrieval occurred on October 13, 1987, when a UFO blew up and its debris was collected by the Soviet military. However, on July 18, 2003, the Russian newspaper *Pravda* ran a story claiming that the "exploded" UFO found at Omsk was actually one of the rocket stages from the launch of a military satellite from the Plesetsk Cosmodrome. The newspaper reported that the second-stage of the carrier rocket separated and fell to the ground. "The separation of the second stage happens thousands of miles far from the Cosmodrome. It is possible to see something only during sunset or before dawn, when it is night on Earth, but the rocket's tail of gas is lit by the sunlight, according to reporter Yevgeniya Lifantyeva. The reporter asserted than in Russia such events "can be seen only in Omsk and on the outskirts of the city." Ufologist Anfalov, who has collected interesting data on alleged UFO crashes, also reported that a UFO exploded in 1981 in the forbidden Kola Peninsula area. According to Anfalov, Soviet military experts collected the fragments of the object. Anfalov's report was published in *Chetvertoye Izmereniye i NLO* newspaper (Issue 8, 1996), and created a stir. Anfalov is also known for identifying the military base from which the Monchegorsk Object was transferred to Monchegorsk - the Veschevo Air Force base, and he also was the first to disclose the date of the Omsk Incident - October 13, 1987.

The Soviet government had assigned the task of creating their "Star Wars" program to NPO Energia and a group of military-industrial enterprises. On August 24, 1996, NPO Energia (now known as RSC Energia) celebrated its 50th anniversary as a pioneer in the field of space technology. The legendary Academician Sergei P. Korolev founded what has become today a private Russian corporation. During the 1970's and 1980's Energia was engaged in complicated space warfare projects. Two combat spacecraft were developed, using the same design, but equipped with different types of onboard weapons complexes, including laser and missile systems.

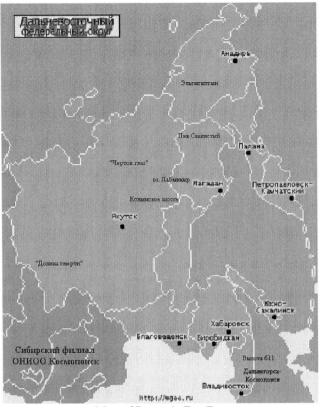

Map of Russia's Far East

In the early 1990's, Russia's Space Missile Defence Forces became involved in the projects. Victor Smirnov, Colonel General in charge, mentioned several entities engaged in the projects: the Vympel JSC, Kometa R&P Associates, Research Institute for Electronic Devices, and the Research Institute for Long-Range Radio Communications Systems (*Space Missile Defence Forces: Yesterday, Today, Tomorrow*, 1997). Of course, there are others (such as the mysterious Izhevsk Electromechanical Works) he never mentioned. Ufologists have wondered if these agencies have used information gleaned from studying extraterrestrial technologies to develop their projects. In July 1997, Russian President Yeltsin issued a decree ordering that the Space Missile Defence Forces, Russian Space Forces, and Strategic Rocket Forces be consolidated into one centralized military branch, which would be known as the Strategic Rocket Forces. The new agency would consist of rocket forces; military units and facilities for spacecraft launches and control; and special defence forces for space defence. This reorganization was completed prior to January 1998.

In August of 2000, the world learned that Russia intended to cut its arsenal of nuclear rockets and merge its armed forces. Russia's armed forces would be restructured into just three branches of the military (land, sea and air), rather than four (the fourth being the Strategic Rocket Forces). President Vladimir Putin decided to merge the Strategic Rocket Forces with the Russian Air Force. The aim was to put greater emphasis on the navy's submarine based missile deterrent. Over time, Russia's navy is certain to become one of the leading naval forces in the world. This new emphasis on water power underscores another interesting fact in Russian ufology – that there have been hundreds of very significant sightings of strange objects and strange being by naval personnel over the years. This includes sightings of both airborne objects and so-called USOs, unidentified submersible objects.

Russia's naval forces, however, have been no more willing to cooperate with ufologists on the release of information about their encounters with UFOs and USOs. Will we ever get to see the priceless paranormal phenomena files collected by Soviet Naval intelligence? Will we ever find out what was truly collected by Soviet Armed Forces between 1980 and 1989, when paranormal phenomena became a focus of monumental, comprehensive research? As more former KGB officers assume the reigns of power in today's Russia, the answers to our questions are not clear. Yet President Putin makes it clear in his speeches that he supports democracy in Russia, while the opposition to his rule has continued unabated. Meanwhile, Russia and Iran jointly begun to study UFOS observed over Iran in 2005. There are interesting rumours coming out from Russia that Putin would declassify certain UFO files. The situation is far from being clear. Russian newspaper *Novaya gazeta* reported on October 26, 1998 that the Defence Ministry houses a group of specialists studying "paranormal phenomena," such as UFOs and occult practices. According to the newspaper, Major-General Aleksei Savin, who heads the unit, allegedly founded the group in the late 1980s at the behest of former General Staff Chief of Staff Mikhail Moiseev. The unit reportedly conducts experiments on humans, specifically military cadets. Allegedly, it also won support from the highest levels of the Defence Ministry, when some of its staff "predicted" the ascent of Anatolii Kvashnin to Moiseev's position.

A CHRONOLOGY OF NOTABLE SIGHTINGS, 1962-1992

1962. June. Lesozavodsk, Soviet Far East. Two witnesses, Nechayev and Sindeyev, were fishing in a river close to the Chino-Soviet border (militarized area). Shortly before midnight they observed a crimson-colored luminescent sphere. It moved toward them noiselessly and slowly, some 13 feet off the ground. The sphere stopped a short distance away, hovered for a few moments, and then flew away slowly.

1968. Riga area, Soviet Latvia. In May of that year, Soviet soldier Novitzky and three of his comrades witnesses three artillery battalions firing on an object hovering high in the sky above them. Its size was several times less than the visible disk of the sun. Ten missiles were fired but all of them blew up before reaching the object. The UFO later zoomed away into the sky and disappeared.

1970. Kapustin Yar Cosmodrome. On the night after several new kinds of rockets were test launched, a UFO alarmed sentries at the Cosmodrome, and their shouts awoke others. The sky was clear and starry, and a gigantic black object, dirigible-like, hovered over the rockets standing on their launch pads. The UFO emitted a thin, needle-like green ray. It seemed to be scanning and detecting the positions of rockets. A panicked sentry fired at the UFO, causing the ray to suddenly vanish. Then, several soldiers in the vicinity began screaming in pain, suffering intense headaches that had come upon them as soon as the green ray was shut off.

1978. January. Soviet Arctic areas. According to Pavel Popovich, during their flight between Medveziye and Nadim, the crew of a Yak-40 airplane observed a very bright sphere. It flew right at them, growing in size as it approached. Then, just before an imminent collision, the sphere veered off and zoomed upward.

1978. Baikonur Cosmodrome, Leninsk. A UFO hovered over one of the launch facilities. Alarmed sentries fired at it. The UFO responded by shutting down all communications and electronics at the base. As the object left the area, the Cosmodrome was left in utter darkness from the sudden power outage.

1978. Gatchina region, Lenigrad oblast. A military engineer, expert in the missile and space exploration technology, saw strange looking, cone-shaped "sacks" were hovering around local power cables. The color and sizes of the "sacks" changed from transparent to dark, and they became bigger. Later the "sacks" ascended, and became smaller, as if sucked away. Igor Filatov, the eyewitness, then observed three flattened discs, silver-colored and containing portholes. They hovered over the cables for 30 seconds and then disappeared in the westerly direction, moving against the wind. The same witness reported another UFO sighting on the 31st of October of the same year. For this second sighting, there were hundreds of other witnesses, as well. While riding in a train, Filatov noticed a "ray" up in the sky, which later turned into a cigar-shaped object. It hovered for a moment, and slowly descended, changing color from grey to white. The object looked somewhat like a rocket, but there was a fiery sphere next to it and later, a second sphere appeared. Thus, the object's appearance kept changing.

1979. A UFO incident took occurred in the Tver area, in the town of Toropetz, in September 1979. Aleksandr Alekseyev was serving in the paratrooper troops of the Spetznaz when an announcement was made over the loudspeaker that the First Mounted Army settlement's radars had picked up a UFO and that a jet interceptor had also spotted it. The order had come in for the troops to observe the UFO but that no hostile move should be made against it. The object returned to the area the next evening and hovered over Alekseyev's regiment. The UFO, which looked like an upside-down plate, moved erratically, hovered, descended rapidly, and made sharp left and right turns. After about five minutes, it flew away in the south-western direction.

1980. This unusual incident was reported by V. Pupkov, a Lieutenant Colonel (Retired), and took place at the Domna airfield, in the Trans-Baikal military district, in December. In the late evening hours, a UFO suddenly appeared over the airfield. The object, shaped like a large ring, was red in color, and luminescent. It pulsated and emitted several reddish rays toward the ground. A MIG-23 was scrambled, and its pilot, Colonel Antonetz, reported the UFO to be flying at an altitude of 13,000 feet. The object slowly dimmed, and disappeared. Soon after, a special commission arrived at the airfield, investigated, and asked witnesses to sign oaths of secrecy. Whatever information the commission collected about the incident was never made public, and the current whereabouts of their report about the incident are unknown. After the fall of communism in the USSR, Colonel Antonetz was appointed commander of Ukraine's Air Force. Another incident took place in the area two years later, which will be discussed in our chapter on underwater UFOs.

1980s. Exact year unknown. Lake Ladoga area, Morye Village. On several occasions UFOs visited the test range. They hovered over it for 10 to 15 minutes each time. The air defence units opened fire, but scored no hits.

1984. End of October. Sea of Laptev area in Russia's northern territories. Valery Lukin, head of an expedition to the Arctic and Antarctic areas, received a report that a UFO was reported in the area. Border guards confirmed that they had observed a fire or brilliant light about 20 miles from the base airport. Lukin and others took a helicopter up. They observed a sphere that emitted a raspberry-colored radiance. It was an "internal" radiance (i.e. an inner light source). The light was not projected outward. The UFO would not allow them to approach. When the helicopter was about three minutes away from reaching it, the object suddenly vanished. The stunned men circled the area for half an hour, but found nothing.

1984. Two Soviet jet fighters fired on an unidentified object, moving at the altitude of 65,000 feet, over the eastern shore of the Caspian Sea. When the object approached the city of Krasnovodsk, a helicopter opened fire on it, but to no avail. The object continued its flight.

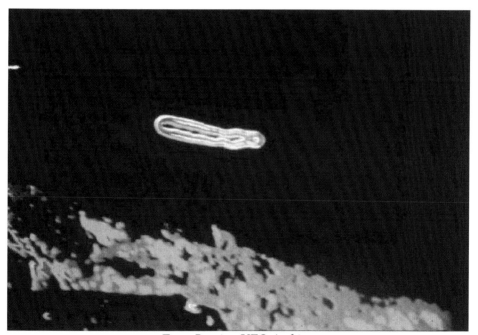

From Russian UFO Archives

1986. On August 18, 1986, Sergei Smirnov, an engineer and former Soviet military officer, received orders to guide a column of trucks to a certain testing site. He was seated in the front vehicle, next to a driver, a Kazakh, who spoke very little Russian. The weather was quite hot. Suddenly Smirnov felt fear as he observed straight in front of him, at the distance of about 2,000 feet, at the altitude of about 10 or 12 feet, a steely-looking disc. Its diameter was 500 to 600 feet. There were no portholes or other features visible. Smirnov felt ill, being overcome by a strong feeling of impending death. The Kazakh, who obviously felt the same way, screamed something in his language, released the wheel of the truck, and cowered on the bottom of the cabin. The truck swerved out of control, slid into a swamp, and its engine stalled. Smirnov climbed out of the cabin, and got stuck in the dirt up to his knees. At that time the object ascended at great speed and was gone in a mere moment, leaving behind only a column of dust. The Kazakh driver was very ill by then. Smirnov took him to the hospital. Later he wrote a report about the incident.

1987. April. Kizil Arvat airfield in the Turkestan military district. Lieutenant Colonel Ivan Ivanovich Zhdanov and other officers were walking to the headquarters building at around midnight when they noticed a strange object overhead. The sky was clear, starry, and across it, noiselessly and slowly, moved what looked like a group of white lights flying in a cluster formation. Obviously the lights were affixed to some kind of larger object, but the men could not determine its size or altitude, as they could see nothing but the lights themselves. The object could possibly have been in orbit. All who observed the object estimated that it was gigantic. The officers decided not to write any reports, agreeing to call what they saw a "satellite." 1989. Siberia. On October 28 of that memorable year, radar at the Irkutsk, Bratsk, and Zhigalovsk airports, as well as local anti-aircraft military units, registered numerous UFOs zooming across the sky for over three hours. The objects moved in complicated trajectories, traversing the flight paths of manmade aircraft, and sometimes flying closely behind the jets. Some objects flew directly toward jets. This incident was revealed in a Ukrainian newspaper *Kiyevskiye Vedomosti* (December 25, 1997). More detailed information about the strange incident that day had appeared in the Soviet magazine *Vozdushni Transport* on November 2nd, 1989. The article mentioned that UFOs also followed a Korean aircraft. Among Soviet aircraft the article mentioned An-12, An-24, An-26, and Tu-154 airplanes. No UFO approached any aircraft closer than 12-18 miles, which is considered a safe distance.

1990. In December, in Kuybishev, long-range radar picked up a blip on its screen at a range of 60 miles. The shape, size, and other readings were comparable with those of a strategic bomber. The automatic friend or foe system failed, so they couldn't tell if the object was hostile or not. The object remained on radar screens for 2 1/2 minutes, before suddenly separating into smaller objects. The largest object had a triangular shape and headed toward the radar post. Stopping overhead and hovering at 300 feet, the smooth, black triangle emitted a flash that destroyed a short-range radar array and melted it to the ground. Witnesses said the object was about 45 feet long and 10 feet thick. It had no openings or portholes. It hovered above the radar installation for about 90 minutes and then took off and disappeared completely in the night sky.

1990. February 24, six in the morning, near the city of Odessa. A UFO hovered over a border guard post. It was silvery in color, like tin foil. The UFO looked somewhat like the surface of the moon with its upper part cut off. Its bottom part revealed a small semi-spherical cut. The object, which rotated rapidly, had a luminescence described as like a raging fire. One side of the UFO was illuminated along its length by a powerful light source. Radar was able to detect the object, which hovered overhead for nearly two hours. The nearby military post also reported that, at one point, a smaller "module" separated from the main UFO.

1990. Early summer. Port of Loksa, Estonia. A. Maksimovich, Soviet Navy officer, reported a strange bright object that hovered noiselessly in the clear sky. For four hours, he observed it through a looking glass. The UFO was an extremely bright sphere that changed colours from time to time. Although radar could not detect it, many Navy men and their commander observed the object at length. 1990. In the city of Grozny, Major Ryabishev was ordered to fly his fighter jet to the area where a UFO was pinpointed by ground radar. Upon arrival, he found nothing and turned around to head back to base. Then, he noticed two giant cigar-shaped objects flying behind the jet. He turned his jet to approach the UFOs, but they vanished instantly. Nonetheless, ground radar had picked up both of the objects.

1990. Near the end of the year, Colonel Nikolai Chaga was conducting a night training flight in the area of Lipetsk and Dobriy. The sky became strangely illuminated as the craft was ready to land. The pilot observed an elliptical formation that resembled a dirigible, with a bright light at its "nose." It seemed to Chaga that the object was hovering quite close to him, at an altitude of about 10,000 feet. The Colonel reported this situation to the flight control center. They already knew about it, as a civilian pilot who flew the Moscow-Voronezh route, reported the same UFO. Chaga wanted to find out more about the UFO, and he asked the control center for permission to approach the object, but the response was "Nyet!" Meanwhile the UFO changed its shape into something that reminded him of a whale, but instead of a tail it had white rays steaming into different directions. Later it became known that many military pilots observed the same, but were afraid to report the situation, so as not to be considered mentally unstable [the crude Russian expression used by Chaga was *choknutiye*]. UFOs frequented the Lipetsk area for the next two months. Chaga collected drawings of the objects done by his colleagues and photographs taken by onboard cameras. The mysterious objects usually appeared during training flights. "They" were careful, as if not to cause accidents. Most were lentil-shaped, but some were sphere-shaped. Colonel Vladimir Litvin almost collided with several "spheres" while flying a target practice mission in his MIG-29. Five blue-green spheres were flying "low and slow" in a precise formation, each equally spaced from the others. The largest sphere was in front – in the lead position. The MIG's onboard equipment did not register the presence of the spheres. The area of the training battle was closed to all air traffic except for the two MIGs taking part in the exercise. Yet somehow, the UFOs were there, and the Litvin's MIG was about to collide with one or more of them. Suddenly, the front most UFO directed a green ray at the MIG's cockpit which temporarily blinded Litvin. He managed to activate the color filter of his protective helmet and turned his jet away. Looking back where the spheres had been, he noticed that they had vanished. Litvin decided not to file a report and checked his jet for damages, finding none. Later, he discovered that his onboard equipment had photographed the UFO. Chaga checked the film and confirmed its authenticity.

Chaga wanted to publish the photos in 1990, but was advised that it would not be wise to do so. One year later, he was contacted by Marina Popovich, who asked for the photos. Chaga gave her the photos when he visited Moscow to receive his Distinguished Pilot of the USSR rank. Marina Popovich kept the only remaining pictures, as the ones at the flight control center were destroyed as per the policy to keep photos in storage only for one year. Marina turned the photos over to the *Komsomol'skaya Pravda* newspaper, which ran the story about the incident on April 7, 2005.

1990. An article by Vladimir Ajaja in *NLO Magazine* (1999) told the story of a giant, pulsating triangular UFO detected on military radar over Samara on September 13, 1990. The huge, black triangle "swallowed" the radar's waves at a distance of about three miles. When local officers came out of their underground facility to look at the sky, they saw the UFO flying very low over the area, at the altitude of about 32 feet. Its bottom part was smooth but non-reflective. The observers could see no apertures, portholes, or landing equipment. Each side of the triangle was about 50 feet long, and its thickness was about 9 feet. It was established later that the object emitted powerful radiation. It also fired some type of destructive ray that smashed the radar's antenna, setting it ablaze. What was extremely interesting about the ray is that it "curved" around a corporal who happened to be standing directly in its path. After the ray went around the soldier, it destroyed the antenna array.

The UFO, which was absolutely noiseless, later landed and remained on the ground in plain view for about an hour and a half. It was later determined that, while the UFO was on the ground, two of the soldiers suffered "missing time." Later, their whereabouts during those 90 minutes could not be verified. The two soldiers believed that they had been at their posts the whole time, but other witnesses said they had not. When the men and their belongings were examined, it was discovered that the serial numbers on one man's bayonet and the other man's machine-gun had both been removed by some unknown means. Ufologist Pavel Kirillov researched the story and published his findings in *Tainy XX Veka* magazine (Issue # 6). His account is as follows: Shortly after the midnight hour, a large object appeared on the radar screen. The UFO was approaching a local Soviet radar station and did not acknowledge inquiries from the automatic identification control system. Furthermore, the object transformed itself; it dissipated into small fragments, creating a cloud of sorts. Then, having collected all the fragments into one mass, the UFO resumed its movement. Now the displays clearly showed a glimmering isosceles triangle. But at the distance of three miles from the station, the object disappeared. A group of officers ascended from the underground command center to the observation deck. And just as they did, an identified object approximately 9 feet long flew right over their heads. Its bottom portion was but 32 feet away from the officers. It emitted three light-bluish rays upwards. This mysterious triangle circled over the station, and landed nearby, close to the fence.

Next, an incredible occurrence took place: the antenna, located inside the fenced area, caught fire. It fell to the side, and burned as if it was made from wood. Some unknown force shattered the mechanisms of the antenna's drive, and scattered nearby. The wagon where they were kept was melted, and the paint blackened and swelled up like bubbles. The aluminium parts of the antenna literally oozed as drops of melted matter. The energy impulse generated by the triangle [Kirillov believes it to be the source] caused the damages from the distance of 469 feet. The impulse was indeed a powerful concentrated force. The triangle remained by the station for an hour and a half. It is not known what other damages it had caused at the military site.

1992. Soviet Far East. Radar followed the flight of the new Russian SU-27 fighter plane, when it suddenly vanished from all radar screens. The territory's air defence headquarters reported that its staff had detected a UFO in the area at the time of the jet's disappearance. For a month, an intensive search failed to find any wreckage of the plane or to account for its mysterious disappearance.

It is not often that UFO researchers can reach quick agreement on any issue in ufology, but the one thing that most of them do agree on is that pilots, either civilian or military, along with other trained military personnel, are very likely the most reliable witnesses to UFO events. Because of the huge size of the former Soviet military machine, it comes as no surprise that so many UFO sightings have come from Soviet military personnel. These thousands of military witnesses remain as mystified as the rest of us as to the exact nature and origin of these mysterious aerial visitors. Another highly credible group of UFO witnesses are the Soviet Union's cosmonauts. Amazingly enough, as we learn in our next chapter, cosmonaut UFO reports were quite numerous, and they remain mostly unexplained even today.

CHAPTER 4.

SOVIET COSMONAUTS AND UFOs

EARLY VISITORS

When Sputnik, the world's first artificial satellite, was launched from the designated space-vehicle launching site Baikonur Cosmodrome atop a Soviet Sputnik (R-7) rocket, nothing out of the ordinary was reported before, during, or after its launch. It seemed that the mankind's first milestone on the path to space exploration had passed without undue significance. But beginning with the launch of Sputnik 2 carrying the dog Laika on board from the Baikonur Cosmodrome in November 1957, strange encounters with the unknown became a regular part of the Soviet space program.

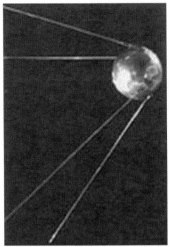

First Soviet Satellite Launch 1957

On the day of Sputnik 2's launch, about an hour before the take-off, a strange, glowing object appeared a short distance away from the Baikonur Cosmodrome. The strange visitor was spherical in shape, and it hovered at a low altitude, remaining in a stationary position for some time before suddenly vanishing. A few days later, L. Corrales, a scientist in Venezuela, was taking photographs of Sputnik 2 in flight when he observed an unidentified object flying alongside the satellite. The UFO at times would approach to within a very close distance of Sputnik 2 and then would slow down and fall behind before catching back up to it again. The strange object was definitely not a part of the rocket assembly. Is it possible that Earth's mysterious ET visitors, that have reportedly shown an interest in our space faring activities, were monitoring the first journey of a living being (the dog Laika) into outer space?

A Launch from the Plesetsk Cosmodrome

UFOs OVER SOVIET COSMODROMES

Following Sputnik 2, almost every launch of a Soviet space vehicle was accompanied by reports of the appearance of one or more UFOs in the vicinity of the launch site. Although the USSR was not the only place on earth experiencing such sightings, Soviet citizens were not allowed to discuss UFOs. It remained a forbidden subject to the general populace. When thousands of people began witnessing these unusual objects, Soviet authorities countered by publishing reports and commentaries ridiculing all ET theories. To derail any "unhealthy" conclusions by its citizens, Soviet scientific officials attributed each and every incident to mundane causes such as ball lightning, a Soviet rocket or missile, the Aurora Borealis, etc.

Soviet Cosmonaut Poster

But what explanation could be given when leading Soviet scientists observed UFOs? In 1982, M.L. Gaponov, a noted scientist involved in geophysical and medical-biological research, observed a gigantic, cigar-shaped UFO hovering over the Star City Cosmodrome. A participant in international geophysical scientific expeditions to the North Pole, Gaponov was working in the Dubna Cosmonaut Training Center at the time of his sighting. Furthermore, Gaponov was by no means the only Soviet scientist to gaze upon anomalous phenomena, as we will shortly learn. While publically telling its citizens that UFOs and aliens were nothing more than hostile bourgeois propaganda, the Soviet government, working under tight lid of secrecy, conducted extensive research into all significant anomalous phenomena brought to its attention. Most of the secret documents and findings generated during decades of research into the paranormal have yet to be released to the general public, even so many years after the collapse of the USSR. However, UFOs do not appear to care much about terrestrial politics, and sightings continued after the demise of the Soviet

Union. In the early 1990s, for example, former Commander of the Russian Military Space Forces, General Vladimir Ivanov, reported three unidentified objects flying at high altitude near the Baikonur Cosmodrome and lighting up military radar screens in the area. Although it could not be determined what the nature of the objects was, they were definitely not any type of known aircraft.

SIGHTINGS IN SPACE

Throughout the tumultuous history of the Soviet space program, its cosmonauts have observed many unusual phenomena. Occasionally, they have even talked about it, despite the official seal of secrecy imposed by the USSR. Highly-decorated cosmonaut Vladimir Lyakhov, who logged 333 days in space during his 27 year career, told the story of a very unusual phenomenon he observed from his Soyuz spaceship while looking down upon the Earth. He saw two gigantic pillars of water rise from the waters of the Indian Ocean and crash into each other, forming a huge mountain of water that subsequently vanished in an instant (published in *Tekhnika-Molodezhi*, Issue 3, 1980). Cosmonaut Vladimir Kovalyonok reported a very similar pillar of water whose height he estimated at over 62 miles in the Timor Sea near Australia(*NLO Magazine*, 10/11, 1996).

Yevgeny Khrunov, a scientist and cosmonaut, remarked in a 1979 article in *Tekhnika-Molodezhi* (Issue 3) that he conceded the fact that thousands of people observe UFOs and that the properties of UFOs simply astound the imagination. As this was in the pre-perestroika times, Khrunov could not speak freely.

Cosmonaut Aleksei Gubarev, going a step further, admitted that he believed in aliens. Interestingly, he said that his belief in aliens was confirmed by information gathered and held by "the Americans" (*Tekhnika-Molodezhi*, Issue 1, 1980,). Valery Rozhdestvensky, a cosmonaut who says he personally does not believe aliens are visiting the Earth, nonetheless made an interesting revelation about a bizarre event during a Soviet orbital flight. According to an article in *Tekhnika-Molodezhi* (Issue 10, 1980), cosmonauts reported that a "small, green man" floated up to their Soyuz spacecraft while in orbit and casually knocked on the porthole.

Over the years, Russian UFO researchers have managed to collect quite a bit of information about cosmonaut encounters with the unknown. An article published in *Spektra* newspaper (Issue 8, Leningrad, 1992) lists several cases, including comments made in 1976 by cosmonaut Vladimir Kubasov, who told a reporter that he and other cosmonauts have "numerous facts" that prove this existence of UFOs. His comments were made in the context of discussion about the September 1976 encounter over Tehran, Iran, between an Iranian F-4 jet fighter and an intensely bright UFO. In 1978 Vladimir Kovalyonok observed a strange object on August 15 from the Salyut 6 space station. The UFO approached and distanced itself repeatedly. Valery Ryumin and Leonid Popov, while aboard the same station in June 1980 observed a formation of white glowing dots that took-off in the area of Moscow, and flew into space above their station. They reported it to the ground control.

On September 2, 1978, Soviet cosmonauts Kovalyonok and Ivanchenkov observed a shadow from their Salyut 6 on strange clouds below. The clouds were of eerie orange-reddish color and the shadow changed its dimension inexplicably during the sighting. This was reported in *NLO Magazine* in the October/November 1996 issue. The source was G. Lisov, a noted researcher and journalist, whose work in ufology is highly respected.

Also in 1978, on August 25, both cosmonauts observed iridescent clouds, with colours that included green, purple, reddish, blue, and even violet. Other Soviet cosmonauts (V. Sevastyanov and P. Klimuk) reported silvery clouds. The origin of these strange clouds remains unexplained. Sevastyanov was mesmerized by their dull, occasionally pearly-white appearance. The structure of such clouds was either very thin (or bright) on the edges of the pitch-dark sky, or porous, resembling a swan's wing. These high-atmospheric clouds are said to be an incredible spectacle. Russian astronomer Vitold Tsesarsky first reported them in 1885. The clouds are the highest in the Earth's atmosphere, located at the altitude of between 40 and 55 miles. They consist of diffused particles whose nature is still unclear. Cosmonaut Georgy Grechko was able to photograph an "ice-floe" moving through the air over these high-altitude clouds. At first, he was shocked, but he later found out that under certain atmospheric conditions, an optical phenomenon

occurs that appears to be ice flowing through the air. Another strange phenomenon that remains unexplained is the occasional "magnification" of Earth-based objects, as seen with the naked eye from space. Cosmonaut Vitaly Sevastyanov reported that as he flew over the city of Sochi in his spacecraft on a clear and sunny day, he could see the city's harbour and his own home in vivid, close-up detail, without using any device for magnification. As difficult as it may be to believe, Sevastyanov claims to have seen clearly from space the small two-story building in which he grew up. Cosmonaut Yuri Glazkov, while in space over Brazil, could discern a small roadway, and a second later, saw a blue bus moving along the road. He could not explain how was able to do it, but insisted that he did see it. Georgy Grechko and Yuri Romanenko also reported to the Tsentr ground control center that while in their orbital station over the Falkland Islands, they had actually observed huge letters. The photograph they took was delivered to Earth by visiting cosmonauts Dzhanibekov and Makarov. Grechko also reported a strange being of gigantic dimensions over Mongolia In his interview with *Vechernyaya Moskva* newspaper (1978), Romanenko recalled that in December of 1977, he and Grechko had observed an object that chased the Salyut 6 orbital station. It was a small, metallic body whose size difficult to estimate. Romanenko was able to draw a picture of it. Later he recanted his story and said the object was nothing more than a "waste capsule." Grechko, too, first discussed his UFO observations publicly, only to later deny them.

Plesetsk Cosmodrome Launch of a Soyuz rocket

Lebedev observed on the monitor's screen of the Salyut 7 an unusual, teardrop-shaped object. It flew between the orbital space station and another ship identified as "Progressor 14," from somewhere above. The cosmonauts reported the sighting to ground controllers. An interesting interview was published in *Sputnik* magazine. The subject of it was UFOS through the eyes of cosmonauts. It contained stories by ten Soviet and American space explorers. All of the space travellers except one refuted the possibility of UFOs visiting our galaxy. The one believer was Yevgeny Khrunov, who stated that it is not possible to deny the presence of UFOs in our galaxy. Thousands of people have observed them, he noted. Perhaps they are but optical illusions, he added, but some of their flight characteristics, such as changing their direction of flight by 90 degrees, boggle the imagination.

RUSSIAN PILOT-COSMONAUT ALEKSEI LEONOV AND U.S. INTELLIGENCE REPORT ON UFOs

Perhaps a key to an accurate understanding of cosmonaut UFO encounters is the experience of pilot-cosmonaut Aleksei Leonov. In this section is presented information previously unavailable in the West about this distinguished, intelligent space explorer, one of the first Soviet cosmonauts and one of the last surviving original cosmonauts. Leonov's views about UFOs first appeared in a declassified report from the U.S. Department of Defence Intelligence. The report number is 2 723 1209 70, and the date is August 19, 1970.

The report made note of a lecture given by Leonov on May 18, 1970 at the Tokai University in Yokogama. Leonov spoke about "Soviet Space Development," during which he talked about Soviet achievement in space and the USSR's future plans for space exploration, including a mammoth orbital space station. As an aside during his presentation, Leonov stated that he did not believe UFOs were extraterrestrial spacecraft.

It is quite likely that Leonov was acting on instructions from his government to deliberately mislead people in the West about UFO sightings in the USSR. The subject remained strictly off limits in the Soviet state. Several years before Leonov's Japan speech, a group of Soviet scientists and military researchers made a serious effort to conduct UFO investigations independent of the government, only to be ruthlessly crushed by Soviet officials. UFOs were clearly not open for discussion. Among other points he made in his Japan lecture, Leonov spoke about improvements to the Soviet space capsule braking equipment and then broached a subject that was of great interest to U.S. military intelligence. He stated that U.S. astronauts had confirmed data about the moon that the USSR had previously gathered. This statement interested U.S. intelligence because the Americans were aware of early (and classified) Soviet attempts to reach the moon. Leonov revealed that the Soviet Union had a well-coordinated program for travel to the moon and had compiled complete and detailed data concerning conditions on the moon through its "moon station."

Aleksei Leonov (Courtesy NASA)

According to Leonov, the USSR had photographs of the moon's dark side and complete data on the make-up and characteristics of its surface, its gravity field, etc.

"The U.S. astronauts who landed on the Moon only confirmed what we already knew" he said. Then, Leonov addressed the Japanese audience on the subject of UFOs. The speaker said he did not believe in the existence of unidentified flying objects. Why, he asked, would the flying saucers be seen only over the United States, France and Italy? He said there is no record of any Soviet observatories, which are manned by highly trained technicians, ever having seen a To UFO researchers in Russia, Leonov's statements about UFOs proved the extent to which the Soviet Union went to hide UFO truth. Of course astronomers had seen UFOs. A later chapter specifically lists UFO reports and observations by Soviet astronomers. These astronomer sightings had been published in the Soviet media in the 1960s, well before Leonov's statements in Japan. Yet, the Soviet newspaper *Pravda*, on February 29, 1968, insisted that Soviet astronomers had never seen any "flying saucers." Both cosmonaut Leonov and the newspaper were obviously deliberately misleading their audiences. The true facts conclusively prove that UFOs had definitely been reported by Soviet astronomers and were of interest to them.

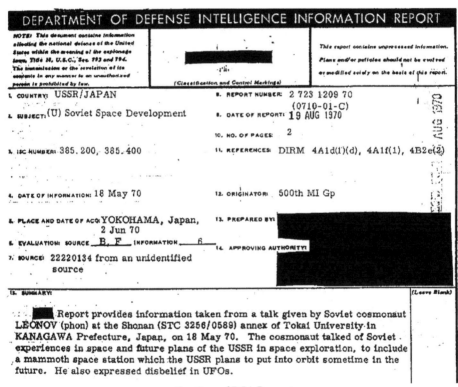

Portion of DIA Report

As someone so highly placed in the Soviet space program, Leonov would have known about the UFO activity that was being reported throughout the USSR, including reports made by astronomers. He also obviously knew about UFO sightings by cosmonauts.

THIRTY YEARS LATER: LEONOV'S INTERVIEWS, OATHS, AND REVELATIONS

On March 23, 2005, fourteen years after the USSR collapsed, Leonov was interviewed on the occasion of the 40th anniversary of his space walk. At a press conference organized by a Russian publication *Drugoye Vremya* (RIAN Agency), Leonov said that all humans desperately desire the existence of other beings in the cosmos, but alas, he said, at least within our solar system, there is no intelligent life. He added emphasis by saying, "I declare it with full responsibility." Leonov added, "As a military person, I headed a commission for the research of unusual space phenomena, and I swear to you, not even one occurrence had been established by us." Leonov said that the unusual objects observed from the Earth, as a rule, were either meteorological phenomena or resulted from exhaust trails from rocket launches. "Crosses with gigantic rings around them, especially in the clear, wintry weather, could be observed for an extended period of time in the area of the Plesetsk Cosmodrome in the Saratov region and over Baikonur after the launch of the Soyuz launch vehicles. Many people saw them, and took the rings to be UFOs -- retold to each other, and thus legends were born."

Leonov also argued, "Till now, nowhere in the world has there been taken even one clear photograph, where one could look at, and unambiguously assert that, yes, this is a UFO. Why are there no such photographs now, when almost everyone has a photo camera in their mobile telephone?" This was, as far as we could establish, the first time that pilot-cosmonaut Leonov mentioned a "commission "(also referred to as "committee" elsewhere) to study UFOs, of which he was the head. As far as we can determine, the commission was not part of the Soviet government's secretive UFO study group called SETKA. The questions remain: What commission did Leonov head? Where are its findings? What cases did it investigate? Next, Leonov was interviewed by Russian magazine *Biznes* (issue 25, June 19, 2006). We will translate Leonov's statements as closely as possible; every word, we believe, had been carefully chosen. He said that for a long time he headed a "committee" that investigated unidentified flying objects.

Leonov said he is certain that in our solar system, there is no intelligent life other than on Earth. There may be life at the level of microbes, such as in the water that has been discovered on Mars. There is intelligent life, undoubtedly, somewhere in the universe, but it is beyond our capabilities for space travel. The closest star to our galaxy is five light years away. Imagine, travelling five years at the speed of light. We do not have the technology to do so, for now. However, Leonov conceded that he believes extraterrestrials have visited Earth in the distant past. He stated that almost every religion in the world has stories of "enlightened" beings that arrived on Earth from the heavens, gathered groups of followers, and then ascended back into the sky." On April 29, 2009, an interview with Leonov was published at the Russian *Kaleidoskop* website. It is a fascinating piece of information, because Leonov is clearly trying to discredit Marina Popovich, the distinguished Soviet test pilot, author, scientist, and UFO researcher [We will discuss her career later in this chapter.]. Leonov also argues against the credibility of other Soviet cosmonauts who report UFOs. Leonov said, "When I had worked in the Cosmonauts Training Centre [Star City, 19 miles northeast of Moscow], I headed the Commission for UFOs, and collected all evidence. Unfortunately, there has not been one fact that would not raise doubts. But when one listens to Marina Popovich, one gets such cheerful notion that around us not only do the flying saucers fly about, but also do humanoids walk with red lanterns and a siren." Leonov reiterates that there is no intelligent life within the solar system. Those are his exact words. Then, he added, "There is life that can have lowest forms, but in our understanding, there is no intelligent life. There are various testimonies, but no scientific corroboration for them. At the same time, there are numerous artefacts on Earth that demonstrate that someone had visited our planet. But that happened long ago. Written language on Earth has been in existence no more than four thousand years. Prior to that, everything was conveyed through words, and every person would add something. In my understanding, religion, no matter who worships what, has a common foundation -- it is enlightenment, ascension. No matter what one takes, Hinduism of Russian Orthodox Christianity, we see that [someone] 'arrived,' 'flew in,' 'told,' 'created students and disciples,' and 'ascended with thunder and lightning's.' A solution suggests itself -- four to five thousand years ago someone had been here. The writing tradition did not even preserve that. But there remain phenomena and testimonies that force doubts whether or not intelligent beings visited the Earth. Most likely, they did. However, so far we do not see them. There is much talk, that Grechko had seen them, that during the flight they were accompanied by UFOs; that, allegedly Volodya Kovalyonok had seen them, too, and talked [with them or about them?].

"But in fact, when one begins to look in depth, it turns out that these objects are ours, manually made. Pails, cylinders made from polished duralumin that had been thrown away from the station were poorly hermetized, and thus retained their shapes, and from the side they looked like unknown objects. Nothing more and nowhere else had appeared. But people, who go about and talk about this, use their privileges and fame." Then, Leonov directly mentions Marina Popovich. "About ten years ago, Marina Popovich, who today is the president of the Central Asian and Kazakhstan collegium of ufologists, wakes us up at one o'clock at night, and beckons to look at a UFO. We ran to the balcony. Yes, there is a saucer moving over the forest. I tell Marina, we are erecting a building there and are using a big horizontal crane 22 stories tall. Her daughter as well as my daughter, they ran to see; come there [and see] the crane. One month later, there was a ufological congress in [Saint] Petersburg. After the congress, I read in *Znaniye* magazine -- On such and such date, at such coordinates a UFO was observed. All our family had observed, plus we invited the Leonov family, who also observed and confirmed. I meet [later] with Marina, and ask, 'Why? It is not true.' She responds to me, 'Yes, not true, but interesting.' But now, when she makes a speech and starts saying about something, I just smile, and think, 'You go ahead and listen, but everything will be completely different, if they arrive.'"
More questions arise after Leonov's interview. Why does he launch an attack on Marina's credibility? While Marina is attacked, what of her former husband, Pavel Popovich, one of Russia's most famous cosmonauts and Leonov's former colleague? Why is Leonov silent about Pavel Popovich, who, as we shall discuss later, has made significant contributions to Soviet, Russian and Ukrainian UFOlogy? Could it be that Marina's research is particularly worrisome to Leonov, and that perhaps she has uncovered something that bothers him and the "commission" he once was in charge

of? What artefacts does Leonov mention in his interview? He does believe in the possibility that ancient astronauts visited earth, which Russian ufologists refer to as *paleocontact*. What does he know of Kovalyonok's and Savinikh's observations in 1981 and what has Leonov heard about the alleged contact described in our book based on Cosmonaut Beregovoy's revelations as reported in the Russian media? What about other observations reported by Kovalyonok during his years in space? How does Leonov know that everything will be completely different if "they arrive," and different in what way?

On May 29, 2009, in an interview with the Russian *Izvestiya* newspaper, Leonov was asked whether UFO enthusiasts try to correspond with him. His response was, "I am fed up with them! Today, there is not even one occurrence, for which one could not find a natural explanation. But people very much want not to be alone. I do not exclude the possibility of the existence of extraterrestrials. Moreover, I think that someone had visited the Earth sometime ago. There are too many signs of the interference of other beings, more developed than human beings. But all the evidence about has to be collected in fragments, because the writing exists several thousand years, and prior to that, everything was recorded by oral tradition." On May 30, 2009, another interview with Leonov was published, this time in the Ukrainian newspaper *Fakty i kommentarii*. Leonov was asked whether, while in space, he observed UFOs. He again mentioned the UFO commission he headed, and his duty to collect all evidence. He reiterated that there has not been a single fact that would not raise doubts, but significantly, he avoided the question about whether he ever observed UFOs in space.

Leonov went on to repeat the story of Marina Popovich and the crane. A few more details were added -- "Indeed, we see radiance that if one really wishes to, could be mistaken a saucer....There is a projector [on the crane] that they turn on at night. When clouds are low, the ray rests in the clouds, creating a glowing circle that resembles a UFO." At the end of the story Leonov asks us to forgive Marina Popovich. Then he adds that he is certain that within the solar system there is no intelligent life, except for here on earth. "Man is the apex of what the Creator has created. And, of course, our planet." Leonov was interviewed by *Russia Today* on July 20, 2009. When asked about UFOs, the cosmonaut replied: "Belief in UFOs is just as stupid as the claim that the Americans never landed on the Moon." But he said that for him, there is still one phenomenon he cannot explain -- crop circles. Leonov stated that "it's not a hoax, and you can't fake one. What is it? No one has been able to explain."

MARINA POPOVICH

Marina is a distinguished test pilot, a scientist with a doctorate degree in flight technology from the University of Leningrad, a Lieutenant Colonel, and a highly decorated aviator. As of this writing, she heads a private aviation company and is also a journalist and published author of several books. Her efforts on behalf of ufology have led to disclosure of many previously hidden UFO incidents in the former Soviet Union.

Cosmonaut Turned Ufologist Marina Popovich

Marina personally observed UFOs three times in her life, once during an expedition to the Pamir Mountains in search of the Yeti. All forty people in the expedition, including her daughter, observed a UFO from their camp located at an altitude of 13,000 feet up the mountain. They saw a spherical object hover over a nearby gorge and then emit a ray before vanishing. On another occasion, she and her husband observed a giant UFO over Mitino, on the outskirts of Moscow. It was a giant, elongated object, over 800 feet long. An airplane flying below it was barely visible. Marina estimated the object to be at the altitude of 12 miles, and, as it flew, it left behind a "vortex" trail.

Marina's third, and most recent, UFO sighting is probably the one that is so often disparaged by former cosmonaut Leonov. She claims to have observed a UFO in June 1996, at 3 a.m. The object made no sound, but displayed complex manoeuvres and emitted pulse-like bursts of illumination. Marina woke up her spouse and guests so that they also could observe the object. Did the "guests" she mentioned include Leonov and his family. We have no way to confirm the truthfulness of either her account or Leonov's account. Years ago, Marina Popovich was close to graduating from cosmonaut training when she was dropped from the program after Pavel Popovich, the general to whom she was married, convinced officials that she was not suited for space flights. By doing so, he probably saved her health. If anyone is qualified to define what a UFO is, it would be this remarkable woman. She flew all Soviet aircraft, from AN-22 transport planes to MIG-21 supersonic jets. She holds 90 flight records. Marina, a clear, level-headed person, is quick to say that she believes 90 percent of UFO sightings are not really UFOs at all and have conventional explanations. However, the other ten percent is what intrigues her. In a recent interview, Marina mentioned a photographic analysis lab in Tver that was given the task of interpreting UFO photographs sent to them. The lab concluded conventional explanation.

Some of her beliefs may seem unusual, but she espouses them firmly. She believes that a number of famous writers and artists -- including Jules Verne, Ray Bradbury, and Leonardo Da Vinci – were used as "mediums" by advanced extraterrestrials that sent messages to our planet through them about important technological innovations. She also believes that former Soviet President Mikhael Gorbachev functioned as an "extraterrestrial front man," receiving messages from outer space that motivated him to carry out profound historical changes. When Paul Stonehill met Marina in 1991, she expressed her belief that eventually top secret Soviet files on UFOs would become public. Functioning somewhat as a spokesperson for Soviet UFO study groups, she said that it would be a long while before all such secret files will be open for inspection. She was kind enough to share information and photographs with the Russian Ufology Research Center, founded by Stonehill in Los Angeles.

During her visit, Marina acknowledged being aware of over 14,000 UFO sightings that took place in the USSR between 1966 and 1991. Speaking at the Whole Life Expo in Los Angeles in 1991, she confirmed what many in the West had suspected – that outspoken UFO advocates in the Soviet Union lost their jobs and/or were involuntarily committed to psychiatric hospitals. In Los Angeles, Marina Popovich expressed her serious ecological concerns regarding environmental damage that has occurred in the lands comprising the former Soviet Union. She stated her sadness in seeing rivers drying up, lakes and ponds dying, and widespread areas damaged by toxic chemical spills. She stated that Russia's ecology was already suffering even before the Chernobyl incident. The economic plight of the former USSR, and its rising poverty, concern her greatly. As for the ten percent of UFOs that cannot be explained, Marina believes them to be extraterrestrial spacecraft. As a trained pilot who has witnessed UFOs herself, she is certain that human beings are not the only intelligent creatures in the universe and that these others have indeed been visiting our neck of the woods.

In 1991 Marina showed Paul Stonehill a photograph that the Soviet Mars probe Phobos 2 took before its demise. The photo depicts a gigantic cylindrical object approximately 15 miles long. After the last frame depicting this strange object was radio-transmitted back to earth, the Soviet probe, which was about to land two research packages on the surface of Phobos, suddenly and inexplicably lost all computer functions and vanished without a trace. Marina stated that Soviet space officials (*Glavkosmos*) knew all along that Phobos 2 was destroyed by a mechanism of artificial intelligence from somewhere other than Earth. After learning of what really happened to the probe, Marina and other Russians, including Professor Valeriy

Burdakov, tried their best to tell the world about the strange incident, but few would listen. We will say more about the Phobos 2 incident later in this book.

Another person of interest in our search for UFO truth is someone who knows both Marina Popovich and Aleksei Leonov quite well. Valentin Vasilyevich Petukhov of the Ukraine had a distinguished Communist Party career in the city of Yevpatoria on the Black Sea. From 1967 to 1980 he headed the city's Communist Party Committee, and thus, controlled the city. Before that, he was the deputy secretary, i.e., second in command. The cosmonauts arrived to Yevpatoria because during the Soviet era, the city housed a special secret facility for cosmonaut training, as well as space tracking and flight control center at the Kalamitsky Bay. The cosmonauts had a nickname for Petukhov; they called him Papa Valya.

He has great memories about "Lyosha" Leonov. At the same time, Petukhov's family befriended Marina Popovich, who was then married to Pavel Popovich. They were really close friends, he revealed in the interview with Ukrainian newspaper *Bul'var Gordona* on March 27, 2009. Petukhov described Marina as "a famous test pilot -- a brave, wilful, and valiant woman." She came to Yevpatoria as the commander of an aircraft flown in for repairs in the city's aviation works of the Black Sea Navy's air force (SAM-20). She presented Petukhov's family with her book, and many photographs.

FAIRY TALES?

In writing this chapter, the authors consulted dozens of Russian and Ukrainian sources. We believe that we have stumbled upon a possible explanation for Leonov's disparaging statements about UFOs and about Marina Popovich. In an April 2008 post at a Russian UFO discussion forum (*www.ufolog.ru/forum*), a person named Vlad, claiming to have a scientific and military background, stated that he had conversations with those who served in the Rocket Forces, the air defence, pilots, KGB personnel, and even submariners. According to "Vlad," almost everyone he spoke with told him, strictly off the record, that either they personally had encountered UFOs or that their colleagues had. As an example, Vlad mentions an acquaintance of his in the air defence forces, who told him that UFOs were often spotted on military radar screens and that their radar signatures were quite different from those of conventional aircraft. Obviously, UFOs were well known in Russia, despite attempts by officials such as Leonov to discredit them and muddle the issue. Also in his post, Vlad said that while serving in the Russian Army, he repeatedly and personally observed that the regiment's officer on duty maintained a "log of the flight of satellites." Vlad wondered why an infantry regiment, whose only means of observation were binoculars, would be keeping track of satellites. Having once taken a look at the mysterious log, Vlad saw that the entries in it had nothing to do with satellites but rather were observations of other mysterious objects in the sky. In his post, Vlad also refers to Marina Popovich, noting that she claims to have witnessed UFOs on three separate occasions. "Think about it," wrote Vlad, "Why would she lie to the entire nation? Has she nothing better to do than study a made-up fiction?" "Moreover, let us remember our very famous ufologist Ajaja." Vlad continued, "He is a former military man, and had begun his UFO research under direct orders from the Russian Navy HQ, as too many reports about UFOs came there from military seamen." His first work was titled "Hydrosphere Aspects of the UFO problem." Vlad added that Ajaja could write much and tediously, but what for? The matter is clear, anyway. Vlad concluded his post by going back to Leonov. "Regardless of all his doubtless merits, he is but an all-Russia story-teller of fairy tales with a kind smile. But a story-teller against his will. Once he said something without thinking it through, and now he has to 'save face.' That is why he swears oaths, although all realize what kind of oaths these are." The most vexing aspect for Leonov, according to Vlad, is that he would like to take his words back, but it is too late.

Vlad mentioned that he, too, had observed something unusual in the sky. Whom should he believe, he asks, his own eyes or Leonov. And, by the way, he added, Leonov talks very intricately, with cunning, when he states that he personally has not seen any UFOs, but he does not talk for anyone else. Vlad concluded his post with a question: "I think I have clarified the situation?" He certainly did for the authors of this article.

A LEGENDARY PERSON

Leonov told Russian newspaper *Izvestiya* on May 29, 2009 that he does not consider himself to be a legendary personality. Despite his illustrious career and position in the Soviet hierarchy, Aleksei Arkhipovich Leonov was not just a *Homo Sovieticus*. He was born in Siberia, in May of 1934. His father was arrested in 1937, accused of being "an enemy of the people." Two years later, he was acquitted, but those years were very harsh on Aleksei and his family, which included eight children. The family was viewed as "enemies of the people," lowest of the low, and as he recalled, a number of his neighbours simply came into their home and took whatever they wanted, including little Aleksei's clothing. Later in life, Leonov was expected to become a professional artist. However, he loved aviation, too, and the young man was soon flying jets and studying engineering. In 1959, the 25-year-old Leonov was picked as one of the first twenty cosmonauts.

Soviet Cosmonauts, Brezhnev and Castro

As his career unfolded, he became the first person to step out of a spacecraft and walk in space, in 1965. In 1975, he was commander of the Soyuz spacecraft that took part in the first rendezvous between Soviet and United States spacecraft. He was Hero of the Soviet Union, pilot, cosmonaut, military scientist, writer, artist and talented artist (painter).

During the Soviet era, Leonov one purchased a U.S.-made Ford automobile, but since it was considered improper for cosmonauts to drive American automobiles, he was forced to sell it. Once, Leonov helped female cosmonaut Savitskaya sneak out of her assigned quarters before her scheduled flight, and he took her along back streets to several stores so that she could buy materials to sew together a blouse, which she planned to smuggle on board her ship. Leonov and Savitskaya sewed lead pieces into the sleeves, so that she could wear the blouse and surprise her colleagues during the flight's weightlessness. We wonder if Leonov ever spoke with Savitskaya about the experience she and her colleagues had in 1984, when they claimed "angels" entered the Soviet spacecraft. He has never spoken about it. In his 35 years of working at the Cosmonaut Training Center, how many other stories about UFOs and

aliens has Leonov heard but chooses not to reveal? It is said that before the Baikonur launches, Leonov had a special tradition. He would gently push the cosmonauts with his knee "under their backsides" before they would climb the ladder to their spacecraft. This ritual became an important "superstition" for him. So Leonov is superstitious, like most other cosmonauts. Very few people know that when Sergey Korolyov died, three cosmonauts made a secret pact to bury his ashes on the moon. Sergey Pavlovich Korolyov was a designer of guided missiles, rockets and spacecraft, former prisoner of the Gulag, this victim of Stalin's purges became the multi-talented chief designer of launch vehicles during the early years of the Soviet Union's space program.

Cosmonaut Marina Popovich

The cosmonauts knew that the Central Committee of the Communist Party would not let them take the ashes to the moon. The Soviet leaders would surely want Lenin's ashes to be first on the moon. Nonetheless, the three cosmonauts acquired Korolyov's ashes and hid them in a special container kept by Yuri Gagarin. As the years progressed, Gagarin died, and so did Komarov, leaving only Leonov presumably still holding the ashes. The Soviets, of course, never did officially land on the moon, and Korolyov's ashes were eventually lost. Leonov strongly rejects claims that the American moon missions were faked. He is adamant that the Americans were on the moon, as the Soviets closely monitored every phase of the U.S. moon missions. Leonov and his colleagues monitored the moon missions with great interest and were fluent in their praise for the Americans.

Soviet "Flight to the Moon" Commemorative stamp

Leonov had himself been in training for the Soviet's planned manned moon mission. As the Soviet lunar team commander, he was actually in charge of the training for the mission. The training was extremely harsh, and three Soviet cosmonauts lost their lives in the process. Then, after Korolyov's death, the program was shut down, and the way was cleared for Americans to become first to the moon. In 1992, Leonov, Major General of the Soviet Air Force, was released from the Armed Forces, five years before his scheduled retirement.

Upset because the government apparently decided that it no longer needed his services, he decided to dedicate himself to painting. But the life of an artist was not to be, as he was soon hired to be president of Alfa-Kapital, an investment fund. The company knew of his connections with the military-industrial complex and of his seasoned managerial skills. In 1998, the year of the Asian crisis and Russia's default, Leonov became vice president of Alfa-Bank and significantly expanded the bank. He travelled to the United States on many occasions, as a businessman.

Leonov now lives in the house he designed himself, near Star City. His painting studio is on the third floor. Leonov is involved in philanthropy, including helping children with heart diseases. His paintings have raised substantial amounts for charity. He said in a recent interview that he often dreams of flying into deep space, and the dream makes him feel very sad. As of this writing, he is in his late seventies and has developed significant heart problems, but his adventuring spirit is still strong. In April of 2009, during a cosmonauts' meeting with then Russia's President Dmitry Medvedev, Leonov was able to save the Cosmonaut Training Center training aircraft from being turned over to the Russian Air Force for its transportation needs. Medvedev treated Leonov with great respect during the discussions about the future of the aircraft.

Leonov considers alien invaders to be a threat. But the invaders he is afraid of are meteorites (in his words, akin to the Tunguska phenomenon). What would happen if a meteorite was to fall on Moscow or London? Yet, virtually no attention is paid to the issue. Leonov calls for a new international prevention system to be created (Izvestiya, May 29, 2009). This is more important than travel to Mars, added Pilot-Cosmonaut. Despite his age he continues to be a pioneer in many fields and his highly respected by all that know him or have worked with him. He is a true hero of Russia in every sense of the word, although we disagree with his opinion of Marina Popovich. Whether he knows more about the UFO phenomenon that he has publicly stated remains to be seen but his many comments on the possibility of ancient astronauts is a curious one and nothing he says would surprise us.

PILOT COSMONAUT PAVEL POPOVICH AND UFOS: GOLDEN EAGLE, AGRESSOR, AND COSMONAUT NUMBER "FOUR."

On September 30, 2009, Pavel Romanovich Popovich died in Crimea, Ukraine, after suffering a stroke at the age of 79. He was the first Ukrainian born cosmonaut in history, always proud of his heritage, and deeply in love with his native land. Twice in his life, he received the "Hero of the Soviet Union" award, the highest distinction in the USSR, awarded personally or collectively for heroic feats in service to the Soviet state and society. Rising to the rank of General-Major of Aviation, Popovich received many other awards during his long career. In terms of ufology, he, along with Vladimir Ajaja, were at one time Mutual UFO Network (MUFON) representatives in post-Soviet Russia.

Cosmonaut Pavel Popovich

Greatly respected by almost all who knew him, Popovich was described as being kind, nice, and decent. Possessed of a great sense of humour, he was always ready to help others. His life was intertwined with the turbulent history of UFO research in the Soviet Union after 1978 and after the fall of Communist rule, as well as after the Union created following the Bolshevik revolution. Pavel's father was a peasant who worked all his life in a sugar processing plant. The boy, who had endured harsh realities of famine in the 1930s Ukraine and the terrors of Nazi occupation several years later, probably never dreamed that he would fly spacecraft. He certainly would have never imagined that one day astronomers would name a small planet in his honour. But looking at his life, it is clear the sky beckoned him. Popovich was born in the Kiev region on October 5, 1929. Although he was strong and healthy as a boy, he suffered from rickets during the 1933 famine in the Ukraine, but survived. In 1941, his hometown of Uzin was occupied by German troops, and Pavel was forced by a Nazi officer living in his house to learn the German language. If the boy did not answer in German, the Nazi would beat his hand with a stick. Not one to take his punishment lying down, Pavel secretly took revenge by slashing the Nazi's automobile tires and damaging some of his weapons. Nonetheless, Pavel did learn German, which helped him later in life, especially in college.

At the age of 22, he graduated as a construction engineer from a technical school and also received a pilot's degree from an amateur pilots' club school. Popovich continued education at an aviation college. Upon graduation in 1954 Popovich joined the Soviet Air Force, and in 1960, while assigned to special aviation training, joined the first Soviet cosmonaut detachment. Popovich underwent a full course of training for space flights on board the *Vostok* spacecraft. Popovich was the number "four" cosmonaut in the history of manned spaceflights, and as of this writing, the only survivor of the original four. His predecessors -- Gagarin, Titov and Nikolayev – are all deceased.

Yuri Gagarin and Pavel Popovich, since both lived under Nazi occupation, ran the risk of being deemed unworthy of the honour of being Soviet cosmonauts. Sad was the fate of many who had the misfortune to live in the occupied territories, as they were later branded as traitors and sent to the Gulag. The KGB took several months to study biographies of each of the future cosmonauts, but someone must have had the courage to overlook that the two young men lived under Nazi rule in their childhood, allowing them to continue their training. Popovich made his first spaceflight aboard the *Vostok 4* spaceship in August of 1962. Later, he was trained for a spaceflight under the auspices of the Soviet moon research program, but after the moon program was abandoned, Popovich underwent training for flights aboard Soyuz spaceships. As a result, he flew into space a second time as chief pilot of the *Soyuz 14* spaceship in July 1974, a secret mission that was part of the Soviet "Star Wars" program for exploring the military uses of space technology. For the secret mission, Popovich's call name for this was *Berkut1* (Golden Eagle). Members of the U.S. space program had a different codename for Popovich – "the aggressor." Having docked with the secret military orbital station *Almaz 2* (which had been given the code name *Salyut 3*), Popovich and his engineer, Colonel Artyukhin, conducted military intelligence operations.

They had at their disposal powerful optical equipment (including infrared), 14 special cameras, and even a thirty millimetre cannon. One of the tasks Popovich and his colleagues were given was to spy on the American Skylab station and its three U. S. astronauts. A much more savoury project for the cosmonauts was the sampling of new space food items for spaceflights. For the record, they really liked the new food. The cosmonauts sent their intelligence dispatches to Earth in special capsules, thus creating the first parcel service from space. However, the parcel space mail program was later shut down. Popovich continued his education, and, between the years 1980 to1989, he served as deputy chief of the Gagarin Cosmonaut Training Center. Then, in 1993, he was promoted to the rank of Air Force Major-General in reserve.

Pavel Popovich, Later in Life

PRESIDENT OF THE UFO ASSOCIATION

In 1990, the Soviet Union's very first official civilian UFO research organization was formed, carrying the name *Soyuzufotsentr* (All-Union Ufological Association). Its director was V. Ajaja, former naval officer and submariner, who had a long history as an independent UFO researcher and lecturer. The new organization's president, Pavel Popovich clearly stated in interviews that, although he agreed to direct the organization at the request of several friends who were UFO researchers, he did not consider himself to be an expert in the field of ufology. As it turned out, Popovich was instrumental in helping those who tried to research the subject, albeit independently, or as part of secret Soviet UFO research programs. His authority and reputation in the former USSR had greatly helped Ajaja's efforts to keep the organization viable and afloat in the turbulent and stormy waters of the post-1991 Russian reality.

POPOVICH AND SETKA: A SECRET SOVIET UFO RESEARCH PROGRAM

In the 1980s, the Soviet government's secret UFO research program, SETKA, gave birth to another group, in which Pavel Popovich played a key role. In 1984, Vsevolod Troitsky, corresponding member of the USSR Academy of Sciences, established a commission to study anomalous phenomena. Earlier, in 1982, he published an article

(Issue 10, *Nauka i religiya* or *Science and Religion* magazine), where he described complex anomalous phenomena (in the atmosphere, hydrosphere, and space) that have been observed but cannot be explained and need to be researched further, for the sake of science and human society.

There are two opinions about the origin and purpose of these governmental UFO study groups. According to respected Russian researcher Yuri Stroganov, the Soviet State attempted to increase the ranks of informants through the creation of so-called "anomalous phenomena commissions." The commissions, according to Stroganov, proved to be another successful effort to pump out information from different strata of the population. Due to the previous debunking efforts directed against the UFO phenomenon by the Academy of Sciences, eyewitnesses were not too eager to contact representatives of any State organization. The newly born "anomalous phenomena commissions" were seen as "independent action" organizations, making them appear more worthy of the public's trust. Soviet citizens believed these groups to be independent, when they were in reality a "grab" by the government to collect information and research about UFOs that had previously been accessible only to independent researchers. Stroganov ties these commissions to the SETKA-MO. The commissions first appeared five years prior to the removal of the ban on UFO information in the USSR, and during their existence, the information collected had been, according to their members, input into computers. Where the data went thereafter hasn't been explained.

The Deputy Chairman of the leading Anomalous Phenomena Commission was none other than the distinguished Soviet cosmonaut Pavel Popovich. According to Stroganov, Popovich made a strikingly improbable statement at the first conference of the All-Union Ufological Association, of which he was President. Popovich told the gathering that he was a man of little competence concerning issues of ufology. He has also stated that his role would be to act as a buffer between the Association and the State. Popovich acted precisely as he claimed he would. He was a modest man who had helped many researchers, and as he stated in his interviews, he did not pretend to be an expert in the field of ufology. According to Popovich, most of the information about anomalous phenomena came from military personnel, including pilots - trusted, sane, and healthy people. Many reports were nonsensical and could be dismissed, but many others were historically significant. Government agencies started collecting UFO data during World War II. For example, during the Battle of Kursk, Soviet aviators and witnesses on the ground observed mysterious objects in the sky. U.S. Air Force pilots had encountered a cigar-shaped object that emitted blinding rays around it, forcing the pilots to catapult, and abandon their aircraft. Popovich first revealed this incident in the April 10, 2009 interview to the Ukrainian web portal Donbass UA. Another view is that of Mikhail Gershtein, Russia's leading UFO researcher. He wrote in his books, such as *Tayni prishel'tsev I NLO* (2006), that in February of 1984, by the decision of VSNTO (All-Union Council of Scientific Technical Societies), a Central Commission for Anomalous Phenomena in the Environment was created, which functioned within the VSNTO Committee for environmental problems. The Chairman was Corresponding Member of the USSR Academy of Sciences V. Troitsky, and his deputies were Corresponding Member of the same Academy N. Zheltukhin, G. Pisarenko of the Ukraine Academy of Sciences, and General-Major of

Aviation, Pilot-Cosmonaut Pavel Popovich. There were other notable persons including A. Mordvin-Shodro, a Soviet ufologist and military officer, and scientists I. Lisevich, N. Petrovich, L, Gindilis, and E. Ermilov. Soviet newspapers *Trud*, *Sovetskaya Rossiya*, *Izvestiya*, and *Sotsisalisticheskaya Industriya* published information about the Commission, including interviews with its leaders. The tasks and goals were stated, and the address to which reports should be sent was published - -*101000, Moscow, Post Office, POB 764*. According to Gershtein, the Commission was born because those in charge of the academic research of the SETKA program had basically gotten rid of all true UFO enthusiasts in their group. Only the debunkers together with military specialists from secret military institutes remained in the program. Ufology enthusiasts were to be controlled and allowed to work only on specific, assigned projects, with no leakage of information allowed.

The GALAKTIKA program, like a powerful vacuum cleaner, sucked in tons of information, but nothing ever came out. Neither non-military ufologists, nor military ones, received any coherent explanation. Even when an unusual phenomenon could have been easily explained as a rocket launch, an official explanation was never released, because in those years, everything was secret or military classified information. The debunkers in the SETKA-AN program were right to state that most of UFO sightings were easily explained as mankind's technological activity and that no more than ten percent were truly unidentified. But, they were wrong to state that all of the remaining ten percent (the truly unexplained sightings) were not of physical objects but of some other phenomena. They were also wrong to say that, in no case, can UFOs be extraterrestrial in origin. These official debunkers usually spent much time deriding their civilian counterparts, the amateur ufologists. Meanwhile, these unofficial, independent UFO researchers began to unite under the protection of popular magazines and scientific technical societies in those years. The UFO enthusiasts did not take the derision from the government passively, and they did an end run around the Academy of Sciences, going directly for information to the military coordinators of the GALAKTIKA-MO program. The initiative to create the Commission was supported by military researchers, who were tired of fruitless activities of the academic debunkers. Of course, the Commission was to include also those who served the Ministry of Defence research (Lieutenant-General G. S. Legasov and Lieutenant-General V. P. Balashov). And that is how the Commission came to be. And Pavel Popovich did play a role in its workings, although due to oaths of secrecy by which he was bound, he could not reveal all he knew.

As for "real anomalies" it was Popovich who did reveal to journalists a few examples. On May 29 1984, *Trud* newspaper published V. Vostrukhin's article *Chto zhe eto bilo?* Popovich told the author about a case that took place on March 27, 1983 in Gorky (and investigated by the Commission's Gorky section), where a strange object was spotted near the city airport. The airport's radars registered the object but could not identify it. The altitude of the object's flight was no more than half a mile, and the speed was around 120 miles per hour. The witness, flight controller A. Shushkin, who had observed the object, said its size was similar to that of an IL-14 aircraft fuselage, but it had no wings. It was a light-grey, metallic, cigar-shaped object that moved slowly across the sky and was seen for about 40 minutes. At a distance of 18 to 24 miles northeast of the airport, it suddenly disappeared from radar screens. Another researcher, Shushkin, later said the date of this UFO sighting was actually March 28 not March 29, and that the object flew at an altitude of between 1,300 and 2,000 feet, disappearing about ten seconds after it was first sighted.

Another, somewhat more dramatic, episode took place in January 1978, and was reported in *Sotsialisticheskaya Industriya* newspaper on August 6, 1984 (I. Mosin's article *Zagadki nebesnikh yavleniy*). Popovich told the author that during the flight of a YAK-40 over the area between two settlements, Medvezhye and Nadim, the crew noticed a very large, round object approaching their aircraft very rapidly. Moments later, it appeared directly in front of the plane, and its size grew rapidly as it approached. A crash appeared to be imminent, but suddenly the object veered off to the right, just barely missing the aircraft.

THE KGB UFO FILES

On October 24, 1991, a file consisting of secret UFO documents from the KGB (dubbed the "blue" folder) were given to former cosmonaut Pavel Popovich, who was then the President of the All-Union Ufological Association in Russia. It was the culmination of an effort by Popovich to persuade the KGB to release some of its UFO information, most of which had been compiled by the KGB's divisions assigned to counterintelligence and to the defence of the country's defence installations. The file was accompanied by a letter written by N.A. Sham, the Deputy Chairman of the Committee for State Security USSR (KGB). The blue file, containing 124 pages of printed text, included copies of UFO reports sent to the KGB and consisted of handwritten reports, typed testimonies, notes from KGB informers, crude drawings, and eyewitness reports of UFOs. The release of the blue file to Popovich was a landmark in Soviet UFO research. This episode of cooperation between the KGB and UFO researchers was without precedent.

The letter included with the blue file was addressed in this manner:
"Committee of State Security of the USSR, 24.10.91, ref. number 1953/III, to comrade Popovich." The letter read as follows:

Dear Pavel Romanovich:

The Committee of State Security is not engaged in regular gathering and analysis of the information on the anomalous phenomena (the so-called unidentified flying objects). At the same time the information about cases of observation of such phenomena comes to KGB of the USSR from the various organizations and citizens. We direct to you a copy of appropriate materials. Vice-president of the Committee,

N. A. Sham.

Chetvertoye izmereniye i NLO newspaper (Issue 2, 1998, Yaroslavl, Russia) published an interesting article written by Vladimir Ajaja as a response to criticism that he has kept secret UFO data from the public, among other issues. In the article, Ajaja mentioned that in the early 1990s, the KGB, upon the request of Pavel Popovich (who was then President of the Ufological Association) gave the organization headed by

Ajaja, some 1300 documents related to UFOs. Among these documents were reports from official agencies, from commanders of military units, and from private citizens. It seems likely that Ajaja's description is of the same batch of documents of given to

Pavel Popovich by KGB in 1991. According to Ajaja, the Lyubyanka (KGB headquarters) was getting rid of an "unnecessary headache," and Russian ufologists benefited by expanding their database of UFO knowledge.

POPOVICH AND ROSWELL CRASH

A serious effort by Soviets and Americans to study the UFO phenomenon jointly and to share information was initiated in 1991. The Joint American-Soviet Aerial Anomaly Federation (JASAAF) was formed, thanks to the efforts of Dr. Richard Haines. The co-signers to the document establishing the federation included the Mutual UFO Network (MUFON), J. Allen Hynek center for UFO Studies, and the Fund for UFO Research in America. In the USSR, the co-signers were the All-Union Inter-branch Scientific and Coordinative UFO Center (*Soyuzufotsentr*), and the Scientific Research Institute for the Study of Anomalous Phenomena. The co-directors were Vladimir Ajaja in Moscow, and Dr. Vladimir Rubtsov in Kharkov (or Kharkiv, as it is known today) in Ukraine. Haines, a retired NASA scientist, travelled several times to the former Soviet Union. The Federation was to be a bridge for serious investigators of both nations. Actually, the Federation translated and published some of Felix Zigel's works, and created an outstanding file of UFO phenomena-related news clippings and articles from the USSR.

In 1992, at Dr. Haines' request, Pavel Popovich, head of the All-Russian Ufological Association, contacted two Russian ministries regarding the Roswell documents. Dr. Haines wanted to find out whether the Soviet-era archives contained documents pertaining to the Roswell Crash. The replies that Popovich received were unusually quick by Russian beaurocratic standards. His letter to the Ministry of Defence of the Russian Federation was dated June 8, 1993 and the reply from the Ministry was dated September 17, 1993. It said that the officials of the Central Archive of the Ministry of Defence had conducted a search of the materials of interest to Popovich but did not find any materials pertinent to the Roswell UFO crash. The second reply came from the Ministry of Security of the Russian Federation, dated September 14, 1993, stating that no materials could be located pertaining to the reported crash of a "flying saucer" near Roswell, New Mexico, USA, in the year 1947.

Soviet intelligence was quite active in the United States in 1940s, and the Roswell crash would certainly have attracted their attention. It was alleged that Stalin had a great interest in the event, and he reportedly showed some of his top scientists a large number of documents and books that he had collected on the subject. Of course, the replies Popovich received about Roswell materials may mean nothing. It is quite possible that Roswell evidence was hidden in secret archives that have not yet been made available to researchers. It is also possible that there is a joint effort by the governments of Russian and the U. S. to conceal such documents and to deny their existence. Yet another, more mundane explanation, is that the Soviets either simply lost the documents regarding the Roswell crash or perhaps a greedy Russian official sold the documents during the confused years following the fall of communism. Having failed to find anything on Roswell, Popovich nonetheless succeeded in uncovering information about other Russian UFO cases.

REVELATIONS

After every interview that he gave, Pavel Popovich was required to sign a special document, stating that he did not reveal any state secrets. He has never been able to make full disclosure about what he knows, as he is a military person and, as such, loyal to his oaths.

In August of 2006, Popovich gave an interview to *Bul'var Gordona*, a Ukrainian magazine. (Issue 31[67]) in which he was asked whether he thought mankind was the only intelligent species in the universe. Unlike other cosmonauts who avoid answering such questions, Popovich did reply, electing to give his strong opinion that other intelligent races exist in outer space. As part of his response, the former cosmonaut told the interviewer a "legend." He said that a very long time ago, there existed another planet, a gigantic one, in our solar system, not far from Earth. Larger than Saturn and inhabited by a very advanced civilization, the planet is called "Phaeton" by some science fiction writers, while others call it "Moonah." The planet's inhabitants knew how to use thermonuclear energy and used Earth as a test range. But one day, a tragedy occurred – a series of nuclear explosions were accidentally detonated on the planet, causing a planetary catastrophe. A large chunk of Moonah was blasted into space and was captured by the Earth's gravitational field, becoming our moon. The shock waves from the explosion turned our planet by ninety degrees and caused the Great Flood recorded in so many ancient manuscripts, including the Bible. This scenario was confirmed when Antarctica was explored and scientists discovered remains of palm trees, crocodiles, and other "out of place" artefacts. Following the catastrophe, the larger part of Moonah flew off toward the outer reaches of our solar system, finally decelerating and settling into an orbit around our sun at the very outskirts of its gravitational pull. Due to their advanced technology, not all of Moonah's civilization perished.

Popovich stated that although he was telling a legend, he had read about scientific speculation that a giant planet may actually exist on the very edge of our solar system, invisible from Earth due to the great distance. If the legend was born long before the scientific discovery, does it mean it was based on concrete facts? Also, why have researchers throughout the world found so many ancient artefacts and rock drawings that seem to represent people in spacesuits and objects in the sky that look like UFOs? Then Popovich added that if the legend of Moonah is true, its inhabitants no doubt visit Earth from time to time. They have established an intermediate base in the area of Saturn, and they have had three bases on Earth -- one in the Andes, an underwater base in the Indian Ocean trench, and a former base in the Himalayas, which was the fabled "Shambala." Although the Andes base was removed after being nearly discovered by humans, the other two bases still remain.

Regarding the Indian Ocean base, Popovich said that a careful reading of the logs of ships travelling over the Indian Ocean trench reveals many sightings of UFO-like objects entering and leaving the waters in the area. The ships' logs contain observations such as "a fiery body entered the waters" and "a fiery body ascended from the waters." Popovich believes that whoever is behind the UFOs has an underwater base at the bottom of the Indian Ocean trench. When Popovich was asked why these intelligent visitors to the Earth would not establish contacts with us, Popovich said we are not ready for the contact. Despite our many advances in all fields of human endeavour, we have yet to bridge the vast gulf of communication and cooperation between humans of different races, religions, creeds, and beliefs. Hence, the "visitors" will not communicate with us until we are "ripe" for such contact. Also during the interview, Pavel Popovich told of his own UFO sighting, which he in 1978, while aboard an airplane flying at 34,000 feet, travelling from Washington to Moscow. Sitting by the window, Popovich recalled that although he really did not have anything to look at but clouds and the ocean, something urged him to keep looking outside. About one mile from the plane and some ten degrees higher, he observed an object that looked like a white, isosceles triangle. The cosmonaut screamed and ran to tell the crew of the airliner. Neither the onboard radar nor any ground radar registered the strange object hovering alongside the aircraft. The plane's crew also observed the object and determined that it measured over 300 feet on its longest side. The object did not resemble any known, conventional or unconventional aircraft, Popovich added.

The UFO moved rapidly, travelling nearly twice the speed of the airplane, which flew at about 600 miles per hour. It quickly overtook the plane and zoomed off into the distance, eventually disappearing from view. None of the observers were able to hazard a guess as to what it was. At the time of this sighting, Popovich was part of a delegation from the USSR Academy of Sciences, returning from to Moscow from Pittsburgh, where they attended the International Gagarin Readings conference. Also on board the plane with Popovich were a number of Soviet academicians, who had also observed the UFO.

In another interview (for Ukrainian newspaper *Fakty*, 2001), Popovich said that when the sighting occurred, the speed of the airplane was approximately 559 miles per hour, while the object travelled at the speed of over 600 miles per hour. The object vanished from the sight after overtaking the aircraft. When interviewed by *Ultra*, a Finnish magazine, in 1993 (Issue number 5), Popovich disclosed additional details. He said the UFO he sighted was "transparent" and that the sighting occurred at an altitude of 39,000 feet. Popovich said that although many UFOs are actually secret weapons or experimental aircraft, he did not think what he saw fits into this category. He is inclined to believe it was something unexplained, stating that there are many questions for which humans still have no answers. For example, he said, science has yet to fully explain what generates ball lightning. We know it is a blob of plasma, but it does not fall apart. It somehow stays intact and occurs in different sizes, varying from several inches to dozens of feet. Ball lightning behaves very strangely. It can fly into the window's upper pane, pour from the electrical outlet, fly around the room, and then depart or explode. Its colours are varied and can even be absolutely black. No one knows its nature, but annually there are about eleven thousand instances of ball lightnings. Popovich added that there are many other regularly-occurring phenomena which cannot yet be explained by modern science. Given our limited knowledge in these areas, is it any wonder that the extraterrestrials are able to so easily evade us? Regarding persons who claim to have experienced contact with extraterrestrials, Pavel Popovich has stated that he does not believe any such contact event to be true. He states that the self-proclaimed contactees are merely seeking publicity. On another occasion, Popovich stated that 95 percent of everything written about UFOs is nonsense. However, during the interview, an interesting titbit came out. He said that during his time at Star City, a group of scientists from Nizhny Novgorod, the fifth largest city in Russia, visited the cosmonauts and told them that there exists another, identical solar system that rotates precisely at a 90 degree angle relative to the plane of rotation of our own solar system. In the same interview with *Bul'var Gordona*, Popovich was asked a question whether he, a pilot and cosmonaut who grew up in an admittedly atheistic society, believed in a Supreme Being. He replied that he was a baptized Christian, and that in 1974, during a flight with cosmonaut Artyukhin, while admiring the heavens through the spacecraft's porthole, he finally grasped the significance of intelligent design in the cosmos. He said that looking at the universe from space causes one to understand how infinite it is. Popovich recalled the thought that suddenly struck him, "Someone created it and someone directs it all." Who has created the laws of celestial mechanics, he thought? All we did was to use those laws -- to discern them and exploit them. At that point, he decided that regardless of what various people or groups call Him, there is a Supreme Creator of everything. His marriage to fellow cosmonaut Marina Popovich ended in divorce after thirty years; after which Pavel married a Ukrainian woman, Alevtina Fyodorovna. Proud of his Ukranian heritage, he served as the president of the Ukrainian society "Slavutich" in Moscow.

Pavel lived his final years in a settlement near Ostankino (Moscow), dubbed Star Village because 36 former cosmonauts reside there. Fond of fishing, he had fished throughout the former Soviet Union, but he most fondly recalled fishing for perch in the Dnepr River. In addition to his fishing, Popovich loved watching boxing and enjoyed playing billiards. For many years, Popovich had been the chairman of the board of the All-Russia Institute of Agricultural Aero-Photo-Geodesic Studies, a group that monitors Russian soil and ecology). He remained in that post until his death. He had a dream that he spoke of often -- to be able to fly a spacecraft into space again, to look at Earth once more from orbit, and to enjoy once more that incredible sight. Until his death, his nights were filled with dreams about exploring outer space and about the space missions in which he had taken part. After his passing, the name of Pavel Popovich was given to a mountain ridge in Antarctica and to a minor planet.

GEORGY GRECHKO

Dr. Georgy Mikhailovich Grechko, Hero of the Soviet Union and a former Soviet cosmonaut, flight engineer, and scientist was born on 25 May 1931 in Leningrad. Graduated with honours from the Leningrad Institute of Mechanics in 1955, he became an assistant to the Soviet Union's chief space rocket designer Sergey Korolyov. Grechko calculated the trajectory for the launch of the first Soviet satellite (Sputnik). In the mid-1960s, he was among 13 men selected from the Korolyov Design Bureau for the first Cosmonaut Detachment. He worked on the Soviet Lunar probes and flew three space flights --Soyuz 17, Soyuz 26, and Soyuz T-14. Cosmonauts Grechko and Romanenko set a space endurance record of 96 days aboard Salyut 6 station, which they first boarded on December 11, 1977. Dr. Grechko resigned from the space program in 1992 to lecture on atmospheric physics at the Russian Academy of Sciences.

Dr. Grechko made the very strange assertion that our planet would be visited by extraterrestrials in the year 2012, sometime between December 21st and 23rd. He said that he had no doubts about it. The retired Soviet cosmonaut is certain that humanoid civilizations exist elsewhere and believes that higher intelligences guide human affairs. Former Soviet cosmonauts are highly trained and skilled explorers. Many of them are scientists and engineers. Many of them seem to have strong opinions or knowledge about extraterrestrials? What sources of information about ETs are available to them that are unknown to the rest of society?

SOVIET LUNAR SECRETS

An interview published in 1991 in the Russian *Megapolis Express* newspaper may shed some light on a subject that remains secret even today. During an interview with ex-KGB officer Vadim Petrov, journalist Alexander Sidorko uncovered evidence about a top secret group of cosmonauts known as "test cosmonauts," whose lives were essentially expendable. Petrov told Sidorko that his job in the KGB was to safeguard the identities of these cosmonauts. Very few people knew of their existence. Among those who knew were the General Secretary of the Communist Party; the chief of the KGB; Petrov; and a select few medical doctors, spaceship designers, and operators –a total of only about 15 people.

Supposedly, the detachment of test-cosmonauts was created even before Yuri Gagarin's flight. The chief of the KGB at the time, Semichastniy, came up with the idea. Brezhnev removed Semichastny in 1967, as part of Kremlin power struggles, and replaced him with Yuri Andropov, who was rumoured to be interested in UFOlogy and SETKA findings in later years. These test-cosmonauts were supposedly "sneaked" aboard "unmanned" Soviet orbital stations to ensure that all systems remained operational, that the necessary data was collected, and that all the objectives of the space station were accomplished. The failure of these "unmanned" space stations was not an option, and supposedly, the Soviets were willing to sacrifice a few test cosmonauts to ensure that the orbital platforms remained in operation and remained viable. Only KGB volunteers were accepted for the secret detachment. Acceptance followed a screening process. Even those who did not make it to be test cosmonauts were sworn to secrecy. Vadim Petrov began his career with the test-cosmonaut detachment in 1969, at the time that the Soviet *Lunokhod* (Moonwalker) project was in progress. *Lunokhod*, the pride of Soviet science, was an "unmanned" moon exploration vehicle. The two test-cosmonauts in training for the flight to the moon were known as Number 13 and Number 14. Petrov told Sidorko that in his opinion, prior to the *Lunokhod* project, test-cosmonauts may have been used on a dozen other missions, although their role was never revealed. It was common knowledge to those involved in the *Lunokhod* project that the men behind the faceless numbers would never return to Earth. They were to arrive at the moon in a separate module. They would then descend to the lunar surface, locate the *Lunokhod* vehicle that had previously landed, and carry out important maintenance on it. They were to repair the chassis, align the tuning of solar batteries, and provide the corrected directions for television cameras. Supposedly, the lateral camera shots of the *Lunokhod* were taken by test-cosmonauts.

Lunokhod 1 (NASA Photo)

According to Petrov, the KGB officers in charge of the program actually wept. The volunteers were heroes who guided the craft to the moon and carried out the *Lunokhod* program objectives. Whether drugged "zombies," or psyched-up heroes, their alleged death was a tragic episode in the history of Soviet space exploration – unless the whole thing is a hoax, as some people have suggested.

FLYING SAUCERS WILL HELP YOU

UFOs and aliens were not forbidden subjects for Soviet cosmonauts, as long as the cosmonauts were very circumspect. Yuri Malishev, a highly decorated veteran of the program, revealed that he knew of thousands of people who had observed UFOs. He stated that it is the nature of UFOs that remains elusive, not the objects themselves. He said their visits to Earth will continue and that the visitors have chosen not to establish contact with humanity. Earth will continue to be observed, he said, but the UFO beings will not initiate any form of interaction with us. This was stated by

Malishev in *Tekhnika- Molodezhi*, Issue # 11, 1981. Then he added something quite unexpected. He said that aliens and their "flying saucers" have long ago entered the world of space exploration, and that their presence has to be accounted for even in the Soviet space flight simulators. Every space flight is completely imitated on Earth using the space simulator. The simulator is supposed to include data on any event, no matter how rare, that could conceivably happen while cosmonauts are in the orbit. Sometimes an instructor fails to enter the data necessary and the simulated mission cannot continue. When the information needed to correct the mishap remains elusive or unavailable, the instructor remarks, in a sarcastic fashion, "A flying saucer is on its way, and you will receive all that you need." Then, the simulator hatch opens and the required information, referred to as "a parcel from aliens," is given to the trainees. Is this just a gimmick used in the training of cosmonauts, or is it based on secret information known only to those involved in the space program?

SECRETS OF THE FIFTH EXPEDITION

Soyuz T-4 was launched into orbit on March 12, 1981, piloted by Vladimir Vasilyevich Kovalyonok, Commander, and Viktor Petrovich Savinikh, Flight Engineer. On March 13, the spaceship successfully docked with the Salyut 6 orbital station. Salyut 6 was the second generation of space platforms built by the Soviets, launched on September 29, 1977. The first crew of cosmonauts went aboard Salyut 6 in December 1977, and the final crew departed in May 1981. Soviet spaceships of the Soyuz and Progress class came in frequently, as Salyut 6 was one of the most active of all Soviet space stations. Replacement craft were sent to the platform in an effort to support longer and longer stays aboard the station. Professor A.I. Lazarev designed the expedition's programs for scientific research. The watch crew of Kovalyonok and Savinikh was given the special task of confirming unusual findings brought back by the watch crews of the Second, Third, and Fourth Expeditions. The "silvery clouds" mentioned earlier irked Soviet scientists. That much is admitted in a book written by Professor Lazarev, Kovalyonok and astrophysicist S.A. Avakyan, *Issledovaniye Zemli s pilotiruyemikh kosmicheskikh korabley* or *Study of Earth from Manned Spaceships* (Leningrad, Gidrometeoizdat, 1987). Mysteriously, all information about what happened aboard Salyut 6 from May 14 to 18 is missing from the book. The last entry states that on May 3, 1981, the crew observed "a ray-like structure" southwest of Australia. In actuality, during the "missing" period from May 14 to May 18, cosmonauts Kovalenok and Savinikh reportedly observed an unidentified alien spaceship in one of the strangest of several paranormal incidents aboard Salyut 6. Information about the sighting appeared in at least one Soviet publication in the 1990's, *O zagadkah NLO*, Issue 1 (Estonia, 1990). Lieutenant General Georgy Timofeyevich Beregovoy (1921 1995) headed training programs for Soviet cosmonauts at the Yuri Gagarin Cosmonaut Training Center between 1972 and 1987. He was a highly decorated military pilot and himself a veteran cosmonaut. Beregovoy played a prominent role in a high-level, secret meeting held in Moscow, in the Gosplan building, after Kovalyonok and Savinikh came back to Earth from Salyut 6. Beregovoy reportedly presented a report about what occurred aboard the Salyut 6 to a crowd of 200 Communist Party leaders, scientists, space exploration experts, and members of the official UFO Study Commission (headed by Pavel Popovich). As the audience watched in astonishment, Beregovoy allegedly showed them a film taken by the cosmonauts showing several "aliens" floating out of their spaceship without any protective suits and seemingly without breathing equipment. The strange creatures approached the Salyut before moving away. Following the showing of the film, information about the contact reportedly was leaked to the West. There are other interesting accounts of the May 1981 sighting and some additional observations by Kovalyonok. It is noteworthy that Kovalyonok tried to present another account to Italian interviewers some years ago. Beregovoy went on to play an important role in the Russian military space program and edited an important book, the *English-Russian Dictionary on Advanced Aerospace Systems* (Moscow, Military Publishing House, 1993). Another Soviet publication, *Informatzionniy Byuleten NLO* (October 1, 1990) contained an account of a conversation between the crews of Salyut 6 and Soyuz 4 on May 5, 1981. Kovalenok reported seeing an explosion from space. While orbiting over Cape Town, South Africa, the cosmonaut saw a brightly burning sphere that was elongated like a melon, moving perpendicularly to the Soviet ship. Two explosions suddenly rocked the strange sphere, one aft and one stern.

UFOS AND THE ABORTED MISSION OF SOYUZ 18-1

Oleg Makarov, a cosmonaut, scientist, writer, and twice decorated Hero of the Soviet Union, died of a heart attack in Moscow in 2003. The cosmonaut who flew two space missions with Makarov, Vasily Lazarev, died of alcohol poisoning in 1990. These men were involved in one of the most fascinating mysteries of the Soviet space program -- the aborted Soyuz 18-1 mission in 1975. Author Paul Stonehill has been following the story for many years and has collected some fascinating facts about the mission to the Salyut 4 station. The mission is referred to as Soyuz 18-1 or, sometimes Soyuz 18a, since the next Soyuz mission, in May 1975, was officially called Soyuz 18. In the Soviet Union, only successful missions were given numbers. The Soviets in 1975 desperately wanted to compete with the U.S. Skylab missions and establish their own space station program. Cosmonauts Lazarev and Makarov were selected for the Soyuz 1 mission. Both were distinguished personalities. Makarov, a graduate of the Bauman Moscow Higher Technical School, had worked in Special Design Bureau Number One, under the legendary Sergey Korolyov. He was selected to be a cosmonaut in 1966. Makarov was engaged in the aborted Soviet lunar program and was in training for a circumlunar flight. He participated in the Soyuz 12 spaceflight in 1973, commanded by Vasily Lazarev. That was the first Soviet manned mission following the Soyuz 11 tragedy, wherein three cosmonauts were killed during Re-entry. Makarov and Lazarev returned to Earth safely, after two days in space. In later years, Makarov worked for RSC Energia (former Special Design Bureau), playing a role in the MIR space station and also in the Buran shuttle. Lazarev, Soviet Air Force colonel, fighter pilot, and surgeon, remained a cosmonaut until 1980s, but did not fly again after the aborted Soyuz 18-1 launch he commanded. Makarov and Lazarev were tough, intelligent cosmonauts. And they knew how to keep secrets, too.

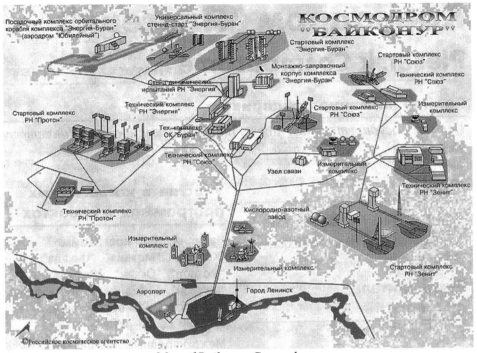

Map of Baikonur Cosmodrome

UFO SIGHTING: APRIL 5, 1975 -- UFO AT THE BAIKONUR LAUNCH

In 1961, the Vostok 1 spacecraft, carrying the world's first space traveller, was launched from the Baikonur Cosmodrome, the world's oldest and largest operational space launch facility. Fourteen years later, in 1975, something highly unusual happened at Baikonur. On the morning of April 5, preparations were underway for the launch of the Soyuz 18-1 spacecraft. The weather was clear, and the cosmonauts that comprised its crew felt great. Their mission was to dock with the Salyut 4 orbital station, relieve the crew of Gubayov and Grechko, and work at the station for sixty days. According to the retired Soviet colonel Kolchin, a respected auth or and researcher, a few minutes before the Soyuz 18-1 launch, Lieutenant Colonel V. Ilyin had observed a cross-shaped UFO of a transparent, greyish color, hovering at a high altitude in the sky, over the launching area. As he and his chauffeur watched the peculiar object, the Soyuz lifted off the launch pad. The weather over Kazakhstan is usually clear most of the year, and he could clearly observe all phases of the rocket's flight. At the 120th second, the *bokovushki* (boosters) separated in a proper fashion and flew off to the sides, in a cross-like manner. Lieutenant Colonel recalled that after that, one could observe, with the unaided eye, a luminescent dot. It was the main engine, and then the dot disappeared, too. At the 150th second, the nose flailing (*golovnoy obtekatel*) separated. But this time, after the *bokovushki* separated, the rocket diverted from its normal trajectory, as was apparent by its trail. So, this was only minutes into the flight, when the separation problems occurred with the Soyuz booster. Ilyin remembered the "grey cross" he had observed in the zenith.

But the object was not there anymore. His chauffer, Gena, confirmed that he, too, saw the greyish cross. Vladimir Ajaja, Russia's eminent ufologist, mentioned this episode in his book *Inaya Zhizn'* (Moscow, 1998). He added that we would probably never find out whether the observed UFO had any role in the failure of the mission. There are other questions about this doomed mission for which we may never find answers.

THE DOOMED FLIGHT

The four strap-on boosters separated, followed by the nose flailing and the escape rocket. At 261st seconds after their lift-off, the time came for the third stage to break away from the second stage. It was then that the cosmonauts encountered a violent swaying motion that was followed by a loud siren and a red *avariya nositelya* "booster failure" warning light on the control panel. The lower stage had only partially separated. The third stage had ignited right on schedule, thus threatening to send the spacecraft crashing onto the taiga below. The crew sent repeated requests to mission control to initiate the abort sequence. Finally, Syuz-18-1 was separated from the wayward booster. Hence, the spacecraft's main engine engaged and pulled clear. The spacecraft's descent module separated from the rest of Soyuz at a high altitude. Following a ballistic trajectory, Lazarev and Makarov were subjected to a horrifying 20g re-entry, twice the normal g-load. The cosmonauts most likely suffered injuries as a result. But then the deceleration forces decreased, and their spacecraft's parachute system was activated, as well as the soft-landing rockets. Finally, the Soyuz command module, containing the exhausted crew, having separated from the booster and plunged back to Earth, came to rest on an Altai mountainside.

Baikonur Cosmodrome, courtesy of Vadim Chernobrov

According to Ajaja (and the official report) the suborbital flight had lasted 21 minutes and 27 seconds, reached the altitude of 119 miles per hour, and flew 978 miles altogether.

VADIM ILYIN'S INFORMATION

Russian journalist Vadim Ilyin published an article in issue 16 of NLO, a popular St. Petersburg magazine, in 2004. *Kosmonavtov spas NLO* ("Cosmonauts Were Rescued By a UFO") was the article heading. He claimed to reveal heretofore unavailable information. Vadim Ilyin stated that at the 260th second, the voice of P. Klimuk, the communications operator at mission control, was suddenly cut off, and the crew heard, strange radio interference for a moment. Then, they seemed to reacquire mission control, but the voice was very weak and muffled. It sounded less like human speech and more like computer generated speech designed to mimic human speech. The cosmonauts could not understand the contents of the transmission. A few seconds later they heard the siren and saw the "booster failure" warning light on the control panel. According to Vadim Ilyin, the cosmonauts heard the same strange sounds again after the 270th second of the flight. The crew's communication with mission control was sometimes normal and other times cut off, replaced by what sounded like an awkward, computerized imitation of a human voice. The cosmonauts wondered how an outsider could break into the radio communication channel designated exclusively for the Soviet space missions.

THE LANDING SITE

In this book, we have described a number of unusual sightings and observations from Altai. This is another one. Although there was doubt as to where exactly the two cosmonauts from the aborted Soyuz 18-1 landed, it was actually near the town of Gorno-Altaisk, about 1,000 miles from their launch point at Baikonur, and not far from the border with Red China. According to sources, the cosmonauts thought they had landed in China, which was considered enemy territory at the time. When they opened the hatch, the cosmonauts discovered a snow-covered landscape. Their capsule's parachute was caught either in a tree or a rocky ledge, and the spacecraft dangled suspended over a ravine that was about 2,000 feet deep. Makarov managed to determine their position, calculating that they landed in the Altai Mountains, very close to Chinese territory. To be certain that their secrets did not fall prey to prying Chinese eyes, Makarov and Lazarev reportedly later burned all their onboard documents. Still a dazed from their hard landing, the cosmonauts managed to crawl out of their dangling capsule. Researcher Vadim Ilyin stated that the men were so exhausted that they could barely move. Later, they put on their thermal clothing, and switched on their distress signal. They dug down into the deep snow, gathered some twigs, and were able to light a fire. The temperatures that night were sub-zero.

UFO SIGHTING

Ilyin claims that not long after the cosmonauts lit the fire, night fell and several airplanes flew over them, signalling that the landing site had been found, and flew away.

A strong wind cleared away most of the clouds in the area and then calmed down. Suddenly, Makarov and Lazarev heard an increasing audible whistling sound, and at the same time, they saw among the stars above them a bizarre, luminescent object, hovering in the night sky. Its shape was unclear, seeming to be just a large, bright spot of light with a slightly violet hue. Its altitude was uncertain. The object hovered over them for about 30 seconds, and then, as if confirming that all was in order, it disappeared as suddenly as it had appeared.

According to Ilyin, Vasily Lazarev supposedly told German journalists in 1996 that he has since become convinced that what they observed that night in 1975 was indeed a UFO and that the same UFO had tried to contact them while they were in orbit, using their communications channel. Further, Lazarev expressed his belief that the UFO was responsible for "guiding" them to a safe landing in the Altai Mountains – and that because of the assistance, they survived the ordeal. Asked why neither he nor Makarov said anything about the UFO upon their return to Baikonur, Lazarev replied that under Soviet rule, any cosmonaut attempting to report a UFO encounter would almost certainly be grounded and possibly also removed from the cosmonaut program. He also revealed that the tape recordings of all their capsule communications were carefully studied, but he never knew what the tapes revealed. Also, he heard that the tape later disappeared under mysterious circumstances. Vadim Ilyin's story has been called into question because of the fact that Vasily Lazarev died in 1990, and therefore could not have given an interview to German journalists in 1996. Could it have been that the date was a typo? Or perhaps the 1996 article contained information from an interview with Lazarev prior to his death? Unfortunately, nobody knows the identities of the German journalists who supposedly interviewed him.

THE GEOLOGIST

Former cosmonaut L. Smirenniy added more to the Soyuz 18-1 UFO encounter story in his memoirs published in 2007. A scientist at Moscow's Research and Technical Center for Radiation-Chemical Safety and Hygiene, Smirenniy was also a member of the International Academy of Astronautics. In his memoirs, Smirenniy states that he discussed the Soyuz 18-1 incident with legendary Soviet test pilot, S. N. Anokhin, who had worked in the S.P. Korolyov design bureau and headed a team of the "test-cosmonauts." Anokhin revealed to Smirenniy that he carefully analyzed all of Makarov's actions during the mission and concluded that the cosmonaut behaved exceptionally courageously. Smirenniy, who had himself trained in centrifuges, knew that after their 20-g re-entry, the Soyuz 18-1 cosmonauts would be badly shaken and possibly injured. Makarov told Smirenniy that mission commander Lazarev had tried to find out from mission control where they would land after aborting the mission, but it seemed that the ground controllers could not hear their inquiries. Lazarev asked his engineer to determine where they would land. "It would be China or the Pacific Ocean" came back Makarov's sarcastic reply, who added some strong Russian expressions about the failed mission and complained about the engines. They did not realize that their conversations were being heard by mission control, although they could not hear the ground. Makarov's harsh comments about the engines' emergency performance enraged V. P. Glushko, who was the general designer of the mission and chief developer of the engines. He ordered the transmission of communications to be limited and stated that Makarov would never fly again. He was wrong.

Cosmonauts before Launch

Smirenniy also revealed interesting new details about the rescue of the cosmonauts. He said that the Lazarev and Makarov were initially spotted by a geologist who was surveying the area in a helicopter. Supposedly, the small copter landed on a nearby slope, and a young man jumped out, trudged through deep snow, and offered his help to the fallen cosmonauts. Because the helicopter carrying the geologist arrived in the evening, it could not take the cosmonauts away. The three cosmonauts were forced to spend the night in freezing temperatures. The next morning their rescuers had returned, but the helicopter commander pilot was hesitant to take the cosmonauts on board his ship. Makarov told the pilot that he could not take the geologist away without also taking them, and the pilot finally allowed them to go on board.

CONCLUSION

We probably will never find out what really had happened in April of 1975 during the failed Soyuz 18-1 mission, which was the only case of a manned booster accident at high altitude. Vasili Lazarev never flew again aboard Soviet spacecraft. He was discharged from the cosmonaut corps due to illness, and remained a colonel in the reserves. Oleg Makarov had two more flights into space, the last in 1980. The aborted

Soyuz mission was dubbed the "April 5 Anomaly," and the Soviet government did not acknowledge it until April 7, 1975. Both cosmonauts were eventually awarded the Order of Lenin for their conduct, despite efforts by some officials to deny them the honour. Also, after the personal intervention of Leonid Brezhnev, they were given monetary compensation.

A model of the Salyut 7 space station, with a Soyuz spacecraft docked at the front port (left) and a Progress spacecraft at the rear port (right). The display is in front of one of the pavilions of the Exhibition of Soviet National Economic Achievement.

THE SALYUT-7 INCIDENT

A strange thing happened in 1984 aboard the Soviet orbital station Salyut 7. The incident, quite embarrassing to the Marxist-Leninist regime of the time, was hushed up for years. In 1998, Russian *NLO Magazine* (Issue 9) carried an account of the incident. The crew, at the time of the incident, consisted of six people - Leonid Kizil, Oleg At'kov, Vladimir Solovyew, Svetlana Savitskaya, Igor Volk, and Vladimir Dzhanibekov. The incident began on the 155th day of the station's flight. The crew was busy with planned experiments, tests, and scientific observations. They were about to start medical experiments. All of them were experienced, skilled cosmonauts. Then, something happened that was totally outside their experience, knowledge, and understanding. In front of the Salyut 7 station, seemingly from nowhere, there suddenly appeared a huge, orange cloud of gas. The cosmonauts immediately informed the *Tsentr upravleniya poletom* (Soviet Mission Control Center), and, while astonished ground controllers analyzed the report, Salyut 7 entered the cloud. The cosmonauts inside Salyut had the impression that the orange cloud actually permeated the hull of the space station and entered inside.

Russian Stamp Featuring Djanibekov, Savitskaya, and Volk

Engulfed by the mysterious orange glow, they were temporarily blinded and lost contact with mission control. Moments later, when their sight returned, the cosmonauts stumbled to the station's portholes and saw something that stupefied them. Inside the orange cloud, they could discern seven gigantic humanoid forms hovering out in space. Each being possessed two large wings and seemed to have extremely bright "halos" over their "heads," thereby closely resembling the "angels" of religious literature. The cosmonauts, despite being travellers from a society that eschewed religious mysticism, could not help but believe that they had encountered a group of Biblical angels. In a moment, the crew's Marxist-Leninist ideals and anti-religion sentiments were shaken to the core. Then, another amazing thing happened. The "angels" smiled at the cosmonauts, who were still staring at them out the portholes. When the angels smiled, it brought intense, overwhelming feelings of joy and rapture to the inner beings of the crew members. "What wonderful smiles the angels had," one of the cosmonauts said later. "No human could smile like that." Locked by those smiles into an ecstasy of joy and well-being, the crew seemed unaware of the passing of time. After about ten minutes, their rapture seemed to be dashed to the ground, as the heavenly apparitions suddenly vanished, along with the orange cloud that had surrounded their appearance. The crew of Salyut 7 was left with the feeling of an intense, devastating loss. It was not until then that they realized mission control was demanding to know what had happened and what their status was. When they reported what happened, the Soviets immediately classified the report as top secret. A special team of doctors was assembled to study, from the ground, cosmonauts' well-being. The crew's space experiments and mission activities were suspended, and they were instructed to take a long and detailed series of tests intended to measure their physical and mental health. When the tests were concluded, the results confirmed that the cosmonauts were well and of sound mind.

The Soviet Union then swept this strange incident under the proverbial carpet, fearing embarrassment and ridicule. The Politburo took elaborate steps to make sure that the report remained secret for all time. The crew of the Salyut 7 was warned to keep silent. They were instructed to never suggest to anyone that "angels" may exist.

WHISPER IN SPACE

There are other episodes of Soviet space exploration that are not discussed even in today's Russia. One such incident is the so-called "space whisper." An anonymous former cosmonaut, referred to only as "Cosmonaut X," first revealed that the mysterious episode was well known to many in the Soviet Union's space program. According to the story, a Soviet spacecraft was orbiting over the Southern hemisphere, when the two cosmonauts aboard suddenly perceived that someone (or something) was whispering a message to them. The mission commander said he suddenly felt as if someone else was standing right alongside him, but there was nobody there. He also described feeling that an invisible being was staring at his back - and that it was a "hard" (i.e. uncomfortable) gaze. The cosmonaut had no doubt he was being observed. A second later, his comrade, the flight engineer, who was looking out the porthole, turned around and looked around him. Both men were dumbfounded and unable to speak. The cosmonauts, who had known each other for many years and were good friends, were said to be pragmatic, scientific persons that were not given to mysticism. They were both atheists and also avid readers of science fiction. After the incident, they compared their impressions of what had just happened. As it turned out, each of them heard a slightly different version of the same whispered "message." Each version was "personalized" to the man hearing it.

Cosmonaut X said the "whisper" seemed to come from the very depths of his inner consciousness, and he heard the voice say in perfect Russian, "You arrived here too early, and you did it in a wrong fashion. Trust me, for I am your ancestor on the maternal side. Do you remember? She told you, back when you were a child, about your great-grandfather, who had founded the Ds plant in the Urals? Son, you should not be here. Go back to Earth. Do not violate the laws of the Creator. Son, you must return ... return ... return..." The whisper also told the cosmonaut a very private story, as if to prove his knowledge of things known only to members of his family. The story concerned the same great-grandfather. The whisper came back to them one more time, repeating, in essence, the earlier message. For their remaining time in orbit, both men reported feeling an "alien presence" in the station with them. When the cosmonauts returned to Earth two days later, they faced a dilemma -- to report the incident or not. If they did, their career could end immediately. They would likely be considered mentally unstable for further flights into space. Although they told their colleagues, the other cosmonauts kept somewhat silent about the incident – or at least said nothing to their superiors.

Cosmonaut X and his colleague spent endless hours trying to determine exactly what they had experienced. They were inclined to believe that an alien intelligence, using some king of hypnosis, delivered a message advising mankind to stop its space exploration efforts. To convince the cosmonauts of the reality of their contact, the alien intelligence reached into their subconscious and plucked out memories of which only they were aware. They felt the alien intelligence has the ability to probe human thought and memory. Their ability to extract data from the human brain seems to indicate that "they" have been studying human civilization for a long time – perhaps thousands of years.

Or, is this what really happened? Is it possible that the souls or spirits of the departed are able to make contact with us in outer space? Did departed relatives truly visit Soviet crews in space? This possibility chipped away at the cosmonauts' atheism and their modernistic, scientific view of the world. Did their experience mean that life continues after death and that the consciousness continues to exist on some other plane of existence? There must be a hierarchy to such planes, and at the top of the hierarchy would be the Creator, as the "great-grandfather" informed the cosmonaut. Although both cosmonauts strongly felt that they should report the strange episode, they finally decided not to report it. Other cosmonauts, however, who also heard the "whisper," supposedly did officially report it. As a result, special medical teams were introduced into the training program. Highly skilled medical hypnotherapists began to explore cosmonauts' psyches prior to space flight. The entire cosmonaut fight-training program underwent changes due to this strange anomaly.

Cosmonaut X, who has since retired, never heard what conclusions Russian scientists came up with to explain the phenomenon (*Press-Extra* newspaper, Issue 135, 1997). He did say that the whisper changed his whole outlook on life and the universe. He now feels that outer space is teeming with intelligent life and that the cosmos is much more complicated than we imagine. Our present knowledge does not allow us to understand the essence of most processes taking place in the universe. Our abilities are still quite primitive and limited. But those who have heard the "whisper" have been left with the strong impression that death is not the end and that all things continue, just as time and space are endless.

RUSSIAN SPACE PROGRAM AND UFOs

Russian ufologists Valery and Roman Uvarov interviewed Musa Manarov and Gennady Strekalov, two Russian cosmonauts, for *Anomaliya* newspaper (Issue 13, 1996). The cosmonauts were asked about a film Marina Popovich showed to Russian ufologists. The film, reportedly taken in 1991 by Manarov while in Earth orbit, showed a strange object outside the MIR space station. On May 16, 1996, Manarov broke his silence about the case. He stated that he put his camera up against a porthole in the MIR and was filming the docking of another Russian craft through the porthole, in order to later analyze the docking procedure. Suddenly, Manarov noticed something unusual. The Russian ship seemed to have a strange, antenna-like object protruding from the bottom part of the ship, where no such equipment should be. Then, the antenna-like object, whose size was hard to determine, seemed to separate itself from the ship and then start to rotate. Manarov is convinced that the object was not part of the original equipment for any Russian spacecraft.

After separating, the object moved behind the Russian craft, but Manarov could still see it. The object remained in view several minutes. Manarov is hesitant to estimate the dimensions of the object he filmed, but he thinks it might have been about three feet in length. Were it larger than three feet, the Americans and Russians, who routinely track large space debris, would have picked it up on radar, although there are cases when radar is not able to register UFOs.

In his interview with Radio Echo on December, 4, 2011, Manarov repeated his assertion that he filmed an object that revolved by itself and flew alongside the MIR station. He reiterated that he remains uncertain of its geometric size. He said it is difficult for him to speculate about what the object was; however, it did seem to conform to the laws of physics in its movements, unlike some reported characteristics of UFOs. It had no lights and made no sudden turns or other strange manoeuvres. It simply drifted past his position and seemed to clearly not be space trash. In disclosing his sighting, Manarov also revealed interesting information about Russian policies for cosmonauts. Before embarking on a space flight, they must sign documents promising that any video they shoot in space will not be used "against the interests" of the State or the cosmonaut corps. Manarov entered the cosmonaut service in 1978, and back then, UFOs were strictly taboo. Nonetheless, Manarov remains personally interested in the UFO phenomenon, but does not pursue UFO research because he feels there are too many dishonest people who hurt the field's credibility. Asked if cosmonauts might have imagined some of the strange phenomena they've reported, Manarov replies that only strict pragmatists make it into the program. Cosmonauts, due to their background and training, are not prone to imagine things to explain events in a mystical manner. Regarding the American space program, Manarov says he has never personally never spoken to American astronauts about UFOs. He simply never had the time to do so when in their company. Manarov also stated that he personally has never been admonished not to reveal any UFO secrets, nor does he believe his life would be at risk if he did. Manarov and another cosmonaut, Gennady Strekalov, had another strange sighting during a flight in 1990. Strekalov has said that he saw strange phenomena several times, but is hesitant to classify them as UFOs. He acknowledges that some of his colleagues claim to have seen "flying saucers," and he envies them. Although he did not provide details about their sightings, Strekalov did describe the strange sighting that he and Manarov had in 1990.

While in orbit over Newfoundland, they spotted a very strange, multicoloured sphere that he later described as "beautiful" and having a "perfect shape." Atmospheric conditions were clear with optimum visibility, and Strekalov and Manarov continued viewing the sphere, watching it change colours, for a total of about ten seconds. Then suddenly, it vanished. Strekalov reported the incident to mission control, but did not refer to it as a "UFO." Cosmonauts must be cautious, he said. Cosmonaut Vladimir Dezhurov observed another strange phenomenon that Strekalov mentioned in 1995. He saw perfectly shaped clouds, with even edges, as if someone intentionally carved them that way. Manarov, too, had observed similar clouds during his missions. Another respected source of information about Russian space observations is V. M. Trankov. In a 1995 interview with *Anomaliya* newspaper (Issue 13), Trankov revealed that while monitoring television transmissions from the Russian orbital stations, he saw a number of very strange phenomena. At the time of his observations, he was posted at the Coordinating Center of the Russian Space Forces. Among what he saw over the years: strange pulsations; unexplained luminescence; fog-like zones; and saucer-like shapes. According to Trankov, all these phenomena were recorded on magnetic tape and are kept in Russia's Central Space Science archives. He mentioned that the same objects recorded on the ground were also frequently recorded in space by cosmonauts. He emphasized that all recordings of these sightings still exist in the archives, but he would not elaborate further.

Trankov said he knew of no contacts with the Americans about anomalous phenomena, but he hoped that would happen. Overall, Trankov was quite cautious in his statements during this interview, but did admit that there have been many cosmonaut sightings, and he added that there are numerous unidentified phenomena in nature, for the study of which no instruments currently exist. Therefore these unexplained forces remain hidden to us. Rumours have persisted for years that American astronauts have encountered UFOs during their various space missions; however, NASA has apparently slammed the lid of secrecy much more tightly than Russia has. There seem to be many more, solid, fact-based cases regarding Soviet cosmonaut sightings than have surfaced in the U.S. It is obvious from the accounts featured in this chapter that Soviet cosmonauts have observed unusual phenomenon, perhaps sometimes but not always resulting from the physical and mental rigors of space flight. There are a number of sightings made by Soviet cosmonauts that certainly remain totally unidentified, and like most things in the former USSR, there will undoubtedly be more to learn about such incidents in the future, when more files are declassified and when more former cosmonauts speak about what they experienced.

CHAPTER 5.

CIA, ESPIONAGE, AND SOVIET UFOs

That the UFO phenomenon in the former Soviet Union attracted the attention of U.S. intelligence agencies is a fact that few will dispute. And, anyone who is inclined to dispute this fact needs only to browse through the recently declassified CIA documents. We can discover much about Soviet UFO secrecy by studying the reports of foreign intelligence services. Although few Soviet files pertaining to UFOs have been released so far, files about Soviet UFO encounters have been declassified in the United States, too, and the information contained there sheds much light on the subject.

As it turns out, the CIA had a very keen interest in Soviet UFOs and in those involved in studying the phenomenon (whether officially or not) behind the Iron Curtain. In this chapter, we examine CIA document releases pertaining to the Soviet UFO phenomenon, in order to learn more about UFOs in the USSR and about the activities of the CIA in monitoring those UFO sightings.

Title: USSR AND SATELLITE MENTION OF FLYING SAUCERS
Pub Date: August 21, 1952
Release Date: November 161978
Case Number: F-1975-03653
MEMORANDUM FOR: Deputy Director (Intelligence)
SUBJECT: USSR and Satellite Mention of Flying Saucers

This curious CIA document, released in 1978, was a memorandum prepared for the CIA's Deputy Director of Intelligence. Although full of deletions, it states that a search of files had thus far produced "no factual evidence" that the subject had been mentioned in the Soviet satellite countries within the past two years. The document notes, "It is believed that a derisive comment was made in a Russian newspaper in 1948 on this subject, but so far that article has not been found." There is a mention of a single radio broadcast about UFOs on June 10, 1951, and the document appends the content of the broadcast. In summarizing the broadcast, the document states that U.S. officials had confirmed that UFOs are aircraft used by the U.S. for studying the stratosphere, and that the U.S. government was aware that UFOs are conventional objects and are harmless. However, the broadcast claimed, the Americans have "refrained" from denying all the "false reports" about UFOs in order to fan the "war hysteria" among the citizens of the United States. This was reported to the CIA as being the first instance of a Soviet radio broadcast dealing with unidentified flying objects, although in truth, there may have been others.

Portion of CIA document

Curiously, top Soviet scientists tried to convince Stalin that UFOs were indeed quite harmless or at least did not pose a threat to the armed forces and security of the nation. Were Soviet agitation and propaganda agents prompting these scientists to take this position? Or, was Stalin sending a signal to UFO researchers in the West? Getting back to the curious memorandum, we find mentioned a State Department cable received from Budapest that quoted from the August 14th copy of Szabad *Nep*: "Flying saucer stories are another American attempt to fan war hysteria." A radar detection of "saucers" is quoted in the article, and it comments on the ridiculous aspects of the mystery. The article concludes that UFOs are nothing but American rulers' propaganda to prove the Western countries are "threatening." Perhaps they meant "threatened." The memorandum concludes that the FBID (Foreign Broadcast Information Department) had been requested to alert field stations to any mention of flying saucers by Iron Curtain countries.

Title: ENGINEER CLAIMS 'SAUCER' PLANS ARE IN SOVIET
HANDS; SIGHTINGS IN AFRICA, IRAN,
PAUL STONEHILL and PHILIP MANTLE
144
Pub Date: August 17, 1953
Release Date: November 16, 1978
Case Number: F-1975-036

This article definitely attracted the Agency's attention in 1953. We have summarized it below.

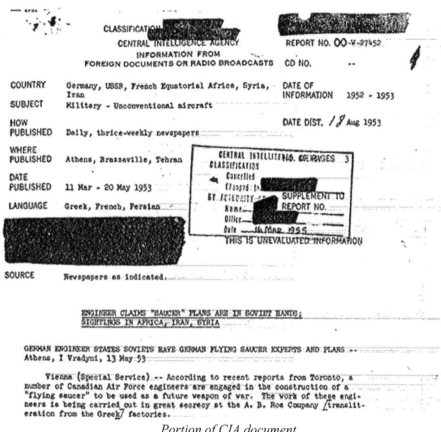

Portion of CIA document

GERMAN ENGINEER STATES SOVIETS HAVE GERMAN FLYING SAUCER EXPERTS AND PLANS

Athens, I Vredyni, May 13, 1953

The information contained in this CIA document was obtained by the Agency from a Greek source. The document was analyzed in Vienna, by some entity called "Special Service." The document states that according to recent reports from Toronto, a number of Canadian Air Force engineers were engaged in the construction of a "flying saucer" to be used as a future weapon of war. The work of these engineers is being carried out in great secrecy at the A. V. Row Company (transliteration from the Greek) factories. [The reference is to the Avrocar, a saucer-like, vertical take-off aircraft designed by the Avro Aircraft Ltd. of Canada.] The article stated that "flying saucers" have been known to be an actuality since the possibility of their construction was found in plans drawn by German engineers toward the end of World War II. George Klein, a German engineer, stated that although many people believe the "flying saucers" to be a post-war development, they were actually in the planning stage in German aircraft factories as early as 1941.Klein said that he was an engineer in the Ministry of Albert Speer [who, in 1942, was Reich's Minister for Armament and Ammunition for the Third Reich] and was present at the first experimental flight of a "flying saucer." During the experiment, Klein reported, the saucer reached an altitude of 41,000 feet within 3 minutes at a speed of about 1,300 miles per hour. Klein emphasized that German plans called for the speed of these saucers to eventually reach around 2,500 miles per hour. One difficulty, according to Klein, was the problem of obtaining materials to be used for the construction of the saucers, but German engineers toward the end of 1945 had removed even that obstacle, and construction of the aircraft was scheduled to commence. Klein went on to state that three experimental models had been readied for tests by the end of 1944, built according to two completely different principles of aerodynamics.

One type of the craft disc shaped, with an interior cabin, and was built at the "Mite" factories, which had also built the V-2 rockets. This was confirmed by a Soviet eyewitness who was a POW at the Mite. This model was about 140 feet in diameter (although this does not confirm the Soviet eyewitness's account; the size he mentioned was much smaller). The other model had the shape of a ring, with raised sides and a spherically shaped pilot' placed on the outside, in the center of the ring. This model was built at the Habermol and Schreiver factories. However, the locations mentioned above, became quite familiar to those ufologists who had pursued the German "trail," whether in the West and in the USSR. Both models had an ability to take off vertically and to land in an extremely restricted area, just as helicopters do today. During the last few days of the war, when every hope for Nazi victory had been abandoned, the engineers in the group stationed in Prague carried out orders to completely destroy their plans of the experimental aircraft, before the Red Army marched in [Paul Stonehill's grandfather was one of the Soviet soldiers who battled Nazis to liberate Prague from German occupation]. The engineers at the Mite factories in Breslau, however, had not been warned in sufficient time, and Soviet forces therefore succeeded in seizing their archives. Captured plans, as well as engineering personnel, were immediately transferred to the Soviet Union, under heavy guard. Among the captured Nazi engineers was the creator of the Stuka JU-87 dive bomber - the man who later developed MIG 13 and 15 aircraft in the Soviet Union.

Also according to Klein, there was an alleged Central Intelligence Agency operation in the Urals, and German scientists were reportedly working in the USSR on another secret program. An American agent involved in the operation, who escaped from Soviet Russia, mentioned five flying saucers being built by the Soviets.

1. On a warm, starry and moonlit evening in August 1953, three flying objects were observed moving over Ayuta P1 camp which was 10 km southeast of the southern perimeter of Shakhty, about 600 meters west of the Rostov-Novoshakhtinsk highway, about 2 km southeast of the Ayuta mines and about 3.5 km east of Ayuta. The first flying object was observed at about 2145, the second at about 2215, and a third one was observed by fellow P1 at about 2345. The objects moved from southeast to northwest, at a deviation of 70 to 75 degrees from the vertical line, and crossed approximately north of the camp. The fiery gleam accompanying the object disappeared over the partially lighted installations of the Ayuta mines. While moving over the camp, the course of the object deviated from the vertical line by about 70 degrees to the north. The flight altitude could not be estimated. No sound was heard while the objects were overhead.

Portion of CIA document

Title: *FLYING OBJECTS SEEN IN SHAKHTY AREA, 1953*
Pub Date: *August 8, 1955*
Release Date: *November 16, 1978*
Case Number: *F-1975-03653*
USSR *(Rostov Oblast)*

The Agency deleted classification status of the report. The date of content was August 1953. The information in the report was obtained in late September of 1954. Source of information was deleted from the declassified report. Shakhty, which is a small town in a coal mining area, is about an hour and a drive half from Rostov (south of Moscow on the Don River east of Ukraine). The report states that on a warm, starry, moonlit evening in August 1953, three flying objects were observed moving over an Ayuta "camp," six miles southeast of the southern perimeter of Shakhty, about 2,000 feet west of the Rostov-Novoshakhtinsk highway, about one mile southeast of the Ayuta mines and about 2 miles from Ayuta. The objects were sighted at different times starting at 9:45 p.m. The fiery gleam accompanying the object disappeared over the partially lighted installations of the Ayuta mines. The objects moved from southeast to northwest at a deviation of 60 to 75 degrees from the vertical line, and crossed approximately north of the camp. The flight altitude could not be estimated. No sound was heard while the objects were overhead. The speed of the phenomena could not be compared with that of aircraft or Soviet jet fighters.

rockets, similar to F weapons. After The first object was observed departing toward the Ayuta mines for 5 or 4 seconds. The second body was seen for 6 or 7 seconds after passing the camp. It also disappeared in the direction of the Ayuta mines. No statement could be made about the third object. The two objects observed had a fiery gleam in a reddish color which was similar to that of planet Mars. It looked like a comet or a shooting star. The approach of the phenomenon was not observed. On the day following the evening observation, the individual "PKs" differed considerably in their opinions about the phenomena. Immediately after the observation, source and sub-source believed the objects observed were the objects disappeared, no detonations were heard.

Field Consent. All previous reports on flying objects observed in the Shakhty area mentioned that loud noise accompanied the action. The description of the noises indicated that the body was propelled by a rocket or fitted with a pulse-jet engine. See [the CIA deleted whatever followed]. The object mentioned in the present report possibly flew at such a high altitude that the sound of the engines could not be heard. Another possibility is that a different phenomenon was observed, which, however appears rather improbable. Another field consent added that the observation reported agrees with previous information and indicates that a ramjet or a rocket engine propelled the body.

Questions, upon reading the above report: What came from the Ayuta mines? Who were "PKs"? What were the "F weapons"? What powerful rockets and jets were developed by the Soviets in 1953 to propel craft at incomparable speeds? Others have discussed Soviet super-secret rocket and spacecraft development of the Stalin era [a still forbidden subject; most files or documents have been heretofore unavailable to researchers]. Perhaps the Agency was also interested in the same subject 45 years ago. Here's another report that seems to support this view.

Title: FAST MOVING FLYING OBJECTS OVER STALINGRAD IN
SPRING 1954
Pub Date: August 1, 1956
Release Date: November 16, 1978
Case Number: F-1975-03653

The report was taken from someone who, in the spring of 1954, was hospitalized at a Soviet military hospital in Stalingrad (now Volgograd). The narrator, along with other patients, observed the flight of an unknown object from horizon to horizon. The object appeared to be climbing. The narrator could not describe the object, but he recalled that it took approximately one minute for the object to leave the range of his vision. The object caused a great amount of vibration in the air and made a screeching, whistling noise, which was different from the noise made by an artillery shell. The narrator reiterated that he did not see the object itself, but did see the disturbance in the air, which seemed to envelop it.

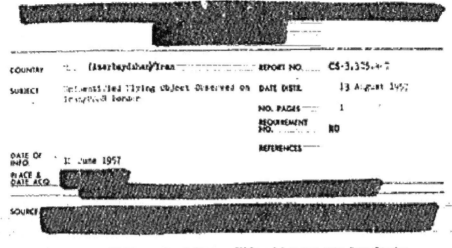

Title: UNIDENTIFIED FLYING OBJECT OBSERVED ON IRAN/USSR
BORDER
Pub Date: August 12, 1957
Release Date: November 16, 1978
Case Number: F-1975-03653

On 12 June at 11:00 a.m. local time, a flying object was seen in Iranian Juifa, travelling on a course from Nakhichevan (N 39-15, E. [unclear text]), USSR. The object appeared to be a ball about two feet in diameter and had a tail of one foot in length. It travelled at high speed at a height of about 2,000 feet and was visible for only a few seconds. [The] trail left by the object drifted over Iranian Juifa from the USSR and [unclear] of a trail about 5 to 10 centimetres in diameter. Field Comment: [Name deleted] also reported seeing a flying object at the same time and described it about the size of a football and moving at a height of 2,000 meters. He said the smoke track left behind the object was visible for about 15 minutes.

UFOs seem to have kept coming to the Iranian-Soviet border. We are yet to learn what has attracted them to the area; obviously, the CIA was interested, too. Could the Agency's interest be aroused also because of the oil fields in the area? One year before the case mentioned here, something else drew the Agency's attention: Case

Number: F-1975-03653, February 7, 1956; Release Date: November 16, 1978. Here the Agency was interested in an object sighted over Baku, capital of the Soviet Azerbaijan. The actual sighting took place on October 4, 1955, and the Office of Scientific Intelligence prepared its analysis of it. There was another document, declassified by CIA, dealing with the same area:

Title: SIGHTING OF UNUSUAL PHENOMENON ON HORIZON
NEAR IRANIAN/USSR BORDER
Pub Date: September 27, 1966
Release Date: November 16, 1978
Case Number: F-1975-03653

The document, the testimony of a nameless witness, describes an unusual phenomenon - a brilliant white sphere on the horizon, some 25 miles away from the Mehrabad airport. The UFO seemed to be expanding in size, was clearly visible, and was sighted by another aircraft, too.

Title: MAYBE THERE IS NO UFO
Pub Date: December 25, 1967
Release Date: October 31, 1987
Case Number: F-1990-01473

The Agency is interested in the report about the creation in November of 1967 of the committee for the investigation of unidentified flying objects. This committee, a part of the DOSAAF is under the command of the Air Force General Porfiri Stolyarov. General Stolyarov recommended that the photographic method be used. The data obtained during the investigation would be correlated to the Pulkovo Laboratory and the Crinca Astronomical Observatory. The observation has been entrusted to a chain of astronomical observatories all over the USSR, as well as civil aviation. It is interesting that the CIA took so long to declassify this document mentioning General Stolyarov and the committee.

Title: FLYING PHENOMENA (UFO's) - SOURCE-SOVETSKAYA
LATVIYA - THE DIRECTOR OF ...
Pub Date: December 9, 1967
Release Date: October 31, 1987
Case Number: F-1984-01392

Unfortunately, the CIA document is virtually impossible to read, containing numerous deletions. But something definitely attracted the Agency's attention to a Soviet publication. It was Dr. Zigel, previously mentioned in this book, that attracted the Agency's attention in 1968.

Title: DATA FROM CRS AND FROM FBIS ON ZIGEL, F. YU., DR.
OF TECHNICAL SCIENCES WRITES
Pub Date: December 31, 1968
Release Date: November 16, 1978
Case Number: F-1975-03653

Actually, the CIA was interested in his articles published in Soviet magazines. His subjects ranged from the Tunguska Meteorite to a "Dialogue on Mars." But, of course, the Agency's fascination with Dr. Zigel's views did not end there. An 11-page document was published the same year.

Title: NOTHING BUT THE FACTS ON UFOs OR WHICH NOVOSTI
WRITER DO YOU READ?
Pub Date: April 8, 1968
Release Date: November 16, 1978
Case Number: F-1975-03653

"Unidentified Flying Objects" by Feliks Zigel, Doctor of Science (Technology), assistant professor, Moscow Aviation Institute, appeared in the February 1968 issue of *Soviet Life* (counterpart to USIA), for which APN supplies all materials (APN, the Soviet "unofficial" news agency). The other article, espousing views of Soviet debunkers, was titled "Flying Saucers? They are a myth!" by Villen Lyustiberg, and appeared in the February 16th issue of *Moskovsky Komsomolets*.

By the way, as we previously noted, the late 1960s had seen crucial battles for openness in the area of UFO studies in the USSR. There was an obvious conflict with proponents and opponents (including top military brass) on both sides. The Agency was quite interested, too, and collected whatever information was available. Villen Lyustiberg's article laughed off UFOs and accused the United States of publishing accounts of UFOs to divert people's attention from its failures and aggressions. What surprised the Agency was the fact that the Soviets actually published two conflicting views about a subject. A truly mysterious document is revealed in the following CIA document. Alas, it is also full of deletions.

(TITLE DELETED) – USSR - UFO SIGHTINGS - SOMEONE
MUST HAVE MADE A POLITICAL DECISION
Pub Date: May 7, 1975
Release Date: May 18, 1989
Case Number: F-1985-00010

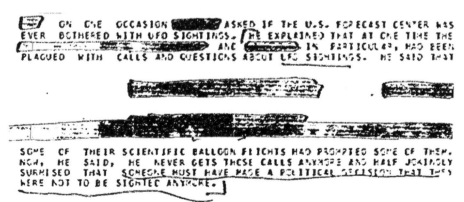

Portion of CIA Document

Despite numerous deletions in this article, what remains is most interesting. A person whose name is deleted asked whether the "U.S. Forecast Center" [presumably the CIA's forecast center] was ever "bothered" by reports of UFO sightings [presumably in the USSR]. He explained that at one time two groups or offices whose names are deleted, in particular, had been plagued with calls and questions about UFO sightings [the word "sightings" was underlined]. He said that their scientific balloon flights had prompted some of [the sightings]. Now, he said, he never gets these calls anymore, and half jokingly surmised that someone must have made a political decision that they were not to be sighted anymore. Unfortunately, it is most probable that UFO researchers will never find out all that was deleted from this interesting 1975 document.

Title: USSR NATIONAL AFFAIRS SCIENTIFIC AFFAIRS
'UNUSUAL' NATURAL PHENOMENON OBSERVE
Pub Date: September 22, 1977
Release Date: November 16, 1978
Case Number: F-1975-03653

In this document the CIA's attention is directed to the Petrozavodsk phenomenon. Moscow TASS information service is the source of the brief mention of the phenomena. Descriptions of a "huge star" and "medusa" were given. Just as we became curious in the late 1980s with all the UFO glasnost developments in the USSR, so did the Agency.

Title: USSR: MEDIA REPORT MULTITUDE OF UFO SIGHTINGS
Pub Date: November 21, 1989
Release Date: July 31, 1991
Case Number: F-1990-00393

Among publications mentioned in the document is one by Anatoly Listratov (*Sotsialisticheskaya Industriya*, September 30, 1989), whose findings we have mentioned elsewhere in this book. Although we will not list here every single declassified CIA document dealing with Soviet UFOs, suffice it to say that the Agency was very interested in reports of UFOs whether in statements from top military brass or in reports in the Soviet media. The CIA also took particular interest in a report issued by a joint Sino-Soviet UFO research group:

Title: USSR, PRC SCIENTISTS IN JOINT STUDY OF UFOs
Pub Date: May 20, 1990
Release Date: May 31, 1994
Case Number: F-1990-01096

We already know that the People's Republic of China has joined the space race, and its astronauts may soon orbit the Earth. Here is what worried the Agency in 1990. The source of the report was the Moscow Domestic Service in Russia on May 21, 1990.

A report from Vladivostok: scientists of the PRC and the Soviet Far East have begun joint study of UFOs. The first meeting of ufologists of the two countries has ended in the small maritime town of Dalnegorsk. Soviet and Chinese specialists of anomalous phenomena have mapped out a program for investigating incidents that are already known and have also arranged to directly exchange video and photographic materials on new similar phenomena. Dalnegorsk has not been chosen by chance as the place for such meeting. (There have been a number of cases of visual observation of UFOs over Dalnegorsk and one crash in 1986; see Chapter 1).

Title: 1. OVERVIEW OF THE ACADEMY OF SCIENCES OF THE
UKRAINIAN SSR
Pub Date: January 9, 1990
Release Date: August 27, 1997
Case Number: F-1993-02057

We cannot ignore this document. The information that remains after numerous deletions is enough to arouse one's curiosity. Someone connected with the CIA paid a visit to the Ukrainian Academy of Sciences (probably, in September of 1989). Someone, a Soviet whose name is deleted in the document, asked about U.S. research in the area of unidentified flying objects [underlined]. The unnamed Soviet person also said that the Academy has several organizations that follow the subject and that some scientists think this is a serious research. Who was this unnamed scientist? What happened to the findings of "several organizations?" There are no answers in our possession. The more declassified intelligence files we look into, the more questions arise. Apparently, CIA and other intelligence agencies had as many questions but more answers than we do. We can only hope that that more files will be released in the future, which in turn will answer more of our questions.

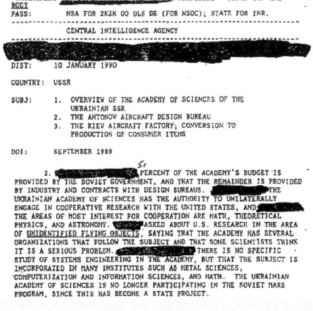

Portion of CIA document

CHAPTER 6

KGB AND ITS UFO FILES

THE DECLASSIFIED FILES

On October 24, 1991, a batch of documents was presented to the President of the All-Union Ufological Association, former Soviet cosmonaut Pavel Popovich. The files consisted of 124 pages and contained copies of UFO reports sent to the KGB. Deputy Chairman of the Committee for State Security USSR, N.A. Sham, wrote an accompanying letter. The Russian Ufology Research Center was able to obtain two copies of the files. The reports consist of handwritten reports, typed testimonies, notes from the KGB informers, crude drawings, and eyewitness reports. Of course, few Russian ufologists believe that the released documents comprised all of the KGB's UFO files.

The letter, accompanying the released documents, is of an interest to historians of the Soviet Union. It stated the following:

Dear Pavel Romanovich,
The State Security Committee has never been engaged in systematic gathering
and analysis of information of anomalous phenomena (the so-called
unidentified flying objects). At the same time, the SSC of the USSR has been
receiving statements from a number of persons and agencies regarding cases
of observations of the above phenomena. We forward you copies of such
statements. At an earlier date, the same material was sent to the Central Machine
Building research Institute in the city of Kaliningrad.
Appendix: Ref. materials on 124 pages, declassified, to the addressee only.
N.A. Sham
Deputy Chairman of the Committee
October 24, 1991
The cases mentioned in the reports consist of the following:
Page 3--Petropavlovsk City, October 20, 1982
Page 24--Cities of Kursk, Voronezh, Yelts, October 17, 1983
Page 34--Guzen settlement February 3, 1985
Page 39--The Khabarovsk region May 25, 1985
Page 42--The Maritime Province November 12, 1985
Page 50--Magadan City November 25, 1986
Page 56--The Tiksi Peninsula August 14, 1987
Page 66--Mineralniye Vodi City December 14, 1987
Page 73--Nevinnomisovsk City December 30, 1987
Page 75--The Kamchatka region 1987-1988
Page 78--Khabarovsk City May 6, 1988
Page 85--Magadan City October 1, 1988
Page 87--Sochi City July 26, 1989
Page 92--The Kapustin Yar July 28, 1989

Deputy Chairman of the Committee for State Security USSR, N.A. Sham

During the 9-year period (1982-1990) covered by the KGB document releases, sightings occurred all over the immense country, from Kursk City in the European part to Kamchatka in the East and from the Tiksi Peninsula in the North to the resort town of Sochi on the Black Sea coast. In analyzing these documents, we used the originals, although some of them have been abridged.

Below is the transcript of a radio exchange between air-traffic controller R. Stepanian and the crews of three flights that were in the area of the Sochi airport on July 26, 1989. The flights were designated Flight 138, Flight 397 and Flight 500. The Controller's words are marked "TOWER." The Exchange started at 11:31 a.m.

JULY 26, 1989, SOCHI AIRPORT ZONE

TOWER: Go ahead, Flight 138.
FLIGHT 183: Do you observe two objects hanging at our left?
TOWER: To the left? What altitude?
FLIGHT 183: Our altitude, right, about 31-37 miles ahead of us.
TOWER: Flight 138, you are clear of traffic now. Do you observe anything on your left?
FLIGHT 183: There was one object, and then another one appeared nearby. They are flying away from us. The distance is already about 50 miles.
TOWER: What is their shape like?

FLIGHT 183: One is oblong, like a dirigible, the other is kind of spherical.

TOWER: Are they abeam?

FLIGHT 183: Yes, right ahead but they are moving away quickly - the distance is 49-55 miles.

TOWER: Flight 397, do you observe anything abeam, 49-55 miles to the left of you?

FLIGHT 397: 18 miles abeam?

TOWER: About 24 miles from the left to the right.

FLIGHT 183: Flight 397, they must be moving from left to right.

FLIGHT 397: No, we do not observe them; I'll look at the radar display.

FLIGHT 183: Flight 397, they are 15 miles to the right and behind you.

FLIGHT 397: We do not see them. There are clouds.

FLIGHT 183: Look above the clouds. They are sort of zigzagging.

FLIGHT 397: Flight 397, I've sighted two spots against the clouds.

TOWER: Which zone?

FLIGHT 397: About 27 miles from Sochi, 30 degrees behind me.

FLIGHT 183: This is Flight 138. One is nearly square; the other is diamondshaped. They are flying apart now.

TOWER: Flight 138; keep us advised on these objects.

FLIGHT 183: They are hanging close together over there. They are probably about 4 miles ahead of us already.

TOWER: Are they moving?

FLIGHT 183: Yes, they were 24 miles away - now they are about 62 miles away, moving from left to right. Request clearance to climb to 36,000 feet.

TOWER: Flight 138, climb to level 36,000 feet and keep us advised on these objects.

FLIGHT 183: Flight 138, Roger, climbing to 36,000 feet. Control Tower, do you see them on the radar display?

TOWER: Negative.

FLIGHT 183: Right. Now they've made a turn and are moving aside.

TOWER: Flight 138, do you still see them?

FLIGHT 183: They are behind us and to the left. The distance between us is increasing. They have moved away too quickly. One moment they were close to us and the other they were already far behind.

TOWER: Flight 138; advise which way they are moving.

FLIGHT 183: Now they are behind me and to the left.

TOWER: Flight 138; is everything all right with you?

FLIGHT 183: Affirmative, everything is all right.

TOWER: Roger, Flight 500, do you see anything?

FLIGHT 500: Flight 500. There is nothing in sight, either on the right or on the left.

TOWER: Roger.

OCTOBER 17, 1983, IN THE VICINITY OF THE CITIES OF KURSK, VORONEZH, AND YELTS

Radar at Georgiu-Dezh did not register the UFO. Witnesses are certain that the object they saw was not a star or other heavenly body. The UFO was sighted at sunrise, when no stars were visible in the sky. At about 7 a.m., the UFO zoomed up and out of sight. The UFO was seen by numerous military personnel in Kursk, Voronezh, and Yelts. Colonel Skrypnik reported all of the information regarding the UFO observation through the chain of command to Colonel Galitisn of the Moscow Air Defence District.

MAY 23, 1985 KHABAROVSK REGION REPORT

While a bomber regiment was carrying out routine flight operations, an elliptical-shaped UFO was sighted from the control tower at 10:35 p.m. A pale orange in color, the object moved noiselessly from west to east at a height of between 6,500 and 9,800 feet and a speed close to 400 MPH. The object was surrounded by a "halo" of light. The sighting lasted 13 minutes, during which radar showed nothing. The object's flight was characterized by periods of complete motionlessness, followed by sudden descents. Two hours later, a similar object was sighted for 10 minutes. Long-range aircraft passed below it at the height of 2,600 – 3,900 feet. The UFO emitted beams of light up and down. The downward beams were brighter.

Colonel V. Alifanov
Flight Commander

NOVEMBER 3, 1985 VLADIVOSTOK CITY VICINITY

"At 20 hrs 30 min I stopped hunting in the estuary of the river Razdolnaya, jumped into my motorboat *Dnepr* and started the engine *Vikhr*. The engine worked smoothly, trouble-fee. At that moment I noticed a UFO moving at a great speed from north to south at an altitude much higher than that used by planes. It looked somewhat larger than a star and sent a beam of light to the earth at an acute angle. The beam was rather long; yet it did not reach the ground and died away in the air. "When the UFO flew up closer, the boat's engine suddenly stopped. I pumped in some petrol, increased the injection, and pulled at the starting cord. The engine started. While it was running, I noticed some luminescence coming from the base of the high-voltage coils, where they were tapped to the spark plugs of the upper and lower cylinders. The upper plug shone brighter. Five or seven seconds later the engine died abruptly without dropping speed. At that moment the UFO was right over my boat. "After the UFO had moved a little farther to the South in the direction of Vladivostok, my companion A. Khripunov and I noticed a satellite over it. Both the UFO and the satellite were moving at about the same speed and in the same direction. When the UFO approached Vladivostok, its beam disappeared, and the object itself was no longer visible. The satellite moved on, it was clearly seen against the sky although it was much smaller than the UFO. "We got into the boat and pushed it away from the bank. Try as I might, the engine would not start. The wind and the stream carried the boat to the opposite bank. I stepped out of the boat onto a shallow place and made another attempt to start the engine, changed the plugs but petrol splashed on the first and on the second sets. Changing the second set of plugs noticed that they did not give off a spark. We used oars to row to the estuary and chose a place for rest. "I gave the engine a close scrutiny. I cleaned the contacts of all circuits, changed part of the circuit and the high-voltage wires. A weak spark appeared in the lower cylinder; it showed up periodically at each turn of the flywheel -once, after several unsuccessful attempts. There was still no spark in the upper cylinder. We decided to row, hoping to meet someone. We met some fishermen at 9 a.m. who lent us an old coil. I checked all the contacts once again - nothing had changed in the lower cylinder; the spark was weak but regular. When I changed the coils, there was no spark in the upper cylinder at all; yet I felt the spark with my hand when the plug was out. "Then I took a spare booster, which I had already tried at night, put it into a pot, covered it with a lid and heated it for half an hour on a primus-stove. Then I put the booster in position. After the first turn of the flywheel I felt a strong electric discharge in my hand. I adjusted the gaps, connected the plugs, grounded them and saw good sparks on the plugs. I screwed in the plugs, splashed a little clean petrol into both cylinders for an easier start and started the engine at the first attempt. It was 3 p.m. 45 minutes later I was in Vladivostok."

V. Alexandrov
Captain 3rd Rank

NOVEMBER 25, 1986, VICINITY OF THE CITY OF MAGADAN

At 12:50 p.m. Moscow time on November 25, 1986, both government and civilian air controllers detected an unidentified target about 50 miles from Magadan, with an azimuth of 85 degrees. The target's speed was 372 miles per hour. At the same time, an Antonov-12 aircraft (Flight 11421) flew nearby at an altitude of 23,600 feet. The aircraft was advised about the target on a collision course and was instructed to perform a starboard diversion turn. The crew of this aircraft, at 12:53, observed an identified target on the flight radar scope, flying along the same course at a distance of 93 miles. The target was observed for a second time when the aircraft was over the Tahtayamsk, and the crew reported the fact to ground control. After the aircraft and the target passed each other, the latter also turned to starboard in the direction of the Bay of Shelihov area, and picked up its speed to between 550 and 600 miles per hour. At 12:58, the target's speed again increased, reaching 1864 miles per hour, heading from the Kamchatka Peninsula. It disappeared from the radarscopes at a distance of 93 miles from the coastline. Military personnel of the Magadan Airport photographed the target's path. A written statement was taken from the crew navigator of the Antonov-12 aircraft, who had observed the target.

DECEMBER, 1987 - SEPTEMBER, 1988, VICINITY OF THE SHIVELUCH VOLCANO, KAMCHATKA

The personnel at a variety of observation posts had been systematically sighting ball-shaped UFOs during missile launches. In particular, the objects looked like small, slowly rising fires, changing color from red to white. The sightings lasted from 30 seconds to 7 minutes. One officer suggested their appearance correlated with the scheduled launch of test missiles. He noticed that UFOs did not appear when the launch time was altered. However, balls the size of a football were sighted without any relation to launching, e.g. on December 16, 1987, an hour after a warhead had fallen to the ground. An orange ball was moving slowly and noiselessly from North to

South. It was freezing and there was no wind. On December 21, 1987 the ball appeared at 7 p.m. while the launch took place at 10 p.m. The next day, there was no launch at all. However, the ball appeared at 6:35 p.m. It pulsed and changed color from red to blue to white.

On July 26, 1988, a strange ball with a blurred outline was sighted immediately before a launch. The situation was repeated at night, on September 9-10, 1989. This time, the UFO appeared five minutes before the launch. It was a silver ball which appeared to the naked eye as being larger than the Moon. The object disappeared right after the missile was launched. The radio operator noticed degradation in the transmission of ultra-short waves. Anti-aircraft facilities and radio instruments of the control complex did not register any unidentified flying objects. Specialists suggested several hypotheses to explain the phenomena observed. They thought the objects might be:

• Ball-shaped concentrations of electric charges in the atmosphere
• Balloons lit by the rays of the setting sun
• Holograms at the crossing of laser beams.

These suggestions are purely theoretical. There are no facts to prove them.

Signed: Unit Commander
KGB Helicopter and Search Team in Action

JULY 28, 1989 VICINITY OF THE TOWN OF KAPUSTIN YAR, ASTRAKHAN REGION

Servicemen from two army units sighted a UFO for two hours from different vantage points at about midnight. Those who were closest to it made drawings of the objects.

Below are extracts from the eyewitness reports. "I climbed the aerial support and observed the object from a height of 19 feet above the ground. One could clearly see a powerful blinking signal that resembled a camera flash in the night sky. The object flew over the unit's logistics yard and moved in the direction of the rocket weapons depot, 1,000 feet away. It hovered over the depot at a height of 65 feet. The UFO's hull shone with a dim green light that looked like phosphorus. It was a disc, 13-16 feet in diameter, with a semi-spherical top. "While the object was hovering over the depot, a bright beam appeared from the bottom of the disc, where the flash had been before, and made two or three circles. Then the object, still flashing, moved in the direction of the railway station. But soon it returned to the rocket weapons depot and hovered over it at a height of 200-230 feet. Two hours after the initial sighting, the object flew in the direction of the town of Akhtubinsk and disappeared from sight. "The light at the bottom of the disc did not flash regularly; it was as if photographs were being taken. Nor did the object move evenly. Sometimes it rushed sideways or upwards and other times it moved smoothly and hovered here and there. I attach a drawing of the UFO's outline and the beam." -- *Ensign V. Voloshin, Communications Officer-on-Duty*

"For two hours Ensign V.Voloshin and I had been observing the object together as it moved and hovered. I confirm everything he reported." – *Private D. Tishchayev*

"Besides the object in the sky, I sighted a ball of fire rising toward it from the ground. When the UFO rushed in my direction, I physically sensed its approach. The object pulled up suddenly. I saw that a plane attempted to approach the object, but the latter gained speed quickly and left the plane behind." -- *Private G. Kulik*

"I sighted the blinking UFO from a distance of 3 km (1.8 miles). Bright light flashed from the ground over the place where it was hovering. The light moved to the left and right. Another object rose, from there. The higher it rose, the dimmer the light grew. At the end of the second hour of observation I noticed a third object at a height of 1,000 to 1,300 feet. It gave flashes of red light at constant intervals. Then colored lights ran over it like on a Christmas tree and I could make out that it was cigar-shaped. The 'cigar' flew to the first UFO, and together they disappeared beyond the horizon." -- *Ensign A. Levin*

REPORT ABOUT OBSERVATION OF AN ANOMALOUS PHENOMENON IN THE TIKSI PENINSULA AREA

On August 14, 1987, the [name deleted] radar outpost of the air defence commander HQ sighted an unidentified target at an altitude of 1000 feet, its speed reaching 248 miles per hour. Six minutes later, the target disappeared from the radar screen. Half an hour later, the target was again sighted, now closer to the Tiksi. A military helicopter sent to the location did not find the unidentified target. The helicopter's commander, Captain Zikeyev, observed two inversion trails going into the clouds. He then returned to the airport. AN-12 airplane on a weather reconnaissance mission was ordered to the site of the target. Colonel Lobanov, the flight commander, upon reaching an altitude of 13,000 feet, observed an odd-shaped, transparent cloud. Its color was emerald, with a violet tint. Inside the cloud, he saw dark spots. The cloud seemed to move, and the colonel saw two inversion trails behind it. The ground control for the air defence unit registered that when the helicopter and the airplane approached the unidentified target, radio communication deteriorated due to interference. The target disappeared from the radar screens shortly thereafter.

[Note: similar strange clouds were observed over the Chukotka in the 1990. Groups of strange "aircraft" were seen exiting from the center of a circle formed by the clouds and then disappearing into the clouds once again. The "aircraft" appeared nine times. When the photos taken by observers were developed, they saw a cigar-shaped object, with several black dots in the background. The seamen who observed the phenomenon suffered headaches and became weak after the incident. Apparently, the KGB, just as those who sent Soviet cosmonauts Kovalenok and Savinkh after the silvery clouds, had a keen interest in these "cloud phenomena."

THE BESHTAU MOUNTAIN CASE

On December 15, 1987, an airplane on a flight from Volgograd to Tbilisi reported that shortly after 11 p.m. the crew observed a flying object approaching from directly ahead. The object resembled an airplane with its headlights turned off, but radar indicated no other craft in the area at the time of the sighting. The "UFO: [term was used by the KGB officer who compiled the report] suddenly vanished. Some five minutes later, the UFO was observed from another airplane. The crew reported that there was a fiery trail behind it, emitting sparks. The UFO "ceased to exist" after a "blast" – some kind of an explosion. Ten minutes later, someone called the local airport to report that an airplane had caught fire in the sky and could be seen burning while still flying. A fiery "train" followed the airplane. Then, observers saw a blast but heard no noise - and the plane disappeared. The person who alerted the local airport went to look for debris or remnants but did not find any. The KGB officer checked with the local military and found out that the area restricted for passenger airplane flight that night was through Guriyev-Astrakhan line only.

An eyewitness, identified as Sergey Sergeyevich Karapetyan, stated that the "airplane" was of gigantic size, much larger than any airplane. The object more closely resembled a rocket, but it descended very slowly and finally went down somewhere at the Beshtau Mountains. Sergeant-Major Varyutin reported to his superiors that the object he and another sergeant had observed that night resembled an airplane, flew at a slow speed, and had powerful searchlight that illuminated the area in front of it. The object moved noiselessly.

KGB Insignia

153

KAMCHATKA

The KGB was also concerned with reports coming from the Kamchatka area between 1987 and 1988. Strange objects had been flying over the secret combat field "Kura." The unidentified objects were small spheres, changing in color from red to white. The officers who reported the incidents to the KGB noted that the objects "existed" for close to three minutes. They appeared at the time of the secret testing of "heavy, manufactured articles [missiles]," and the objects did not come down (as the "articles" would). But a warrant officer and some soldiers observed a fiery sphere one-hour after the tests. It moved through the air noiselessly and slowly; the weather was cold, and there was no wind. The same sphere was observed after another secret test. The unidentified object was measured from afar. It flew in a vertical and a horizontal pattern at different times. Sometimes it pulsated, and its colours changed from red to blue to white. Among different objects observed by military, there was one that resembled a silvery moon. A cone-shaped ray pointed downwards from the object. There seemed to be a smoke-like substance around the object. When the "article" was tested, and made its way upward into the air, the object vanished. Radio communications became degraded. At the same time, the KGB agent "Shestakov," who was visually following the "article," observed a radiant dot in at the slope of a mountain ridge. The dot emitted a reddish ray, narrow at the origin point, becoming wider as it reached the area of the testing. As the dot illuminated the rocket that was rising into the sky, the strange beam disappeared. Local radar registered nothing unusual. Just as the test range experts failed to come up with explanations as to the origin of the objects, the report also cannot explain who or what flew over the forbidden areas of Kamchatka during secret tests.

KGB QUESTIONS AN EYEWITNESS

Boris A. is a former Soviet scientist who currently resides in Chicago. He told me of a sighting he had in December 1982. The UFO he observed was very similar to the ones that seen during the famous Greek UFO wave of 1981. A KGB investigation of the sighting ensued and reveals the extent to which the secret police was interested in the phenomena. The incident took place in Kiev, shortly before New Year's Day. Boris' friends invited him to their parents' home in Rusanovka, a suburb of Kiev. The sighting occurred as Boris was leaving his friends parents' place. His wife, Lena, had forgotten her cigarettes upstairs, and Boris went back to get them. At that time, a man came running past them, pointing at the sky. When they looked up where he was pointing, they saw the UFO. The object was passing slowly over Kiev at low altitude. Shaped like a mushroom and measuring about 1,200 feet in length, the UFO was stunningly beautiful. The "cap" of the mushroom was the object's "nose-cone," located at the front end. It seemed that the "cap" was the machinery for propulsion. In any event, the "cap" glowed and dispelled some sort of inversion trail. The UFO had a delicately violet color was luminous. The violet color seemed to be iridescent with subtle tints and hues. The "cap" of this mushroom reminded Boris of a glowing cigarette tip; that is, it was brighter than the rest of the object and was of a somewhat different color. The top of the ship was definitely not of a violet color. Boris found it difficult to give a verbal description for the front part of the UFO.

The next day, he met Lena at the Institute of Plant Physiology of the Ukrainian SSR Academy of Sciences, where she worked. They told all her co-workers about their sighting, but nobody would believe them. There was an unexpected confirmation of their ac count. *Chervonniy Prapor*, a local newspaper, published a brief news report that confirmed the UFO sighting. The newspaper also informed the readers that radar at both of Kiev's airports detected the object. Also, in the newspaper report, a telephone number was provided to contact "a team from the Academy of Sciences" whose members were very much interested in talking to witnesses of the UFO. So, Lena and Boris called them. A few days later, a group of tough-looking KGB agents arrived to talk to them, stating that they were very interested in hearing about the UFO. Boris spoke with a muscular, square-jawed young agent with a sharp gaze underneath his straight brows. Boris thought he looked like a stereotypical "villain" (as in movies), and unfortunately, he did turn out to be villanous. The interrogator began with questioning that had nothing to do with the UFO. He demanded to know what Boris was doing at the Institute of Plant Physiology, since his *komandirovochnoye oudostovereniye* (warrant for travelling on official business) did not permit him to be there. The tough KGB man told Boris that he did not have the proper security clearance to be there. Stunned, Boris asked the interrogator if he had come to defend the social status quo or to find out about the UFO sighting. An argument ensued, and Boris told him to "go to hell." As if Boris had given a secret password, the cursing seemed to please the KGB agent, and the previous line of questioning was dropped. The agent called into the room another member of the interrogation team, a young woman, and the two KGB agents proceeded with questioning that was more appropriate for a witness to a UFO sighting. They quickly established the direction of the UFO's flight, its speed, and its angle to the horizon. But the agents said it was difficult for them to accept the description of the colours that Boris had attributed to the UFO, as no one else had described the UFO in that manner. Boris tried to explain to them that their task was to collect information, and not to believe or disbelieve a witness. Later, however, they interviewed Lena, and she confirmed the description that Boris had previously given of the UFO. After the interview, Boris never saw the agents again, although they promised that they would contact him. To this day, Boris recalls that the UFO he saw was very beautiful and pleasing to look at. Boris' report is yet another confirmation that the government- authorized entities empowered to "study" the UFO phenomenon in the former USSR existed, in reality, to obstruct and deter genuine research.

YURI ANDROPOV, THE KGB AND UFOS

The word *pravda* means truth in Russian. Perhaps there is some truth in the report published in the Russian newspaper *Pravda* on April 1, 2003. *Pravda* reported that the KGB had enlisted about 4 million soldiers to watch the skies in search of UFOs until the dissolution of the KGB and the Soviet Union in 1990. Was the newspaper describing the top secret SETKA programs? And, if so, what was the role of the KGB in SETKA? Yuri Andropov, leader of the Soviet Union's KGB showed an acute interest in UFOs and ordered (according to *Pravda*) the creation of a program that lasted 13 years and used soldiers to monitor the Soviet sky in search of unexplained flying objects.

Stunning information came to light in 2003. M. Chizhikov's *V stole Andropova lezhala papka s sekretami inoplanetyan* or *Andropov's desk* had a file with secret information about extraterrestrials, which was published in the *Komsomolskaya Pravda* newspaper, on March 19, 2003. In this article, Igor Sinitsin, who worked with Andropov for six years as his aide in the Politburo, revealed that the Soviet leader maintained a file on UFOs and consulted it as part of his daily routine. General-Secretary of the Communist Party of the Soviet Union Yuri Andropov, the ascetic Soviet leader and feared, formerlong-time head of the KGB, had a keen personal interest in UFOs. Andropov kept a file on the UFO phenomena always near at hand in his desk. Sinitsin, who exposed the information, mentioned that one of his responsibilities was to monitor the foreign press, and he brought Andropov a *Stern Magazine* piece about UFOs. The year was 1977, and the Petrozavodsk Phenomenon was on the minds of Western observers, underground ufologists, and KGB officers. Sinitsin was hesitant about presenting the piece from *Stern* to his grim superior, lest he be considered a lunatic, but Andropov's reaction was quite unexpected. Andropov handed Sinitsin the text of an official report he had ordered from the counter-espionage directorate. The text described an incident in Astrakhan where an Army officer had seen a UFO while fishing. The 1978 case we describe below was the case that interested former chief of the Soviet secret police. His "reign" of power between 1967 and 1983 was well-known for its draconian suppression of political dissidents. Andropov, as we learned after the fall of the USSR, was definitely interested in UFOs. Because of him, the case was turned to the SETKA-AN program (via the Military Industrial Commission), according to Andropov's assistant Igor Sinitsin. The officer who had witnessed the phenomenon had sent his report to the Chairman of the KGB.

We collected this information from a number of sources. This officer, prior to his career in the KGB, served in a Soviet Air Force bomber regiment and knew astronomy and navigation (he was a navigator of the bomber squadron). In brief, on June 26, 1978, K. Medzhidov, a KGB officer in the military counterintelligence directorate, along with several companions, was aboard a cutter watercraft in the Volga floodplains, about one mile away from Mumra settlement, in the Astrakhan Region. Late in the evening, they noticed a bright dot in the starry sky, in the area of the North Star. It was larger and brighter than other celestial bodies. A few minutes later the dot descended sharply, increasing in size and reaching an altitude of about 1,900 feet. Thereafter, it moved eastward.

As the dot descended, the dot acquired the shape of a saucer (turned at an angle, resembling an elliptical body, like a Frisbee. The observers clearly saw it was a physical object of a bright, bluish-silver color. As it levelled out into a horizontal position, the object's size seemed to grow to around 500 feet, and in the middle of it Medzhidov saw two bright lights (like the headlights of an automobile). The left one emitted a sharply focused, bright ray toward the ground, projected down at a 30-degree angle. The ray was rotating around. The impression was that it did not reach the ground. Its color was bright white (Medzhidov wore tinted glasses, and recalled a rosy hue).

As the object approached them, the observers discerned a weak halo, that later became bright white in color. The object stopped over them, and the radiance around the observers and the cutter increased. A minute later, the air mass under the object stirred, as well as (seemingly) the object. Two minutes later the object suddenly vanished. The halo, poorly visible, remained, and it dissipated in the sky in the next twenty minutes. Medzhidov called three other companions from the bunk room, when the object became visible. All of them observed the phenomenon. The KGB officer verified his observations with all of his companions and kept a precise timing of the occurrence. He stressed that no alcoholic drinks were consumed aboard the cutter. In the archive of the SETKA-AN program, this case is registered under number 96. V. Migulin received the report among the first military UFO observations sent to the Academy of Sciences. According to Sinitsin, it was Andropov who was instrumental in the creation of the SETKA programs. Sinitsin added that the KGB controlled what was published on this subject in many other countries. Both military and civilian UFO research centres were created under its direction.

The KGB files that have so far been released are undoubtedly only the tip of the iceberg, but if nothing else, they do provide a fascinating glimpse into the study of UFOs by this organization. Without a doubt, like their counterparts at the CIA, the KGB has files on U.S. UFO sightings as well. It is hoped that greater openness in the former USSR will allow access to all such files, and that they will fall into the hands of genuine UFO researchers. As stated at the beginning of this chapter, on October 24th, 1991, documents were provided to former Soviet cosmonaut Pavel Popovich, who was then President of the All-Union Ufological Association in Russia. These files contained copies of UFO reports collected by the KGB. An accompanying letter was written by the Deputy Chairman of the Committee for State Security USSR, N.A. Sham. The files consisted of handwritten reports, typed testimonies, and notes from KGB informers, crude drawings and eyewitness reports of UFOs. This cooperation between UFO researchers and the KGB was unprecedented and was a landmark in UFO research in the Soviet Union and possibly the world. Sixteen years later we have managed to catch up with the now former Deputy Commander of the KGB, and published here for the first time is an interview with the man himself. [Translated by Paul Stonehill and reproduced with the kind permission of NTV.]

In June 2007, author Philip Mantle was asked for an interview by NTV. NTV is one of the largest TV companies in Russia. Mantle said, "Apparently they were making a new UFO documentary and wanted to discuss with me my research into the Alien Autopsy film and the book I had co-authored with Paul Stonehill, *Mysterious Sky: Soviet UFO Phenomenon*." "The journalist Aleksey Egorov, along with his cameraman and translator Elena Volkovaya, duly arrived, and the interview took place at my home in West Yorkshire. After the interview, we discussed many things, and Aleksey informed me that he had interviewed the former Deputy Chairman of the KGB, Nikolay Sham, and discussed with him their release of official KGB UFO files to Russian UFO researchers. Aleksey went on to say that he could provide me with a transcript of his interview with Nikolay Sham. This duly arrived via email and was quickly translated by my colleague Paul Stonehill. Nothing has been omitted from the following interview, although Paul Stonehill has inserted a few things in brackets for clarification purposes only, "Mantle said.

KGB letter to Pavel Popovich

Nikolay Alekseyevich Sham was born in 1940. He was in the KGB from 1966 to 1991. Beginning in 1974, he worked in the central administration of the KGB. He was involved with the operational, technical and scientific projects. In 1986, he was with the commission that investigated the Chernobyl disaster. His rank was deputy chief of the 6th Directorate of the KGB, responsible for researching revolutionary scientific ideas and high-tech innovations, and protecting them from foreign agents. This KGB directorate is also where the Soviet economic espionage against other nations originated. Sham left the KGB in 1992 due to health reasons. In 1999, he headed a private corporation, Greenmaster, involved in the production of various devices using defence industry technologies. Later, he was the General Director of First Leasing Company (2003). He is often mentioned in Russian media in connection with paranormal phenomena.

In 1991, the former KGB Major-General, Nikolay Sham, who for a time served as a KGB deputy chairman, turned over to cosmonaut Popovich a 127- page record of UFO sightings reported in the territory of the former Soviet Union and in the Russian Federation.

Nikolay Alekseyevich Sham

INTERVIEW:

Nikolay Alekseyevich Sham is referred to as SHAM.

Alexey Egorov referred to as (AG).

AG: Nikolay Alekseyevich, this document here from the KGB, sent to Cosmonaut
Pavel Popovich; did you send it?

SHAM: Quite right.

AG: What year was it?

SHAM: It was in '91; the document's registration indicates so, that is why the
year was '91.

AG: Hence, you sent a complete file of documents from the KGB?

SHAM: Quite right. I simply [unintelligible] story, why the accumulation of
these documents took place specifically in the KGB. There was a special decree
of the Government and the Central Committee of the Communist Party
of the Soviet Union about the commencement of the research of these phenomena
that occur in nature. According to this decree, all law enforcement
agencies (KGB, Ministry of Defence, Ministry of Interior Affairs, and the
border guards) had to inform and report to the Center about facts they had
been receiving regarding all such phenomena in nature. And all the agencies
had factually accumulated the information.

But the KGB was not engaged in research of such issues; it is just that
some administration, some special department, if they would get some eyewitnesses
of all that was happening in the atmosphere... they would take
explanations and mostly hand-written materials that were sent there, describing
how they saw [phenomena], what they felt during [sightings]; describing
the background of the event, and so on. All that we had eventually accumulated
... accumulated, and by the same decree a few academic institutes were
obliged to undertake [measures] in order to research all these effects, various
phenomena, and come to some conclusion of every incident.

The main institute in the Academy of Sciences selected and appointed [to
head the research] was the Institute of Space Studies. All interesting facts
were always addressed. Experts, scientists left for the place of the incident,
asked questions, took soil samples, took various measurements, and so on;

and reached some conclusion based on the results of the event or a fact (that was being researched-P.S.). This work was conducted for several years, and some time in mid '85- '86, in that area, it was completed, this work ... and produced was a report about all the events that were registered through a number of years over the territory of the Soviet Union. I remember that report; I held it in my hands. Of course, I do not remember all of the details there, but from what I remember now, up to 70 percent of all phenomena that were somehow registered had been explained.

AG: They were explained from the point of view of classical science?

SHAM: Quite right.

AG: And, [the remaining] 30 percent?

SHAM: Well, 30 percent ... of those 30 percent, half were explained; not just one explanation, but variations of it could be explained this way, or that way. But not in the sense that again, [it was] some extraterrestrial civilization, its manifestation, and so on. No. And some 10-15 percent could not be explained at all ... what it was, what effects, manifestations, what kind of phenomena occurred in nature, atmosphere, and so on.

AG: Do you remember any examples of what could not be explained?

SHAM: Mostly it ... things that could not be explained, when some object materialized. Observed was a materialized object, mostly they were spots, some luminescent points, something else of different configurations and so on. As for materialized objects, that truly, if they were photographed, they had a materialized background in the shape of a saucer, some cylinder, or something similar. All such things, of course, could not have been explained; what it was, how one can comprehend all of it. That is what I remember from everything that took place back then. Moreover, all these sharp increases in public interest, they take place periodically. Time after time, the same question ... you are fifth or sixth party that come with the same question. Also, from the West I was approached, why? Because these materials; this digest, travel all over the world.

AG: All comes from this letter, because after this letter, the KGB secret files were sent to ufologists.

SHAM: No, there was not any secret document.

AG: That is, the documents were not secret before?

SHAM: Of course ... quite right. Imagine, some citizen saw some luminescent loop, and he wrote about it. The officer on duty of some administration or a special department received this information, registered in the logbook, wrote an accompanying letter, and sent to the Center. What secrets are here? No secrets at all. On the other hand, the explanation for all such phenomena in most cases ... you understand, tests were conducted, launches were performed, airplanes fly about, helicopters fly about, and the space is full of [manmade] objects and fragments of the space objects that periodically descend and enter the dense layers of the atmosphere. That is on one hand. On another hand, so-called mirage phenomena - mirages. You know, you have heard of mirages. Things related to crashes, disasters; aircraft crash when [the craft] falls apart in flight and falls to the ground and so on. That is, a multitude of things that due to some optic distortions and so on, sometimes create such background, that really it can appear that you are in some fairy tale world, and are surrounded humanoids, that another civilization attacks the Earth, and so on. In all of my life I have never met such a fact or event, or something similar, as a result of which one could with some certainty and credibility say, that this was appearance of an extraterrestrial civilization. In all of my life, regretfully, nothing like that happened. At the same time, if we, for example, will find explanations for all of that … Here in Russia now, for some years there is research, various experiments; at their core lies, to say generally, registration of the Galactic and Universal influence on the Earth. If one can imagine this entire world…

AG: In this file people write… I saw a strange object, a luminescent cloud. This is not a hallucination; here he exactly…

SHAM: And I want to address this point … how one can explain such things. Here, based on the results of the work that is being performed here in Russia. What is the heart of the problem? If we imagine this Earth where we live -- it is constantly subjected to the effects of the external environment. In fact, we have … we have gravitational fields. Further … we have the sun, and the gigantic energy of the sun comes to the Earth. Correct? Then, we have heavy planets, we have galaxy, we have so-called relic radiation; we have a tremendous amount of electromagnetic fields with different frequencies, and so on. And human being, it is also such a being that has everything moving inside, shifts.

You know, there is some aura around a human being; a human being emits some radiation, and so forth and so forth. As a principle, one cannot exclude that in conjunction with certain factors and creation of certain fields, with manifestation of certain electromagnetic fields with certain frequencies there comes some influence on human beings. And results of these studies demonstrate, really definitely and truly demonstrate, that a human being, entering into the area of influence of such natural phenomena … he starts changing, this human being. That is, in principle, he comes to the point where he ceases to comprehend. That is, entering into the field, into this zone, that can continue for dozens of minutes … he becomes inadequate, this human being.

AG: Can the same objects often be called hallucinations?

SHAM: Quite so … in the mind of the human being affected by all that, it can [be a hallucination], on one hand. On the other hand, because the Earth, too, is not of one origin - that is, there are so-called break-up lines. What is the break-up line? To speak figuratively, it is electrolyte. In the fissure, there is electrolyte. And as this is electrolyte, and imagine, there is some movement of this firmness, naturally it comes [movement], currents are registered, and the mechanism…of the equipment in the cables registers currents up to 27 amperes!

AG: Can you imagine the power that comes as a result of these waves, radiation, that comes from the very Earth?

SHAM: Neutron streams. Neutron streams, they come from space, neutron streams come from the Earth. And this gigantic energy component in variousshapes …and what is a human being in comparison to all this power as such?The water, too … it is the stuff that, as it is said, the original mother of all thatexists.

AG: These accumulated documents the ufologists nicknamed the Blue File …
Do you know the fate of the Blue File? What happened with it, after ufologists
were given these documents?

SHAM: Also, there was some interest two - three years ago in the same subject,
in this file. I offered them to just meet, I know some ufologists, I offered
to meet them in order to … and I organized this meeting; I do not know what
happened after that, but I did previously speak with these comrades on the
subject of all these documents. And they said, generally, with regret, with
resentment, they told me that all of the materials that had been accumulated in
the institutes and so on, it did, to say figuratively, left Russia.

AG: They say, for five hundred dollars…

SHAM: In fact…with such [great] resentment I was told of all these things.
Indeed, some unscrupulous people used the situation, the lawlessness and
uncertainty that existed in the country and tried to make business out of it.
And in fact, these materials left the country.

AG: I can give this example. The letter was addressed to Pavel Popovich.
Three days ago, we posed a question to Popovich, and he said - let me go
through this file, I want to understand, what is there, because he [Popovich]
did not see.

SHAM: In this case, it was, so to say, the enthusiasts of this field [ufology],
they are in the world, enthusiasts of this field, because a human being in its
essence is such, he needs something that is always certain, that is why people
have sorts of hobbies…

AG: How seriously can we take these here shots [photos] of flying saucers?

SHAM: Firstly, I know absolutely nothing about this. This is the first thing. I
can only comment that in the Soviet Union during the period of, so to say,
blooming of the rocket-space system industry here, every year more than 100
satellites of various types had been launched. We had that main spacecraft
that is still with us, the piloted Soyuz craft, and its descending capsule. At the
same time, our other organizations developed completely different systems,
including [those for] evacuation of the crew and landings. These systems had
been tested, and really they were in their essence, unique, these systems. It
seems to me, one of the emergency breakdown situations connected to the
experimental work to develop these systems, is depicted in this film. This is
most likely. Usually, when there was an emergency breakdown situation,
naturally, the site would be sealed off, and experts would arrive there. In
principle, all these developments were conducted in the interests of the Minis
try of Defence, interests of the Armed Forces. They were not the only developments;
they were done in the interests of the Ministry of Defence.

AG: And that, precisely, is what could have taken place?

SHAM: Quite right. That very Buran [a Soviet attempt to create a spaceshuttle
like vehicle] that we created, the orbital craft, it was preceded by a
bunch of experiments, connected with tests of various models and so on and
so forth. That is, we had a massive volume of undertakings in that direction;
various undertakings. Long-term orbital stations, like Mir, this currently international
… All of this was preceded by military developments, they were
completed these military developments, they were in use and so on

AG: If this here autopsy took place, would you be informed? [Most likely the

TNT TV show *The Secret KGB Files* broadcast in the USA in 1998].

SHAM: Of course, naturally ... Such event, it just could have gone unnoticed, could not have. Why? Because the KGB, counterintelligence, it was concerned with all our military-industrial sites, that is why ...such event, if it truly took place, of course the KGB would have been in the know. I have no doubts about that whatsoever. That is why here, whatever is taking place [in the film], and I do not know what it is. Why? Because, in reality, experiments did take place....

And then, we had lots of programs for the study of the planets of the Solar system. If you look at all the apparatuses, which descend, be it on Mars, be it Venus, or our moonwalkers and so on. And there, imagine, how many experiments were conducted here on Earth to supply this or other Martian program, or a program connected with launch of our apparatuses to Venus? These apparatuses were of various shapes. Mostly, of course, they were spherical. Why? Because, for example, it lands on Venus with a parachute, naturally, the best is the spherical shape. As for the strategic weapons that we had created ... Strategic weapons, before they are added to the armoury, they [weapons] go through a whole series of design experiments. When it flies, the missile, one part separates, the second part separates, the third...There are emergency landings, with breakdowns, and the missile has these discs, these parts... There can be anything, in fact ... and in all the cases, you can imagine, you prepare for turning over for utilization some strategic complex.

And suddenly, in the final stage, an emergency breakdown takes place. The chief, general designer, he has to understand the reason for this breakdown, that is why all fragments were always collected. And always, special units were dispatched....

NG: Nikolay Alekseyevich, in 1991, with this file, at that moment, what was your position in the KGB?

SHAM: From September '91 I was Deputy Chairman of KGB and remained at that position until June of '92. And then left because of health reasons.

AG: In your service, what did you oversee or control that is connected with what we now call UFO; what units and projects were under your control?

SHAM: That subject of UFO appeared in mid '70s. I already mentioned.... From mid-'70s there was a sharp increase, related to these unidentified flying objects. There was a resolution of the government and Central Committee of the Communist Party of the Soviet Union to conduct related projects to bring clarity to these phenomena that took place in the country. This resolution was made, and all law enforcement agencies - Ministry of defence, KGB, Ministry of Interior Affairs - were obliged to receive information from citizens regarding such events and send this information to the center.

Thus, this system was created, worked out, and from all the corners of the nation, wherever something happened, related to such events and phenomena, all this came to us, to the Center. And from the Academy side, several institutes were obliged to conduct research of the phenomena that were registered on Earth.

The Institute for Space Studies was designated to be the main one. And
for several years this work had been conducted; it was completed some time
in mid '80s; a report, a fundamental report was produced, where, generally,
all collected matters, related to the events in this or that corner of the country,
all were put on shelves, systemized, materials were related to every (appropriate-
P.S.) event, location of the event, time of the event, what eyewitnesses,
what did they observe, what did they feel at the time, what effects and what
shape the thing had-all this was systemized; they even made tabular shapes,
shapes and silhouettes (outlines-P.S.) of UFOs that had appeared in the atmosphere.
In most cases, experts went to the most interesting sites. Performed appropriate
measurements, conducted questioning of eyewitnesses, and
conducted various researches of sorts, and so on. And as a result some conclusion
was made for every event.

I remember, around seventy percent of the events were provided with
real and objective explanations. What were they connected with? Tests of
aviation technology, missile technology, launches of space objects, parts of
spacecraft objects falling into the atmosphere, aircraft technology disasters,
some cataclysms in nature connected with something being discarded and so
on. That is, everywhere they found an explanation.

But in thirty percent of cases, it is as if half of an explanation was given,
but not a single one, meaning that yes, something took place, but facts that
certainly confirm what is, are not sufficient. And in some instances, simply
due to lack of information and due to dearth of any material proof at the incident
site, no conclusions were made.

The annual report was completed somewhere in mid '80s. The KGB itself,
naturally, did not research these issues; we did not have such direction.
There simply was collection, gathering; and periodically the materials, as they
say, were dumped into the Institute of Space Studies or other departments,
depending again on the contents of an event, as they say. That is what took
place.

AG: Who took the lead in the government to issue resolutions; was it Brezhnev
himself; did it fascinate him, was he interested in it? Why all of a sudden
in the mid '70s this resolution came about, and who took the lead?

SHAM: I do not know about taking lead. After all, at the time we had a military-
industrial commission, and in that, many things were originated there.
But who specifically at the military-industrial commission all of a sudden
took the lead, I do not remember ... Most likely it [the initiative] could had
been the military-industrial commission, or, let's assume, we had the rocket space
technology field; the Ministry of General Engineering Industry, it could
have come from there. Or, for example, from the same Academy of Sciences.
That is, where would the initiative come from? Well, the initiative came
about because the media, as they say, began to play up with things, as such.
And since it began to play up, our government and Party always reacted to
such things. I cannot say who took the lead with the release of the resolution.
The topic was named, I recall, SETKA-AN [A sharp increase in UFO activity
in 1977-78 had forced the appropriate departments with the USSR Academy
of Sciences to agree to a research program to look into anomalous phenomena.
The code name for this program was SETKA-AN.], the name of this

subject, the SETKA-AN program. And since then…

AG: Why SETKA-AN?

SHAM: I do not know why it was exactly SETKA-AN. I cannot say. That did not interest us; what was interesting was why? Because…As a matter of principle, all these things, [unclear] … that take place in the atmosphere, and that assume such various forms, all this, generally, first of all are connected with, of course, power engineering, with electromagnetic fields, with massive radiation that surround us. This radiation … just the enumeration, as they say, God knows how much there is, starting with … [unclear] … was given a Noble Prize for discovering this relic radiation. This scientists had discovered first, launching a specialized satellite, and see how the Americans had developed that topic, and received a Noble Prize for it. And our program was terminated, did not get to be developed.

End of interview.

You don't have to be Einstein to see that Sham is still quite guarded all these years later. It is nonetheless interesting to note that he readily admits that a large percentage of things did remain unidentified and he did clarify what western researchers had speculated about for years, the fact that the Soviets used UFO stories to mask weapons testing. The reason for this is that they were breaking a number of international treaties at the time. In concluding this chapter, is important for readers in the West to understand that because the Soviet Union was a totalitarian state built on secrecy and lies, the KGB was omnipresent. For example, the USSR Academy of Sciences had a special "First Department," actually a secret police outpost that spied and collected information. Every Soviet state institution had such outposts. The files collected by KGB scientists are out of reach of Russian researchers. Without a doubt, UFO reports and observations are hidden in such files. One wonders what secrets they contain and whether they still remain in Russia. Allegedly, some files and video films have become property of Western television producers. UFO researchers, like the authors of this book, are interviewed occasionally for such programs, but researchers are never given the actual films for independent study. Of course, no documents in the possession of such producers are given to independent researchers. That is why we will abstain from commenting on such "KGB files" productions. But we urge television producers that claim to possess KGB UFO files to turn them over to serious researchers for a comprehensive, detailed examination. There are such entities as MUFON and the J. Allen Hynek Center for UFO Studies in the West; and Gherman Kolchin, the RIAP, Aleksandr Plaksin, Mikhail Gershtein and other well-regarded and experienced researchers in the East who could join forces for the task. This is the only way to establish authenticity of the documents and films.

CHAPTER 7.

MYSTERIOUS OCEANS:

UNIDENTIFIED SUBMERSIBLE OBJECTS IN RUSSIAN AND INTERNATIONAL WATERS INTRODUCTION

The late Alexandr Al'fredovich Gorbovsky -- Russian historian, social scientist and writer -- worked for 20 years in the USSR's Academy of Sciences. For many people in the Soviet Union, his 1966 book, *Zagadki Drevney Istorii* (*Enigmas of Ancient History*), opened the doors to the fascinating but forbidden world of the paranormal, delving into topics such as ufology, mysteries of ancient history, and paleocontact [the Russian term for theories about ancient astronauts having visited Earth in antiquity]. In his book, Gorbovsky mentioned an incident that took place in the ancient Mediterranean during which people observed a strange underwater vehicle surfacing at high speed. The object rose from the water and shortly thereafter disappeared into the sky. This was certainly one of the first recorded instances of a USO, unidentified submersible object.

In this chapter, we will discuss USO cases occurring in the waters of the former Soviet Union. It should be noted that some of the most accurate of the observers and researchers of this fascinating phenomenon reveal their secrets very reluctantly, if at all. Secret files of the Soviet Navy contain much valuable information about UFO and USO sightings. Soviet military researchers had been quite efficient at keeping these files largely inaccessible, even long after the fall of communism. But after years of compiling information with the help of our colleagues in the former Soviet Union, modern Russia, Ukraine, and other newly independent countries, we have been able to collect some incredible stories.

It is worth mentioning that the Soviet Navy carefully guarded its secrets, and spoke out [or lashed out] against writers and journalists that gave a paranormal slant to the subject of USOs. For example, Rear Admiral M. Rudnitsky reacted with scorn to an article about USOs published in *Tekhnika-Molodezhi* magazine (Issue 9, 1972). A typical argument used by Soviet Navy officials is that if intelligent beings have resided underwater for thousands of years, they would surely have tried to contact us. Yet there's no record of such contacts. Yerokhin, a perceptive Siberian engineer interested in USO phenomenon, however, is of the opinion that a mysterious fluorescence observed in the sea may be exactly such an attempt to establish communications between an underwater civilization and us. Regardless of the Soviet Navy's attempts to diminish public interest in this sensitive subject, the topic of USOs simply will not go away. Nikolai Nepomnyaschy's 1998 book *Iz sekretnikh arkhivov razvedok mira* (*From Secret Archives of the World Intelligence Services*) mentions a key USO event that occurred in Argentina in 1960. The Argentine navy detected a strange underwater object and proceeded to bombard it and try, unsuccessfully, to capture it. The Soviets, upon hearing of the case, demonstrated a keen interest in the case and in other USO events. Nikita Khrushchev, then still the General Secretary of the Central Committee of the Communist Party of the Soviet Union, sent an inquiry to the Soviet attaché in Argentina.

Leonid Breshnev with Soviet Navy in the Black Sea

Since 1991, author Paul Stonehill has published a number of articles about USOs observed by Russian mariners, sailors and seamen in the waters of the Russian Empire, the USSR, as well as in international waters. Some of Paul's articles were written in Russian, but most were in English. The articles have also been translated into many other languages. One of Paul Stonehill's most popular articles in Russian described the *podvodniye lodki-fantomi* [phantom submarine] cases in the northern seas. A number of Russian publications have reprinted his articles.

Soviet Navy Poster

Among Russian researchers of the UFO and USO phenomena, one finds such prolific writers as Vladimir Ajaja, Mikhail Gershtein, and Vadim Chernobrov; Valentin Psalomschikov and Aleksandr Petukhov; Konstantin Khazanovich; and late Russian scientists and researchers Feliks Zigel, Alexander Kuzovkin, Colonel Gherman Kolchin, and historian Vadim Vilinbakhov. In recent years, such researchers as Colonel V.P. Pravdivtsev, a scientist and TV producer, and Captain 1st Rank E. P. Litvinov, a UFO researcher, have contributed to the study of the USO phenomenon in Russia.

In August of 2006, Pavel Popovich, that famous Soviet cosmonaut who had helped Vladimir Ajaja and other devotees promote UFO research in the USSR, and who was prominent in helping them obtain the KGB UFO files in the early 1990s, was interviewed by *Bul'var Gordona*, a popular Ukrainian newspaper, (Issue 31[67]). Popovich stated that the inhabitants of Phaeton or Moonah [a theoretical planet that supposedly existed near Earth in antiquity but later was pushed to the outer edge of our solar system by a nuclear catastrophe] probably visit Earth from time to time. He said the visitors' intermediate base is located in the area of Saturn, and they have three bases on Earth. One of them is in the Andes, the other in the Indian Ocean trench, and the third one is located in the Himalayas, the famous Shambala.

Pavel Popovich

The base in the Andes, according to Popovich, was shut down by the extraterrestrial visitors because human civilization came too close to them. But they do have an underwater base at the bottom of the Indian Ocean trench. While we do not know the source of the late cosmonaut's knowledge, this chapter will present Russian and Soviet observations of USOs and UFOs from all corners of the world, and let the readers decide, whether the presence of such bases is possible.

In 2006, a documentary film titled *Tayna tryokh okeanov* (Mystery of Three Oceans) directed and written by V. Pravdivtsev was broadcast on Russian television. It featured several Russian Navy officers who knew about USO encounters and presented some of the cases mentioned in Paul Stonehill's articles through the years, as well as cases and sightings that had been mentioned by other Russian researchers.

In 2008, Russian television (First Channel) broadcast a documentary film *NLO. Podvodniye prisheltsi* (*UFO. Underwater Aliens*). The same year, another Russian TV channel (REN-TV), broadcast a film titled *NLO: ukhod pod vodu* (*UFO: The Underwater Departure*). This media attention proves that there is definite interest in Russia regarding USOs, as well as UFOs in general.

Soviet Submarine, 1990

In 2009, media outlets both in Russia and in the West reported that the Russian Navy planned to declassify its secret UFO and USO files. Of course, those in Russia who guard their Navy's secrets also found out about the reports and issued a response. On July 30th, 2009, the Main Staff of Russian Federation's Navy said there are no official documents of encounters between Soviet ships and submarines with unidentified objects. The Russian naval command said that rumours sometimes arise because commanding officers of ships and submarines are required to report all "unidentified" objects that are observed visually or on radar screens. However, typically these "unknowns" are actually schools of fish, floating trash, or natural phenomena that are mistaken for USOs or UFOs.

Thus hopes were shattered that the Russian navy would declassify its secret UFO files. The word used by Russians is столкновение (*stolknoveniye*); it can be translated as collision, conflict, encounter, jostle, or smash. We do not believe that in Russia, anything related to the nation's Navy intelligence and counterintelligence files will be declassified in the near future. Ufologist Vladimir Ajaja, who has done much to promote UFO and USO research, states that neither he nor any of his respected colleagues have received any information about pending releases of secret files from the Russian navy. Sightings of strange "swimmers" -- beings dressed in tight, silvery uniforms and swimming in freezing cold water -- was reported by M. Shteynberg in 1992 in *Anomaliya* magazine and further investigated and corroborated by Paul Stonehill through the years. Most likely the "swimmers" incident was picked up by Western media from Paul's articles, published in Russian and English years ago -- for instance, in *Pravda* newspaper in 2008 as well as in our books about Soviet UFOs. But no secret USO files have been declassified; for Russia and its Navy guard their secrets very well. And lest we forget, the Russian Navy will become the world's second largest in 20 years' time, according to its commander-in-chief, Admiral Vladimir Masorin, who was speaking ahead of Russia's Navy Day in 2009.

One such secret lies in the deep waters of Lake Baikal in southern Siberia. Something definitely bothers the Russians about this lake, as is evident by a number of recent expeditions there. Not long ago, Vladimir Putin, then Russia's Prime Minister, as well as several key scientists, descended in a submersible craft, to the bottom of the mysterious lake. At the same time, someone keeps leaking information to the various media claiming that the Russian Navy will be releasing new information. This seems unlikely. Yet, we should all remain vigilant for new announcements about USOs not just from Russia but from all other nations that study oceans, seas, and lakes of our planet. We should pay special attention to news from Mariana Trench and Java Trench, as well as reports from the Pacific and Arctic oceans.

Judging by information about Russian underwater sightings, including statements of its Navy officers and intelligence operatives, it is safe to conclude that the Soviets (before 1991), and the Russians (now) are preoccupied with the strange unidentified objects and unearthly creatures lurking in their waters. Let's look at some of these sightings, reports, and statements. Most of the information in this book has never been presented outside of Russia's borders, and is little known even to those inside the borders of that country.

AJAJA, POPOVICH AND HISTORY OF SOVIET USO RESEARCH

Vladimir Georgiyevich Ajaja is a prominent personality in the history of Russian UFO research. When he first became active in the field, he earned the ire of the Communist Party, which intensely disliked those who studied forbidden subjects. Among other annoyances to the Party was the very real possibility that, while looking for UFOs, Ajaja and other independent UFO researchers would stumble upon Soviet secret military tests and rocket launches. In reporting their findings about "UFOs," foreign intelligence agents listened with great interest, trying to "read between the lines." Hence, they feared, the Soviets' new secret weapons would become known to all the world.

Soviet Military Photo of a Disc-Shaped UFO Emerging from the Ocean

Also, as history had demonstrated, the Kremlin had not been able to control unidentified flying and submersible objects. The strange craft crossed the Soviet Union's borders at will, hovered over its nuclear sites and test ranges, chased its fighter jets, and seemingly thumbed their noses at all attempts to thwart their purposes. Soviet censorship could repeat on a daily basis through its media and functionaries that UFOs do not exist, but all the power the Politburo had, including its secret police and its formidable armed forces, were not able to restrict the movements of UFOs and USOs. These objects exhibited no regard whatsoever for the USSR or any Earthly authority.

At one time in his arduous and tumultuous life, Vladimir Ajaja, who was a scientist as well as later a ufologist, served as the head of the underwater exploration expedition aboard the Soviet *Severyanka* submarine. Ajaja actually designed many features of the vessel. During their expedition, he and his fellow crew members observed very unusual creatures down below, including one that looked like a lyre [the musical instrument] and had green tentacles.

When his urge to research and discuss the forbidden subject of UFOs got him fired from his job, it was the Soviet Navy that provided Ajaja with employment and an enviable opportunity to study UFOs and USOs. Other mainstream Soviet marine researchers would not touch such "questionable" subject as UFOs. In his search for the information, two sources helped Ajaja -- the Russian translation of Charles Berlitz's book *The Bermuda Triangle* which mentioned UFOs [he could find no other books on the subject in the Soviet libraries], and Vice-Admiral Y.V. Ivanov, head of the Naval Intelligence Directorate. Ajaja found out that the Soviet Naval Intelligence had long considered UFOs to be a subject worthy of serious investigation.

But his newly found conviction put him on thin ice. Ajaja's efforts to study and promote ufology made him a target of science "officialdom" and Communist Party functionaries. His credibility was attacked in the Soviet media, and his published works were blacklisted. In addition, his lectures were outlawed, and he was fired from several jobs for his UFO positions. Again, his comrades in the Navy helped him land a job and write about UFOs for their practical use. Ideology took a back seat to practical matters of national defence. Because as a young man Ajaja attended the M.V. Frunze Higher Naval School [the oldest Russian naval officers commissioning schools], served in the Soviet Navy, and later participated in oceanographic research, he still had friends among those who were in charge of Russia's maritime power. He was even presented with opportunities to question Navy intelligence officers who were responsible for their Navy's UFO and USO studies. Vladimir Ajaja as we mentioned before, wrote a monograph about UFOs for Soviet Navy. And, with the help of his highly placed Soviet Navy buddies, he was able to write a piece about the Bermuda Triangle for *Nauka I Zhizhn*, a respected Soviet scientific magazine.

In 1976, Ajaja had a fascinating meeting at the Department of Underwater Research of the Oceanographic Commission of the USSR Academy of Sciences. The date was November 17, and among those present were the Chairman of the Department P. Borovikov, his deputy, E. Kukharkov, and twenty-nine other people. They came to hear V. Ajaja's lecture about UFOs and the associated underwater phenomenon. At the time, Vladimir Ajaja was a deputy to Chairman P. Borovikov. After Ajaja's lecture, these present decided to include collection of UFO sightings over bodies of water, and in the depths of the planet's hydrosphere, into the planned activities of the Department. Such collected data was to be researched and analyzed. Another curious episode took place the same year. Pirogovsky Reservoir Basin is located four miles from Moscow. In August of 1976, A. Troitsky and six other eyewitnesses observed a silvery metallic disc over the reservoir. It was about eight times as large as the lunar disc. The object moved slowly at the altitude of several dozen feet. On its lateral surface, they observed two revolving stripes. When the object hovered over the witnesses, a black hatch opened its lower side, and a small thin cylinder came forth. The lower portion of the cylinder started moving in circles, but the upper portion remained attached to the object.

Secret Soviet Submarine Base in Balaklava

We should point out that it is quite possible that Ajaja has not revealed all that he knows about the underwater UFO phenomenon. In 1966, he and other authors published a curious book, titled *Submarines in Scientific Research* (Nauka, 1966). Briefly mentioned there is that V. G. Ajaja, N.I. Tarasov, A.K. Tokarev, and E.V. Shishkov performed "intriguing" research in the area of hydrobiology. Ajaja never really discussed what that intriguing research was; obviously, some areas of the Soviet UFO phenomena remain secret in modern Russia. In one of his recent interviews, Ajaja revealed observations of fiery spheres underwater in the Pacific Ocean. One of the Soviet nuclear submarines of the Soviet Pacific Fleet, while on battle patrol, using hydro acoustics, discovered six unknown objects in the water next to it. The objects could not be classified.

The sub tried to get away from the fiery spheres, but they moved as the sub moved, remaining in the same position relative to the submarine. Although it violated the rules for battle patrols, the submarine commander was forced to surface. As the Soviet submarine broke the surface of the water, all six USOs flew out of the ocean and disappeared into the sky. Ajaja stated that he learned of this incident in a document he saw in the Main Staff of the Soviet Navy. He recounted the incident in his books, lectures, and television appearances (such as the September 26, 1992 Russian TV program *NLOneobyavlenniy visit* (*UFO-An Unannounced Visit*).

One interesting and significant episode that has been brought up by Ajaja several times in various publications (including *NLO Magazine*, 1999) took place on October 7, 1977. Volga, a floating service base (submarine depot ship) for Soviet submarines in the Barents Sea was "visited" by nine strange shining discs. The UFOs descended and circled around the base; no radio signal could be sent out or received by frantic Soviet Naval officers. This "dance" lasted fully for 18 minutes, after which the UFOs vanished. As a result of the incident, the very same day, Vladimir Ajaja was invited to meet with deputy Commander-in-Chief of the Soviet Navy, Admiral N.I. Smirnov, who Smirnov oversaw all scientific research for the Navy. He asked Ajaja to listen to the recording of the report of the operational officer on duty with the Northern Fleet. Ajaja heard in the recording that Captain 3rd Rank Tarankin was urgently called to the ship's battle information center. The radar indicated that an aerial target was approaching the base from a distance of approximately 60 miles. While the seamen were quickly responding to the emergency on the depot ship, radiometer technicians had detected the target. The signal indicated that what seemed to be a group of helicopters was approaching the floating base. Where would they come from? The base was far away from the shore, and Soviet helicopters based on airfields would not reach it; as for foreign helicopter aircraft carriers, there were none in the Barents Sea, according to intelligence reports. Tarankin ran to the bridge. An expanding radiance approached the ship from north-east. As the objects came into view, observers saw nine, shiny discs that were definitely not helicopters. Among those who witnessed the flight of the discs was the ship's captain, Tarankin. As the discs approached Volga's masts, they began an eerie circle dance (*khorovod* in Russian).

For eighteen minutes, radio operators tried in vain to contact the main base of the Northern Fleet in Severomorsk. Captain Tarankin issued the following unusual order over the ship's radio -- all onboard personnel were to observe the objects, make drawings, take photographs, and generally remember what they saw, so that when they returned to their main base, no one could accuse the captain of losing his mind. At the nineteenth minute, the UFOs had left, radio communications were restored, and radiograms were sent to the main base. One hour later, a reconnaissance plane arrived at the site, but by then the objects were long gone. Obviously, this incident greatly concerned those in charge of the Soviet Navy.

Interest in the phenomena was further ramped up in December 1976 when three Soviet Naval Captains observed a UFO on their way to Moscow. Consequently, Admiral N.I. Smirnov contacted deputy chief of the Main Staff of the Navy, N. P. Navoytsev and ordered that all fleets and flotillas should implement the SETKA Instruction for UFO observations. Vladimir Ajaja provided the exact language of the Instruction (directive) that later was issued to the Soviet armed forces as part of the secret SETKA program mentioned throughout this book; according to some sources, he actually wrote the Instruction for the Soviet Navy, at the request of the chief of Soviet Navy's intelligence, Vice Admiral Y. V. Ivanov (who was also at the time the Deputy Commander of Soviet Navy Main Staff). The Instruction, or *Metodicheskiye Ukazaniya*, (as part of the SETKA-MO program) became an official directive for the Soviet Navy, signed by Deputy Commander of the Main Headquarters of the Navy, Vice Admiral Saakyan. This document was signed by Rear Admiral Mars Iskanderov (another graduate of the Frunze Higher Naval School) for the dissemination in the

Northern Fleet. We will mention this fleet in relation to a number of significant USO/UFO sightings over the years. It was deputy chief of the Main Staff of the Navy, N. P. Navoytsev, who signed the directive to implement the Instruction after the Volga incident. Initially, the Instruction was put into practice aboard hydrographic, scientific research, and reconnaissance ships. Later, the Instruction was adopted as the SETKA directive (through the *Goskomgidromet SSSR*, or State Committee of the USSR for hydrometeorology and environmental control). One of the first sightings reported under the Instruction was an object sighted on September 20, 1977, by the watch officer of a high-speed Soviet nuclear submarine (*Project 705*) returning from tests in the Severodvinsk shipbuilding yard. Severodvinsk, located in the delta of the Northern Dvina, was built to make the Northern Fleet independent of the Baltic shipyards and serves as the principal Russian shipyard for the nation's Northern Fleet. The watch officer, Captain-Engineer 2nd Rank noticed a rapidly-moving, bright "star" in the sky. The object moved from the north southward, toward Petrozavodsk and Leningrad. The star stretched itself out and transformed itself into a long, glowing ribbon.

The watch officer thought that it was a cylinder that flew over him; one of the ends of this cylinder suddenly became asymmetrical. Out of this cylinder came small objects that resembled, from the distance, small peas. It was hard to estimate their size. But the altitude, at which the UFO moved, was enormous. The peas did not follow the cylinder, but flew into various directions. The watch officer recorded this unusual phenomenon in the submarine's log. Later it was determined that one hour later this "UFO" was observed over Petrozavodsk. This Petrozavodsk Phenomenon was the impetus leading to the creation of the SETKA program in the USSR. The Instruction, signed by Saakyan, mentions two military units, where the most credible and "serious" UFO data collected by Soviet troops had to be sent to immediately: Unit 67947 (Mitischi town, Moscow region); and Unit 62728 (Leningrad).

Serious data that was to be sent right away included the following: physical traces of anomalous phenomena, death of military personnel (as a result of contacts with the anomalous phenomena), and breakdown of technology. In his brochure *Vnimaniye: NLO* or *Attention: UFOs*, Ajaja stated that the UFO wave of 1989, still in progress in 1991 when it was published, had swept away ideological and censorship barriers which were placed against ufology in the USSR. In this book, we mention many observations of unidentified objects, flying and submersible, recorded by Russian mariners and scientists during this "wave" of sightings. Because of the many years when UFOs were a forbidden topic, the country was totally unprepared for the sudden surfacing of hundreds and even thousands of UFO reports. So, Ajaja helped organize the *SOYUZUFOTSENTR* in 1990, the very first official civilian Soviet UFO research organization to promote scientific study of UFO phenomena. It broke away from its cradle, the Soviet Academy of Sciences, largely because Vladimir Ajaja was convinced that those responsible for the UFO research within the Academy actually prevented true and unbiased research. This was later confirmed, when the story became public of how SETKA had manipulated UFO information in order to obscure the truth and mislead the public. In 1984, by the decision of VSNTO (All-Union Council of Scientific Technical Societies), a Central Commission for Anomalous Phenomena in the Environment was established.

We will often mention in this chapter several cases reported to and researched by the Leningrad (Saint Petersburg) branch of this Commission. One such report was filed by A. Golotikin, a mechanic from Leningrad (now Saint Petersburg). In 1980 he worked aboard *Brilliant*, a large fishing freezer trawler. On January 24, the trawler was operating at the distance of about 20 to 30 miles from the Western Sahara coast. At 13:00, while Golotikin and other crew members were on the deck, they observed a black object, shaped like a cigar. The object flew toward the ship; it moved much slower than usual aircraft, and emitted no sounds. The crew observed it for five to seven minutes through binoculars. They were amazed that upon approaching the trawler, the object immediately disappeared. This sighting was mentioned in the 2001 article written by Valentin Psalomschikov, and published in *NLO Magazine*.

Vladimir Ajaja was dedicated to the promotion of UFO research. On January 16, 1979, he took the Instruction he had written for the Soviet Armed Forces to those who had trained the nation's cosmonauts. It was Pilot-Cosmonaut V. Shatalov, the Deputy Air Force Commander for Cosmonaut Training, who was the recipient of Ajaja's Instruction. No one among independent Russian UFO researchers knows whether the Instruction was adopted for UFO observations by Soviet cosmonauts. But Ajaja was allowed to conduct his lectures in the Soviet Space Research Institute and the Mission Control Center. In 1984, Pavel Popovich said "Today there is a great compilation of observations of flying objects, and it is time to understand what we are dealing with. There is no sense to hide one's head in the sand, like an ostrich, and deny everything. The inexplicable must be researched." He was interviewed by I. Mosin, of *Sotsialisticheskaya Industriya* newspaper, on August 5th, for his article "Zagadki nebesnikh yavleniy" (Mysteries of Celestial Phenomena). Vladimir Ajaja and Pavel Popovich played an important role in the history of Soviet UFO and USO research. Most likely, they knew more than has been revealed in their writings and interviews.

GHOSTS OF THE OCEAN: SOVIET NAVY'S INVESTIGATION OF *KVAKERI* – UNDERWATER CROAKING SOUNDS

The Cold War was raging at the end of the 1960s, and dangers for both sides of the ruthless (and frequently invisible) war lurked in the skies, on land, and underwater. One particularly strange underwater phenomenon attracted the attention of the Soviet Navy's High Command in the late 1960s. Soviet nuclear-powered submarines encountered strange sounds emanating from moving objects at great depths. Listening to underwater sound is known as hydro acoustic monitoring, and Soviet monitors heard the strange signals that resembled frogs croaking. They dubbed the objects *kvakeri*, and the term was officially accepted in the Soviet Navy's documents. *Kvakat*, in Russian means "to croak."

It was the Soviet Minister of Defence, Marshal Andrei Antonovich Grechko, who ordered the creation of a special research team by the Intelligence Directorate of the Soviet Navy to investigate various paranormal phenomena such as the *kvakeri*. Sergey Georgiyevich Gorshkov, a Soviet naval commander during the Cold War who oversaw the expansion of the Soviet Navy into a global force and at the time was Commander-in-Chief of the Soviet Navy and Admiral of the Fleet of the Soviet Union, spared no effort in researching this phenomenon that obstructed the navy's operations.

Consequently in the USSR, a special top secret research program into the *kvakeri* phenomenon was started in the late 1960s and lasted until the early 1980s. But it was not the only unusual underwater phenomenon of interest to the Soviet Navy.

The Commander-in-Chief ordered a series of oceanic expeditions to research the *kvakeri* and other phenomena. Soviet officers in the top secret naval research program, who were all highly-education and professional people, performed their duties eagerly, visiting different Soviet fleets and collecting all available information. The *kvakeri* were found to operate as far as away the area around the Philippines and in the northern seas close to the USSR, but they were most active in the Atlantic Ocean. One research expedition, in April 1970, involved the *Khariton Laptev*, a reconnaissance vessel codenamed SSV 503 [the ship was removed from active service in 1992]. This was precisely at the time that a Soviet nuclear submarine, the K-8, perished in the North Atlantic. The reconnaissance ship, which was participating in a secret mission, stopped its sonar operations, rushed to help the submarine and was able to save many of the crew. It is believed that the *kvakeri* had a particular interest in nuclear-powered submarines, as will be discussed later. However, the *kvakeri* research program was stopped abruptly when the phenomenon ceased to "bother" Soviet ships in the Atlantic Ocean.

So, what were those mysterious *kvakeri*? A small Russian newspaper, *Podmoskoviye-Nedelya*, published a very interesting article on August 8, 2001 by Vadim Kulinchenko, a retired Soviet naval officer and submariner who had also been a senior officer in the Main Staff of the Russian Navy. He was the first former Soviet Navy officer to reveal details about the *kvakeri*. Kulinchenko said that the gist of the *kvakeri* phenomenon is similar to the UFO phenomenon. Many people have witnessed mysterious objects, but no one has been able to prove their existence. Kulinchenko recalled the stir created by reports of strange, unidentified noises that accompanied Soviet subs in their secret missions in unfriendly waters. It was almost as if the captains of underwater missile cruisers, returning from their missions in the Atlantic Ocean, had conspired to submit similar reports of peculiar noises.

SOVIET INTEREST IN UFOS, USOS, AND SEA CREATURES

Other former Soviet military officers and researchers revealed more information in the years that followed about this very unusual phenomenon. Among them is the last Commander-in-Chief of the Soviet Navy and president of the Russian Union of Submariners, Admiral Vladimir Nikolayevich Chernavin, who commanded the Northern Fleet between 1977 and 1981. Chernavin stated that the instruction regarding UFOs and USOs, written by Vladimir Ajaja for the Soviet Navy (as part of the Soviet Union's highly secretive SETKA-MO UFO research program), was not unique to the USSR. The Americans had similar instructions to collect information about anomalous (paranormal) phenomena. Chernavin also stated that there is no proof Ajaja was privy to the results of the *kvakeri* research.

Soviet Navy – Pacific Fleet

Some Soviet military researchers believed that the *kvakeri* were USOs. Yet many specialists in the research groups who had studied the phenomenon disagreed with this conclusion.

Nuclear submarines drove the Cold War's most furious phase of the arms race. According to Vice Admiral Viktor Patrushev, Chief of Operations on the General Staff of the Russian Navy and professor of the Academy of Military Sciences, the Soviets built 243 nuclear submarines of various classes as well as over 1,000 diesel submarines. Some of these submarines must have really been of interest to the *kvakeri*, for the course and bearing indicators of the Soviet naval vessels demonstrated that the objects circled the subs and changed the frequency and tone of their signals. The Soviets had never been able to establish the source of the sound. It came from different sides, and the tone constantly changed. It was as if the objects were inviting the submarines to engage in "conversations."

The *kvakeri* reacted especially actively, yet never aggressively, to the acoustic dispatches from the submarines. They would accompany Soviet submarines until the latter would exit a certain area. Then, producing the "croaking" sound for the last time, the objects would disappear. There was never any confrontation with the objects in the long years of their interaction; yet the Soviet commanders and submarine crews were tense and under stress when the *kvakeri* accompanied their vessels.

TECHNOLOGY MADE IN AMERICA

Were the *kvakeri* "made in the USA?" America was the chief suspect as the origin of the *kvakeri* because the Soviet Navy surmised that its vessels were encountering an advanced U.S. submarine tracking technology. Rear Admiral Vladlen Naumov believes that the *kvakeri* were U.S. Navy sonic underwater buoys. Naumov points to SOSUS, an acronym for Sound Surveillance System, a chain of underwater listening posts across the North Atlantic Ocean near Greenland, Iceland and the UK. It was operated by the U.S. Navy to track Soviet submarines in the Atlantic (and other oceans).

Naumov has studied the experience of Soviet nuclear submarines armed with ballistic missiles designed to strike at strategic military–industrial targets of a potential adversary. In September 1975, as a Captain 1st Rank, Naumov was given command of the K-182 submarine cruiser. A Delta II–class Project 667BD submarine, the K-182 was launched in January 1975 and commissioned on 30 September 1975. Project 667BD submarine cruisers were actively utilized in the Soviet and, later, Russian navies from February 1973 through to April 1996. Naumov was able to hear the *kvakeri* during his missions, and he claims that he established a procedure to evade the "sonic underwater buoys." According to Naumov, during its service history the K-182 was approached by the *kvakeri* 72 times and was able to cut contact with them 72 times. Consequently there was great interest from the Soviet High Command, which paid close attention to his submarine. Naumov's opinion is shared by an anonymous Soviet submariner, who expressed his opinion in one of the Russian forums dedicated to the *kvakeri* phenomenon. This person wrote that on a number of occasions he heard sounds emitted by *kvakeri* through the sound channel of the Soviet MGK-300 Rubin submarine towed array sonar. He recorded the sounds and analyzed them during the years he served aboard the submarines of the 3rd Division. This was in the mid-1970s, when the *kvakeri* phenomenon was in its heyday. At the beginning of the 1980s, he personally observed the phenomenon and became convinced that it was actually caused by an aerial buoy, dropped from U.S. Navy PS or PM aircraft. He heard the familiar *kvakeri* sounds through the sonar sound channel of a surface vessel. An aircraft would drop the buoy, and the Soviets at once would hear the *kvakeri* sounds from precisely the direction where the buoy had "landed."

It is significant, added the writer, that the sonar operators of surface vessels had not been given instructions to study the *kvakeri*. Or, he added, the results of such studies could have been so mundane and clear that only the submariners would still carry romantic recollections about the *kvakeri* phenomenon. As for the naval intelligence service, it apparently still secretly dismisses the *kvakeri* phenomenon and probably curses it. The writer also mentioned that the *kvakeri*-emitted sounds always reminded him of the typical dry knocking sound of wooden spoons, as made by spoon players in Russian folk music. All other sounds, he believes, are "from another opera" -- that is, of another origin. As for the *kvakeri* conduct, according to him, it can be completely understood if we are to recall that the buoys contained water-filled cell batteries, and as such batteries discharged, the signals emitted became longer.

FORNICATING LOBSTERS AND OTHER HYPOTHESES

Not everyone in the Soviet Navy shared Vladlen Naumov's conclusions. According to E. Ibragimov, a Soviet captain involved in the research, the *kvakeri* possessed amazing manoeuvrability. They could move at speeds reaching 150–200 knots (up to 229 miles per hour), remaining at nose angle in relationship to a submarine. Another former Soviet submariner, who calls himself Dima the Guru, recalled that the *kvakeri* were heard differently aboard submerged subs.

One time he heard something like a purr, rushing about outside the submarine; the estimated speed of the object was close to 80 knots (92 MPH). Sometimes he felt, but did not hear, a sound he describes as "sh-shshookhhh," as if somewhere close something huge had rushed by -- something obviously that was not a living creature. "How could it live at such speed?" he asked. On occasions, "something" small would lurk around the sub. Dima mentioned that the "guys" who had served aboard the strategic Soviet subs (*strategi* in Russian naval slang), as people who value their secretiveness, gave a semi mystical status to this phenomenon in their conversations. On the contrary, the "guys" from the multi-mission subs treated the *kvakeri* with rather cynical humour, saying that "playful lobsters were fornicating." Sonar stations working in direct listening mode registered sharp changes of bearing in relationship to the objects. In the active mode, they detected objects up to hundreds of feet in size, but only briefly. Dima added that while "on the surface," he had never seen or heard anything about the *kvakeri*. He said he thinks that the experimental manned submarines we know today are not capable of matching the speed of the objects.

According to Admiral Anatoly Alexandrovich Komaritsin, Chief of the Main Directorate (navigation and oceanography) of the Ministry of Defence of the Russian Federation, the Soviets tried to locate and detect the *kvakeri* formations with their acoustical stations. Sometimes, after moving through the area of the *kvakeri* activity, Soviet submarines came to the bases, and the crew discovered that the subs' rubber surfaces were covered with some biological mass. This mass would emit light for a long time, but under the sunlight, the luminescence would eventually disappear. Sonar stations working in direct listening mode registered sharp changes of bearing in relationship to the objects. In active mode, they sighted objects up to hundreds of feet in size, but only briefly. A former Soviet submariner, who stated his name as Sergey Vasilyevich, wrote about his experience with the *kvakeri* in 1985, while serving aboard the K-433 Soviet nuclear submarine in the northern region of the Pacific Ocean.

The K-433 was a Project 667BDR Kalmar class Delta III nuclear-powered ballistic missile submarine of the Soviet Navy and is presently, under the name *Svyatoy Georgiy Pobedonosets*, part of the modern Russian Navy. At a depth of approximately 328 feet, after an hour of "croaking" by *kvakeri*, the submarine encountered and collided with something soft and viscous. The sound was similar to the one that raw meat makes when dropped on a cutting board, but the "piece of meat" was so huge that it forced the submarine cruiser (of 13,000-ton displacement) to shudder and shake.

Sergey Vasilyevich also recalled the incident that took place in 1989 when he was serving aboard the submarine K-211 in the Sea of Japan. The K-211 was also a Project 667BDR Kalmar-class Delta III nuclear-powered ballistic missile submarine; now, as part of the Russian Navy, its name is *Petropavlovsk-Kamchatski*. The submarine joined the Soviet fleet in 1980 and, as of 2009, is active in the Russian Pacific Fleet. At a depth of 328 feet, the Russian sonar operators discovered two underwater targets that caught up with and overtook the submarine cruiser. They moved at a speed of 50 knots (57 MPH), while the Soviet submarine moved at 10 knots (12 MPH). The submarine's commander joked, "Your glorious sonar operators, oh commander of radio engineering, discovered an underwater airplane!" Another former Soviet submariner shared his views on a website forum that discussed the *kvakeri* phenomenon: "You cannot even imagine what took place in the Main Staff of the Soviet Navy during *perestroika* and fraternization when the issue of the *kvakeri* was discussed with NATO. Realistically, NATO thought the *kvakeri* were our weapons, while we thought they were NATO's. It appears they were someone else's. The point is, neither could we build things at that level (that is why we thought about geniuses from NATO), nor could NATO (that is why they thought, 'What in damnation did the Soviets invent?')."

A NATURAL PROPERTY OF WATER

The Russian newspaper *Argumenty I fakty* published an article about *kvakeri* in its June 9, 2010 issue. The author, Yuliya Garmatina, mentioned that eyewitnesses referred to *kvakeri* as "ghosts of the ocean." Many Soviet submarines encountered such ghosts. It seemed to some submariners that the *kvakeri* wanted to ram their vessel and then disappear, as if to dissolve. Sometimes "it," as Garmatina was told, would glow, creating shapes in the water. Garmatina also presented the views of a prominent Russian scientist on the origin of *kvakeri*. This scientist, Aleksandr Smirnov, from the Moscow State Institute of Radio Mechanics, Electronics and Automation (*Moskovskiy Gosuderastvenniy Institut Radiotekhniki, Eletroniki I Avtomatiki*), is an expert on the properties of water. He considers *kvakeri* to be a natural water phenomenon. According to Smirnov, the appearance of *kvakeri* is associated with a change in the structure of water. Depending on the temperature (which can change due to the sun's radiation, weather conditions and currents), water acquires different characteristics. Among them is its ability to change volume, and this change creates the croaking sounds and luminescence. This process is invisible on a small scale, but in the huge expanse of the ocean, it is displayed distinctively.

A passing vessel disturbs water and stimulates its transition from one state into another. The luminescence of the water can be explained from the point of view of physics; in short, it is visible when there is a concentration of the energy of a large number of disturbed molecules. The process can start in one area and gradually spread, creating revolving radiant spiral wheels, circles, etc. Smirnov finds confirmations of his theory in the fact that *kvakeri* are spread all over the global oceans, do not have permanent coordinates, and travel with water currents. They are not really dangerous, although the phenomenon does generate electromagnetic radiation that can interfere with the functioning of electronic equipment.

WARNING OF ECOLOGICAL CATASTROPHE

According to the World Nuclear Association, at the end of the Cold War in 1989 there were over 400 nuclear powered submarines operational or being built worldwide. At least 300 of these submarines have now been scrapped, and some on order have been cancelled due to weapons reduction programs. Today, the U.S., Russia, Great Britain, France and China possess, in total, 160 such submarines. The Arctic has become a graveyard for the once mighty and feared fleet of Soviet nuclear-powered submarines. Perhaps the *kvakeri* were attracted to the nuclear submarines in general because of the unpredictable ecological hazards posed to the environment by such vessels. Nuclear submarines everywhere are extremely prone to disaster. Soviet and Russian nuclear submarines have used enriched uranium for fuel (some as highly enriched as 90 per cent). The spent fuel is tremendously radioactive and contains unburned, highly enriched uranium, plutonium and fission products. Russian submarines in the Arctic are corroding and sinking as their reactor compartments fill with water, foreshadowing a possible ecological catastrophe.

SOVIET RESEARCH PROGRAM TERMINATED

At the close of 1970s, a scientific conference on the *kvakeri* was conducted by the Soviet Navy, but the participants were not able to reach any definitive conclusions. The Soviets even attempted to communicate with the *kvakeri*, but were never able to identify whether the reaction from the phenomenon was intelligent. Some believed the sound was that emitted by killer whales during mating; yet, the *kvakeri* disappeared by 1985 and killer whales keep on mating. Other researchers (such as those at the Russian Academy of Sciences – St Petersburg, who had been involved in the *kvakeri* project) believed that the mysterious phenomenon was an unknown creature with a high level of intelligence—not a mythical creature, but an undiscovered underwater animal. Perhaps the Soviet Navy, not interested in ichthyology, accepted this point of view, because in the early 1980s the *kvakeri* research program was abruptly terminated. Special research groups were disbanded, and the officers who had worked there were given other assignments. All the collected information and data were marked Top Secret and locked away in naval archives. Neither Vadim Kulinchenko nor other former Soviet officers of his rank know why the program was shut down. The reasons why the results of the research have been classified are quite obvious -- Soviet and Russian state military secrets are involved.

RESEARCH FILES REMAIN CLASSIFIED

We repeat -- in Russia, anything related to the nation's naval intelligence and counterintelligence files will not be declassified any time soon. The reasons are obvious. Former chief of the information (naval intelligence) centre of Russia's Northern Fleet, Captain 1st Rank Anatoly Smolovsky, stated: "The Russian Navy Main Staff has information about 15,000 sounds of unknown nature, registered by Soviet and Russian seamen. This information pertains to Russian nuclear submarine cruisers' routes, and, as such, is in direct relationship with Russia's security. Hence, such data will remain secret in the near future." Smolovsky's made this comment in an article by Andrei Moiseyenko and Natalya Lebedeva, published in the Russian newspaper *Komsomol'skaya Pravda–Vladivostok* (November 2, 2008) titled "NLO: kvakayuschiye v okeane" (UFO: Those Who Croak in the Ocean). As for the former submariner Kulinchenko, he tried to collect whatever information was available short of opening the secret files. All these years since the disintegration of the Soviet Union and, still, very little information about the *kvakeri* has leaked out. Those who have researched the phenomenon still have widely differing opinions as to its nature. Apparently the phenomenon is not being researched officially at present, but there are those in Russia who are dedicated to finding out the truth about the mysterious *kvakeri*. After all, they could come back.

THE "SWIMMERS" OF 1982, LAKE BAIKAL OF SIBERIA, LAKE ISSYK-KUL OF CENTRAL ASIA AND OTHER ABODES OF MYSTERIOUS HUMANOIDS

Boris Pavlovich Grabovsky was a Soviet engineer who invented the first fully electronic TV transmitting tube and authored the book *Kosmicheskiy Biofactor*. In the late 1930s, he conducted an intriguing interview with a reluctant witness to an amazing episode of our planet's mysterious past. The interviewee and his friends had explored a cave near Lake Issyk Kul, located in Kyrgyzstan. Inside the cave, the men discovered three human skeletons, each more than 9 feet tall. The skeletons were adorned with decorations that looked like bats [flying mammals] made from silver. The men became greatly frightened and kept silent about their discovery for many long years. They melted down the silver decorations, but kept a small piece in its original form. Soviet scientists who later studied the piece said they could not determine its age.

Interestingly, a Kyrgyz legend does mention a submerged city in the Issyk Kul. The city's ruler was a creature with "long, asinine ears." Lake Issyk Kul, which means "the hot lake" in the Turkic languages of Central Asia, is one of the largest alpine lakes in the world. The Trans-Ili Ala-Tau and the Terskey Ala-Tau mountain ranges stretch along the north shore of the huge deep-water lake; south of the lake, two mountain ranges of the Tian Shan, separated by the valley of the Naryn, stretch in the same direction. From the days of antiquity, the shores of the lake and its waters have held many secrets and mysteries. There are caves of Stone Age people; burial mounds of ancient nomads and Scythian kings; open-air temples and many strange rock drawings; ruins of long forgotten cities; and remnants of lost civilizations buried underwater.

The earliest mention of gigantic beings dates back to early 1900's. Several boys in the country of Georgia (at the time, part of the Russian Empire) discovered a cave inside a mountain, full of humanoid skeletons. Each skeleton was about 9 feet tall. To get to the cave, the boys had to dive into a lake. George Papashvili and his wife recalled the incident in the 1925 book *Anything Can Happen,* (New York, St. Martin's Press). In the summer of 1982 Mark Shteynberg, along with Lieutenant Colonel Gennady Zverev, were conducting routine training of the reconnaissance divers ("frogmen") of the Turkestan and Central Asian military regions. The training exercises had been taking place at the Issyk Kul Lake.

Quite unexpectedly, the officers were paid a visit by a very important official, Major-General V. Demyanenko, commander of the Military Diver Service of the Engineer Forces of the Ministry of Defence, USSR. He arrived to inform the local officers of an extraordinary event that had occurred during similar training exercises in the Trans-Baikal and West Siberian military regions. There, during their military training dives, the frogmen had encountered mysterious underwater swimmers -- human-like, except that their size was much larger (almost 9 feet tall). The swimmers were clad in tight-fitting silvery suits, despite icy-cold water temperatures. At the depth of 164 feet, these "swimmers" had neither scuba diving equipment ("aqualungs"), nor any other equipment – only sphere-like helmets concealing their heads.

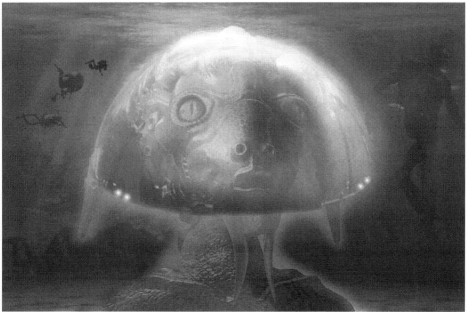

Artist impression of 'the swimmers'. Copyright Daniel Ramirez

The local military commander, who was quite alarmed by such encounters, decided to capture one of the creatures. To complete the mission, a special group of seven divers, under the command of an officer, had been dispatched. As the frogman tried to cover the creature with a net, the entire group was thrown out of the deep waters to the surface by a powerful, invisible force.

Due to the sudden decompression, all the members of the ill-fated expedition were stricken by aeroembolism. The only remedial treatment available consisted of an immediate confinement under decompression conditions in a pressure chamber. They had several such pressure chambers in the military region, but only one in working condition. It could contain no more than two persons at a time. The local commanding officer ordered that all four frogmen be squeezed into the chamber. As a result, three of them, including the leader of the group, died, and the rest became invalids -- terrible consequences caused by the usual Soviet military inefficiency and incompetence.

The major-general rushed to the Issyk Kul to warn the local military against similar "devil-may-care" actions. Although the Issyk Kul Lake is shallower than the Baikal Lake, the depth of the former was sufficient to contain similar mysterious creatures. Did the major-general know something that Officer Shteynberg did not? A short time later, the staff headquarters of the Turkmenistan military region had received an order from the Commander-in-Chief of the Land Forces. The order consisted of detailed analysis of the Baikal Lake events and reprimands. It was supplemented by an information bulletin from the headquarters of the Engineer Forces of the Ministry of Defence, USSR. The bulletin listed numerous deepwater lakes where there had been registered sightings of anomalous phenomena -- appearances of underwater creatures analogous to the Baikal type, descent and surfacing of giant discs and spheres, powerful luminescence emanating from the deep, etc. Such documents, without exception, were highly classified and "for the eyes only" of a very limited circle of military officers. The purpose for such documents was "to prevent unnecessary encounters...."

The territory under the military unit jurisdiction, where Shteynberg had served, contained an anomalous water reservoir, the Sarez Lake in the Pamir area, roughly a mile deep. Sarez was visible to those stationed at a "tracking point" in the Pamir Mountains, where Soviets tracked the movements of American SDI satellites. Super powerful instruments, equipment and devices of the Soviet military sub-unit had repeatedly registered disc-like objects, plunging down into the lake and later surfacing for lift-off. Lake Sarez, located deep in the Pamir Mountains of Tajikistan, was created in 1911 when a strong earthquake triggered a massive landslide that, in turn, became a huge dam along the Murghob River, now called the Usoi Dam. The area experiences considerable seismic activity. It is possible that part of the right bank may slump into the lake, creating a gigantic wave that will top over and possibly breach the natural dam, creating a catastrophic flood downstream reaching all the way to the Aral Sea. Since the year 2004, the lake has been monitored for surging water levels or other events that might cause the dam to fail. According to a Soviet military report mentioned by Mark Shteynberg, UFOs have been "monitoring" Sarez since the 1980s. According to V. Pravdivtsev, a Russian colonel, scientist, and film director, most USO observations during the 1980s were registered in the northern seas of the Soviet Union. This was disclosed in "Kto vi, ikhtiandri" (Who Are You, Fish Men?), his article in the *Na Grani Nevozmozhnogo*, newspaper [Issue 4 (232), 2000]. For example, Russian ufologists had confirmed that, in the years 1980 and 1981 alone, residents of the Kola Peninsula had observed numerous USOs ascending from the sea. Apparently, Central Asia had been of interest to UFOs and USOs, too.

Here are some examples. In February of 1990, in the Ak Suu Gorge near the Issyk Kul, local shepherds observed a large sphere at an altitude of 2,300 feet. The sphere separated into four parts that flew into different directions, only to recombine into a sphere half a minute later. This was repeated three times, and afterward, the sphere flew toward the lake. This report was published in Mikhail Yeltsin's 1992 book *K razgdake NLO* or *To find meaning of UFOs*. On June 20, 1990, an expedition of the SAKKUFON research organization made its way to the Tien Shan Mountains, on the Sino-Soviet border.

It was comprised of scientists, military personnel, civilians, KGB officers, and ufologists. Two eyewitnesses, members of the expedition, observed a triangular UFO over the Issyk Kul Lake. The object, which had bright, luminescent lights, hovered at an altitude of only about 65 feet. It suddenly turned around and then vanished. Later it flew over the main group of the expedition. Mikhail Demidenko, a Russian writer who passed away in 2003, read Shteynberg's account in 1992, and recalled that while on an assignment from the Union of Writers in 1986 in Irkutsk (Siberia), he spent some time at the Baikal Lake. There he learned from local fishermen that some years before, they observed Soviet frogmen being propelled out of the lake and up to 50 feet into the air. The locals never found out how the frogmen were able to accomplish such incredible feats.

Demidenko thought it might be the same episode where the seven frogmen had been expelled from underwater while trying to capture one of the mysterious "swimmers." He contacted his sources in the highest echelons of the Russian Army, but to no avail. Finally, the writer did speak with a colonel from the Chief Logistics Directorate who tried to help him. Demidenko found out from him later that such information would be kept in special archives that required top clearance. Demidenko was a true humanitarian who hated totalitarianism of any kind -- a tolerant man who survived the Nazi occupation and remembered the horror of Nazi atrocities against Soviet Jews. As a young man Demidenko, upon graduation from a military college, became a translator and interpreter of Chinese. He was dispatched by the General Staff of the Soviet Army to Red China's Air Force headquarters and also served in North Korea during the war. Later, Demidenko travelled through China to Western Tibet, and when he became a well-known author and scriptwriter, he visited a number of countries in Southeast Asia, and Europe. In his travels, he collected fascinating stories that he later included in his books, including *Po sledam SS v Tibet* (*Following the SS trail into Tibet*), published in 1999.

In 1954, Demidenko was accompanying high-ranking Beijing and Soviet military commanders as they inspected Red Chinese troops in Xinjiang Province (Uygur Autonomous Region), and Western Tibet, where the group spent a night in a Lamaist monastery. There, Demidenko met an old monk, who was a Russian-speaking Mongol. Among many fascinating subjects, the monk told him of the caves in the Tibetan mountains where 9-foot tall giants remained in an anaesthesia-induced sleep. One day they may wake-up, according to the monk. Later, Demidenko heard stories that Red Chinese troops broke into one such sacred cave, removed the "sleeping amphibian giants," and publicly hanged them. Demidenko had great connections in the Asian, East German, and Russian armed forces. As Demidenko's well-researched book points out, the occult oriented Nazis were quite aware of the giants and of legends about the underground cities of Tibet. That is why Hitler sent his SS expeditions to Tibet, as he was certain that these giants-demigods would somehow bolster his bizarre theories of Aryan supremacy. We should add that in 1904 there had been numerous UFO reports in the Lake Baikal area. Witnesses saw in the sky black objects with searchlights; objects with strange "wheels" that rotated and opened; multi-colored lights; and cigar-shaped objects with "signal" lights. Observers said the objects performed complex manoeuvres and landings. For example, workers for the Trans-Baikal railroad claimed they saw mysterious "spheres" with rotating searchlights.

A very unusual incident took place in May of 1964 in the area of the lake. An anti-aircraft missile unit, located about 15 miles from Ulan-Ude, was attacked by an unknown force during the night of May 17-18. There was a glow that ascended over Lake Baikal in the evening on the 17th, and spread over the area. It was no sunset. The military decided that the taiga was ablaze. Later, they lost radio communication with the outside world due to strong interference.

Over the horizon, from the direction of the lake, a fiery orange sphere ascended. Like a living organism, the sphere pulsated, emitting a very strong radiance. The sphere was approximately the size of the midday sun, but not as bright, and one could view it without the use of dark lenses. The military unit sounded the alarm. As the time went on, radio communications remained unavailable, and the soldiers were only able to use the regular phone line to report to their commanding officer. The fiery sphere continued its advance. The luminosity it radiated, like a burning fog, enveloped everything in its way. The commanding officer ordered that radiation be measured every thirty minutes and reports be sent to the command center. Soldiers put on gasmasks and other protective means. But there was no radiation. The sphere approached the unit's position at the height of a telegraph post, stopping along the way. As it approached, the brightness of the body diminished, as if it gave away all of its energy to the radiance it emitted. When the first "tongues" of the radiance, as if luminescent fog or another substance, started to envelop the military position, the commander ordered the men to stop taking measurements, lock ventilation locks, turn on the autonomous life support system, and hide. They did so and remained in hiding until the perceived danger had passed. KGB agents arrived on site shortly after the incident and conducted an investigation. Those involved never learned any more about what phenomenon they had encountered at the lake.

Another incident reported by V. Pupkov, a Lieutenant Colonel (Retired), took place at the Domna airfield in the Trans-Baikal military district, in December 1980. In the late evening hours, a red, luminescent UFO shaped like a ring suddenly appeared over the airfield. The UFO pulsated, and emitted several reddish rays to the ground. A MIG-23 was scrambled. Colonel Antonetz, who flew it, reported the UFO to be at the altitude of 13,000 feet. The object slowly dimmed, and disappeared. Soon thereafter a special commission arrived in the airfield, investigated, and took signed secrecy oaths. No one found out what happened to the collected information. Colonel Antonetz later, after the fall of the USSR, was appointed Commander of Ukraine's Air Force. The Republic of Buryatia is located in central part of the continent of Asia. The total area of the republic is 218 square miles, about the size of Germany. It is bounded by Irkutsk and Chita regions, Republic of Tuva and Mongolia and is bordered by one of the greatest and magnificent lakes in the world, Lake Baikal.

According to the Buryat legends, Lake Baikal has no bottom. The lake is connected with all oceans, seas, and rivers. In its depths is a silver castle of Erlik-Khan, the Ruler of Destinies. Russian historian and writer Aleksey Tivanenko, who resides in the city of Ulan Ude of the Buryatia republic [part of the Russian Federation, 62 miles from Lake Baikal], has researched the history of this Siberian lake. He states that UFOs have been observed over Baikal for at least the past two centuries.

There are eyewitness reports in 19th century newspapers, as well as in the ancient legends of the Buryat people. For example, the Irkutsk Chronicles of N. S. Romanov, dating back to 1884, contain description of a gigantic glowing sphere with numerous portholes seen hovering over Baikal. Numerous eyewitnesses saw the phenomenon. At that time, there were no airplanes, dirigibles, or meteorological balloons in the area that could be mistaken for UFOs. Tivanenko, and other people who live in the area of Lake Baikal, frequently observe UFOs over the lake, and over Buryatia. In the autumn of 1965, a gigantic cigar-shaped, radiant object flew across Baikal, leaving behind a typical inversion layer, just as a jet aircraft would. No sound of any kind was heard. The diameter of the UFO was estimated to be around 820 feet. While approaching the Hamar-Badan mountain range, the UFO dispatched three small radiant spheres from its bottom part. The smaller craft were yellow, pink, and blue, and they flew in different directions at the same speed as the cigar-shaped object. Many years later, historian Tivanenko found a report about this UFO in an official bulletin of the Commission for Anomalous Phenomena.

There is a story well-known to denizens of Buryatia. On one of the mountains surrounding the Kudara-Somon settlement, a manned apparatus had landed. Humanoid beings dressed in shining spacesuits exited the craft. Some locals, among them a district militia [police] officer on motorcycle, set out to the UFO landing site, but when the humans approached, the object lifted off at a high rate of speed and flew away toward Mongolia. Tivanenko continues to research odd incidents in the area, as reported in an article published in *People* newspaper (July 17, 2009 issue). In it, Tivanenko described recent sightings of orange spheres over the lake. The objects moved noiselessly, approaching each other and then departing. A reader later commented that he had observed the UFOs on the very same Saturday. They followed one another, and glowed like searchlights, at altitudes much lower than those of satellites. Also, unlike satellites, the objects vanished instantly. He had observed similar objects in the previous year. The Borisoglebsk Giant case may also have a direct connection to the mysterious "swimmers." Again, we must delve into the secret Soviet SETKA program. Eduard A. Yermilov, a distinguished Russian scientist in the prestigious Radio-Physics Science Research Institute, had been involved with the SETKA (the Galaktika-AN) program and investigated the 1982 case that very likely involved a humanoid "giant" of the same type.

Borisoglebsk, located in the Voronezh region, is one of the most active areas for UFO sightings, according to A. Plaksin, an expert with the Defence Ministry of the Russian Federation, and a former leading participant of the SETKA program. A special military commission was created in the 1980s specifically to study the UFOs in the area. The objects sighted and reported by military observers varied in size from tennis ball size to 650 feet long, and they manoeuvred at speeds ranging from 0 to 372 miles per hour at altitudes ranging up to 12 miles. And so, E. Yermilov, a scientist from Gor'ky who worked for SETKA, according to both Colonel Gherman Kolchin and Mikhail Gershtein, reported that on May 26, 1982, during the loss of communications with a MIG-21 aircraft and its subsequent crash, a UFO was sighted at the altitude of 5000 feet.

A search and recovery operation was organized. On May 27, the search team, which included Junior Sergeant A. A. Panyukov and Private A. Yu. Kunin, while in the Povorino area forest, walked into a clearing where they observed a humanoid entity. The being was no less than 11 feet tall, dressed in silvery clothing with a green hue. After the entity fled the site of the incident, the eyewitnesses observed an explosion behind the trees and the flight of a luminescent object that left a slightly glowing trail. The object disappeared beyond the tree line. This episode was confirmed by Colonel Kolchin, in his 1997 book *Fenomen NLO-vzglyad iz Rossii* or *UFO Phenomenon: A View From Russia*. E. Yermilov also told about strange Borisoglebsk aircraft breakdowns to Gherman Kolchin and Arvid Mordvin-Schadro, who were at the time chiefs of the Leningrad Commission for Anomalous Phenomena of the Geographic Society of the USSR.

The mysterious "swimmers" have not disappeared from Russia's waters. *Komsomol'skaya Pravda* carried an article on the phenomenon by A. Pavlov in its December 1, 2000 issue. The report also described a close relationship that had developed between local Russian military and UFO researchers, among the latter, Dr. Dvuzhilni, famous for his research into the Dalnegorsk Crash case, which we mentioned in chapter one. Among the documents provided by the commander of the Far Eastern Air Defence District to local ufologists was one that mentioned an encounter with mysterious beings in 1990. A military brigade at the Timofeyevka settlement was dispatched due to an alarm raised by a sentry who fired a warning shot at two creatures that suddenly came out of a nearby oak grove. The sentry observed two beings, about 8 feet tall and clad in silvery overalls. Right after the warning shot, the "silvery ones" immediately ran back into the forest. The soil was wet because a recent rain, and the Russian counterintelligence officers who came to the site, discovered the footprints of huge, shapeless "feet." There have been other fascinating reports of sightings of creatures that may be those mysterious "swimmers." Yekaterina Vorontsova published a curious article in *NLO Magazine*, Issue 3, in 2001. She mentioned that the Russian intelligence services had declassified KGB files pertaining to the UFO phenomenon. This document release was separate from the September 1991 files declassified by KGB and turned over to Pavel Popovich. According to the materials presented in Vorontsova's article, in 1984 in the Baltic Sea, unusual, "huge" fish had been observed by crew of a Soviet submarine. The witnesses said the "fish" actually looked more like 9-foot-tall humanoids dressed in silver suits. Of course, humans could not be swimming around without diving suits at a depth of 1,300 feet. We have been unsuccessful in our attempts to contact the author of this article, Yekaterina Vorontsova, in hopes of obtaining more information about the case and about the reported KGB document releases. Our request to *NLO Magazine* to put us in contact with the author did not receive a response.

UFO over Murmansk, 1978

In another fascinating case, B. Borovikov hunted Black Sea sharks for many years until a very disturbing encounter put an end to his hobby. Diving in the Anapa area, he descended to the depth of 26 feet, where he saw gigantic, humanoid beings rising up from below. They were milky-white with human-appearing faces, but the bottom half of their bodies had something that resembled fish tails. The creature that was swimming ahead of its companions noticed Borovikov and stopped. It had giant bulging eyes, almost as if magnified by thick lenses. The other two creatures joined the leader, who then waved its hand [it was definitely a hand with membranes] towards the diver. The creatures approached the diver, and stopped a short distance away, turned around slowly, and swam away. Borovikov's experience was published in the book *XX vek: khronika neobjasnimogo* (Moscow, 1996). In another sighting, D. Povaliyayev was hang-gliding over Kavgolovo (Leningrad area) in the early 1990's. There are lakes in the area, and in one of them, the skydiver noticed three giant "fish." He descended, and was able to discern that the creatures were "swimmers" dressed in silvery costumes. He mentioned the episode in *Letuchi Gollandets*, published in 1995. There also have been many UFO sightings in the Kavgolovo area.

THE NIVATA-KAVACHAS

Perhaps the answer as to the identity of the "swimmers" can be found in Hindu mythology. Indra is the god of the firmament, the personification of the Earth's atmosphere. In the *Vedas*, he stands in the first rank among the gods. Arjuna ("White") was Indra's son and had four brothers.

When the five brothers went into exile for thirteen years, Arjuna continued on a pilgrimage to the Himalayan Mountains to placate the gods and to obtain from them celestial weapons for use in war. Although he initially battled Shiva [wearing a disguise], having found out his true identity, Arjuna then worshipped him. Shiva gave him the *pasupata* (a missile-like warhead), one of his most powerful weapons. Indra, as well as other deities, came to Arjuna and gave him their own powerful weapons. Indra carried Arjuna in his transportation vehicle to Indra's heaven. There, Arjuna was immersed in learning on the proper use of the weapons presented to him and made a promise to Indra that he would never discharge those celestial weapons at mortals, except when all my other arms failed.

Later, Indra sent him on a mission against the Daityas [Titans] of the sea. Daityas were descendants of the goddess Diti by Kasyapa. They are a race of demons and giants, who warred against the gods and interfered with sacrifices. Kasyapa's sons by Diti became Asuras (Daityas), and his sons by Aditi (one of Diti's sisters) became Devas (Aditeyas). Nivata-Kavachas, translated from Sanskrit as either "clothed in impenetrable armour" (or as "of practical application - layer - garment") were a class of Daityas descended from Prahlada (a son of Hiranyakasipu). The Sanskrit word Ni-Vata-Kavacha, according to Jijith Nadumuri Ravi, means Ni (no) – vata (air) – Kavacha (casing, shelter, garment, and coat-ofmail) -- sheltered in airless capsules, or wearing garments without air. Some researchers consider this a description of a spacesuit. Ravi believes that it either describes their air-tight garments or their air-tight dwellings. Ravi is a researcher and writer in India whose website, as of this writing, was at: *http://ancientvoice.wikidot.com*.

Now, Hiranyakasipu, in his wars with the gods, had wrested the sovereignty of heaven from Indra and dwelt there in luxury. After the death of his father, Prahlada became king of the Daityas. According to the *Mahabharata*, this celestial race of Asura (Danava) demons, in Vedic mythology, were thirty million in number and dwelt in the depths of the oceans. The Danavas were the sons of Danu. They revolted against the gods, but were defeated. After their defeat, the Danavas were cast into the deepest oceans and locked there forever by Indra. As per Hindu mythology, Nivata-Kavachas were the Danavas or demons. They were humanoid, with fish-like characteristics. In the *Mahabharata*, Nivata-Kavachas' destruction is described as one of the exploits of Arjuna. Indra told him to do battle the Nivata-Kavachas, his enemies, whose strength increased. The gods were fearful of these demons. My enemies, those Danavas named Nivata-Kavachas, dwelled in the womb of the ocean. They number thirty million, are notorious, and are all of equal form and strength and splendour. For his battle against the sea demons, Arjuna used a car or chariot, a vehicle of some sort, driven by Matali. Arjuna tried using several weapons, but in order to win the battle, Arjuna had to discharge "that celestial weapon which I had learned from Indra -- even the dreadful and flaming Visoshana" Arjuna also used "illusion-creating weapons" ["an illusion of arms capable of bewildering all beings"] against the Asuras, who ["of unrivalled prowess"] also used "horrible illusion weapons," as well as tectonic and ultrasound weapons of their own. As they battled with the "illusion-creating weapons," the world around them "displayed itself," then would be "devoured by darkness," only to disappear from view, submerged underwater.

Attacked by the "fierce" Nivata-Kavachas, Arjuna fought them and sent them to Yama (the lord of death) mansion. The final annihilation of the daityas seemed at hand. But then they used "illusion," and Arjuna could not see the danavas any more. (*Mahabharata*, Book III, Chapter 167). At the end, Arjuna won the battle. The Nivata-Kavachas were destroyed. But, perhaps, some of them managed to escape, and have operated in the oceans, seas, rivers and lakes of our planet.

The city of the demons, destroyed by Arjuna, was the Daitya city of Hiranyapura "on the other side of the ocean." It used to belong to the celestial deities, but they were overpowered and driven out by Nivata-Kavachas." Hiranyapura was the capital city of the Nivata-Kavachas, and it situated on the other side of the great lake [Caspian Sea, Aral or some other large lake, which could also be Lake Baikal]. Jijith Nadumuri Ravi does not have enough information to say precisely which one, but it should be closer to the Deva territories in Tibet (near Manasa Lake and Kailasa range), while the Deva territories lied to the opposite side of the lake. It was a city superior to the one the lord of celestials, Purandara, had possessed. But only Arjuna was able to overpower the Nivata-Kavachas. "Then, in order to carry out their slaughter, Indra rendered unto thee those weapons. The gods had been unable to slay these, who have been slain by thee." As Arjuna's car entered the city, he noticed that "when the Danava hosts had been destroyed, all their females began to bewail in that city, like unto cranes in autumn. Then, with Matali entered in that city, terrifying, with the rattling of my car, the wives of the Nivata-Kavachas. Beholding that excellent city, superior to the city of the celestials themselves. But what if the city was located elsewhere? According to the Indian researcher Ravi, it was. Naga refers to a tribe called Nagas who were a group of people spread throughout India during the period of the epic *Mahabharata*. They were also considered as one of the supernatural races like Kinnaras and Yakshas. Vishnu, the younger brother of Deva king Indra, had slain the Nagas in the great lake. Indra asked Arjuna to slay the tribe of Nivata-kavachas, a clan of Asuras, living in the vicinity of the same lake. But could it have been Lake Baikal?

Sometime back, in March 2006, Jijith Nadumuri Ravi has written several articles speculating about the possibility that the exotic tribes like Devas, Yakshas, Gandharvas, etc, mentioned in Mahabharata were aliens or an ancient human civilization that interacted heavily with aliens. *Mahabharata* considers their territory as trans-Himalayan. Again, Ravi places them in Tibet, in the surrounding the Kailasa Range and Manasa Lake (Manasa-sarovara, Manasarovara), since these two are mentioned in Mahabharata as abodes of these tribes. These geographical entities have retained their name even to current times (Manasasarovara, Kailasa). Hence they are easily identifiable even today by the same name. However, there is a tribe called the Manasas, mentioned in a region (Dwipa) called Saka-Dwipa, which is identified by many as falling further north so can be identified with places in Mongolia or Siberia.

Nivata Kavachas lived next to a large lake. But it is difficult to identify which one, since to the north of Himalayas there are several large lakes in Tibet, Central Asia, Russia and West Asia. Obviously the Caspian Sea is the biggest of them. If we include the Siberia region, then Lake Baikal too is a possibility. Ancient literature describe Nivata-Kavachas as living not just near the lake but *under* the lake or sea, though it is considered by many as an exaggeration.

If we take this literally, then their city Hiranyapura has to be considered as an underwater city or perhaps even a submerged spaceship. We now know that the Nivata-Kavachas were destroyed by Arjuna. But, perhaps, some of them managed to escape and have operated in the oceans, seas, rivers and lakes of our planet. We are certain that mankind will find that out soon enough.

RUSSIAN SUBMARINES AND USOs

V.V. Krapiva, a researcher and writer who resides in Odessa, Ukraine, years ago attended numerous lectures presented by veteran officers of Soviet nuclear-powered submarines. The officers served in the Soviet North, aboard secret naval installations and bases. The lectures sometimes veered off from the planned presentations, and many spellbinding tales were told as a result. Some lecturers recalled instances of Soviet sonar-operators (military hydro acoustics technicians) who "heard" strange "targets" at great depths. Sometimes it sounded as if Soviet Navy submarines were being chased by other "submarines." The pursuers changed their speed at will, with velocities that were much greater than any other similar vessel in the world could produce at that time. Lieutenant-Commander Oleg Sokolov told his audience that while on duty aboard his submarine, he had observed the ascent of a strange object from the water. He was not able to identify it, because he viewed it through his ships periscope. This underwater "take off" took place in the early 1960's. An interesting observation of a UFO was recorded by a crew of a Soviet nuclear submarine in 1965. This case is on file in the Colonel Kolchin archives. All those who had observed the UFO, were ordered to report the details and provide drawings to the Special Department (i.e., Naval Intelligence). The submarine was to rendezvous with a ship in the Atlantic Ocean. They arrived to the meeting place an hour and a half ahead of schedule, and the captain allowed his crew to go up to the outside deck. No ships were in the area, and the sky was starry and cloudless. Then the watchman observed a cigar-shaped object moving noiselessly through the sky. Although the submarine was in international waters at the time, the Soviets assumed the unidentified object was American and decided to dive immediately. But their onboard radar did not detect anything, and the captain decided to stay hold his position. Suddenly three rays shot out from the UFO, and the Soviet submariners noticed something very unusual around the object.

The UFO had no gondolas and no horizontal or vertical rudders. The object was about 650-800 feet long, and Soviet submariners were not familiar with this type of airship, for those used by the U.S. Air Force were much smaller. Then, something strange happened. The UFO slowly descended to the surface of the ocean, its searchlights still on, about half a mile from the submarine, and dived underwater. The submarine's sonar registered a strange, intense hissing sound, as the UFO submerged, followed by silence. A similar object was observed in 1964 by well-known Soviet UFO researcher and author A.S. Kuzovkin, which originally inspired him to engage UFO research. He was a physicist and researched ecology of anomalous phenomena for *Vokrug Sveta*, a very popular Soviet magazine.

Aleksandr Sergeyevich Kuzovkin, who passed away in 2001, was a well known Soviet and Russian researcher of UFO phenomenon. From 1977 through 1988 Kuzovkin worked with Feliks Zigel. In 1989-90, as a leading expert on UFO photography and the photography of "invisible" beings, he conducted a seminar together with E. Semyonov (*Ecology of the Unknown*). By 1990, Kuzovkin had collected over ten thousand reports of Soviet UFO sightings. He believed that Earth was a living organism, maimed and injured by uncaring, greedy humans. He was afraid that our hullabaloo around anomalous phenomena and UFOs, as well as our interference in their affair could cause unpredictable consequences. Kuzovkin mentioned in his interviews that Russian science still refused to consider the UFO phenomenon as anything serious, while research groups in the United States knew the seriousness of it. Ufological research was also taken seriously in Europe, and in China, he argued. In 1993, Kuzovkin officially rejected any further research into the study of anomalous phenomena, and burned most of Kuzovkin's archives and photographs of UFOs. Kuzovkin mentioned in his writings (*Ekho Planeti*, Russia, 1990) that while visiting Sevastopol, a port city in Ukraine, he met with local marine scientists who had descended into the depths of the Black Sea in deep-water bathyscaphes. They observed, among other things, an object that resembled a wheel, as large as a ten-story building, standing vertically underwater. The scientists saw and later described to Kuzovkin that the "wheel" that would remain immobile for a while and then would move into a horizontal position, rotate, and depart.

Another well-known Russian researcher of the paranormal and author Aleksandr Petukhov, mentioned a USO incident from 1951. It took place in the territorial waters of the USSR. A Soviet submarine encountered a strange underwater object of gigantic size; it did not react to the submarine communication to identify itself, and continued an unhurried movement towards the nation's shores. The captain of the submarine ordered depth bombs to be dropped onto the site where USO was located. The unidentified object did not react to the attack, and continued its course, at the same speed. After a while, it unexpectedly and abruptly ascended to the surface of the sea. At a depth of about 160 feet, it stopped its ascent, changed the course, and departed. In July 1978, at between 7:30 and 8:40 a.m., a pearl-white UFO that looked like a flattened out sphere was sighted in the Mediterranean. The object, which had three protruding, antenna-like constructions on its bottom portion, was moving from east to west. The coordinates for the sighting were 37 degrees north (latitude) and 3 degrees, 40 minutes east (longitude). The captain of the Soviet ship *Yargora* immediately sent a radiogram about it to the Soviet Academy of Sciences. No reply to the radiogram ever came from the Academy. This sighting was mentioned in the 2001 article written by Valentin Psalomschikov, and published in *NLO Magazine*. An unnamed Russian source mentioned that *Yargora*'s Captain Cherepanov sent a telegram from the ship to Moscow, Soviet Academy of Sciences, regarding the sighting.

UFO Photographed Over Sea

On December 26, 2002, Russian newspaper *Zhizn* published an article about Soviet observations of UFOs. Yevgeny Litvinov, Chairman of the Anomalous Phenomena Commission of the Russian Geographical Society in Saint Petersburg, made a presentation at the society's monthly meeting. Formerly named the Leningrad Commission for Anomalous Phenomena of the Geographic Society of the USSR, it was organized in 1980. The society had studied tens of thousands of cases UFO sightings, and had reached the conclusion that UFOs are real.

Litvinov recalled that his experience with UFOs had begun when he was a Soviet Navy officer. He did not take seriously any published UFO-related information until the winter of 1979-80, when several incidents rocked the Northern Fleet, forcing the Soviet General Staff to reconsider its dismissive attitude toward UFOs. The strange objects visited a Soviet submarine base at the Western Dvina every week over a six month period. The craft were shaped like disks and hovered over the armament test area, used for testing mines, torpedoes, and nuclear weapons. The UFOs also flew all around the top secret Soviet military base. While the military personnel observed these flying saucers, the radar systems on the ground did not register anything. Captain Beregovoy, head of the Naval Intelligence for the Northern Fleet, ordered that photographs of the UFOs be taken, but to no avail. The film turned out to be inadvertently exposed each time. Initially the Soviets suspected the objects were some kind of NATO spy technology, but Russian scientists explained to the military that NATO, and indeed no nation on Earth, possessed any technology of that sophistication. To prevent panic, those in command told their military personnel that the UFOs were actually Soviet-made experimental aircraft engaged in test missions. Of course, high-ranking officers knew better.

Some rather serious encounters took place that same winter. The crew of a Soviet Project 671 submarine ("Victor" class sub, per NATO classification), commanded by Aleksey Korzhev encountered a UFO. The submarine was on its way back to base, alternately surfacing and then descending to 650 feet, in an effort to remain undetected by spy satellites. Suddenly, the sub received a report of an incoming aircraft headed straight for their position, despite the fact that the weather was not conducive to air traffic. Then, about 160 feet from the sub, a silvery disc appeared, hovering ahead of the sub and matching its speed and course, but staying a bit ahead of it.

As the crew looked at it, they were mesmerized by it. Next, the UFO emitted a ray of bright, white light that, contrary to the laws of physics, did not reach the water's surface immediately but rather descended as is if slow motion. Korzhev immediately ordered a change in the ship's course. As the submarine moved away, the disc slowly ascended and disappeared into the clouds. Litvinov said the Soviets thought the UFO wanted to scan the submarine, which happened to be carrying some new weapon technologies aboard. Mikhail Soroka, a paranormal phenomena researcher from Kiyiv, Ukraine, described the same incident in more detail in an interview he gave to the *FAKTY* newspaper (December, 2007). Soroka said that the nuclear submarine was actually being accompanied by a Soviet surface vessel during the mission. When the sub surfaced, a large object appeared in the sky, whose shape was that of a mushroom with its cap turned down. Its bottom part was bathed in white light, above which shone a yellow light, then a pale red light, and finally a bright red light at the very top. The object approached the two Soviet ships, and then directed toward one of them a ray or searchlight. Then the object unexpectedly disappeared. This encounter was disclosed by Aleksey Korzhev, Captain 1st rank, added Soroka. He also mentioned that Soviet Navy intelligence believed that UFOs generally tended to appear near military vessels and coastal installations. Later, when Litvinov was part of the special commission of the Soviet Navy's Main Staff, he was able to read dozens of UFO reports that came from the intelligence channels. One report described a UFO landing in the Motovsky Bay (located in the Barents Sea). Years later, a leakage of liquid radioactive waste from a spent fuel storage facility took place in the Motovsky Bay and Litsa Fjord.

Zapadnaya Litsa is the largest and most important Russian naval base for nuclear-powered submarines. The base is located on the Litsa Fjord at the westernmost point of the Kola Peninsula, about 27 miles from the Norwegian border. The Litsa Fjord heads into the Kola Peninsula interior from the Motovsky Fjord, just across from the south-eastern coast of the Rybachiy Peninsula. Few people in the West know exactly what was going on there during Soviet rule. Multiple UFO sightings occurred and yet no radar station in the vicinity could detect the object. Soviet experts theorized that the UFOs were surrounded by some type of ionized cloud, which prevented them from being detected by radar.

Another incident, mentioned by Litvinov to Zhizn, comes from the archives of the Russia's Geographic Society. It took place in the Mediterranean, in November 1976. Soviet diesel submarine Project 641 ("Foxtrot," per NATO classification) navigated through the Gibraltar channel and then surfaced. It was at 2:00 am, and the sea was absolutely still. The captain, the watch officer, and signalman came to the submarine deck to verify the vessel's coordinates. Suddenly, they noticed a radiant, silvery sphere to the left, over the horizon. The sphere ascended rapidly, and suddenly they saw right in front of the submarine, displayed on the water, a radiant map of the Mediterranean – believed to have been projected by the UFO. The map image appeared at precisely the moment when the submarine navigator was trying to determine the ships location using the position of stars. The impression was that someone aboard the UFO read the Russia navigator's thoughts and displayed the map in response. Interestingly, the radiant map also indicated the sub's position. Shortly after the UFO flew away, the map disappeared.

Litvinov revealed in the interview that he is convinced that UFOs exist. However, he puts aside his personal convictions when he considers the truthfulness of data regarding UFO sightings. He has developed a complex method for systematic selection (as is done by intelligence officers). His scale of credible authenticity is based on 350 criteria. Litvinov has concluded that out of all data he examined, about seventy percent are explainable, being caused by natural phenomena or confusion on the part of the witnesses. But the other thirty percent are legitimate observations of real UFOs. There are too many of them to simply wave them away. His database contains ten thousand observations and incidents. Litvinov stated that most often UFOs are observed over military installations, areas of ecological disasters, and geological faults.

In the 1970s, reports issued by Rear Admiral Viktor A. Domislovsky, chief of the Pacific Fleet's Intelligence Department, described an unknown, gigantic cylindrical object sighted by the Soviet Navy in "faraway" regions of Pacific Ocean. The object was 2,600-3,000 feet long. When it hovered over the ocean, smaller objects exited from one of its ends ["like bees from a beehive"] and descended into the waters. Some time later, they re-entered the larger ship. After the smaller objects thus "loaded" inside, the UFO would fly away and disappear over the horizon. This information was revealed in Vladimir Ajaja's interviews with the Russian media. Our research confirmed that Domislovsky was in charge of the Fleet's intelligence from 1970 to 1975. A distinguished WWII veteran and former submariner who passed away in 1979, he had been involved with Navy intelligence since 1953, serving from the Baltic to the Pacific. According to *MosNews.com* (July 16, 2009), former Rear Admiral and nuclear submarine commander Yury Beketov was quoted describing events that occurred in the Bermuda Triangle. "We repeatedly observed that the instruments detected the movements of material objects at unimaginable speed, around 230 knots (400 km. per hour [250 MPH]). It's hard to reach that speed on the surface – only in the air … The beings that created those material objects significantly exceed us in development." Russian Naval intelligence expert and Captain 1st Rank Igor Barklay noted that the unidentified objects were most often spotted in deep water near where military forces are concentrated – off the Bahamas, Bermuda, Puerto Rico and the east coast of the United States.

The February issue of the remarkable Belarus newspaper *Sekretniye Issledovaniya* (Issue 3[212]), contained an article written by Valeriya Peresilkina. Titled "Zagadki glubin" (Secrets of the depths), it lists cases of USOs observed by the Russian Navy in the various seas of our planet. The author mentions Captain 1st Rank (retired) Yuri Vinogradov who served in the Soviet Navy from 1975 to 2000. He, a top expert in his field, had been involved in a number of submarine search and recovery operations, was a veteran of "high-risk" units, and was a participant in four long-range missions. He had been to the Devil's Sea, also know as the Dragon Triangle, located between Japan, Guam, and northern Philippines. Some call this area the "Pacific Bermuda Triangle." In the 1980s, Vinogradov had participated in the search and rescue operations of the Soviet Pacific Fleet (submarines and surface vessels had been used for such missions). Twice he and other officers had observed, on the sonar screen, a USO that had moved at great speed, and disappeared in the depths.

In March of 2010 Wayne Frey, author of the book *Russian Submarines: Guardians of the Motherland* and a member of Russian Saint Petersburg Submarine Club, wrote to Paul Stonehill about Russian USOs. Frey interviewed Russian submarine officers for his book. During the course of the conversation with a former officer, Captain 2nd Rank, who had served 25 years aboard nuclear submarines of the Northern Fleet, Frey asked if Russian submarines on patrol ever made contact with or detected submerged objects that were too deep, too fast, or sounded irregular enough to not be easily classified by conventional means. His answer was "yes." These incidents were recorded and handed over to authorities upon return. But everything had to have an explanation. Anything unknown was simply classified "biological," as if it were simply a form of marine life. In the time of the Soviet Union, one did not want to stir up any trouble with the KGB. Therefore, on return to port, the records would be simply filed away and not talked about.

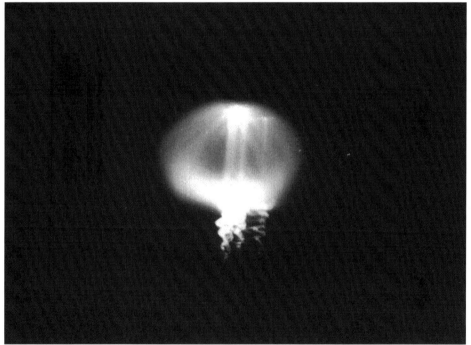

Photo Taken Aboard the Ship Komsomolets Karelii

USO SIGHTINGS IN INTERNATIONAL WATERS

In August 1965, a crew of the steamship *Raduga*, while navigating in the Red Sea, observed a most unusual phenomenon. At about two miles away, a fiery sphere dashed out from under the water and hovered over the surface of the sea, illuminating it. The sphere was about 20 feet in diameter, and it hovered above the sea at an altitude of 500 feet. A gigantic pillar of water ascended upwards, as the sphere emerged from the sea and collapsed some moments later. This observation was mentioned in a number of Russian publications.

There was another fascinating sighting, in the summer of 1972. A "shape shifting" UFO was observed by Soviet seamen aboard *Musson*, a Soviet scientific ship. The vessel was at the time approximately 300 miles from the Bermuda Islands. Early in the morning, Vagin – electrician, radio operator, and one of the navigators -- observed an elliptical body moving through the cloudless sky. The object moved through at a great altitude, slowly from northwest to southeast. Reaching the horizon, the UFO changed its shape to that of a wheel, and then, distancing itself from the Soviet vessel, the object again became an elongated elliptical body of a silvery-white color. All three observers looked at the object until it disappeared from view. This sighting was mentioned in a 2001 article by Valentin Psalomschikov in *NLO Magazine*. In 1976, the crew of the Soviet scientific research vessel *Vladimir Vorobyov* observed eight revolving white radial rays, each around 650 feet long. They emanated from a massive object, located by acoustic depth finder at the depth of 65 feet under the ship. The depth of the Bengal Bay in that area was 557 feet. This phenomenon lasted for thirty minutes. When the rays initially appeared, sleeping sailors were awakened, overcome by great fear. This incident was reported in a number of Russian publications.

On February 28, 1977, Soviet newspaper *Vechernyaya Odessa* published an interview with captain of the ship *Anton Makarenko*. His name was Yevgeny Lisenko, and he told the reporters that while sailing the Malak Strait in Indonesian waters, five members of the crew had witnessed an amazing spectacle. It was 2:00 am when they observed a radiant wheel with "spikes." The center of the revolutions was behind the ship, and the radius of the revolutions was around twelve miles. The "wheel" was underwater. They observed the phenomenon for about 50 hours. Initially, there were glowing spots among the waves. Their numbers increased, and they became lines, about 20 feet wide, stretching to the horizon. The distance between the distinct lines was about 130 feet. Everything became bright, as if the moon had appeared in the sky. The luminescence was cold, silvery, and quite bright. The lines began moving, as if spikes of a gigantic wheel, recalled the captain. The revolution was not rapid, even, and up to the very horizon. Seasoned Soviet sailors felt dizziness and became nauseated, as if they were on a merry-go-round. The revolution accelerated, and the ends of the "rays" became bent. Finally, they broke into separate spots, and disappeared. Several fascinating reports came from the area of South Georgia Island. Located southeast of the Falklands, the UK-ruled South Georgia is lost in the midst of the Southern Ocean, one of the most remote regions on our planet. South Georgia lies between 35.47' to 38.01' west and 53.58' to 54.53' south within the Polar Front. The Antarctic continent is 1,000 miles to the south.

Glaciers coat more than half the island. A great site dedicated to Russian seafarers is *www.morehod.ru*. In its forum section, pertaining to the "UFO at sea" theme, we found interesting recollections of former Soviet sailors. On January 5, 2011, one of them, "Delmar," mentioned that seasoned seamen who had worked on fishing vessels in the vicinity of South Georgia Island had often encountered underwater light. Its diameter was about a mile, and it would disappear suddenly. "Delmar" said that similar stories were told to him by people who were not acquainted with each other. He also stated that while sailing in the Caribbean Sea on several occasions, he would see, at night, an object on radar screen.

It would be next to the ship, invisible to the eye, but quite visible on the screen. Delmar is absolutely sure it was not radar interference. He also recalled that once, in the same sea, they encountered a phantom ship. It sailed without any illumination at the speed of about eight knots. The phantom ship did not register on the AIS [the Automatic Identification System, an automated tracking system used aboard ships]. Its length was about 328 feet. The vessel was visible only on the radar. The 2006 Russian documentary film about USOs, produced by Vitaly Pravdivtsev (aired on the *Rossiya* television channel) contained interviews with Viktor Berezhnoy. Captain First Rank, veteran of the Soviet Navy's intelligence service. Berezhnoy recalled periodic reports (i.e. accounts of eyewitnesses) he received in his capacity as head of flotilla intelligence. He mentioned that it would be wrong to think that the unidentified flying objects were observed only in the North. They were observed throughout the Atlantic Ocean and even in the southern Atlantic, in the vicinity of the Antarctic. In particular, Berezhnoy remembers one case of UFOs near South Georgia Island. The fishermen, who had observed the object that ascended from the water, had enough time to photograph it. Despite strong winds, the object remained in the same place for quite a long time. This was neither a cloud not an air balloon. Other strange flying craft were observed over the island. Berezhnoy provides description of one, based on the testimony received. The disk hovered over the island, and was visible for a long period of time, before and after sunset. During the two hour period, the object had a spherical shape and attached to the object was a protruding equilateral triangle. At night this triangle not only glowed, but at its base lights were observed (as if engines were a work) although the object remained at the same very place.

For years, the authors of this book have heard that captains of Soviet ships reported seeing a bizarre, cone-shaped cloud constantly hovering over the island. There was a photograph, attached to the reports, showing an upward fight of a "saucer" from below the ocean's surface. The object resembled neither a missile nor a torpedo. Right after it ascended, the object became invisible to radar. In December 1977, not far from the same South Georgia Island, the crew of the fishing trawler *Vasily Kiselev* also observed something quite extraordinary. Rising vertically from under the water was a doughnut-shaped object. Its diameter was between 1,000 and 1,600 feet. It hovered at the altitude of two to three miles. The trawler's radar station was immediately rendered inoperative. The object hovered over the area for three hours, and then disappeared instantly. The report came from Dr. Zakharov, the ship's medic, who described the object as a mushroom-shaped body ascending from the water, leaving a trail of smoke behind. The object changed its angle of inclination to the horizon as it hovered above and then abruptly disappeared, leaving no traces behind. As the crew observed the UFO, they also noticed that the onboard radio station and radio direction-finder malfunctioned. This report was sent to the VSNTO (All-Union Council of Scientific Technical Societies), the Central Commission for Anomalous Phenomena in the Environment.

Siberian engineer Yerokhin, who is very much interested in USOs, recalls an article published in the *Soviet Nedelya* newspaper in 1977(issue 18). The article mentioned that scientists aboard the ship Vladimir Vorobyev reported a bright white spot revolving around the ship at the depth of 550 feet.

Its radius, according to Yerokhin, was approximately 500-650 feet. It rotated counterclockwise and then separated into eight portions. The sonic depth finder registered the presence of something at the depth of 65 feet under the keel. The light moved in a wave-like manner, in the shape of eight rotating and bending rays (something like turbine blades). In a 1977 book by M. I. Girs, the commander of the underwater experimental vessel *Tinro-2*, described an incident that took place in the early 1970s while the vessel explored in the Atlantic Ocean. In the evening, as darkness was descending upon the ocean, the seamen watched a gigantic luminescent cloud. It was slightly over the horizon, and its shape was almost perfectly round.

In the middle of the cloud they observed a chaotically moving dot, with a "tail." The cloud grew in size, while the "tail" of the dot constantly moved about. When the first cloud dissipated, another one grew in its place, and then a third one. At one point, they covered each other. The clouds were luminescent and resembled the moon, but not nearly as bright. Radio communications were not affected and magnetic compasses aboard the vessel registered normal. Feliks Zigel mentioned the following incident in his books. In 1978, sailors of the Soviet ship *Novokuznetsk* observed a UFO as their vessel was departing from the Ecuadorian bay Guayaquil. A radiogram was sent from the ship on June 15th, reporting that at night, at the bow, four rapidly departing bright white trails were observed. They were about 65 feet in length. At the same time, two other trails (32 feet long) approached the vessel. Soon thereafter, at 3:00 a.m., straight ahead of the ship, a white, luminescent, oblate sphere ascended from the water. It flew around the ship, hovered for a few seconds over the vessel at an altitude of 65 feet, ascended higher, zigzagged, and plunged back into the water.

Another incident involved the Soviet cruise ship *Shota Rustaveli*, which was built in Germany in 1968. While sailing in the Atlantic Ocean in 1978, a large sphere flew over it, and passengers reported that their watches stopped working. This was disclosed in Feliks Zigel's manuscript *Nablyudeniya NLO v SSSR* (1979). On September 21, 1980, a strange flying object was sighted from Viktor Bugayev, in the Atlantic Ocean. Its shape was unusual. The object resembled a cone-shaped cigar, and moved at slow speed from southwest to northeast. Its front end was luminescent due to large fiery shaft of light that was more than half of the length of the object. This fiery shaft of light created an impression that the light was directed to the aft part of the ship. After flying a certain distance, the object, having rotated a bit, hovered motionlessly. It would rotate sporadically. Then, another, identical object separated itself from the first object, and rapidly gaining speed, disappeared to the northwest. Its front end was also luminescent due to large fiery shaft of light. The first object, still hovering, turned off the shaft of light and assumed the color of aluminium. It started moving in the north-easterly direction, increasing its speed. The clear outlines of its body became blurry as the distance increased. Right in the middle of both objects was a dark stripe; it was about 1/6 of the length of the body. The altitude the objects were flying at was about one to two miles. No sound was heard, and the objects left no trails. Thirty crew members observed the objects. The report was published in a number of Russian UFO books, and originally was included in Alexander Kuzovkin's manuscript about statistical UFO data in the USSR (1981).

The following testimony of Alexander G. Globa, a seaman from *Gori*, a Soviet tanker, was published in *Zagadki Sfinksa* magazine (Issue # 3, 1992), Odessa, Ukraine. In June of 1984, *Gori* was navigating in the Mediterranean, twenty nautical miles from the Straight of Gibraltar, at 4 p.m. Globa was on duty, and with him was Second-in-Command S. Bolotov. They were standing watch at the left bridge extension wing, when both men observed a strange polychromatic object. When the object was astern, it stopped suddenly. S. Bolotov was very excited, shaking his binoculars and shouting: "It is a flying saucer, a real saucer; my God, hurry, hurry, look!" Globa looked through his own binoculars and noticed, at a distance over the stern, a flattened out looking object, sort of like an upside-down frying pan. The UFO was gleaming with a greyish metallic shine. The lower portion of the craft had a precise round shape, with a diameter of about 65 feet. Around the lower portion of the object, Globa also observed "waves" of protuberances on the outside plating. The base of the object's body consisted of two semi-discs, the smaller being on top. They slowly revolved in opposing directions. At the circumference of the lower disc, Globa saw numerous shining, bright, beadlike lights. The seaman's attention was cantered on the bottom portion of the UFO. It looked completely even and smooth, its color that of a yolk, and in the middle of it, Globa discerned a round, nucleus-like stain. At the edge of the UFO's bottom, which was plainly visible, was something that looked like a pipe. It glowed with an unnaturally bright, rosy color, like a neon lamp. The top of the middle disc was crowned by a triangular-shaped "something." It seemed that it moved in the same direction as the lower disc, but at a much slower pace. Suddenly, the UFO jumped up several times, as if moved by an invisible wave. Numerous lights illuminated its bottom portion. The crew of *Gori* tried to attract the object's attention using a signal searchlight. By that time Captain Sokolovsky joined his men on the deck. He and his Second-in-Command were watching the object closely. However, it seemed that the UFO's attention was distracted by another ship, approaching from the port side. It was an Arab dry cargo ship on its way to Greece. The crew of the Arab vessel later confirmed that the object hovered over their ship as well. A minute and a half later, the object changed its flight trajectory, listed to the right, gained speed, and ascended rapidly into the sky. Soviet seamen observed that when it rose through the clouds, appearing and disappearing again, it occasionally "glinted" in the sun's rays. The craft then flared up, like a spark, and was gone instantly.

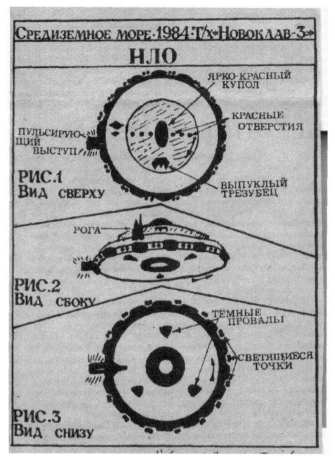

The Gori 1984 Diagram

Also in June of 1984, another Soviet ship reported an interesting phenomenon. *Professor Pavlenko*, built in 1973 with its port of registry at the city of Odessa, was sailing in the Adriatic Sea by Neretva Bay (Bay of Zaton), when its crew observed a bright spot that appeared on the surface of the water and radiated circles of light that pulsated away from it. The circles moved at a velocity of about 300 feet an hour, as reported in issue 6, 1987, of *Vokrug Sveta* magazine.

Mikhail Soroka, interviewed in Kiev's *FAKTY* newspaper in December 2007, that his data indicated Soviet seamen had numerous encounters with unidentified objects. Often, objects would appear unexpectedly, fly over the ships, and then descend into the water without making a splash. If ice was present on the surface of the water, the objects would break through it. Often, these objects emitted luminescence from the depths of the water. Soroka mentioned specific encounters with plunging USOs that followed a similar scenario. Gigantic cylinders appeared in the sky, and smaller UFOs would fly out from their bodies and plunge underwater. Some time later, they returned to the surface and flew back inside the cylinder. Often, after such objects appeared in a certain area, electromagnetic interference would be experienced in the vicinity. In the Kuril Islands, for example, an unfrozen patch of water was found in one of the lakes; its shape was that of a circle with melted edges. Electromagnetic fields there were unusually high. However, no witnesses were found to reveal what really took place there. Soroka described an episode from 1968 that took place near the shores of South America. Soviet scientists aboard *Akademik Kurchatov* (a scientific research ship) tried to bring down into the oceanic depths special equipment. The measuring instruments they submerged were attached to metallic cables. At a depth of 1,600 feet, one of the cables gave way. It just hung in the water, and the device that was attached to it broke off. The same happened with the other two pieces of equipment.

Today, only its anchor remains, as a monument to the vessel's former glory; it is located in Moscow, at the corner of Nakhimovsky Prospekt and Novocheryomushkinskaya Street. But this was no ordinary scientific research vessel. *Akademik Kurchatov* had conducted fifty voyages in all of the planet's oceans, and participated in major international programs. Its last one took place in 1989. The vessel was built in Germany, following initiatives by great Soviet scientists Papanin and Keldish. It became the leading ship of the Soviet Academy of Sciences Oceanology research. The Atlantic Ocean was its main field of research. Indeed, it was a floating institute, well-equipped and intelligently designed; it possessed state-of-the-art manoeuvrability, navigational system, cutters, lifeboats, and a helicopter. The vessel was outfitted with seventeen permanently installed oceanographic deep-sea research winches used to lower scientific instrumentation over the side, enabling up to seven scientific teams to observe the underwater world.

In greater detail, here is what happened during the 1968 voyage of the scientific research vessel *Akademik Kurchatov*. According to Pavel Kirillov (*Tayni XX Veka*, issue 10, 2003), the crew encountered "phantoms of the oceans." It was September 1, 1968, when *Akademik Kurchatov* drifted in the South-East Pacific region, not far from the shores of South America. The South-East Pacific region spans the entire length of the Pacific coast of South America from Panama to Cape Horn, encompassing tropical, sub-tropical, temperate and sub-antarctic systems. The vessel's scientists periodically lowered scientific instrumentation for research purposes. Thick, steel cables carried thermometers, radiometers, plankton nets, soil sampling tubes to the bottom. Experienced operators manned the winches. The weather was fine, and no surprises were expected. Suddenly, when one of the instruments reached the depth of 1,640 feet, the cable moved aside, as if someone pulled it, and sagged. The instrumentation was gone. A minute later, the thick cables carrying a soil sampling tube and bottom dredge were torn off; altogether three cables were torn. This had never happened before during all the voyages of the *Akademik Kurchatov*. When the torn cables were brought up to the deck, distraught Russian scientists were amazed. At the spots where the cables were torn, they saw brightly polished, 6-foot long abrasions. This was as if someone had used a giant file to cut the cable off. The crew of Akademik Kurchatov never did find out who did this to their thick steel winch cables.

Where exactly was the research vessel taking samples? We found an interesting reference in a letter published by *Nature Physical Science* in its July 19, 1971 issue (232, 61-62): "...during the third and fourth cruises of r.v. *Akademik Kurchatov* (1968), material from the South-West Africa and Chile shelves was recovered so that the process of phosphorite formation could be traced in a more detailed manner."

The letter was from G. N. Baturin, a well-known Soviet marine geologist who first developed the concept of phosphorite formation in the up welling zones. But this reference does not confirm Kirillov's account of the incident, only a possible location of where the incident occurred. The article "Sovetskiye moryaki y leaysuchiye tarelki" or "Soviet Seamen and Flying Saucers" mentions UFO sightings that were collected and sent to VSNTO (All-Union Council of Scientific Technical Societies). In 1984, by the decision of VSNTO, the Central Commission for Anomalous Phenomena in the Environment was established in the Soviet Union. This commission had collected reports of UFO and USO sightings from the general population.

One such report came from a Leningrad mechanic, A. Golitikin. In 1980, he had sailed aboard fishing trawler-refrigerator *Brilliant*. On January 24th the trawler was operating some 20 to 30 miles from the coast of Western Africa, At 1 p.m. Golotikin went to the deck, and along with other crew member, observed a black cigar-shaped object, flying toward the ship. The object moved noiselessly and much slower than an airplane would, at an altitude of about one mile. The mariners observed the object for about seven minutes using binoculars. As they watched in amazement, the object approached the trawler and then vanished before their very eyes.

USOs AND UFOs IN THE PACIFIC BERMUDA TRIANGLE

Captain Vinogradov, already mentioned in this chapter, stated that scientists believe there are USO bases in the Devil's Sea, the Okhotsk Sea, and in the Bering Sea. How else can one explain eyewitness testimonies recorded in military reports? Soviet seafarers observed, on more than one occasion, elongated, cigar shaped objects that ascended from the sea. The USOs would silently hover over the ship, and then either fly away or dive back into the sea. Vinogradov, who believes in the existence of an unidentified underwater civilization, mentioned another fact he had personally observed. While on a mission in the Indian Ocean, he and others had seen bright luminescence and narrow rays, emitted by underwater objects. The radiant rays were generated under the surface of the ocean, over some long object, which would descend to great depths at great speeds. Observations and data from onboard equipment indicated that such USOs were able to change their exterior shape and size and separate into several autonomous objects. There are disturbing reports from this Devil's Sea. In 1978, a Soviet floating whaling base, the *Vladivostok*, was in the area. V. Ustimenko conducted agricultural experiments aboard the vessel and was successfully growing wheat seeds. But when *Vladivostok* navigated in the Devil's Sea, the seeds "refused" to grow. They ballooned, burst open, and a white mass would ooze out. People who happened to be in the waters of the Devil's Sea reported feeling tired, worn out, and drained of energy. Some seafarers claim that they never see any wildlife in the area, including dolphins and birds. This information is from Vadim Chernobrov's *Entsiklopedia Neopoznannnogo* (*Encyclopedia of the Unidentified*).

As we describe USOs reported in various parts of the Sea of Okhotsk, we must describe the geographic area. We also want to mention a few historical details about other mysterious phenomena found there, derived from the 1975 digest *Prizraki v okeane* or *Ghosts in the Ocean* written by V. Psalomschikov and A. Stepanyuk. The Sea of Okhotsk makes up the north-western part of the North Pacific Ocean bounded on the west by Asia, north by Russia, and east and southeast by the Kamchatka Peninsula and the Kuril Islands. It is connected with the Sea of Japan by the Tatar and La Perouse straits and with the Pacific Ocean by passages through the Kuril Islands. The sea is less than 5,000 feet (1,524 meters) deep; its deepest point, near the Kuril Islands, is 11,033 feet (3,363 meters). The sea is icebound annually from November to June and has recurrent heavy fogs. In this sea, winter navigation is usually difficult and at times impossible due to ice. The Sea of Okhotsk is the coldest sea of East Asia; in winter the climate and thermal regime over much of the region differ only slightly from those found in the Arctic. Magadan and Korsakov, in the Russian Far East, are the largest harbours; Palana and Yuzhno-Sakhalinsk are also important ports. Except for the small area touching Hokkaido, the sea is completely enclosed by Russian territory.

Japan still maintains a claim to the four southernmost islands of the Kuril Archipelago, including Kunashir, Iturup, Shikotan, and the Habomai rocks. Japan calls them its Northern Territories. In 1902, a Russian patrol cruiser detained a Japanese fishing vessel near the shores of Kamchatka. The Japanese captain swore that he arrived in the Russian waters because his compass was broken. Later it was determined that a big radiant cloud was at fault. It appeared suddenly over the horizon. Russian sailors had encountered such phenomenon on a number of occasions in the Sea of Okhotsk. Once, observed behind a moving ship, an unusual, bright, greenish-white light exploded on the surface of the sea. This glowing spot grew in size and slowly surrounded the ship with a fiery circle. Later it separated itself, and rushed forth; three minutes later reaching the horizon, leaving a bright reflection in the clouds, as the glow of a large city would. The authors of *Prizraki v okeane* probably referred to the 1908 case we describe below. Fishing and crabbing are carried on off West Kamchatka peninsula. Also, a popular Soviet newspaper *Trud*, in its July 13, 1974 issue, had an article titled "Zagadochny svet v okeane" (Mysterious Light in the Ocean). It stated that on occasion sailors and travellers who sailed close to the Kuril Islands observed a bright spot that suddenly appeared in the darkness at the horizon. The spot moved rapidly, increasing in size until it reached a width of up to a quarter of a mile. From the oval spot, a pillar of light shot up into the sky, causing strange electromagnetic disturbances in the vicinity. Compass needles danced around erratically; human hair made crackling noises; bright sparks flew off silk; and some objects glowed. This "magic light" was said to be full of wonders. The phenomenon is well known to people who live in Japan and the Far East. They have a number of names for it, but its true nature remains elusive to scientists.

Perhaps, the phenomenon *Trud* made reference to was observed in the beginning of the 20th century. In 1908, Russian steamship *Okhotsk* was in the Sea of Okhotsk, in the Russian Far East. F. D. Derbek, a Russian Imperial Navy doctor aboard the ship, reported that during the night of October 22, at 11 p.m., a bright, unusual, greenish-white luminescence flared up under the ship's stern. The luminescence quickly expanded, surrounding the bottom of the ship. With the steamship at its center, the brightly lit surface assumed the shape of an oval. It moved with the ship for a while and then separated itself and moved sideways, and then forward, ahead of the vessel. The brightly lit and clearly outlined spot rapidly distanced itself from the *Okhotsk*, and two or three minutes later, it reached the horizon, where it glowed as a bright clear streak, reflecting its light upon clouds. This sighting was reported in several Soviet and Russian magazines.

More strange reports from the area became known through the turbulent years of the 20th century. In September of 1950, two Soviet fighter planes, while in flight over the Sea of Japan, spotted a UFO and attempted to attack it. The incident was observed by crew of a Japanese merchant vessel. One of the planes, having spent all of its ammunition without any results, approached the UFO at a dangerously close distance. Suddenly, the Soviet aircraft began vibrating violently and broke apart into small fragments, apparently as a result of colliding with the some kind of invisible energy field around the UFO. This brief report was published in 1998 in the Russian digest *Okkul'tniye sili SSSR*. Kunashir Island is the southernmost link in a chain of volcanic islands reaching about 621 miles from Japan north to Kamchatka. The islands separate the chilly waters of the Okhotsk Sea from the warmer Pacific Ocean and are controlled by Russia but claimed by Japan. When the Soviet Union took control of the island after World War II, Lyudmila Shevchenko and her husband served on Kunashir Island, where the Russians had a military airfield for test flights over the Pacific Ocean. In 1953, something strange happened over the island, and Shevchenko has remembered ever since. An aircraft was ordered to land. The pilot acknowledged and headed the plane toward the airfield. The airplane was visible from the island, but when it was very close to the runway, the craft began to "fade" out of existence. Finally, it just vanished, as if it had never been there. At the same moment, all radio communications in the area were cut off.

The air unit's commanding officers later got in touch with the Ministry of Defence. Soviet divers were brought in to search the bottom of the sea but found no traces of the vanished aircraft. The case was described in Yuri Smirnov's article "Ischez samolyot" or "Disappearance of an Aircraft") in the *Chetvyortoye izmereniye* newspaper in Yaroslavl, Issue 10, 1992. On September 10 in 1972,the crew of the Soviet cruiser *Varyag* observed an object that "fell" rapidly into the ocean, close to the Kuril Islands in the Pacific Ocean. Initially, the object resembled a sphere, but while descending into the water, it changed its shape to that of cone. No splashes were observed. There is a Koryak settlement on the shore of the Sea of Okhotsk, in Kamchatka, with an unusual name -- Paren' ("Young Fellow" in Russian). According to Academician Dikov of the Soviet Academy of Science, in 1977 a group of geologists observed, for ten minutes, a disc-shaped UFO (about the size of the visible moon). Six rays, narrowing down, extended from the UFO down to Earth. This information appeared in Feliks Zigels' manuscript *Petrozavodskoye Divo* (1980).

In May of 1982, the Soviet frigate SKR-3 was in the Pacific Ocean when its commander, Captain 2nd Rank A. Sokolov and two other crew members observed a UFO. The object ascended from underwater. It was cigar-shaped and about 500-650 feet long. Its ascent out of the water was slow and noiseless. The UFO then hovered at the altitude of 800-1,000 feet, where it seemed to "engage" four engines (four lights in the aft part) and rapidly disappeared in the atmosphere. In filling out the form required for reporting the incident, Sokolov noticed that the form did not have a category for underwater UFOs. The closest option he found was "UFO landing on the water." When the ship returned to base, the captain made his report. This incident was mentioned in the Russian TV documentary about USOs, aired on in 2009.

We found more detailed reports about fascinating sightings from the Soviet Kuril islands. N.S. Krokhmalev reported the first sighting in an article published in Russian newspaper *Chetvertoye izmereniye i NLO*, Issue 6, 1997. In August 1982, Krokhmalev was aboard the *Nikolai Boshnyak* , in the Shikotan island area. The ship was heading to the Yekaterina Strait, between the islands of Iturup and Kunashir. The watch commander invited the crew to observe an interesting phenomenon. An elliptical circle with clearly outlined borders appeared on surface around the ship. The luminescence was like that produced by a TV set. They estimated the size of the luminescence to be 410 feet long and 242 feet wide. No sounds except the ship's engine could be heard. There was an object below the ship at the depth of 9-13 feet. Also, a perfect round circle appeared around the moon, at the same time. The circle on the surface of the sea accompanied the Soviet vessel for two hours, and then disappeared suddenly. The ship's speed was slow at the time. No onboard devices registered anything unusual. Krokhmalev recalled having feelings of depression and perplexity after the sighting.

Another sighting took place in July of 1983, two miles from the Shikotan Island. It occurred during the summer, in the second half of July, early in the morning. Zenit, a fishing vessel from the Sakhalin Island, was moored near the island and waited for the opportunity to load the cargo aboard. Six crewmen stood on the deck. The sun was not out yet, and an early haze covered the horizon. All of a sudden, the men saw a bright, orange-colored sphere, moving slowly from north to south, before disappearing instantly as if someone flipped a switch. The sphere was ten times larger than the visible moon. It was seen for about two minutes. The sea was calm, and the fog was light. The sphere moved low over the horizon, between the Shikotan Island and vessel, and looked somewhat like the reddish disc of the setting sun. This report came from V. P. Krilosov, and can be found in Valentin Golts's archives. Mikhail Gershtein has graciously provided it to us. Golts was a UFO researcher and journalist in Leningrad (Saint Petersburg) and an active participant in the projects of the Leningrad Commission for Anomalous Phenomena of the Geographic Society of the USSR.

Five years went by, and another event took place in the very same location. The *Priroda i anomalniye yavlenia* newspaper published an article about the incident in its Issue 7, 1990. The sighting occurred in October 1988 at about 9 p.m., while Soviet aircraft carrier *Novorossiysk* conducted training exercises. The crew noticed a gigantic body with vague outlines rising from behind the island. There were 36 lights located geometrically along the object's hull. As the UFO ascended, all electronic systems aboard *Novorossiysk* went dead. The ship's diesel engines ceased functioning, and even the portable battery-operated accumulator radio stations would not work. A state of the art modern ship, equipped with the modern electronics was instantly left dead in the water three miles off the island. It was left completely defenceless. The strange event was observed by fishermen on the nearby island. Forty seconds later, the ship's onboard systems came back to life, one after another. The radar did not register any objects. A K-27 helicopter was sent after the UFO, but the strange object flew away, at an amazing speed. The entire incident lasted only about fifteen minutes. On October 21, 1989, another strange object was observed by the inhabitants of the Kuril Islands and the crew of the ship *Egvekinot*. The object flew over Shikotan Island at an altitude of approximately half a mile. The black nucleus, located inside a red sphere, was separated into three parts by silvery rays. Their glimmer was so strong that it reflected in the sea water. During the flight of that UFO, radar screen experienced interferences. This was reported in the 1989 article in the local newspaper *ovetskiy Sakhalin* by V. Plotnikov in his article "NLO ili gazovoye oblako" or "UFO or a Gas Cloud?"

What a fascinating area this really is! Situated in the Central Kuril Islands are a number of small isles and emergent rocks. The largest, Island Yankicha and Island Ryponkicha, are collectively known as Ushishir. Ushishir is the remains of a partially submerged volcano. The Ushishir Islands were favoured by the Ainu, the native people of the Kurils. The numerous thermal pools used to be the site of religious ceremonies been discovered. and feature prominently in many of the legends of the Ainu. Volcano caldera forms the Kraternaya Bay on the Yankicha. Mysterious animals and micro organisms, products of an isolated biosphere, have been discovered in the bay by Russian scientists. But the reasons for variations and mutations of the inhabitants of marine shallow-water hydrothermal ecosystem have not

KAMCHATKA'S MYSTERY

Kamchatka is one of the most fascinating regions of Russia. With an area of 292,000 square miles, the Kamchatka Peninsula separates the Sea of Okhotsk from the Pacific Ocean. Lake Kronotskoye, over 300 feet deep in spots, is the largest lake in Kamchatka and is situated in the inter-mountain depression. A chain of 16 volcanoes goes along Kronotskoye Lake; the highest of them is the dome of Kronotskaya (11,500 feet above sea level). In 1970, a group of hydrologists conducting research at the lake aboard a motor boat had an extremely strange encounter. The scientists included Vadim Psalomschikov and Agarkov [first name unknown], who had met and become friends while attending the Leningrad Hydrometeorological Institute. Agarkov headed the hydrological expedition at the Kronotskoye Lake. It was a pleasant August day. All of a sudden, at a distance of about a half mile from where he scientists worked, a dome of rising water formed and a grey-colored oval object flew out of it. The UFO was about 131-196 feet in diameter. It rose to the altitude of a few hundred feet, at 70 to 80 degrees to the horizon, and hovered motionlessly.

The Russian hydrologists watched in stunned silence for about a minute and a half and then started rowing their disabled boat. The UFO began moving away and disappeared from view at great speed. As the object vanished, the boat's motor roared to life again. Later Agarkov reported that the next year, two of the four eyewitnesses of the UFO sighting perished under very strange circumstances. This sighting was mentioned in the 2001 article written by Valentin Psalomschikov, and published in *NLO Magazine*. Psalomschikov also mentioned that there have been other tragic incidents of close encounters with unidentified submersible objects. He mentioned an incident that took place August 2, 1965 in the Red Sea. About 300 feet from a motor boat carrying six Arab fishermen, an oval object ascended from the sea. The object's diameter was about 200 feet. It hovered for a while, at a low altitude; then it rapidly began a vertical ascent. The resulting wave of displaced water overturned the boat, and one of the fishermen drowned. In the following months, three more of the fishermen died; two of them were diagnosed with cancer of the blood. No one knows whether the USO that came from the waters of the Red Sea was the same one that ascended from the remote lake in the Russian Kamchatka.

MYSTERIES OF RUSSIA'S ARCTIC REGIONS

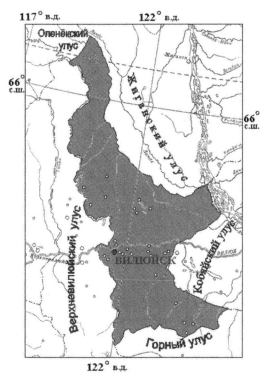

Map of the Location of the Enigmatic Cauldrons (Kosmopoisk Archives)

To the great irritation of the Soviet aviation, civil and military officials, UFOs also frequented forbidden Arctic territories. E. Loginov, the civil aviation minister, asked the legendary Soviet Arctic pilot Akkuratov to describe his experiences after four incidents of direct UFO encounters.

Akkuratov did, and mentioned in the end that the pilots had many more encounters, but were hesitant to report, because the Soviet press had decreed that UFOs do not exist, and those who reported them would be ridiculed. The highly militarized Soviet Arctic has attracted the uninvited guests from outer space, mysterious ocean depths, or other dimensions, wherever the UFOs and USOs come from. Few people in the West know much about Yakutia. The land consists of the thick backwoods of taiga, the seemingly endless tundra, vast mountain chains and the icy Arctic Ocean. Yakutia is an enormous country. It covers 2 million square feet, which is 5 times the size of France. Yakutia's diverse natural environment ranges from Arctic tundra on the coast of the North Arctic Ocean to the rocky mountains of the Aldan plateau. In between are giant expanses of dense taiga forest and boggy lands dotted with dozens of lakes. Much of the country is flat as a result of the massive glaciers of the last ice age when it levelled everything in their path.

The Yakut People

Yakutia borders on the Khabarovsk and Krasnoyarsk territories, Magadan, Amurskaya, and Chita and Irkutsk regions. Yakutia is located on the edge of the Laptevyh and East Siberian Seas, and encompasses the Novosibirskie Islands. The major part is taken up by large mountain systems and plateau. The main rivers are the Lena with its tributaries in the Aldan and Vilyui, Yana, Indgirka, Kolyma, Anabar, Olenek [Arctic Ocean basin]. All these areas experience frequent UFO visits. Yakutia has a long history of paranormal activity. Long distances, lack of infrastructure, inaccessibility to the remote areas, dependence on air transport, and climatic conditions are reasons Yakutia is a place rarely visited by Westerners. In 1993 the Joint USA-CIS Aerial Anomaly Federation published Feliks Y. Zigel's *UFO Sightings over the USSR*-1968 (Volume 1).

It contains the following report about Yakutia sent to F. Zigel by S. N Popov, an Air Force reserve officer. From 1958 through 1965, Popov worked in the Yakut SSR, at the Ust'-Maya airport, as an aviation technician. In March of 1964, as he and three other men exited a club, they observed two very strange discs. At first the discs moved one behind the other. Later, they re-formed and continued their movement in as a pair.

Passing almost over the heads of Popov and his comrades, the discs emitted a low intensity light beam toward the ground. There was indescribable brightness around the discs themselves. It seemed to Popov that the color was that of a dark violet-blue, like the discharge of an electric spark. The edge was an exact circle and stationary as if a dull milky smoke tried to go beyond the limits of the circle, and glass walls would not allow it to leave. When the discs passed over their heads, illuminating the men below, Popov did feel something oppressive, as if a natural disaster was about to take place. Curiously, in 1982 a similar feeling was reported by Krokhmalev. It was, he recalls, a very unpleasant feeling. Popov thought that the Soviets again launched some "novelty" into the space. However, media reported nothing of the sorts. Popov also recalled that in March of 1961, "Comrades Orlova and Tirasenko" observed a milky white disc of a perfect shape in the area where the Maya River empties into the Aldan, across from the Ust'-Maya settlement. Then, in 1964, Comrades Orlova, Kozlova, and Sifronova observed three milky white discs at 62-68 miles from Ust'-Maya upstream, along the Aldan River. The date is 1964, but some other information written by Popov was abbreviated and illegible. S. N. Popov personally heard stories from Soviet aviators who flew to the airport where he was stationed; stories about strange phenomena like "flying saucers" that they had observed. He believed that researchers should interview the personnel of the Yakutsk Territorial Administration about this issue.

Galina Varlamova, a Russian writer and scientist of Evenk origin, urged Russia's UFO researchers to pay close attention to the mythology and oral traditions of the Evenk people. Descendants of this nomadic nation reside in Yakutia. We described some of the Evenk beliefs in chapter two, in reference to the Tunguska Phenomenon. Varlamova has collected Evenk stories for over 15 years, and states that there are numerous stories of encounters with extraterrestrials, ancient astronaut visitations, and an "artificial" origin for mankind. The Evenks viewed such phenomena as "protective spirits," and they communicated with the "spirits" through shamanism. The word "shaman" was actually an Evenk word, borrowed by other cultures. The Evenk shaman's soul, according to tradition, is able to leave the body and travel to other parts of the cosmos. It travels to a mysterious upper world in the sky and a lower world, located under the Earth. The shaman remains in the control, and aware of his surroundings, throughout this cosmic travel, known as *kamlaniye*.

ULYUYU CHERKECHEKH

Now, we will look at the Tungus legends. In the North-West of Yakutia, in the area of Upper Vilyui, lies the area known in antiquity as Ulyuyu Cherkechekh or Valley of Death. Home to the Tungus tribes, it is a mysterious, hard-to-reach area, full of broken stone pieces strewn around for hundreds of miles. Here, the natives have, for ages, told stories of strange sightings. One, deeply carved in their tribal memory, recalls how their land was swallowed by sudden darkness. A mighty, deafening roar shook the area, a powerful hurricane whirled about, and strong blows struck the ground. Lightning lit the sky. When the darkness left, the amazed Tungus saw a giant vertical structure, gleaming in sunlight. It could be seen "from many days away." The structure emitted unpleasant, sharp sounds. It also diminished in size, until it disappeared underground. Those who ventured to the burned-out site never returned.
When the land healed, and the plants, animals, and nomadic hunters came back to the area, they found there a strange dome-like "iron house." It had many lateral supports, but no doors or windows on its smooth surface. Nearby there were other metallic constructions, embedded in the ground. At the spot where the vertical structure stood, the Tungus found a giant vertical "crater." The legends described it in details (and with great awe). The "crater" consisted of three "laughing abysses." An underground land was located in the bowels of the crater, which had its own "waning sun." Suffocating stench came from the "crater," and no tribe settled the area. On occasions, a "revolving island" ascended from the crater. Centuries later the permafrost swallowed the "iron house." An opening was found in its dome. A spiral-like downward slope led to circular galleries; there were many metallic rooms. The rooms were warm even during the coldest winters, but whoever spent a few days inside, soon perished from strange sickness. The elders had banned any travel to the area. Numerous legends tell of the Nyurgun Bootur fiery spheres in the area, disc-like "flying objects," and explosions that caused genetic diseases. The second fiery sphere destroyed the area 600 hundred years later. The sphere had a new name then: "Kyun Erbiye," or "bright celestial messenger."

THE CAULDRONS

The last such "explosion" occurred in September of 1880. A famous explorer of Vilyui in the 19th century, R. Maak, mentioned giant "cauldrons." One such "cauldron" was of enormous proportions. The explorer saw its edge protruding through the ground and several trees that grew on it. Contemporary Russian researchers A. Gutenev and B. Mikhailovski interviewed an elderly nomad, who visited the Valley of Death, and saw a metallic "burrow," where he found frozen, very skinny, black, one-eyed people in iron clothes. In 1933, Mikhail Petrovich Koretsky of Vladivistok, while visiting the Ulyuyu Cherkechekh, was informed by a Yakut guide how 10 years before he discovered several "cauldrons" of perfect spherical shapes. The objects protruded from the ground, and their height was greater than that of a human. The objects looked brand-new. Koretsky described the "cauldrons" he personally saw in 1933-39. They were 20-30 feet in diameter. However, their shapes were not spherical. They were made from a strange metal. No piece could be broken off. The metallic surface of a "cauldron" was covered with some unfamiliar layer, similar to emery paper or sandpaper. But the layer could not be cut through.

Depiction of the Enigmatic Cauldrons (Kosmopoisk Archives)

Vegetation growing immediately around the objects was very strange – it was strikingly more luxuriant, and the grass was unusually tall, twice as tall as a human. Koretsky and five others slept one night inside a "cauldron." Three months later one of them lost all his hair. Koretsky developed strange, tiny, painful spots on the side of the head he slept on while inside the "cauldron." No treatment he tried would get rid of them.

Tungus legends also mention a strange life form, a giant called *Uot UsumuTong uurai*. The name translates as "Criminal alien who bored through the ground and hides there, and whose fiery tornado destroys all around." Serafim Boyev, in a 1997 article published in *NLO Magazine* (Issue 13), described a similar phenomenon in Yakutia. On the right shore of the Vilyui River hunters discovered a source of unusual radiation. One curious hunter spent a night there, attracted by the superb fauna of the area, including gigantic burdocks, trees full of leaves and lianas, and velvety high grass as tall as six feet. All this vegetation was completely out of place in an area of permafrost and sparse vegetation. Upon awaking the next morning, the hunter screamed in terror, for he discovered that all his hair had fallen from his head. But he was determined to find out more about the area. What he found left him dumbfounded. Not far from the clearing where he spent the night, the hunter discovered strange, reddish, metallic-looking semi-spheres protruding from the stony ground. He looked inside one, and froze, for inside were "very skinny, black one-eyed people in iron clothing."

Vadim Chernobrov in Yakutia

A strange phenomenon was observed in Yakutia in 1938. It resembled the Biblical story of the Egyptian darkness that lasted three days. The Siberian darkness occurred on September 18 of 1938, and it took Soviet authorities two years before they issued permission to publish reports about the event. So, at the start of 1940, Soviet meteorologist V.N. Adreyev published his account. He was able to observe the phenomenon in a settlement Khal'mer-Sede on the river Taz. The sky turned completely black; one could not see anything. The origin of this phenomenon is still unknown.

NUCLEAR REALITY

The wilderness, where the Valley of Death once was present became a site of Soviet nuclear testing. Something very strange happened there in the 1950s during the test firing of a 10-kiloton nuclear device, having the explosive force of 1,000 tons of TNT. For some unknown reason, the force of the explosion was magnified thousands of times over. The blast registered a reading of 20 to 30 megatons, equivalent to a million tons of TNT! What caused such a dramatic increase in the force of the explosion no one knows. Russian researchers suppose that the Soviet nuclear testing damaged one of the mysterious underground structures, releasing some type of energy contained in it.

CRYPTOZOOLOGY

Although our book describes the UFO phenomena in the former USSR and modern Russia and the Commonwealth of the Independent States, we cannot ignore reports about unusual creatures that inhabit the far away Yakutia. Perhaps there is a connection between these creatures and UFOs that is still unclear to researchers. Ufologis Vadim Chernobrov collected interesting materials about Yakutia's cryptozoology and published them in the digest *Nad propastyu neraskritikh tayn* or *Over an Abyss of Unsolved Mysteries* (Moscow, 1996). More details were given in an article by Gennady Lisov in *NLO Magazine* (2000).

Both sources describe strange "monsters" and beings in the lakes of Yakutia. Those who want more details should contact Vadim Chernobrov at the Kosmopoisk website, *http://kosmopoisk.org/*.

We will add here that according to Yuri Metelev, a Russian geologist, one of the participants in Metelev's expedition to Yakutia at the end of 1960s was able to discover a small herd of buffalo [bison] in the River Khandiga area. But then the discoverer of this mystery, biologist Boris S. Shlikman, disappeared without a trace somewhere in the mysterious lands of Yakutia.

YAKUTIA'S STRANGE SITES

Ten hours of walking from the Bol'shaya Khatim settlement in Yakutia brings one to a legendary site, where according to local beliefs, people can cure their eye diseases. At the site is a large rock, known as Bottle Rock because it resembles a big mass of compressed broken glass from bottles. According to legend, if one were to press his face to this rock and look inside its semi-transparent depth, one's eyesight will prove. Another strange rock in Yakutia is at a cave, where in 1995 sensational archaeological findings were made. The site is known as Yeleneva Cave, and the name of the rock is Watch Bull. The place is located at the Yenisey River, across from the syanka Village. Among the archaeological discoveries recorded here was an object made entirely from the tusk of a mammoth, dating back 3,000 years. Yet, the last mammoth to die in the area did so not later than 10,000 years ago! Also, the object was made for observation, not as a hunting tool. It contains carvings that indicate a lunar calendar, and its base has carvings that correspond to the twelve months of the year. The ancients in Yakutia apparently were aware of the calendars for both the moon and the Earth. The source for this information is *Entsiklopedia Nepoznannogo* or *Encyclopedia of the Unknown*, compiled by Vadim Chernobrov, and published in Moscow in 1998.

THE KGB INVESTIGATION IN KOLYMA

Kolyma is a remote, harsh, and severe vast piece of Arctic and sub-Arctic territory, with undefined borders, located in the farthest northeast corner of Siberia. It is bounded by the East Siberian Sea and the Arctic Ocean in the north and the Sea of Okhotsk to the south. The extremely remote region gets its name from the Kolyma River and mountain range, parts of which were not discovered until 1926. Later, the Soviet regime built 300 concentration camps in the Kolyma Region. The Kolyma Road was built by many of Stalin's GULAG prisoners that had been exiled to die in this frozen wilderness. It is called the Road of Bones, because the bones of perished political prisoners were found there. In his 2006 book *Tayni NLO i prishel'tsev* or *Secrets of the UFOs and aliens*, Mikhail Gershtein mentioned a UFO sighting report made by a KGB officer. Pyotr Pavlov headed the operational section of the KGB of Yakutsk Autonomous Soviet Socialist Republic in the late 1950s and early 1960s. Numerous UFO reports were made during that period, and they were sent to the KGB. No guidelines regarding secrecy pertaining to such reports were ever sent to local KGB from Moscow. However, local *chekisty*, as KGB operatives were called, did ask the local population to send UFO reports to them. Apparently, so many reports came to Pyotr Pavlov, that he instructed Captain N. Nesterov to collect and classify the data.

The town of Chersky is located at the mouth of the Kolyma River. One summer, when the sun did not set beyond the horizon, five or seven "flying saucers" hovered over the town, at a great altitude, inaccessible to Soviet interceptor jets. The "saucers" were lined up in a straight line. They departed in the same fashion, in a single line formation. And then one day, the KGB received a report about a UFO landing behind the Polar (Arctic) Circle, on the shores of Lena River. Captain Nesterov was dispatched to the area. He questioned five or six people, local inhabitants who had seen the object. They said that a strange object with glowing portholes landed noiselessly on the ground, causing the snow cover to turn reddish for a few moments. After a brief stay on the ground, the object flashed red several times, ascended noiselessly and disappeared. The local KGB notified the Ministry of Defence, USSR. Soon thereafter, a group of senior officers arrived in the area and went to the site of the landing, where they interviewed the witnesses.

Here is a fascinating account that illustrates the complicated nature of the history of the Soviet UFO investigations. The local KGB, headed by Pyotr Pavlov, compiled a report based on all UFO sightings in the area, including photographs taken in 1960 of an impressive, rhomboid-shaped UFO. Pavlov sent one set of documents to the Presidium of the Academy of Sciences, USSR. The other set was sent to the popular Soviet magazine *Ogonyok*. Two or three weeks later, major Soviet newspapers (*Pravda, Izvestiya, Komsomol'skaya Pravda* and more) published articles, authored by notable scientists, debunking reports of UFOs over the Soviet Union. One article even rebuked the KGB of Yakutsk Autonomous Soviet Socialist Republic for sending the UFO report and photos to them.

1999 Kosmopoisk Expedition to Yakutia

The photographs in Pavlov's reports were of a UFO seen at the Tiksi settlement in 1960. Pavlov recalled that in the winter of that year, he was shown two photographs with the same object on each one. The UFO was seen at night over an Arctic meteorological station. The pictures were taken one after another, seconds apart. They clearly show a rhomboid object, moving low over the horizon. The photographer did not see the objects as he was taking the pictures.

Kolyma had been visited by UFOs even earlier, back in 1950. Valentin Ivanovich Akkuratov, senior navigator of the Soviet Arctic Air Force, wrote four reports to the Ministry of Civil Aviation regarding his encounters with UFOs. He addressed those reports to E. Loginov, then Minister of Civil Aviation. One such report, listed in Gherman Kolchin's books, concerned the 1950 incident, when the crew of his aircraft observed a disc-shaped UFO that appeared over the Nizhniye Kresti settlement on

Kolyma (renamed to Chersky settlement in 1963). Chersky is a settlement and the administrative center of Nizhnekolymsky District of the Sakha Republic (Yakutia), Russia, located on the Kolyma River about 1,242 miles east of Yakutsk. The UFO hovered in the southern area of sky over the horizon for three days. It resembled the moon but was smaller in size. The disc showed up at around 3:30 p.m. local time daily, as the settlement's population watched in astonishment. Soviet pilots in the area were among the most amazed observers. At 5:30 p.m. each day, the object would depart to the west, sharply gaining altitude, until it disappeared from view. When the report about this case was received in Moscow, an order came back to approach the object as closely as possible and study it. The "Catalina" aircraft was able to reach the object's altitude of 23,000 feet. The disc was pearly-white with pulsating edges. It had no antennae or other attachments. The Soviet crew noticed that the disk did not seem to react to their approach. It did not change its size, shape, or motion. It continued its previous slow movement from east to west. At the end of the third day, the disc left at its normal departure time but never came back.

The pilots carried out extensive correspondence about this incident with the Main Directorate of the Northern Sea Route, also known as Glavsevmorput. The correspondence and related materials, according to Akkuratov, are still in the archives of the Ministry of the Navy. The importance of the area was largely due to the Zelyoniy Mis harbour. It served the entire Northern Sea Route and, before the 1990s, was the largest Soviet Arctic seaport. It was the sea gateway for Yakutia and Chukotka's Bilibin area, and gained military-strategic prominence for the nation's entire north-eastern territory. Control over Arctic weather meant control over the weather in the Atlantic Ocean, the main battlefield of the Cold War, where long-range aircraft, aircraft carriers and submarines of the USSR faced off against their NATO adversaries.

UFOs AND THE ARCTIC OCEAN

Russian Arctic pilots who fly their aircraft over their nation's most remote areas have observed UFOs much more frequently than pilots who fly over populated areas of Russia. Arctic pilots report that during their encounters with these strange objects, all sound is lost around their aircraft. UFOs appear in foggy weather, as well as in clear weather. In one case, a UFO flew alongside the aircraft piloted by B. Korotkov. As the object maintained a parallel course, the airplane's hull began to degrade, especially around the tail fin, according to an article by A. Myagchenkov and A. Malikov in the 1992 digest *Prishel'tsi raydom*, or *Aliens Are Nearby*. Ukrainian writer A. Kul'sky participated in the UFO research projects of the Kiev group formed to study of anomalous phenomenon. The group had researched a number of cases linked to USOs in the Black Sea area during 1985-1992. But he also recalled one case that took place in the freezing waters of the Arctic Ocean. One evening, while the Soviet Navy was conducting manoeuvres, the sailors observed something that resembled a huge silver bullet ascend from the waters, break through the 9 feet of thick ice cover, and then disappear into the sky. These Navy men were accustomed, due to their military service, to seeing the launches of missiles from the depths of the sea.

However, in this case, the object they saw breaking through the ice was completely different. There was no fiery glow of rocket engines. The velocity at which the object exited the water was much greater than what a missile's velocity would be. Also, missiles are never launched when a thick layer of surface ice is present. This case was revealed in A. Kul'sky's book *Na perekrestkah vselennoy* or *At the Crossroads of the Universe* (Kiev, Ukraine, 1997).

Soviet leaders felt compelled to maintain a continuous military presence in the Arctic. In the 1950s, special studies were conducted by aircraft and drifting research stations of the Northern Sea Route with the ultimate goal of opening more of the Arctic to the Soviet military. The Soviet push into these remote territories was especially intense during the 1960s and 1970s. Soviet scientists were dispatched to conduct numerous research projects in the Arctic. The Northern Sea Route, which stretches approximately 3,100 miles across the Soviet maritime Arctic, from the Atlantic to the Pacific Oceans had been carefully expanded and developed. No other nation could rival the USSR in the field of meteorological observations of the Arctic territories. Soviet leaders knew that the United States could easily reach their Arctic territories with submarines, long-range aircraft, and missiles. Hence, enormous investments had been made to develop the Soviet Arctic and to build up military defences, from the borders of Norway to the Bering Strait. The Soviet Union had fortified its Navy and Air Force in the North. Soviet ice-breakers and specialized Arctic vessels maintained year-round navigation of the Glavsevmorput. And, all during the years of Soviet exploration and development of the Arctic, UFOs and USOs were sighted and tracked. Yet, these unidentified objects were by no means the only unusual phenomenon in the Arctic. A Russian ORT TV documentary from February 2000 revealed a shocking event that occurred to a team of researchers from the top secret Soviet North Pole exploration project called Sever-2 (North-2). Stalin had personally ordered the Sever-2 mission in 1948, and Lavrenty Beria, head of the secret police, was in control of the program.

In 1951, without any explanation, the program was terminated, and all materials pertaining to Sever-2 were quickly removed from Soviet scientific institutions and were buried under a top secret security classification. However, some Russian UFO researchers claim that some of the details of what happened leaked out in 1956. The available facts are presented below. Three Soviet airplanes, with experienced Arctic explorers onboard, had left from Kotelny Island in April 1948. On the way to the North Pole, they noticed unusual phenomena occurring down below them, but there was too much open water and too much fog for them to see very much. Reaching North Pole, the pilots found large stretches of ice that had apparently been broken up into large, jagged chunks. They sought a smooth place to land and finally did so, arriving on April 23, at 4:44 p.m. Moscow time. It was the first ever airplane landing at the North Pole. As the pilots left their aircraft, they encountered very unusual weather conditions, namely a winter thaw that was more appropriate for mainland Russia. The members of the team, all rugged individuals with nerves of steel, became concerned, feeling a sense of imminent danger. They measured the thickness of ice near their landing spot and found it to be 16 feet thick, which reassured them a bit. They set up camp, made plans for their research, and then tried to rest. But their period of rest was quickly interrupted.

The ice around their camp suddenly cracked, and they could see expanding water. A rapid and furious stream was bubbling up toward them, with steam rising from it. The airplane, which was parked near the cracking ice, began to slump over. The flight crew rushed to try to save the plane, while all around them strange, incredible changes were taken place. The first crack in the ice turned into a zigzagging and ever-expanding ravine that broke the camp in two parts. The Arctic explorers tossed equipment over the ravine to the other side and then jumped over to re-establish their camp on more solid footing. But the ice cover was developing more cracks and fissures. The landing strip they had used was breaking up into fragments. Black rivulets of water were visible everywhere. The small hill where the team had placed the Soviet red flag was now obscured by a strange fog. Small ice floes were adrift all around, carried away by powerful stream. The ice was moving at incredible speed.

The Arctic explorers figured out later that the ice floe they were on was moving in circle. The diameter of the circles was 90 nautical miles. They saw how a seal quickly swam near their ice floe and even tried to climb onto the ice floe, but the speed of the stream prohibited the attempt. This was also unusual in that seals do not live at the North Pole. The radius of the circles had diminished. They moved in a centripetal, spiral fashion. The explorers surely feared what fate might await them at the end of this movement. On the third day, the speed of the circular drifting movement diminished, ice fragments began moving straight to the north, the area of water was reduced, and the polar cold was felt again.

Artic Landscape (NOAA Photo)

What exactly did these Soviet polar explorers encounter in the forbidden North? Why was the Sever-2 program abruptly cancelled following this bizarre event?

According to the 2007 book *Planetarny Mif* or *Planetary Myth* by Violeta Violyeva and Dmitry Loginov, we may never know the answers to these questions. There are rumours in Russia of another secret program that also ended abruptly in the late 1970s in the Soviet North. Details about the program, codenamed "Typhoon," remain largely a mystery, but apparently it involved continuous underwater patrols, under the Arctic ice cover, by Soviet submarines, ready to launch intercontinental missiles in the event of a strike on the USSR.

Experts in contemporary Russia are amazed at the incomprehensible scale of the Typhoon mission. The Soviets cut tunnels through the granite mounds; built gigantic, underground storage spaces for spare parts and machinery; built huge, nuclear-proof shelters; designed magnificent roads that seemed to lead nowhere; and built splendid piers with communication towers in the most remote areas. The entire infrastructure for Typhoon was never completed, and the facilities were never utilized. Did the Soviets encounter some unknown force in the Artic that made it impossible for them to complete the project? This information comes from the 2005 book by I. Pavlovich and O. Ratnik called *Igrayuschiye teni* or *Playful Shadows* and a 1998 article by A. Sklyarov called "Podvodniy ledokol strategicheskogo naznacheniya," or Underwater Icebreaker of the Strategic Mission," published in the prestigious magazine *Nauka i Zhizn'* (Issue 7).

Even today, according to its leaders, geopolitically, Russia's most vital national interests are linked to the Arctic. If dangers to the Earth's ecology attract UFOs, then mysterious objects may be interested in the legacy of the Politburo's fascination with Glavsevmorput -- one million abandoned barrels of Soviet-era fuel that have polluted Arctic environment. Development of the Soviet North produced a deep, adverse impact on the Arctic ecosystems. The sharp decrease in military activity after the collapse of the USSR resulted in ugly trash dumps all over the North. The Laptev Sea, a part of the Arctic Ocean, is located off the coastline of Siberia in far northern Russia. The sea is positioned between the Taymyr Peninsula and Severnaya Zemlya in the west, and the New Siberian Islands in the east. In 1978, a UFO appeared next to a Soviet destroyer in the Laptev Sea and temporarily disabled the ship's navigation system. The captain and most of the crew observed a dome-shaped object at an altitude of 100 feet. The UFO sparkled with a bright yellow color and seemed to be semitransparent. After a while, the UFO slowly descended onto the surface of the sea, and glided upon it at great speed, not disturbing the environment. When the object disappeared from sight, the ship's system resumed normal operation. Another ship, located a few miles from the destroyer, observed nearby a strange yellow-colored object that rushed by on the surface of the water. This information was presented in a Russian TV documentary about USOs, aired in 2009.

The *Krasnaya Zvezda* newspaper, the print media mouthpiece of the Soviet Armed Forces, published a curious report in its October 23, 1985 issue about a sighting that took place in the Soviet Polar (Arctic) regions. A group of seamen reported a very bright, yellowish object low over the horizon.

From their vantage point, it seemed the size of a U.S. quarter. Three more similar objects were hovering at an equal distance from the first one. A lieutenant who came from his watch also observed the objects and stated unequivocally that what he saw were not helicopters. As this sighting took place at a time when UFOs were a taboo subject, the article ended with the assertion that what the lieutenant saw was actually the planet Jupiter. But if one of the objects was Jupiter, what were the three other objects that hovered alongside it?

Another amazing sighting occurred in 1980, according to an article by K. Puteyev titled "K vam NLO ne zaletalo?" or "Did a UFO Fly to You?" published in the official newspaper of the Northern Fleet, *Na strazhe Zapolyarya*, in Severodvinsk. The author interviewed Alexander Sczerbina, Captain 2nd Rank, who in 1991 was a specialist with the hydrometeorology unit of the Soviet Northern Fleet. The officer revealed that the unit where he served had collected data about anomalous physical phenomena as part of the SETKAMO research program, mentioned previously in this book. This data collection began in May of 1980. Through the years of gathering data, Sczerbina recalled that there were a dozen or so cases of appearance of "anomalies." Among reported sites where such phenomena was recorded were Kil'din Island, Olenegorsk (a town in the Murmansk Oblast, Russia, located beyond the Arctic Circle), and in the estuary of the Zapadnaya Litsa river. This is where the largest Russian naval base was built for its Northern Fleet. This base is located far in the north of Russia, on the Litsa Fjord at the westernmost point of the Kola Peninsula.

Photo Taken on July 28, 1981 in the Kalinin Region

Upon notification that an anomalous phenomenon had taken place, the unit would collect information, talk with eyewitnesses, attempt to obtain photos and drawings, and get reports form nearby military units. Per the SETKA instructions, all collected information and documents would be sent to the secret research institutes that studied such phenomena. No independent research could be conducted by the hydrometeorology unit, as this was not one of their functions. Sczerbina said that the unit never found out what happened to the information they had submitted to the scientists. In the 1989 incident, they received a report from a submarine garrison about strange lights observed at night over a bay. There were three lights, forming a single line, at 30 degrees to the horizon. The lights would either remain in one location or move rapidly around the sky. One seaman was able to take pictures, but the photo did not reveal the source of the lights. When the collected information was compared with media reports about UFOs over Moscow and Denmark, Sczerbina's colleagues concluded that the cases were very similar. But in 1991, the scientists, who had received the report and data from the hydrometeorology unit, kept their silence, and did not provide any feedback.

In 1984, at the end of October, an unusual incident occurred in the Sea of Laptev area, in Russia's northern territories. Valery Lukin, head of an expedition to the Arctic and Antarctic areas, was notified that a UFO had been reported in the area. Border guards confirmed that they had observed "fire" about 20 miles from the base airport. Lukin and others took a helicopter up, from which they observed a sphere that was emitting a raspberry-colored luminescence. It was described as "internal" luminescence. The UFO would not let them come close, and vanished when the helicopter was three minutes away from reaching it. They circled the area for half an hour, but found nothing. The Bering Strait connects the Arctic Ocean and the Bering Sea. It is located between extreme northeast Asia and extreme northwest North America. In 1990, three UFOs were observed flying out from its waters, at its narrowest part, near St. Lawrence Island, which is part of Alaska, but is actually closer to Russia than to the Alaskan mainland. Among observers was Soviet academician R. F. Avramenko, who viewed the UFOs through binoculars. This case was reported in Vadim Chernobrov's book *Nad propastyu neraskritikh tayn* or *Over the Abyss of Unsolved Mysteries* (Moscow, 1997). Just as a side note, we need to add that Russia's Radio Instrument Building Research Institute under the supervision of Academician Ramiliy Avramenko had reportedly developed a plasma weapon capable of striking any target at altitudes of up to 31 miles.

Something very unusual took place in the waters of the North Sea in 1993, as reported in the February 2 issue of *NLO Magazine*, in an article titled "Incredible 'Russian' submarines." On February 6, 1993, during a powerful storm, a NATO squadron encountered three American destroyers. The Americans sent a radio signal, telling NATO's military vessels not to approach closer than three miles. The NATO ships stopped their progress and waited. Soon thereafter, sixteen flying craft of bright amber color appeared over the American ships. They hovered for a few minutes and then flew away at great speed. A few weeks later there was a report that one of the American destroyers had disappeared during the incident. A massive naval search began, including ships from NATO, the U.S., and Russia.

The American destroyer was never located, but something else was found. On April 15, a Russian anti-submarine vessel reported that it had detected an unidentified underwater object, moving at an approximate speed of 60 knots and measuring about 688 feet by 393 feet. The sighting reportedly occurred in the Barents Sea, according to a 2009 Russian TV documentary about USOs. Alexey B. Blinov, a scientist who headed an Arctic expedition in August of 1995 in the Karsk Sea (a part of the Arctic Ocean), reported another episode in his article published by the *Anomaliya* newspaper (Issue 4, 1996). On August 13, 1995, about 8 p.m., Blinov observed some 328 feet away from his ship, a bright underwater object. It moved perpendicularly to his ship, the *Yakov Smirnitsky*. Another scientist joined Blinov, who directed his attention to the strange object. Initially, Blinov thought they were looking at a beluga whale, but when they observed it closer, it turned out to be a bright round spot, fluorescent, and approximately three meters (10 feet) in diameter. The object's speed was constant and too slow for a whale. It approached the Russian ship, went down under the bottom of the vessel, and some fifteen seconds later, it ascended on the other side, resuming its previous speed and direction. A. Blinov believes the object was definitely of non-natural origin, for it moved vertically and also perpendicular to the current. The object did not seem to cause any electromagnetic interference and also did not seem to affect the humans or wildlife in the vicitnity.

MYSTERIOUS CHUKOTKA

The Chukotka autonomous region is one of the 89 regions of the Russian Federation. Chukotka is located in the far northeast part of Russia. Chukotka is located at the meeting points of two continents, two oceans, and four seas. The Chukotskiy Peninsula is a short distance away from the United States. It is the Russian territory that is the closest to Alaska. The Bering Strait is the only boundary between Chukotka and Alaska. About half of Chukotka's territory lies above the Arctic Circle. Permafrost and tundra cover most of the region, resulting in a harsh climate. The geographical location of the Chukotka peninsula between two oceans yields extreme temperatures and complex atmospheric weather patterns.

Map of Russia Showing Location of Chukotka

Early in the year is when the people of Chukotka, land of the north, typically see UFOs. During the "white nights," when the Sun does not leave the sky, such encounters are rare. Yet, there was a noteworthy exception to this rule in the summer of 1990.

The sighting was by the crew of a ship that was harboured in the Ust-Belaya Village, a large rural community at the shore of the Anadyr River in Chukotka. The crew noticed cumulus clouds that suddenly formed a perfect circle. In the center of the circle, they observed the clear blue sky. The watch officer, Aleksandr Polorotov, took pictures of the event unfolding before their eyes. Suddenly, groups of strange aircraft exited the circle, and flew away, to disappear in the surrounding clouds. The Soviet sailor, who previously served in the Air Force, knew that the "aircraft" he saw were not Soviet and, most likely, not man-made at all. Polorotov was able to take just several pictures before his camera malfunctioned. When the film was developed, a cigar shaped object could be seen on some of the photos. It had a strange luminescence and some "black dots" were also visible at a distance. But the mysterious "aircraft," also observed by seven other crew members, were not in any of the photos. After the sighting, the Soviet crew members experienced general weakness and headaches, as have other witnesses in UFO cases.

To add even more questions to the UFO sighting seen in the vicinity of Ust'-Belaya, it was determined that it came from the mysterious Lake El'gygytgyn, located 62 miles north of the Arctic Circle in northeast Russia (67° 30' N latitude and 172° 05' E longitude). Scientists say the lake was created 3.6 million years ago by a meteorite impact that carved out a 12-mile diameter crater. An international expedition sent to the lake in May, 1998, successfully recovered sediment cores from the center of the 9 mile wide basin, penetrating nearly 42 feet in 574 feet of water depth using a percussion piston corer from the lake ice surface. They discovered a striking similarity between the El'gygytgyn magnetic susceptibility record and the Bermuda Rise, as well as Bahamas Outer Ridge Numerous legends exist about this lake -- tales of strange disappearances, the presence of unknown life forms, and more.

According to one local legend, a shaman capable of levitation resides in the area of the lake. From the description provided, the shaman is dressed in something that modern observers say looks like a modern spacesuit. A noted Russian UFO researcher and proponent of the ancient astronaut hypothesis, Vladimir Avinsky, has collected and analyzed many of the local legends. There is a geographic area of Chukotka where UFOs apparently allow themselves to be photographed. It is bordered by Providence, Lavrenty, and Uelen. In the vicinity of Cape Shmidt, UFOs are invisible to the naked eye, but technology is able to register their presence. In the winter of 1991, radar at the Shmidt Airport, as well as the radar of a lone helicopter in the area, registered the presence of a strange object. The UFO was 18 miles from the settlement, and flew at the altitude of approximately a mile. A helicopter began to approach the object, coming to within a kilometre (half a mile) of it. The indicator on the helicopter's radar clearly showed the object's presence, yet the pilot was not able to see anything.

In the areas of Vankarem, Ust'-Belaya, and El'gygytgyn Lake, UFOs adversely affect humans. For some reason, UFOs tend to be quite aggressive there. However, few people inhabit the above-mentioned areas. Yevgeny Rozhkov, who published an article about the Chukotka UFOs in the July 1992 issue of the *Vostok Rossii* newspaper, is of the opinion that there may be secret UFO bases in those areas.

Around the Shmidt and Anadyr areas, UFOs are rarely seen. Are they afraid of the Russian Air Force? Could there be a research base, something like Nevada's Area 51? Some encounters and sightings in the Russian lakes have sad consequences for those who come close to the unknown reality. We have described the 1982 incident with the "swimmers" elsewhere in this book. But twelve years before that year, another sinister incident took place in yet another remote Russian area.

UFOs AND USOs OF RUSSIA'S FAR EAST

The natives of Priamurye and Primorye (Russian Far Eastern territories) did not consider anomalous phenomena to be anomalous. They knew and accepted poltergeist, the abominable snowman, UFOs, and the "Flying Man." The natives have their own names for these phenomena, which have been present for many years through legends, testimonies, eyewitness reports and written accounts.

The legends of the taiga dwellers vividly describe heavenly "doors" that open up between different worlds. The worlds are located in the "outer, original world," "underground," and in the "Great Beyond." The shamans have detailed descriptions of ancient aircraft (as relayed in the legends of their people). They believe that "flying saucers" are nothing other than *agd ezen adani*, ships of the Sovereigns of the Thunder. The "sovereigns" sometimes took humans with them, sometimes forcibly. Before the First World War, local Udege hunters and their Russian *Staroveri* (descendants of religious dissidents of 18th century Russia) friends observed some very strange phenomena, while hunting together. In several localities, including Annuye and Bikin, they sighted UFOs that moved in the air and mysterious "three bright points" that also moved on the ground. The "goloan," a ball-lightning-like object moved through the sky, and while in flight, it left a smoky or luminous trail. The elders told stories of the *amban khotongon*, or "Devil's fiery skull."

Apparently it fell down to Earth from a UFO. A "skull," appearing near a dwelling, was able to scare people to such an extent that they could neither move nor lie down. To put it in 20th century terms, the" skull" exerted adverse biological and physiological effects on human beings. It was observed that lukewarm water in the presence of such a "skull" immediately began boiling. Kamen'-Ribolov is a village, located on the shores of Lake Khanka, in the Khankay region of Russia's Maritime Province. It was established in 1865 by Russian Cossacks. On June 1, 1899, in the late evening hours, observers saw a blue sphere, about ¾ *arshin* in diameter [*arshin*, an old Russian measure of length, is equal to 28 inches]. The sphere flew in from the south, moving north, at a distance from the moored steamboat Kazak Ussuriyskiy. The sphere was about 300 *sazhens* away from the vessel at approximately the same height (one *sazhen* is equal to 84 inches). The sphere was observed for about twenty minutes. Later in the evening, the sphere returned from the north, now moving south, at the same distance from the ship but at greater speed.

It disappeared eleven minutes later. When the sphere flew back and forth in different directions, as reported by three eyewitnesses from the ship, its color did not change and it emitted no noise. This case was reported in the *Vostochniy Vestnik* newspaper in Vladivostok on July 10, 1899.

Terney is a settlement, located in the north-eastern area of Russia's Maritime Province, about 406 miles from Vladivostok. The land is comprised of hard-to-reach places, wilderness, and wild animals -- taiga, waterfalls, mineral springs, and beautiful lakes. Among the lakes is Lake Blagodatnoye. In 1956, dozens of fishermen who worked at the lake observed a UFO that crashed into Sea of Japan. They described a silvery object with a diameter of one mile flying rapidly over them at an altitude of 20,000 feet. The flight was accompanied by strong grinding sounds and thick smoke. While in flight, the object lost numerous small parts, thin metal threads that resembled horse hairs. The next day, these were picked up by fishermen. The UFO resembled a "hat" with red portholes located around its rim. This incident was reported by K. Pronina in the 2005 article "NLO v Primorye: samiye anomal'niye mesta," or "UFO in the Maritime Province: Most Anomalous Sites." The Zeya River is a northern tributary of the mighty Amur River. One of the main tributaries of the Zeya River is the Urkan River. It runs between the Zeya and Tynda rivers. Regionally it is in the Amur Region of the Russian Federation. It is also almost on the southern border with Yakutia-Sakha Republic of the Russian Federation. UFOs began their visits to the area in the early 1970s. They were sighted quite often, in the spring of 1970, after the military confrontation between China and USSR in 1969 over their border disputes.

Border troops and anti-aircraft units on both sides of the border paid close attention to the UFOs. Later, after the UFOs had flown over Mongolia, the troops there opened fire on the intruders and also reported the presence of additional UFOs. The Mongolians claimed that the routes of UFO flights crossed somewhere over the Soviet territory, 1,031 miles to the northeast of Ulan-Bator. While Soviet radars did pinpoint the precise coordinates, the radar operators could not determine any specific details. All that was established was that it was the same remote area of the Siberian taiga where UFOs had come from and vanished, not far from Urkan River. This was reported in Vadim Chernobrov's *Entsiklopedia Neopoznannnogo* or *Encyclopedia of the Unidentified*, 1998. Vladivostok is Russia's largest port city on the Pacific Ocean, the administrative center of the Maritime Province, and the home port of the Russian Pacific Fleet. According to Vadim Chernobrov, at the end of 1989, a triangular UFO was observed over the Tikhaya Bay, near Vladivostok, in the same Maritime Province of Russia. It was not detected by radar. Russian Navy artillery fire tried to shoot it down, but the UFO changed direction and departed at great speed. Naval aircraft that arrived in the area shortly thereafter could not locate the object.

1977 was another interesting year for UFO and USO sightings. Here is a sighting, described in a letter to the Academy of Sciences, USSR, and abridged for this book. The date was July 7, 1977, precisely at 4 p.m. Moscow time. The ship *Nikolay Ostrovsky* navigated through the Tatar Strait from the Port Vanino and the La Perouse Strait to the Providence harbour.

Port Vanino is a major port in Pacific Russia; it is included into the ten largest ports of Russia as to its cargo-handling volume. Through Port Vanino pass the flows of export and import cargo to and from China, Japan, Australia, the USA, Korea, and other countries as well as cargo going to the northern territories of Russia. Port Vanino operates all year round.

Vladivostok in the 1980s

On that day in July 1977, a very unusual event took place. The weather was cloudy, and the visibility was 5 to 7 miles. To the east of the ship, at an altitude of around 1,000-1,300 feet, the seamen observed a cloud-like formation shaped like a parallelogram. One of the eyewitnesses, radio operator O. M. Dereza, stated in the letter that he shuddered at the thought that whoever was inside the cloud formation, which moved at the same speed as the ship, must have carefully watched and studied the seamen. Dereza could not see anyone in the cloud but somehow felt that "they" heard and understood the Russian language and could even read the seamen's thoughts from a distance. He thought the perfectly shaped parallelogram cloud formation could have been a spaceship from another world. Whatever it was, the cloud formation disappeared at 4:32 p.m. Moscow time. The incident was described in a number of Russian publications; but the original reference comes from a 1982 interview with Academician V. Troitsky in the *Nauka I religiya* magazine (issue 10).

In 1989, a sighting took place in the Maritime province (Primorskiy Krai). It was reported in the *Tikhookeanskaya Gazeta* newspaper (Khabarovsk) on October 21, 1989. The report came from the captain of Soviet tanker *Volgoneft-161*, O. I. Zimakov. The actual sighting occurred on August 2 of that year. The UFO was spotted in the northern part of the sky, at a 35-degree angle to the horizon.

The sphere had a pale yellow color, and it has some sort of luminescence around it, like the moon. The object moved in the north-easterly direction, ascending slightly over the horizon. The observers watched it for about five minutes, and then it disappeared.

KHABAROVSK, 1990

As reported by the Northern News Service, bright red spheres flew across the horizon and darted above the ice-bound Amur River. In Khabarovsk on the evening of March 21, 1990, witnesses reported that the objects kept a fixed distance between each other. The policemen, who observed the UFOs, stated that the objects arrived in force. He tried to videotape them, but the video was plagued by some kind of interference, which caused a lot of flickering and flashing images. Witnesses reported strange objects to the military, the police, and the government officials. One city hospital called for help, stating that a cigar shaped object was hovering above it and causing panic among the patients and personnel. As a patrol car approached the hospital, the UFO flew off. Other witnesses reported a low flying "saucer" with a bright surface and "running lights" all along the hull. The UFO shifted around, its "nose" dipping and rising. The *Suvorovski Natisk* daily paper, mouthpiece of the Far Eastern Military District, asked a spokesman of the air defence headquarters whether they had received any UFO reports. He replied that on March 21, a UFO was detected moving 328-393 feet above ground. It was a black, cigar shaped object 164 feet in length. In its rear part, a ruby-colored glow was observed. The orderly officer phoned this information in to the headquarters. Yet the radars detected nothing.

Ufologists in Vladivostok reported that in January of 1990, Tumnin villagers from the taiga area near the Okhotsk Sea observed a huge spherical body. It drifted slowly to the southeast in a cloudless sky. Then there was an interesting article in January 20, 1990 issue of the *Tikhookeanskaya Zvezda* newspaper, referring to an incident that took place on January 14, in the same village of Tumnin. The eyewitness described an object in the sky that drifted slowly from the horizon and had a huge, semitransparent, egg-shaped body. The eyewitnesses later described the object as a silvery sphere that contained inside it something dense. The chief of the local meteorological station, Y. Kwiatkowski, mentioned that a number of unidentified objects had frequented the area lately. Among them were luminescent balls of red, green, and yellow colours. On November 29, 1989, a luminescent object flew from behind the mountains at a low speed and a low altitude. The object drifted toward the center of the village, and hovered over it. Three multi-colored beams pointed toward the ground. An hour later, a similar object was sighted over Vanino, Sovetskaya Gavan', and Zaveti Ilyicha village. Tumnin Village is located in a fault zone with active geological activity. There are thermal springs. A nearby mountain stands over the site of a magnetic anomaly. Perhaps this is the source of mysterious luminescence that has been reported by local hunters.

In 2004, on January 17, at 3 a.m., the crew of tanker *Fokino* observed a UFO in the area of Dalnegorsk. This settlement is the site of the crashed UFO we described in our first chapter. The object hovered over the mounds of the Kamenka settlement, six miles from Dalnegorsk. The object left toward Japan after three hours of hovering, and manoeuvring in the sky, some two miles from the shore. It was a sphere-shaped UFO, of reddish-orange color. The object was radiant, and resembled a small beacon. Dr. Dvuzhilni, the famous local UFO researcher and scientist, visited the area of the sighting and told the newspaper that on December 30, 2003, a witness who lives in Dalnegorsk had observed a UFO (also about 3 a.m.) not far from there. The object was radiant, pyramid-shaped, about 65 feet by 16 feet in size, and also resembled a beacon.

As it moved toward the Shumniy settlement, the eyewitness, Alexei Kolesnikov, tried to repeat the flashing of the UFO's beacon with his car's headlights. The UFO, as if noticing this signal, descended and began to approach. When it was at the distance of a third of a mile, a passenger in Kolesnikov's car screamed in fear. Kolesnikov stopped the car and turned off the headlights. The UFO immediately turned around and departed toward Shumniy. At the same moment, another object ascended from a hill, and flew toward another settlement, Nizhniye Luzhki. The report was published in the *Komsomolskaya Pravda* (Vladivostok edition) newspaper on January 24, 2004 issue.

According to Russian media, on September 5, 2006, people in Vladivostok observed three radiant spherical UFOs (or perhaps one UFO consisting of three parts?) The next day, a Russian aviator called radio OKAY, a popular local station, to report that what the people saw the day before were aerial targets for Russian SU-27 front line fighter aircraft. But locals insist that the UFOs did not look like targets. The Pacific Fleet's anti-aircraft defence headquarters informed *Komsomolskaya Pravda* reporters on the 8th of September that they had nothing with the objects. According to retired Air Force major Roman Ronin, the Air Force issues warnings before conducting such exercises. According to him, the UFO did resemble a "chandelier" that consisted of SAB-250 aircraft bombs. They are candle bombs, often used for aircraft target practice. The SU-27aircraft must have had powerful aviation cannons aboard. Assuming that there really was target practice that night, the fighter plane would have to be one mile from the target. But there was no aircraft. If it was not visible due to darkness, there would still be a huge explosion when its missile hits the candle bomb. But there was only one explosion, far away from the object.

Ronin observed and counted four lights that approached the object at low speed -- much less than the speed of a missile shot from an aviation cannon or a rocket. And the object periodically vanished and reappeared, as if turned on and off. Other witnesses also reported four lights. Local policeman described the object to the reporters. It hovered over the sea at the altitude of one or two miles. It consisted of ten bright yellow lights (they moved around in circular motion). The object was long; its size impressive. The largest of the objects would slowly dim, and then radiate again.

Three or four times, other smaller objects would approach it. At a distance of 1,600 feet, one smaller object seemed to flare up or explode. Some local people told the policeman that the military put a dirigible in the sky and fired S-300 missiles at it from a local anti-aircraft defence unit. But military experts assured the policeman that such target shooting had never been and is not conducted now in the Maritime Province. Researchers think it was a real UFO, a very large and bright object. The newspaper also reported that there were a number of additional UFO sightings in the area in 2005.

June 1980 Sighting (Russian UFO Archives)

UFOs AND USOs IN CENTRAL ASIA AND MONGOLIA

An interesting UFO sighting took place in early July 1975, in the Soviet Uzbekistan. Four young people who were vacationing on the shores of the Charvak Reservoir woke up at 3 a.m. feeling intense fear. The reason for this fear was quickly apparent -- a radiant sphere ascended from underwater, approximately 2,600 feet from the shore. An eyewitness said the light of the sphere was cold and deadly, hundreds times brighter than the light of a day lamp. As the sphere rose up, concentric circles formed around it. The circles were of different thickness and brightness. This luminescent sphere slowly rose above the lake. The witnesses observed this phenomenon for over 7 minutes, in absolute silence. And all the time, the observers experienced feelings of absolute fear.

Snake Valley is located in the Mongolian Altai Mountains. V. Gorsky was a Soviet major in 1983, while serving in Mongolia. On March 23 of that year, he was in the Snake Valley when Gorsky and two commanding officers observed a silver disk at an altitude of approximately 1,300 feet. Its color was constantly changing, the predominant ones being rose and silver.

With the black starry sky as the background, they clearly saw a blue halo around the object. A narrow ray of light resembling a search light descended to the ground. The impression was that the object was illuminating the area, as if searching for something. Other service members were called, and over 30 people observed the phenomenon. The object remained at the distance of 1-2 miles and "studied" the area for another four minutes. Then the ray disappeared, as did the halo. The disc ascended another 1,300 feet, and hovered there. Then, it suddenly vanished.

There is a lake at the distance of 86 miles from the site of the observation. Gorsky said that off-duty Russian soldiers went there for the fishing. One night, a powerful ray of light from a nearby mountain pass illuminated the fishermen. Later, the ray moved away in an erratic manner, moving vertically and also zigzagging. When dawn came, the ray slowly moved away behind the mountain. When Gorsky looked at the UFO, he felt a sense of overwhelming. It was as if he knew that this object had powers that were way beyond any power on Earth. He published the article "Krutitsa-vertitsa disk goluboy," or "The Blue Disc is Rotating Around" in the Belarusian military newspaper *Vo slavu rodiny* (Minsk, May 22, 1993).

Syr Darya is a river in Central Asia. It rises from two headstreams in the Tien Shan Mountains in Kyrgyzstan and eastern Uzbekistan and flows for approximately 1,379 miles west and northwest through southern Kazakhstan to the Aral Sea. The Aral Sea, located in Uzbekistan and Kazakhstan, formerly part of the former Soviet Union, is historically a saline lake. It is in the center of a large, flat desert basin. Millions of years ago, the area was covered by a massive inland sea. When the waters receded, they left a broad plain of highly saline soil. One of the remnants of the ancient sea was the Aral Sea, the fourth largest inland body of water in the world. The Aral Sea is fed by the Syr Darya and another river, the Amu Darya.

In 1991, strange images of unknown origin were discovered at the bottom of the sea. This happened during the aerial photography expedition of the Kazakh Scientific Research Hydro meteorological Institute. The scientists were taking photos of the Syr Darya flood lands to determine the sources of the loss of the river's waters, before it flows into the Aral Sea. The Soviet Union began irrigating vast areas along both rivers in the early 1950s for cotton production. High volumes of water were diverted causing the rivers to sometimes run dry by the time they reached the Aral Sea. The Aral Sea is highly polluted, largely as the result of industrial projects, weapons testing, and fertilizer runoff that occurred before the break-up of the Soviet Union.

Reporter Ol'ga Khrabrikh, in the March 1, 2011 issue of the *Leninskaya Smena* newspaper, claims that photographs of the coastline and the bottom of the Aral Sea show furrow-like images of gigantic, strange shapes. Some resemble lines, while others look like the outlines of rockets, or trails of huge underwater vehicles. The width of the shapes is anywhere from 6 to 164 feet, while the length is several miles. Some of these bizarre shapes possess intricate geometrical structure. It was Boris Smerdov, at the time a Soviet hydrologist, who requested that the area be photographed in the early 1990s.

He is convinced that the shapes at the bottom of the sea were created by extraterrestrial civilizations utilizing advanced technologies. All the years since the discovery of strange shapes, Smerdov has been trying to find funds for further research but has not succeeded. Over the years, the sea has receded, and some shapes have disappeared because of storms, vegetation, and other factors. The furrows that remain underwater have retained their shapes.

Smerdov mentioned two interesting facts: similar lines resembling furrows are found at the bottom of the Caspian Sea, and local villagers tell stories about sailors in the distant past who deliberately avoided the area where the strange shapes are located, at depth of about 50 feet. A report we received from Russia described strange events that took place in 1958. In June of that year, B. Muratov and his father from the town of Chimbay, Karakalpak ASSR, were coming home after fishing. It was around 9 pm, and the sky was clear. The sun hid beyond the horizon. Suddenly they noticed a huge disc-shaped object approaching them at low altitude from the northeast. It was flying directly toward them. Muratov pointed the object out to his father, who remarked, "Probably an airplane." About 328 feet over them, as the object flew past, they saw that it was no aircraft. It emitted a steady "zing, zing, zing" sound. No other sounds were heard, its diameter was about 82 feet, and it had some time of pipe-like structure attached vertically to the hull. The disc's speed was no more than 155- 186 miles an hour. Its hull was shiny, with one side appearing a bit reddish. Two year later, other local fishermen in the same area observed a similar object.

USO AND UFO SIGHTINGS IN THE BLACK SEA

Novorossiysk is a city in southern Russia and the main Russian port on the Black Sea. In December 1941, Soviet anti-aircraft gunners defending the city against Nazi forces, opened fire on an invisible object. The UFO left a trail in the sky that resembled an inversion trail but seemed more like a smoke screen. The UFO could not be seen through a stereoscopic telescope and naval binoculars, but the impression was that the object was fairly close to the gunners. The best of the observers determined that the object was flying at the altitude of 31 miles, at a distance of 43 miles. Someone in the Navy headquarters demanded that the gunners open fire on the object. The battery commanders concurred, as they visually observed the object's flight. But they had been mistaken as to the proximity of the object, and the artillery fire had no effect. Meanwhile, the slow-moving UFO "dropped" two smaller objects, accompanied by more of the smoke screen.

The next case was mentioned in the 1982 manuscript of well-known Russian ufologist Vadim Vilinbakhov, who passed away in 1982. He was the first Chairman of the Leningrad Commission for Anomalous Phenomena of the Geographic Society of the USSR, and Candidate of Science (History). Vilinbakhov formulated the psychological phenomenon known as "detachment." The gist of it is that people are prone to ignore incomprehensible and frightful phenomena.

Vilinbakhov's manuscript, dated 1982, was titled *NLO v nashem nebe* or *UFOs in Our Sky*, as reported by Mikhail Gershtein. Years ago V.V. Krapiva, Ukrainian researcher and author, met with Professor Korsakov of the Odessa University. The professor told him of a conversation he had with a friend of his, a Soviet Navy officer who had served at the Sevastopol naval base. Back in the 1950's this officer personally sighted a UFO. The object suddenly rose from behind a battle cruiser. The officer was under the impression that the object had surfaced from the depths of the Black Sea. Professor Korsakov had kept a photograph of the object. *Tehnika Molodezhi* (Technology for the Youth in Russian) is a famous and immensely popular Soviet and Russian periodical magazine founded in the 1930s, and still published today. During the Soviet period, it often published positive articles about anomalous phenomena, and even UFOs – as opposed to demeaning, degrading, and debunking at the behest of the prevailing Soviet Communist ideology. The magazine published an article by N. Yerokhin, a Siberian engineer, in its Issue 12, 1991, in which Yerokhin quoted from the 1956 book *Svecheniye Morya* or *Marine Glowing Sea* that described several interesting episodes about giant underwater "wheels" rotating at great speeds; luminescent lines that crossed the ocean from horizon to horizon; and fluorescent spots, ascending from the depths.

Crimea is an autonomous republic in today's independent Ukraine. It is located on the northern coast of the Black Sea, occupying a peninsula of the same name. The Crimean Peninsula's area is 17 000 square miles. It is surrounded by the Black Sea and the Sea of Azov. Kastropol, a Crimean resort about 15 miles from the city of Yalta, is a secluded place. In September of 1964 about 150 vacationers from the resort sailed the Black Sea and observed a shiny disc that appeared over the sea. Its size was somewhat smaller than the moon in the sky. The disc suddenly came to a complete stop in the sky and just hovered. Most, but not all, passengers observed the disc for about three or four minutes, according to a 1979 article by a researcher named Pamirenko, which was mentioned by Colonel Kolchin in his books. Gherman Kolchin, a retired Soviet colonel, was deputy Chairman of the Leningrad Commission for Anomalous Phenomena of the Geographic Society of the USSR. He was an expert in the field of UFO research, and published several books. His book *Fenomen NLO - vzglyad iz Rossii* or *UFO Phenomenon - A View from Russia* was published in 1997. Colonel Kolchin passed away in February of 2007.

His colleague, Arvid Mordvin-Schodro, a former military engineer and expert in aviation technology who had worked in a secret research institution of the Ministry of Defence (NII-115), and was a noted Russian UFO researcher who had several sightings himself. He passed away in 2008.

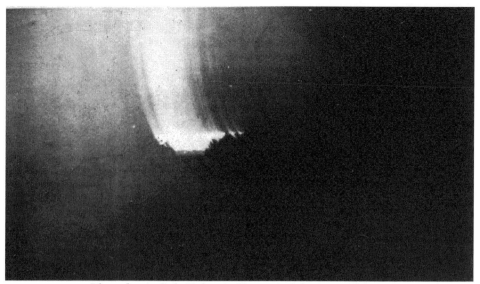

Photo by A. Guk, Taken in Krasnoyarsk region, Siberia

In August of 1965, Soviet astronomer S. Tsekhanovich, was vacationing in a top Soviet resort on the Black Sea, in the Noviy Afon area of northwest Caucasus, when the lecturer from the Moscow Observatory witnessed an unusual object in the sky. She was swimming in the sea, and the air was clear and transparent. Twenty minutes after the sunset, she was swimming back to the shore, which was about 300 feet away. Suddenly she noticed a black spot high on the sky, to the west. A few seconds later, she could discern an elongated object. She thought it was an airplane, but noticed it had no wings and made absolutely no sound while flying. The object, which seemed black in color, flew over the sea, west to east. About 1,300 feet from Tsekhanovich, the object descended to about 300 feet over the sea and then made a sharp 90-degree turn toward the shore, and continued flying north, gaining speed. At that moment, it started turning as if around a longitudinal axis. In its middle, a band of light flashed. Tsekhanovich could now see that the object was disc-shaped. It kept turning, and the light intensified. Then the object's shape seemed to change into a circle. In the center of it was a "porthole," glowing with yellow light. The diameter of the "porthole" was about half the size of the object's diameter. The object continued its flight, gaining altitude, over the shore, until it became a dot and disappeared. The entire sighting lasted about a minute, according to Feliks Zigel's 1967 article "Letayuschiye tarelki-mif ili real'nost'?" or "Flying saucers, Myth or Reality?" Mikhail Gershtein also discussed the case in his books.

Sochi is a resort city located north of Russia's border with Georgia, along the Black Sea near the Caucasus Mountains. Greater Sochi stretches 145 kilometres (90 miles) along the sea and is considered one of the longest cities in Europe. The Lazarevskaya district is located at the northern outskirts of Sochi. In August of 1970, eight eyewitnesses observed around a dozen rectangular objects that appeared suddenly from the direction of the Black Sea. They were of identical size, each the size of the sun's disc.

The objects flew one behind the other, in column formation, and the distance between they were equal to twice the size of each object. Their movement was uneven, but all changes in the movement were synchronized among all the objects, according to historian Vadim Vilinbakhov, as noted in Gherman Kolchin's books.

The Black Sea had its own sightings the next year, such as the one that took place in May 1979. An object ascended from the water a few dozen feet from ships. It was a gigantic shiny, metallic disc that pulled up a huge column of water as it rose out of the sea, before the water came rushing back down. The UFO vanished quickly into the upper reaches of the sky, as reported by S. V. Tyutin in Felix Zigel's manuscript *Petrozavodskoye divo* (1979). Zigel had a photograph of the object in his archives. At 2 am, on August 12 in 1979, Y. Podvyazniy, an engineer, and two companions were on the shore of the Black Sea, to the west of Khosta, a resort area of Russian city of Sochi. They saw a radiant object that moved jerkily, from the direction of the sea. Soon thereafter, the object made a sharp lunge and came to within one mile from the eyewitnesses. They understood that it was neither ship nor boat, but something unusual.

Two of them ran to get a camera and a looking glass. The object moved away to a distance of approximately nine miles. They took nine photos. The observers estimated the object to be between 164 and 229 feet in diameter. It had four glowing portholes. The UFO moved slowly over the surface of the sea at an altitude from 16-65 feet. It moved to the right, flying away at three degrees to the horizon. A patrol vessel, stationed nearby, used its searchlight to illuminate the object, which turned out to be spherical. The UFO lit up momentarily but then quickly dimmed, as the searchlight and all illumination on the patrol ship suddenly powered down, according to Vadim Vilinbakhov's manuscript *UFO in Our Sky*. The ship *Akademik Aleksey Krilov*, a Soviet scientific research vessel was located about five miles away from the peninsula when its crew observed a UFO. The sighting lasted approximately four minutes. The object was a luminescent cloud, inside of which something was "flickering." The sighting was reported in the Soviet Navy newspaper *Flag Rodini* (November 11, 1990). The UFO moved with the speed of an airplane, high up in the sky. Suddenly the flickering "something" moved away from the UFO, and at a considerable distance from it, simply disappeared. Suddenly, the UFO seemed to "explode" and emit a large volume of gases. Moments later, a second explosion occurred.

The SETKA program's instructions also affected Soviet scientific research vessels. Mikhail Gershtein, who has access to the manuscripts of the late Russian UFO researcher Alexandr Kuzovkin, has mentioned in his books one case from 1980. The crew, after encountering UFOs, not only sent their report to the Goskomgidromet (USSR State Committee for Hydrometeorology) of the USSR, as instructed, but also sent radiograms to the Odessa harbour (where their ship Viktor Bugayev was registered), and to the Soviet newspapers *Pravda*, *Izvestiya*, and *Vechernyaya Odessa*. The Goskomgidromet (and its main organization, the Institute of Applied Geophysics), like a number of other Soviet academic institutes and scientific organizations, had participated in the SETKA-AN program. It had its own expert group to research anomalous phenomena (i.e., UFOs and USOs); a not-too-difficult undertaking considering that this Goskomgidromet operated a gigantic net of hydro meteorological stations all over the nation. Its scientists were presumably able to distinguish "an alien spacecraft" from a bright star or another natural phenomenon. And as did their military counterparts, the Goskomgidromet had received precise Metodicheskiye Ukazaniya, or methodical directives regarding collection of anomalous phenomena observations and data, tailored to the non-military entities.

Balaklava was no ordinary Soviet town on the Crimean peninsula in the district of Sevastopol. It contained an underground, formerly classified submarine base that was operational until 1993. The base was virtually indestructible and designed to survive a direct atomic bomb strike. During that Soviet period, Balaklava was one of the most secret residential areas in the nation, because of the "amenity" of having a top secret submarine base. At the end of 1982, during naval exercises, an unidentified target was detected over Balaklava. The UFO would not respond to repeated radio inquiries. Eyewitnesses recalled that the object, moving at an altitude of a regular helicopter flight, had a very sharp nose, and sparks were coming from its tail section. Interceptor-jets were sent after it, but the object descended rapidly and plunged under water at their approach. Soviet Navy vessels, dispatched to the area, could not detect it underwater.

Another UFO sighting took place in July of 1989 over the waters of the Black Sea. A TU-154 aircraft (flight number 85500) was headed to the city of Simferopol. At the altitude of six miles over the sea and a distance of 62 miles north-northwest from the town of Adler, the crew contacted their flight controller to find out what "dirigible" was flying at their altitude. The flight controller assured them there was no dirigible. Yet the pilots clearly observed a cigar-shaped body, its color that of light steel with a silvery tint. Then, another object separated from the UFO. The second craft was originally square-shaped but then shape-shifted, becoming triangular. Its surface later became "blurred," and then it re-formed itself. The two objects ascended, descended, and changed positions. No radar recorded their presence. Five different aircraft observed the objects that day; all information was collected by flight controllers, and sent to the regional center (All-Caucasus Directorate of Civil Aviation), and from there, to the Aeroflot bosses and scientists in Moscow. Even the KGB was informed, and received the report, which was later released among the documents of the so-called Blue File obtained by Soviet Cosmonaut Pavel Popovich from General Sham of the KGB. This case was also mentioned in Mikhail Gershtein's books.

Russian UFO Archives

In 1997, *NLO Magazine* published a letter in which Nikolai Sadkov from the Russian city of Pskov described a highly unusual sighting during his naval service in the Black Sea Fleet. He was part of a crew assigned to recover Soviet torpedoes that did not explode upon reaching their targets during tests at sea. The torpedoes would stay afloat for up to 48 hours, after which they would sink to the bottom. On one occasion, the crew had to recover a secret "Dolphin"-type torpedo. A "special department" (Naval intelligence) representative was with them, as the crew hunted for the torpedo. They located it about two hours later, and in another hour their boat approached it. The torpedo was hardly visible, as the commanding officer guided the vessel toward it. Suddenly, a bell-shaped "spaceship," about 60 feet in diameter, swooped down out of the sky and hovered about 16 feet over the torpedo. A voice, emanating apparently from somewhere in the sky, uttered, in clear Russian language, that no harm would come to them and that everyone had to remain where they currently were. The voice was unusual, commanding, and at the same time gentle. Then, a round platform extended from the bottom part of the "spaceship" and attracted the torpedo to it like a magnet. When the boat's sonar technician ran out with a camera in his hands, eager to take pictures, a thin brightly red ray was emitted from the "spaceship" and touched the technician's head, causing him to fall down. The strange voice reminded the sailors to remain where they are, for nothing bad would happen to them. Some time later, the UFO disappeared, along with the torpedo, zooming away into the sky at a great speed. Two hours later it re-appeared and hovered over the deck of the recovery boat. The torpedo was slowly descended from the bottom part of the "bell" and placed gently on the Soviet boat's deck, after which the "spaceship" disappeared. When the sailors returned to the base, they signed a statement swearing that they would not reveal the incident to anyone.

In another case, on August 11, 1987, several witnesses sighted a triangular object over Sevastopol. It consisted of three lights, laid out in the shape of a triangle. The object had a yellowish illumination around its perimeter and a bright white color inside. The lights shone steady, clear, and cold. The object hovered and moved around the city for three hours – occasionally disappearing and then reappearing, its trajectory changing from time to time. Smaller objects that looked like "capsules" would separate from the main object. The smaller objects would zoom away at great speeds. Then, the larger object moved away from the shore at an incredible velocity. People watching the phenomenon were afraid that it would crush them, but the object stopped dead, and in a short while moved in another direction at the same incredible speed. After a while, it left the area.

Another curious incident is mentioned in Nikolai Nepomnyaschy's 1996 book *Stranniki Vselennoy* (*Wanderers of the Universe*). Academician E. Shnyuyukov recalled an expedition that took place in the early 1990s to the Black Sea. He was aboard a scientific research vessel *Mikhail Lomonosov* when an unidentified submersible object was detected at a depth of between 4,500 and 6,000 feet. Its size was enormous (one mile by two miles); and its shape was elliptical. The sonic depth finder registered the mysterious USO as a dense cloud (up to 885 feet in thickness), but analyses of water taken in the immediate area did not reveal any hydro-chemical anomalies. Here is another fascinating detail: Russian devices that safeguarded barometers against impact with the soil would start functioning immediately upon registering the USO.

On December 12, 2007, Ukrainian newspaper *FAKTY* published a letter from a seaman who served aboard *Balta*, a small vessel of the Ukraine's Navy. In the fall of 2006, Nikolay Sadovnichiy of Sevastopol wrote that the crew of his ship had observed a USO. The sighting took place during Balta's participation in the search expedition for a sunken World War II vessel. The newspaper had contacted the Institute of Archaeology, National Academy of Sciences of Ukraine. The experts at the Institute confirmed that they indeed registered a mysterious object by Crimea's shores. They also claimed to possess a photograph of the object, according to Sergey Voronov, Director of the Department of Ukraine's Department of underwater heritage. The sighting took place during the joint Ukrainian-Russian deep underwater archaeological expedition in the large area within the territorial waters of Ukraine on the southern coast of Crimea, by Ayu-Dag. Ayu-Dag [the Bear mountain, because it looks like a bear lying in water], the sacred mountain worshipped by pagans in antiquity, is located in the sea and is surrounded by the Adalara islands. Among the large coastal rock formations is hidden the country house of famous Russian writer Anton Chekhov. The water is unusually clear and clean in the area.

Triangular UFO Sighting

The expedition was to carry out the detailed study of the region, as well as to locate the sunken ambulance ship *Armenia*. The vessel was sunk by Nazi aircraft in 1941, resulting in the loss of seven thousand souls -- a horrible tragedy. But instead of the WWII vessel at the bottom of the Black Sea, the scientists encountered a USO.

Russian participants in the expedition had provided deep-water scanning equipment. Using it, the scientists are able to "see" objects in the depths of the sea. It was during Voronov's watch that one Russian scientist said that they possibly sighted a Ukrainian submarine. Voronov looked at the screen and saw an object and an inversion trail similar to those left in the sky by jet aircraft. Voronov did not reveal to his Russian colleague that Zaporozhye, the only submarine the Ukrainian Navy had possessed, had stopped its sea voyages long ago. He just said that the unusual outlines of the submarine they sighted very much resembled those of a "flying saucer." But Voronov did not believe in UFOs, and that is why he had a feeling of unreality of the situation. He was sure that nothing of the sort could exist. So, he assumed that this was a Russian submarine.

Voronov returned to Sevastopol, and told of the strange submarine to his acquaintances among Russian officers of Russia's Black Sea Fleet, stationed in the city as per a treaty between two nations. The Russians told him that their submarines had not gone out to the sea for several months. Voronov decided to check if the strange object might be an illusion. The technicians replayed the recorded tape of the scanning of the sea bottom and confirmed that the equipment did register a "saucer." The scientists studied the location for any unusual characteristics and found out that there are three underwater mud volcanoes -- but there are many such formations in the Black Sea.

KARELIA'S MYSTERIES: LAND OF STRANGE PHENOMENA

Some of the most interesting UFO and UFO reports have originated in Karelia, an autonomous republic of northwest Russia between the Gulf of Finland and the White Sea, north of Saint Petersburg. The area was once under Swedish control but was annexed by Russia in 1721. It is full of virgin woods, thousands of picturesque lakes, and hundreds of rivers. There have been many strange phenomena associated with this area of northern Europe. The Kola Peninsula, mentioned more than once in this book, lies north of Karelia. In 1932, a thick black cloud enveloped the Shuknavolok Village. After its disappearance, local peasants discovered a jelly-like substance on the ground. They collected it and later used it as a medicine. Many years later, villagers complained of unusual interferences with their TV and radio broadcasts. The area affected was limited to the village and not any of its immediate neighbours. Lake Onega is situated in the northwest part of the European portion of Russia, northeast of St. Petersburg, between Lake Ladoga and the White Sea. It remains frozen from November to May.

Mikhail Gershtein, in his comments to Konstantin Khazanovich's book *UFO Zone*, mentioned an observation of a triangular UFO over the lake. Nikolay Solovskiy was on a vacation at the shores of Lake Onega in 1973. One evening, he observed a strange triangle-shaped object in the North, which moved slowly, occasionally stopping. Having reached its zenith, it stopped, rotated 180 degrees, and then flew back. The triangle had brightly lit dots, but the witness did not know whether they emitted light, or reflected the sun.

Sprut were in the Kola Bay, aboard their ship, and for an hour and a half they had observed an unknown ellipsoid object slowly moving over the surface of the sea, at the altitude of 1,600-3,200 feet. They observed that the object separated into three spherical objects which sharply increased their speed and flew toward the Norwegian border, according to Gherman Kolchin's archives of the Leningrad Commission for Anomalous Phenomena of the Geographic Society of the USSR.

It is important for our readers to realize the significance of the Kola Bay. It is a 35 mile-long fjord of the Barents Sea that cuts into the northern part of the Kola Peninsula. It is up to four miles wide and has a depth of between 650 and 1,000 feet. There are about 200 battle, transport and fishing boats that have sunk to the bottom of the Kola Bay. They interfere with navigation and present a potential ecological peril. There is a civilian nuclear icebreaker facility and several nuclear installations operated by the Russian Northern Fleet. Serious contamination of Kola Bay has taken place as a result of industrial and military activities. If ecological problems interest the UFOs and USOs, then Kola Bay would be the place they would want to visit. And actually, numerous paranormal phenomena have been reported there. On August 28, 1989, a major USO sighting took place in the area of the Kola Peninsula. The year 1989 is also significant, as numerous sightings had been reported in the Soviet Union, a nation then being transformed by Gorbachev's policies of openness and change.

Another article about the same area appeared in the *Zhizn* newspaper, written by Grigory Tel'nov. He wrote that during the 1980s, a large number of unidentified underwater objects had been sighted in the northern seas of the Soviet Union. Soviet ufologists had analyzed such sightings, obtained from various sources, and concluded that during 1980 and 1981 alone, residents of the Kola Peninsula had observed UFOs at least 36 times, ascending from the waters.

UFOs AND USOs OF LAKE LADOGA AND OTHER KARELIA LAKES

Located in north-western Russian, directly east of St. Petersburg and to the southeast of Finland, Lake Ladoga is Europe's largest freshwater lake. This body of water has been a place of strange mirages and is well known for its anomalous phenomena. Often people hear a mysterious rumbling sound coming from its depths. Local ship captains tell of luminescent lights that sometimes will accompany their vessels out to sea. Tatiana Tyumeneva published an article in *NLO Magazine* (Issue 9, 1998). She has collected information about sightings and paranormal phenomena in the area of the lake. She mentioned that once, in the wintertime, a UFO ascended from the waters, broke through the ice, and quickly disappeared in the sky. Sometimes huge, perfectly round unfrozen patches of clear water appear in the Karelia's lakes, as if UFOs have broken through the ice. T. Tyumeneva personally observed a strange phenomenon in Lake Ladoga, while on her way to the Valaam Archipelago one August night. Standing on the deck of the ship, she noticed that the sky was cloudy and rain was approaching, but she could see no storms in sight. The sky was totally dark – no stars or moon visible. About 164 feet from the ship, Tyumeneva observed a gigantic luminescent area on the surface of the water. Streams of bluish light ascended upwards from the deep. The phenomenon lasted for three minutes, and disappeared as quickly as it appeared.

The surrounding area once again turned pitch black. Valaam is an island in the north-western part of Lake Ladoga. It is 7 miles long and 4 miles wide. In the 10th century a monastery was founded on Valaam. The island was originally just a huge piece of granite, devoid of any plant life. The monks turned it into a prosperous place, full of gardens and fertile soil. The island became an attraction for many famous visitors. There have also been many sightings of UFOs over it, reported throughout the centuries. In August of 1989, members of the Fakt UFO research society in Leningrad received a letter from an eyewitness. While on Valaam Island, she observed a fiery sphere of reddish-gold color. Its diameter approximately equaled two diameters of the sun. The object descended into the waters of the lake. K. Khazanovich, who was the Society's chairman at the time, dispatched Lev Gorokhov and an astronomer to investigate the case. They located a member of the military who observed a similar phenomenon but would not reveal his name. When they asked the commanding officers about the sighting, they claimed that the military was using "descending remote controlled spherical targets" in Lake Ladoga.

Mikhail Gershtein, like the authors of this book, has been fascinated by Lake Ladoga's secrets. He believes there might be an underwater UFO base at the bottom of the lake. Gershtein found interesting data in the Russian academic magazine *Priroda* (Issue 5, 1995), which contained an article written by A. Assinovskaya and A. Nikonova, "Zagadochniye Yavleniya na Ladozhskom Ozere," or "Mysterious Phenomena on Lake Ladoga." Researchers of the Institute of Earth Physics studied very old manuscripts that described strange rumbling sounds in the depths of the lake. Back in 1914, a letter arrived in the Main Physical Observatory in Saint Petersburg, signed by the Valaam monastery's clerk whose name was Polikarp. The letter stated that in the previous five years, the monks had heard a strange phenomenon in the south-western and western parts of Lake Ladoga -- underground rumbling noises that resembled the noise made by canon fire shot from a distance. This rumbling noise was not uniform -- sometimes it was heard in the distance, as if coming from the depths of the waters; and on rarer occasions, it was heard underground, in the western portion of Valaam. The ground would shake slightly. Later, Russian and Soviet seismologists asked the monks to record the exact dates and times when the sound appeared, and the monks did so until 1927. They recorded 125 instances of the rumbling, and during none of those events had any earthquakes been registered in the area. Scientists travelled to Valaam, talked to local residents, and found out that the rumbling was a well known phenomenon there. The locals have a name for it; they call it *barrantida*. This rumbling reminded them of noises made by a passing train.

Another mysterious phenomenon is the sudden boiling of the water in Lake Ladoga. None other than Alexander Dumas, the famous 19th century French novelist who visited the lake, wrote about the "boiling lake, as if in a pot." One local captain informed the *Priroda* journalists that when his ship was on its way to Valaam, it suddenly encountered stormy waters, although there were no weather justifications for it. The rumble originated in the area where Lake Ladoga is the deepest. The authors of the *Priroda* article suppose that troughs located under Lake Ladoga's waters formed as a result of the bottom of the lake cracking up, when it descended to different depths levels, separated by crevices.

The February 19, 1997 sightings took place exactly in the area of the origin of the mysterious underwater phenomena. There is also a luminescence that is observed very often in the very same area, coming from under the surface of the lake.

Let us look at important sightings took place on February 19, 1997. Bright dots became visible over the Ladoga, but radar did not detect them. An air traffic controller called the editorial offices of the *Anomaliya* newspaper to report the sighting. Another witness confirmed the sighting and reported that a military TV operator filmed the objects. Yuri Mefodyevich Raitarovsky, a noted Russian ufologist and chairman of the Ufological Commission of the Planetology Department of the Russian Geographical Society, was able to find the film and turn it over to the newspaper. Mikhail Gershtein, too, investigated the case, and collected much material. As a result, the sightings of strange objects over Lake Ladoga were a subject of discussion for the Leningrad Region's Emergency Commission. Tatiana Sirchenko published some information about this in Issue 13, 2000, of *Anomaliya*. Raitarovsky calculated the objects' size and flight characteristics. There was a cluster of bright lights over the lake, hovering for 15 minutes and 39 seconds, at an altitude of 2 miles. The local air defence units did not conduct any training exercises at the time. The Russian newspaper *Argumenti y fakty* published a gripping account of the Valaam mysteries (September 11, 2002), which also mentioned strange spherical clouds that move over the lake on numerous occasions and fiery spheres that burst out from under the waters of the lake. What are these phenomena? Some researchers say the events could result from underwater earthquakes or volcanic activity. Similar phenomena have been observed at several other small isles in the area.

In a 1967 report sent to the Russian Ufology Center in California, Grigory Demyanovich Oleynikov, captain of the fishing boat *Kama*, told of an unusual sighting he had in the Bay of Viborg, in the Gulf of Finland, in September of 1967. At approximately 1:30 a.m., the captain noticed a luminescent, milky-white object descending through the clouds. This object hovered, after its descent, at an altitude of 1,300 feet or so. The witness described the object as a disc with a diameter of about 50 feet. Its outlines were well defined. The bottom portion of the object contained rectangular formations, like nozzles, that emitted flames. For about two minutes the object remained motionless. It was bright, but not blindingly so, and no components separated from it. It had no reported influence on humans or electronics in the vicinity. The object, which emitted no sound at all, disappeared from sight by suddenly taking off upwards. When the clouds dissipated, the witness observed similar object at a distance of about one mile from Kama. Before the object rapidly ascended, the witness saw that the luminescence in the nozzles increased greatly. Of those aboard the *Kama*, only the captain of Kama observed the object aboard the ship. However, the boatswain of the Soviet ship *Novorosiysk* also observed the object.

Konevets Island (in Soviet hands since 1944) is a desolate isle off the south-western shore of Lake Ladoga, near Vladimirovka village. The nearest town, Priozersk, is some 12 miles away. Priozersk was not present in Soviet maps, however, as it was classified as a secret site due to a military base that was quartered in an abandoned monastery.

The island of Valaam is about 37 miles from the lake. Konevets is four miles long, and about one mile wide; it is almost completely covered with sandy beaches. With the end of the USSR, the military base was shut down, and the monastery was returned to the Saint Petersburg diocese.

Konevets Island is an anomalous zone, where numerous UFOs were sighted throughout the 1990s, as well as in the early part of the 21st century. In February 1997, witnesses saw a huge Belgian triangle-type UFO hovering near the isle for over an hour. On March 28, 2003, observers throughout the Priozersk area saw a similar type of UFO. In the summer of 1993, St. Petersburg researchers had noticed that a large number of dead fish had washed up on the island's shores. In August 2005, a number of UFOs of various shapes had been sighted over the island, according to Vadim Chernobrov and Kosmopoisk research organization files. Chernobrov and his Kosmopoisk colleagues have been collecting information about Karelia's anomalous phenomena for some time. Some of the information listed below pertains to UFOs and USOs seen in and around the lakes in the area.

The Gulf of Finland is an arm of the Baltic Sea bordering Finland, Russia (all the way to Saint Petersburg), and Estonia. The eastern parts of the Gulf of Finland belong to Russia, and some of Russia's most important oil harbours are located farthest in, near Saint Petersburg (including Primorsk). Zheltaya Bukhta (Bay) is located 34 miles from Primorsk. Over twenty years ago, a secret military base was located there by the bay. But now it is an openly accessible area. Russian ufologist Raytarovsky and his colleagues had observed cylindrical and spherical UFOs over the Gulf during their 1996 expedition. The expedition's camp was located across from the Beryzoviy Isle, on Kurenniyeni Cape. In 2006, Vadim Chernobrov and his Kosmopoisk expedition revisited the area for further research. The report of the Raytarovsky expedition, drawings and photographs was published in the Russian newspaper *Anomaliya* in 1996. Kronshtadt is located on Kotlin Island near the head of the Gulf of Finland. For dozens of years UFOs have been sighted in the area, near the local military base. UFOs have also been sighted over Lake Zerkal'noye, not far from Zelenogorsk, a town located in the Karelia Isthmus on the shore of the Gulf of Finland.

UFOs have been sighted near Lake Mednoye, on the Viborg highway near Chernaya Rechka, on a number of occasions. Some UFOs were seen separating into several parts. Mysterious creatures have also been reported lurking in the area, according to the *Komsomolskaya Pravda* newspaper (Issue 98, 2006) and also the archives of the Russian Geographic Society. Another mysterious site is Lake Sukhodol'skoye, located in the Priozersk region, northeast of the Karelia Isthmus. UFOs have been sighted near Gromovo settlement, where there is a military airfield. In the 1990s, there have been numerous reports of UFO sightings and contacts with strange humanoid creatures. This is an area of tectonic activity, containing numerous faults. Anomalous plants and mushrooms have been discovered, some mutated to gigantic size, according to Y. Melnikov, a St. Petersburg geologist who has studied anomalous phenomena in the area. Raitarovsky and colleagues also conducted research in the area in 1994-96, observing radiant spheres and mysterious black balls over the lake and their camp.

Lake Cheremenetskoye, by Luga, is the site of an alleged alien base in the Leningrad area. UFOs have been sighted frequently over the lake, especially at the end of 1990s and in the early 2000, according to members of the Kosmopoisk 2006 expedition to the area, in conjunction with the Russian Geographic Society.

Among reports of sightings sent to Philip Mantle from the former USSR, there is one that pertains to Lake Onega, sent by A. S. Savich and dated February 19, 1982. That day, at 4:54 p.m., a strange luminescence was observed in the sky over the lake. The luminescence was pale-blue, and its shape was that of a cloud. Inside this luminescent cloud, moving at a great speed toward the city was a bright, ellipsoid object – as bright as a star. Ten minutes later, after the bright object disappeared from the sky behind the forest, the luminescent cloud remained in the sky for some time, before it too disappeared from sight. At about 5 p.m., a little to the right from the place where the first bright spot appeared, two more luminescent spots showed up, moving synchronically in the same direction. One of them resembled the first sighting. It was a luminescent ellipsoid, surrounded by a spherical pale-blue haze, but its size was somewhat smaller. Another object had the shape of a luminescent sphere, moving in a spiral-like motion. As it moved, it left a rapidly-disappearing, hazy trail. The altitude of the observed objects was like that of aircraft in flight.

At 5:15 p.m., flying parallel to the ground right over the observers, a luminescent arrow moved toward the city at a great speed, leaving behind a short, luminescent trail. The observed objects did not seem to affect humans or other living organisms in the area; nor was there any noise associated with the flight, according to documents from the USSR Academy of Sciences, Institute of Earth Magnetism, Ionosphere, and Wave Distribution (IZMIRAN). The Institute director was none other than V. Migulin of the SETKA program.

Then there is a no-nonsense but, alas, brief article written by Senior Lieutenant A. Krishtal in the newspaper *Sovetskiy Moryak* (March 30, 1999). He visited the area of the Gulf of Finland, and collected reports about anomalous phenomena from Soviet Navy personnel. Two sailors told him of strange sightings of a "flying saucer" over the lighthouse on the island where their unit was stationed. It was a grey disc, shaped like a bagel, with a hollow middle part. It flew at an angle, up and down. Later an officer confirmed the sighting, and Krishtal recorded it. Also later, Krishtal obtained confirmations of the sighting from Soviet Naval officers aboard other ships in the vicinity of the same island.

MYSTERY OF KORB OZERO

There is a fascinating Soviet incident that took place in a remote lake, and it is a case that is virtually unknown in the West. No coherent explanation has been found so far. The incident was disclosed in a 1966 book by Molodaya Gvardia titled *Mi ukhodim poslednimi* or *We are the Last Ones to Depart*. V. Demidov was the original investigator of the case.

On the morning of April 27, 1961, two inspectors embarked on an inspection of local dams. The same day, in the evening, the dam inspectors arrived at a small lake, known as Korb Ozero, in Karelia. After examining the dam, the inspectors spent the night some three miles from Korb Ozero. The next morning, one of the inspectors, Vasily Brodsky, returned to the lake and discovered something quite amazing. The inspectors had made a series of marks the day before, but the marks were gone. Instead, there was a hole measuring 59 feet wide, 82 feet long, and 16 feet deep. The hole had something like a "mouth," an aperture facing the shore's cliff. The aperture had walls that sloped. As for the lake, there was an area devoid of ice. V. Demidov arrived to the site with a diver, after being summoned by Brodsky's telegram. The diver, A. Tikhonov, searched the bottom of the lake. They found fragments of ice floating in the ice-free water. The color of the fragments was that of an emerald. They also discovered greyish foam in the water and in the foam numerous tiny balls. Demidov, who discovered the foam, stated that the balls were black and resembled burnt millet grain. The balls were hollow inside and were very fragile, easily crumbling between fingers.

According to the investigator, Major Kopeikin, a strange fiber-like material was discovered on some fragments of the floating ice. An analysis of the material performed in the Leningrad technological institute revealed the presence of magnum, aluminium, calcium, barium, and titanium. The balls were analyzed at the same institute. According to Demidov, when studied under the microscope, the balls had a metallic sheen and possessed a crystalline structure. Also, they would not dissolve in any known acid. The experts concluded that the millets were of non-organic origin and were not naturally occurring substances. Divers discovered that the bottom of the lake was covered with mounds of frozen soil and a layer of pieces of the fallen soil. Broken ice chunks were lying over everything. Apparently, whatever occurred there was so instantaneous, that the ice, pressed down by soil, did not have a chance to surface. That would explain the absence of ice on the surface. Also, the divers discovered a mysterious 65-foot long track, at the end of which was a cylinder-like soil formation, about four feet high. It was as if some pipe-like object moved along the bottom, pushing the soil in front of it, and then the object stopped and disappeared. Beyond the unfrozen patch of water, the bottom of the lake was normal in appearance. As reported by Major Kopeikin, the soil that had fallen to the bottom of the lake, contained a tiny plate, its thickness one millimetre, its length two centimetres, and its width half a centimetre. Spectral and chemical analyses demonstrated that the plate consisted of iron and silicon, with additives of platinum, titanium, and aluminium. No unusual radiation was detected. When the emerald-covered ice was delivered to a Leningrad laboratory, the experts who conducted the analysis could not explain the coloration. Also, there was a problem with the volume of the fallen soil. It was less, according to the diver, than the volume of the soil that had been removed from the hole. The ice around the unfrozen patch of water was free of any soil. What happened to the missing soil? Demidov stated in his book that the local residents did not see or hear anything that night. According to Vadim Chernobrov, Russian scientist and author of books about the paranormal, there are still traces of the mysterious force that changed the lake. Interestingly, Yuri Gagarin's space flight took place six months before the incident.

From 1961 through 1979 several expeditions worked in the area of the Korb Lake, and noted ufologist Y. Raitarovsky headed one of them. The expeditions proved beyond any doubt that the body that crashed into the soil was neither a missile, nor ball lighting, nor an explosive, according to *Entsiklopedia Nepoznannogo* or *Encyclopedia of the Unknown*, compiled by Vadim Chernobrov, and published in Moscow in 1998. V. Demidov, former member of the Commission for Anomalous Phenomena, clarified a few things in his 1993 newspaper article "Taina Gluhogo Ozera" or "Mystery of the Remote Lake," published in the *Na strazhe Rodini* newspaper. Initially, the phenomenon was investigated by a group of officers and soldiers. The group included explosives experts, divers, sappers, and helicopter pilots. No explanation was found as to what happened in the lake located at the border of the Leningradsky and Vologodsky regions. Among the information that was not revealed in 1964 were names of high officials involved and the involvement of the KGB. Because of such "guardianship," according to Demidov, it was easy to gain access to top research laboratories, and top experts in meteorites, chemistry, ball lightning, and some "secret" subjects. Not one of them was able to determine the exact nature of the event. Professor Aleskovski, of the USSR Academy of Sciences, who headed chemical research of the Academy, told Demidov that the tiny balls were not of natural formation and that he could not even imagine a technology that would be able to create such material. Demidov was able to determine that neither the Soviet Armed Forces nor the scientific establishment were responsible for the Korb Ozero event. Despite the many unanswered questions, even well-known Soviet dignitaries, such as Cosmonaut G. Titov, could not get scientists interested in investigating the case further. Vice President of the USSR Academy of Sciences, M. Lavrentyev once told Demidov that Soviet scientists do not time to dedicate to suspicious "holes." In science, he said, everyone is concentrated in his own narrow field. N. Kalashnikov hiked to the lake with a group of companions in October of 1993. The lake looked like a cucumber, elongated from north to south. Two tiny huts, used occasionally by hunters and fishermen, stood next to the shore. There was also a very old, abandoned and dilapidated wooden chapel nearby.

They could only stay there a short time, but it was long enough to allow Kalashnikov to collect several kilograms of the soil from the area, and find a strange plate, 20 by 30 centimetres, and 3 to 4 centimetres thick. The plate was square, smooth on one side, but the other side was strangely ribbed. He actually had to dig the plate out of the ground. Kalashnikov took the plate and the soil sample with him. Kalashnikov grew ginseng, the "root of life," in his dacha [cottage]. He placed the soil from the Korb Lake in his garden and forgot about it. Amazingly, over the next couple of years, any ginseng plants he grew in the Korb Lake soil grew to amazing proportions. One ginseng root went from 100 grams when he placed the Korb Lake soil on it, to 253 grams. The miraculous growth was not related to radiation, for there was none whatsoever in Korb Ozero. In addition to being much larger, the ginseng was said to possess "unusual qualities." Kalashnikov hinted that other amazing things were discovered about the soil he brought from the lake, but he did not go into details, promising to tell more in the future.

THE KODUMAA PROJECT

Reportedly, the alleged crash of an extraterrestrial spaceship was investigated in the 1990s by a joint Russian-Finnish expedition of scientists from the Jyvaskyla University (Finland) and Peter the Great Institute of Anthropology and Ethnography (Russia). Supposedly, the Finnish government invested over 110 million Finnish marks in the so-called "Kodumaa Project." This project was reportedly initiated before the disintegration of the USSR. However, evidence verifying the existence of this project is extremely elusive. In 1986 young Leningrad scientists Vladimir Majdanov and Aleksey Knyazev discovered and followed weak traces of radioactivy along a path that ran from Helsinki through Scandinavia, continued toward Kronshtadt, and then abruptly ended in the Volosovo area (USSR). In 1990, scientists from Finland and Sweden reported that the signal, weakest on Soviet territory, became more powerful in the area of the Scandinavia Mountains. Majdanov and Knyazev became convinced that these traces of radioactivity represented the trajectory of a crashed alien ship. But, what happened to its crew and where are the fragments of the ship?

To answer these questions, Swedish and other foreign scientists joined the project. A Swedish satellite performed measurements and studied the radioactive trail in the Arctic Ocean. Researchers concluded that the trail may have been caused by a UFO catastrophe that occurred before the First Ice Age in Europe [Could the incident have somehow caused our Ice Age?]. They speculated that the disaster took place at some point along the trajectory of a huge alien spaceship that entered Earth's atmosphere on approach to a landing in the area of the Scandinavia Ridge. The ship probably impacted upon the ridge, and only a part of the "emergency capsule" reached Volosovo, according to an article published in the *Anomaliya* newspaper (Issue 2, 1997). Knyazev and Majdanov did not have necessary equipment and funds to conduct further research of the suspected crash trajectory. However, they surmised that archaeology might lend support to their hypothesis. They attended an exhibition of Nicholas Roerich's artwork. There, the scientists were drawn to a drawing of an ancient, sacred burial ground. Roerich's archaeological expedition conducted digs in the area of his Volosovo manor, Izvar. Knyazev and Majdanov looked into the documents from Roerich's expedition and obtained an exact description and measurement of the burial ground. According to the two scientists, the measurements matched those of the emergency capsule of American Apollo spaceships. Other interesting details about the burial ground included a "cosmonaut's sitting position" and strange artefacts found there. The artefacts were positioned in a manner that resembled the controls of a spacecraft.

Russian scientists believe that the ETs who survived the crash, or perhaps our human ancestors of the time period, buried the aliens who were killed in the crash and then tried to recover fragments of the ship. The Ice Age forced humans to retreat to the Altai and Pamir areas, and a gigantic glacier dragged fragments of the crashed ship to the Arctic Ocean, partially covering them. It is possible that Nicholas Roerich guessed the same.

Many doctors and scientists observed that the Volosovo indigenous people have different anthropological features than residents of Estonia and Finland, as well as Russia. Ancient Russian manuscripts, and documents of Czar Peter the Great, describe the magic of "Chud sorcerers." The Russian Orthodox Church and Muscovite princes put down uprisings of the local believers of ancient magic. Yet, there are still legends and ancient knowledge in the Baltic, as well as burial grounds shaped like space capsules.

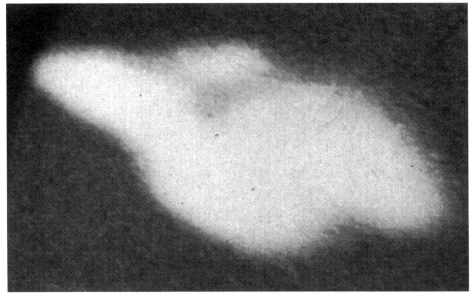

Photo from 1988 in the Area of Sanjeika Village

Could it be that the Soviet military did or even still does have a secret UFO research establishment close to Saint Petersburg? It is rumoured that other countries like the USA and Great Britain have such a facility. Area 51 in the U.S. has become well known for its alleged research into UFO technologies, and RAF Rudloe Manor in England is also rumoured to have officially investigated UFOs. Given the theory that mankind, in its ancient past, has been visited by extraterrestrials (the "Ancient Astronaut" theory), it should be no surprise that in the ancient lands of the former USSR, we find legends of ancient alien visitors.

USO SIGHTINGS IN THE BALTIC SEA

In 1947, Fyodor Pavlyuk served in the Baltic Sea area, guarding artillery battalion 612 (anti-aircraft gunners). It was a clear summer day, when he noticed spherical objects flying from the direction of the sea, at an altitude of 650 feet. Their diameters were also about 650 feet. They moved slowly, rocking, stopping and hovering over the battalion's guns. Two smaller spheres had separated from the original spheres. The smaller objects, around 70 centimetres (28 inches) in diameter, looked like radiant balls, and they proceeded to fly around the artillery guns. Pavlyuk grabbed his rifle, caught up with one of the sphere, and pierced it with the bayonet.

There was a flash, and the bayonet burned up. The small spheres slowly ascended and merged with the larger, original spheres, which subsequently flew away. This case first came to light in the 1991 Russian TV documentary "Ochevidnoye-Neveroyatnoye." For some reason, the Soviets seemed to relax their UFO censorship policy in 1967. During that year, the Soviet press actually began carrying some of the UFO cases that were being reported in the West. Also, there was a TV appeal made to the Soviet populace to send their reports of UFO sightings to Feliks Zigel and his colleagues, as previously mentioned. Even reports about "Soviet UFOs" appeared occasionally on the pages of the newspapers, such as a November 1967 sighting of a gigantic UFO that appeared over the shores of the Baltic Sea, near Liepaja, the third largest city in Latvia. It was a glimmering object, moving through the sky, that clearly was not a cloud, an airplane, or a satellite. It was a huge spherical craft, hovering low over the ground. Its glow was fiery and painful to look at with unprotected eyes. Later, the UFO stirred and quickly vanished over the horizon. Among those who witnessed the incident were several meteorologists, as reported in the *Sovetskaya Latvia* newspaper (December 2, 1967). In October of 1985, there was another interesting sighting over the Baltic Sea, which is a young sea in geological terms. It is located in Northern Europe, from 53°N to 66°N latitude and from 20°E to 26°E longitude. The Soviet ship *Baltiysky-35* was bound from Lubeck to Riga. Those on board the ship observed a bright dot in the sky, with concentric circles of light green color that emanated from it. This case was found in the archive of the Leningrad Commission for Anomalous Phenomena of the Geographic Society of the USSR.

Konstantin Khazanovich considers this event to be a result of the launch of a Soviet ballistic missile from the Murmansk area (the Kola Peninsula). In 2002, Khazanovich (also, an active member of the Leningrad Commission for Anomalous Phenomena of the Geographic Society of the USSR), in his book *UFO Zone*, argued that a number of well-known Russian UFO cases were, in actuality, secret Soviet military tests. As the years went by, Gorbachev's policies changed the Soviet Union. Before the fall of the USSR, a Soviet Navy officer published a fascinating article about sightings of UFOs by Soviet military personnel. Like many other Soviet military officers, Nikolay Dyomin did not consider UFOs to be "optical illusions." The UFOs his colleagues observed were the same saucers, balls and rays as seen throughout the ages in other parts of the world, but recorded with the precision and impartiality of a military report. Quite often, Navy observers utilized special technical means. In some cases, the objects were observed and recorded from different points in their flight dynamics. The sightings, checking and verification by Soviet fleet meteorological officers had positively established that the observed objects were not the results of human technological activity or optical illusions. *AYA* Magazine (Issue 2, 1991).

In early summer of 1990, in port of Loksa (Estonia), A. Maksimovich, Soviet Navy officer, reported a strange, bright object. It hovered noiselessly in the clear sky. For four hours he had observed it through a looking glass. The UFO was spherical, extremely bright, and changed colours. Other crewmembers and their commander watched the UFO. The onboard radar was not able to detect it. The border guard vessel in the vicinity also observed the object but could not detect it on radar.

USO SIGHTINGS OVER THE SEA OF AZOV

Henichesk is a port city along the Sea of Azov in southern Ukraine. On August 8, 1978, at the shore of the sea, near the city, a large group of tourists observed a flying disc-shaped object, three times larger than the visible moon. The object, surrounded by a bright orange glow, had protrusions at the top and bottom, and two rows of portholes. Every 15 seconds smaller discs flew out from its lower protrusion. A blinding explosion accompanied each appearance of the smaller discs. Each such disc hovered motionlessly for about 2-3 seconds and then rapidly departed in the direction of Black Sea. There were between 15 and 20 such discs during the observation period, as reported in Feliks Zigel's 1980 manuscript *Posadki NLO v SSSR* or *UFO Landings in the USSR*. No one knows how many of these USOs and UFOs lurk quietly deep inside our planet's lakes, rivers, seas, and oceans. We are certain, however, that as we continue to explore our world's bodies of water, we will certainly encounter more USOs.

CHAPTER 8.

RUSSIAN ASTRONOMERS AND UFOs

Astronomers are trained observers. Soviet-trained astronomers are no different, but their UFO observations remained largely unknown to the rest of the world until the 1990s. We already know that S. Korolyov sent Professor Burdakov to the Pulkovskaya Observatory with a letter of recommendation, as a "punishment" for his unauthorized UFO lectures. In those years, people reported their UFO sightings to the astronomers, and Burdakov was able to learn of many fascinating cases. What is amazing is the extent to which the Soviets went to hide the facts that the astronomers did see UFOs. We also discussed a declassified U.S. Department of Defence Information Report, dated August 19, 1970. The Americans seemed very interested in Soviet cosmonaut Alexey Leonov's comments during a lecture in Japan. The cosmonaut gave a presentation at the Takai University in Kanagawa Prefecture on May 18, 1970, during which he stated that he did not believe in the existence of unidentified flying objects. He said that there is no record of any of the Soviet astronomical observatories, manned by highly trained technicians, ever having seen a flying saucer. The Soviet newspaper *Pravda* stated, on February 29, 1968, that astronomers who carefully observe the sky day and night "never see flying saucers." In truth, both the cosmonaut and the newspaper concealed the true state of affairs. Not only were UFO reports clearly of interest to Soviet astronomers, but also a number of significant UFO sightings were actually first reported by astronomers!

Back in the 1960s, astronomer Robert Vitolniek reported something quite unusual. He headed the radio observation station of the ionosphere at the Radio-Physical Observatory of the Academy of Sciences, USSR (Latvia branch). On July 26, 1965, he and others studied the ionosphere and silvery clouds from the observation center at the city of Ogra. The astronomers saw an unusually bright "star" moving slowly to the west. Tracking it with a powerful telescope, they saw that the UFO was a lens-shaped disk, about 328 feet in diameter. In the object's center was a clearly defined "bump," like a small sphere. Near the disk, at a distance of approximately 650 feet, they saw three spheres, similar to the one in the "bump," which slowly around the disk. The objects were becoming smaller, apparently moving away from the Earth. Twenty minutes later, the spheres distanced themselves from the disk, flying in different directions. The sphere in the middle of the disk also separated. The spheres were greenish-pearly in color and dull. Vitolniek and other astronomers were certain that they observed neither a rocket nor satellite, as those objects would have moved at much greater velocities. Also, rockets and satellites would not consist of multiple flying objects like the UFO observed by Soviet astronomers in June 1965.

The Pulkovskaya Observatory

According to Mikhail Gershtein, writing in the *ANOMALIYA* newspaper (Issue 20, 1996), on July 18, 1967, the Pulkovskaya astronomer G. Poter observed a strange blast near Kislovodsk. The explosion formed a reddish spherical cloud, surrounded by waves of white luminescence. Poter's colleagues informed him that, several hours before, they observed a flying sickle-shaped object. One month later, another astronomer, A. Sazanov saw another sickle shaped body in the area, with a star-shaped object flying ahead of it. The "sickle" finally changed its shape to a disk and vanished. On September 21, 1968, L. Tsekhanovich, astronomer and lecturer at the Moscow Planetarium also observed a "sickle" for an hour. So did many other local inhabitants. Ufologist Gershtein was able to obtain a statistical analysis of UFO observations, produced by the Institute of Space Research of the Academy of Sciences, USSR. The report, published in 1979, concluded that 7.5% of all UFO sightings in the Soviet Union were reported by astronomers. The astronomers could not be silenced -- not even when Stalin ruled the Soviet Union. Donatas Myaziyauskas, a Lithuanian astrophysicist, mentioned in an interview with the *Komjaunimo tiesa* newspaper that it is not "random observers" who see UFOs and similar phenomena most frequently.

Astronomers and meteorologists report UFOs as well, and as experts, they are better able to describe and classify what they see. On numerous occasions, Lithuanian astronomers observed phenomena they could not identify. So did Myaziyauskas, while working in the Moletsky Observatory. He took photos of a "jumping star," an object that he could never explain.In 1978, Lithuanian scientist Dr. Vitautas Straijis published an article in *Mokslas ir givanimas* magazine. It was titled "Anomalous Phenomena in the Atmosphere and Space," and mentioned some thirty UFO sightings reported from the area of the Vilnius Observatory. The most fascinating one, dated August 20, 1974, actually came from different localities at the same time.

It described a triangle of 460 feet in diameter, which hovered over Raseinyai for 12 hours, at the altitude of about 12 miles. Feliks Zigel's book *UFO Sightings over the USSR-1968* (Volume 1), published by Joint USA-CIS Aerial Anomalies Federation in 1993, contains a fascinating report sent to him by astronomers. Surely a prominent personality of the Soviet space program, Soviet cosmonaut Leonov and his colleagues must have read Zigel's books, available through the black markets of the Soviet Union and other, more sinister places. But it is not right to blame Leonov and other debunkers for his statements in Tokyo, for he was but a Soviet citizen and had to "observe the rules"; he was not the one setting the rules.

On November 30, 1964, in Soviet Azerbaijan, at the Shemakhinsky AstrophysicalObservatory of the Soviet Academy of Sciences in Pirulki, witnesses observed an unusual celestial object, moving from west to north, starting at an altitude of 3 to 4 degrees above the horizon and moving up to 30 degrees. It moved at about one degree per minute. The path passed seven to ten degrees below the constellation Aquila, a little below the head of Draco, and disappeared two or three degrees to the right of Ursa Major. Two parts of the object were easily distinguished -- its head and tail. The head looked like planetary mistiness with a sharp internal edge and a diffused outer edge. Located in the center was a star-shaped object of a third or fourth stellar magnitude that was a point even in an AT-1 astronomic telescope. There was no sound. S. N. Komlev, a Soviet scientist, filed a report filed a report regarding a UFO sighting he had in September of 1981. Komlev, a trained meteorologist, had experience in the observation of atmospheric meteorological phenomena, flights of weather balloons, and more. Komlev sent his report to a Commission for the study of anomalous phenomena (we described such "commissions" elsewhere in the book) in 1985. His testimony is as follows. The night of the observation was at the end of September 1981 [he did not recall the exact date, even during the interview with a member of the Commission], about quarter after midnight Moscow time. S. N. Komlev, a passenger aboard Tu-134 flight from Balkhash to Moscow, observed an unusual phenomenon. The airplane at that time was in the vicinity of the Vnukovo Airport, flying at an altitude of approximately 26,000 feet with a speed of 500 miles per hour. The object was seen by almost all of the passengers, who observed it through the airplane windows. The object was cigar shaped, and Komlev estimated that its size was similar to the size of an airplane hull (if viewed from a distance of 1-2 miles).

Apparently, the object flew about 18 miles above the Tu-134, its speed similar to that of the airplane. Witnesses could not determine the direction of the flight. The color of the object was white-yellowish. The observers did not see any sections or components of the object. Observers saw no residue or inversion. The UFO did not seem to have any effect on the passengers or onboard equipment. The sky at the time was clear; one could see the stars and the ground. The sighting lasted about two minutes. Then the airplane changed its course, and they did not see the object again. The airplane was not allowed to land for an extended period of time. Komlev believed this was a consequence of the appearance of the anomalous phenomenon they had observed. It is clear that the Soviet government attempted to mislead its citizens and Westerners about UFO sightings reported by astronomers and other professional sky watchers. It was obviously a key part of their disinformation campaign, because if trained sky observers are reporting UFOs, then Soviet citizens would be more likely to believe in them. One thing is for sure, just like their counterparts in the West, Soviet astronomers did observe and record UFOs. And like observations made by scientists all over the world, most of these sightings remain unexplained despite all attempts to unravel their mysteries.

CHAPTER 9.

THE PHOBOS MYSTERY

WHAT IS PHOBOS?

In 1959, Iosif Shklovsky, the famous Soviet astrophysicist who co-authored with Carl Sagan the book *Intelligent Life in the Universe*, expressed his opinion that Phobos, a moon of Mars, was of artificial origin and was likely hollow inside. Something he found very puzzling about Phobos was its incredible rotation speed in relation to the orbit of Mars. The two Martian moons, Phobos and Deimos, orbit Mars nearly in the plane of its equator. Phobos goes around once every 7.7 hours, and Deimos goes around every 30.2 hours. Mars itself rotates on its axis once every 24.6 hours; Phobos rotates around its orbit much faster. Planet Mars has the highest orbital eccentricity of any planet in our solar system (not counting the dwarf planet Pluto).

Phobos (meaning "fear" in Greek) is the larger of the two tiny moons of Mars. It is but 13.8 miles (22.2 kilometres) across and has a mass of 1.08×1016. It orbits Mars at a mean distance of 5,600 miles (9,000 kilometres). Its major known feature is a large crater, named Stickney, which is 6.2 miles (10 km) wide. American astronomer Asaph Hall discovered Phobos in 1877. It is also very probable that Jonathan Swift knew about the tiny moonlets, having described them in his literary work. In 1959, Shklovsky reached a conclusion that Phobos must be hollow inside. The Soviet scientist went even further and hypothesized that Phobos is an ET space station.

RACE TO THE MOONLET

Those involved in the Soviet space program, as well as their Western colleagues, have been very much interested in Phobos. On July 12, 1988, the Soviets launched two unmanned probes, Phobos 1 and Phobos 2, in the direction of Mars. The probes were actually a joint creation of Western scientists and their Soviet counterparts. In fact, the project had international participation from its very inception. The Soviet *Izvestiya* newspaper on March 3, 1989 (S. Leskov's article) reported that data from the probes was transmitted to the European Mission Center, to France, and to NASA. Nothing was done by Soviets without the input and recommendations of their global partners. It appears that the Jet Propulsion Laboratory in Pasadena, California, was directly involved, too. In his article, Leskov expressed amazement at the level of global participation. Just as equally amazed were authors of this book, after reviewing TASS documents regarding the failed Phobos mission. Whatever Phobos contains was of the utmost importance to all. The Americans eagerly transferred all their Phobos astrometrical observations to the Soviets. American radio telescopes stationed throughout our planet were made available to aid the Soviet missions (March 11, 1989, *Uchitelskaya Gazeta* newspaper, quoting Y. Kolesnikov from the Flight Control Center). Swiss and French scientists provided a special measuring device for the probes, which they created jointly with the Soviets.

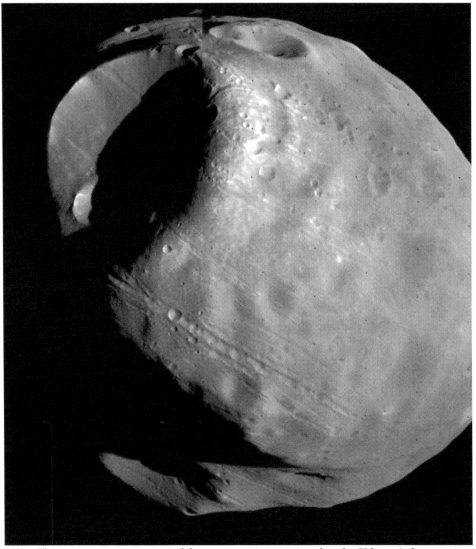

This image is a montage of three separate images taken by Viking 1 during one of its flybys of Phobos in October 1978.

Each probe contained a complicated set of devices, including three television cameras, spectrometer, guidance system, and video recording system. Also, the Phobos 2 probe contained a secret laser device dubbed LIMA-D. Specialists at the Leningrad Institute of Precision Mechanics, together with Eastern European and Finnish scientists, created this mysterious machine. The device was to emit a laser ray at the surface of the moonlet, causing a small explosion, and then gather data on the composition of evaporated materials. Some said this was the most important experiment that the probe was to conduct, according to G. Lomanov, a reporter (*Sotsialisticheskaya Industriya* newspaper, March 26, 1989) By the way, the technical name for Phobos 2 was *Videospektrometricheskiy kompleks* (VSK), and its personal name was "Fregat."

DISASTER

The Phobos 1 spacecraft was lost in September 1988, supposedly, according to the Soviets, due to a radio command error. Phobos 2 was also lost, but before it disappeared, it was able to send images and data to Earth. Phobos 2 arrived in Martian orbit in January 1989. This was the beginning of the mission that included a transfer to an orbit that would make the probe fly in tandem with its namesake moonlet. Furthermore, Phobos was to be explored, and certain equipment was to be placed on the surface of the moonlet. The problems began when the probe aligned itself with the moonlet. On March 28, 1989, the official Soviet news agency TASS made an announcement that Phobos 2 had failed to communicate with Earth as scheduled after completing an operation around the Martian moon Phobos. Scientists at mission control had been unable to establish stable radio contact. In April 1989 Lieutenant Colonel Baberdin published an article in the *Krasnaya Zvezda* newspaper ("Enigmas of Martian Orbits," April 4). He mentioned an unidentified spot on the Martian surface, photographed using the infrared wave range. The Soviet Vremya program mentioned it in its broadcast, and the military had to respond, albeit late. Baberdin stated that astrophysicists and planetologists carefully studied the image and that the mysterious spot was most likely a "shadow" from some space object. This "shadow" was able to sharply lower itself in the Martian atmosphere to where the on-board device of Phobos 2 was able to capture the image. But what exactly the space object was remained unclear.

SENTINELS OF THE RED PLANET

In 1991, Cosmonaut Marina Popovich, during a visit to Los Angeles, showed Paul Stonehill a photograph that Phobos 2 made before its demise. It depicts a gigantic cylindrical object approximately 15 miles long. After that last frame was radio-transmitted back to earth, the probe disappeared. *Aviation Week & Space Technology* magazine (April 10, 1989), quoted a controller at the Kaliningrad control center as saying that the limited signals received after the conclusion of the Phobos 2 imaging session gave him an impression that he was tracking a spin-stabilized spacecraft (a "spinner," in his words). Phobos 2 was in orbit around Mars on March 27, when it failed to re-establish communications with earth. The probe was commanded to change its orientation for an imaging session. Its cameras had to be aimed at the moonlet, and later it was to resume its Earth-pointing orientation to downlink the data. But that never happened. Something struck the object, and sent it into a spin. In the October 1989 issue of *Nature*, results were revealed from several Soviet technical reports regarding the few experiments that Phobos 2 actually completed. Just one paragraph dealt with the loss of the space probe. However, the data did confirm that Phobos 2 was "spinning," either because of a computer malfunction ... or because the space probe was "impacted" by an unknown object.

Glavkosmos was established in 1985, under the Ministry of General Machine Building, as the Soviet Union's contract agency for space affairs by the government of Mikhail Gorbachev. Alexander Dunayev, who was appointed the first Chairman of the Soviet *Glavkosmos* space organization, talked to Leskov on March 29, 1989, according to the *Izvestiya newspaper*, about the probe's failure. According to him, a special commission was created the day before, right after the failure, and it included top space scientists. They came up with seven reasons as to why the probe was lost. The commission was to issue a conclusion. Dunayev later reported that the loss of the probe was not a complete failure, because a range of scientific data was collected during the cruise phase and at the time Phobos 2 was in the Martian orbit. Images of the moonlet and Mars were successfully transmitted on Earth. One image, according to Dunayev, included an odd-shaped object between the spacecraft and Mars. He supposed it was either the debris in the orbit of Phobos or the Phobos autonomous propulsion subsystem that was jettisoned after the spacecraft was injected into Mars orbit. However, Marina Popovich told Paul Stonehill that the *Glavkosmos* knew all along that whatever it was that destroyed the probe was created by an artificial intelligence. In another article by S. Leskov published in *Izvestiya* (November 1, 1990), Professor N. Ivanov, head of the Ballistic Service of the Flight Control Center, mentioned rumours that, after Phobos 2 was supposedly lost, the JPL in Pasadena received some strange signals from the lost probe, contrary to all physical laws. Ivanov did not directly contradict the persistent rumours.

He stated that by this time the lost probe should have ceased all communications and become a frozen derelict. The only other possibility – although not a serious one, he hastened to add -- was that Phobos 2 was dragged away by extraterrestrial, who kept it functioning for their own purposes. Doctor Selivanov of the *Glavkosmos*, who was also interviewed by Leskov, adds that he contacted the American scientists in Pasadena, but they claim that no signals from Phobos 2 were received. We admire the ease with which the Soviets and Americans handled direct communications about space probes, but there is another scientific opinion that is no less important than that of Ivanov's or Selivanov's. Professor Burdakov made direct inquiries about the loss of Phobos 2 probe and discussed the matter with the original designers of the project, as well as those who had tested the spacecraft. Suspicious of official explanations, Professor Burdakov questioned the series of strange events that led to the destruction of Phobos 2. He knew nothing about the photo images taken by Phobos 2 and was unaware that certain individuals in the West had discussed possible "offbeat" reasons why the probe perished. The Professor came up with a hypothesis: if Mars is inhabited, the intelligent beings who exist there would not like the idea of a device placed on the surface of their moonlet for the purpose of constant surveillance. Consequently, in his opinion, they did something about it. Burdakov's views were expressed in an article published in 1992 in a Russian magazine *Quant*. Vyacheslav Kovtunenko was the official head of the Phobos project. In his interview with M. Chernishov of the *Krasny Voin* newspaper (a military publication) dated May 24, 1989, he revealed some details about the probes.

The apparatuses were able to solve complex problems. Apparently the designers found out about certain failures and design shortcomings during the flight, but were eager to proceed with new "expeditions." Roald Sagdeyev, who now resides in the United States and could shed much light on Soviet space secrets, mentioned in the same interview that the work on the project was going well, except for the reluctance of "financial organs" in the West to help his Western partners complete the project. And yet, 13 countries had participated in the project. What was the haste involved? Why all the secrecy surrounding the mission?

Roald Kremnev of the Babakin Space Testing Center, another top scientist involved with the project, mentioned a "swarm of small bodies" around Phobos 2 during the incident. Did they cause the failure? Or, he added in his interview with Chernishov, was the probe's failure somehow due to the alien body registered by the Phobos 2? Kremnev again talked to Leskov on April 14, (*Izvestiya*) and stressed that the most discussed version of the failure is the gigantic object registered three days before the accident. Still, there was no official conclusion. According to Leskov (*Izvestiya*, April 16, 1989), who talked to top scientists involved in the project, the Soviets spent 272 million rubles for the project, and Western partners spent 51 million rubles. The probes cost 51 million rubles -- an enormous amount of money for the time. It took five years, according to official information, to build the probes. What of any weapons aboard? The probe was to be a long-time automatic station on the surface of Phobos. Among the equipment it was to use was a special "jumping probe" or a "hopper," according to Leskov (*Izvestiya*, March 24, 1989). The hopper, which looked a little like a mechanized ladybug, would unfold its spindly legs and literally hop around the moonlet (each stride being about sixty feet in length). Each time that the hopper would land, it was to use its X-rays to study the soil's chemical composition. It also had a device ("penetrometer") to study the moonlet's physical properties and the underlying geological structure. The hopper, according to the Soviets, was also to carry a magnetometer to measure magnetic fields and a gravitometer to measure the moonlet's mass. Most likely this little ingenious "ladybug" had to carry out some other missions, too, and probably was designed to carry some other, more sinister devices. We simply do not have enough information, even years after the demise of Phobos 2.

NO WEAPONS ALLOWED

We already know that a new type of laser weapons was to be used on Phobos. Perhaps this was the reason why it was destroyed before it could complete its mission. Perhaps Man is not the master of the solar system. Perhaps those who have left mysterious and deep tracks on Phobos are the true masters. Phobos has mysterious long parallel grooves across a large part of its surface. They are a few hundred feet wide and a few hundred feet deep and may have been formed by the same impact that caused the crater Stickney or by an alien intelligence. Our scientists are unable to explain the nature of the grooves.

Can they explain how tiny Phobos could generate heat and conventional volcanic activity to account for the presence of numerous craters on its surface? It took the Soviets ten space probes, none of which carried its program to conclusion, to realize that Mars is very inhospitable to human life. Just two Soviet space probes actually made it to the Martian surface. We know about the past failures and recent successes of America's Martian exploration program. We are certain that new space probes will be sent to Mars in the near future. Does it mean that our governments, who know more than we do, are more than eager to reach Mars and its moonlets? Decide for yourself.

Ten years went by, and another spacecraft (America's Mars Polar Lander) was sent to Mars. It contained a strange device onboard, better known as the Light Detection and Ranging (LIDAR). It was created in the Space Research Institute (IKI) of the Russian Academy of Science, under the sponsorship of the Russian Space Agency. This was the first Russian instrument to fly on a United States planetary spacecraft. The LIDAR instrument was to look "for ice and dust clouds." The LIDAR system was a laser sounder located on the Mars Polar Lander deck. It was composed of a sensor and electronics assembly. The LIDAR transmitter used a gallium-aluminium-arsenic laser that emitted energy in pulses at a constant rate and wavelength. The LIDAR had two sounding modes -- active and acoustic:
1.During active sounding, the instrument sent out pulses of light and then timed their return in order to locate and characterize ice and dust hazes to a level of 1-2 miles.
2.An acoustic device, the Planetary Society's Mars Microphone, was part of the LIDAR assembly. Engineers designed the LIDAR to operate in the temperature range from - 100 to 50 degrees Celsius (-148 to 122 degrees Fahrenheit) under lower pressure, near one millibar. It was connected to the board by an RS-422 interface and generated science data up to 25.6 Kb per day for standard operation scenario, which is a limit from the spacecraft. The LIDAR also had a high-pressure variometer for studying the correlation of optical atmospheric characteristics with very low frequency sounds (infrasound) and changing pressure. The laser transmitter was gallium-aluminium-arsenic pulses laser diode emitting one micro Joule in 20-nanosecond long pulses at 890-nanometer wavelength. The laser beam had a linear polarization and a 2-milliradian divergence with the output 54x34 mm2 clear aperture. The laser operated with repetition rate of about 20 to 25 kHz. Outside daylight background irradiance was the main source of noise inside the receiver channel. The background irradiance was reduced by an optical interference filter having a bandwidth of 10 nm (FWHM), at 890 nm with 50 percent transmission and a 15-millimeter clear aperture only. One of the receiver channels had a polarizer. Its axes were coincident with the LIDAR beam polarization. Full sounding distance was 750 meters (2,461 feet) with 16 feet resolution along the trace or the 32-second total integrating time. The single cycle had 10-minute duration.

How powerful can such laser device be? It was not, as far as we know, powerful enough to threaten anything substantial on Mars or Phobos. Similar devices are being used by military for the purpose of precise aim, or to measure distances accurately.

Much more powerful systems are needed to pierce a structure (for example, a metallic hull). And yet even such a weak laser device is able to penetrate a surface. Once it penetrates a surface, it can interact with a system below, destroy its equilibrium, and damage whatever mechanism lies within it. A Russian scientist who is also a participant of the RUFORS Round Table (where news pertaining to ufology is exchanged) actually worked with the creators of the LIDAR (on other projects). They were the same scientists who had designed all of the devices aboard Soviet spacecraft sent to Venus. "Top experts" is how they were described. Their invention was original and exquisite: two "radars," one acoustic, one laser, functioned together. Wherever laser was not capable of operation (fog, clouds, smoke), the sound started its work, for it could penetrate further. Where the environment was denser (for example, water), only acoustic "radar" is capable of providing orientation and communication. Laser needs an ideal, optically transparent environment. The story of the Polar Lander's failure is well-known, although we will probably never learn the true causes of its demise.

2009 was a very interesting year for those interested in Phobos and the secrets it contains. International scientists concluded that year that the interior of Phobos likely contains large voids. This was a very important conclusion based on independent results from two subgroups of the Mars Express Radio Science (MaRS) team who independently analyzed Mars Express (MEX) radio tracking data for the purpose of determining consistently the gravitational attraction of the moon Phobos on the MEX spacecraft, and hence the mass of Phobos. What is hidden inside those voids? On August 6, 2009, in an interview with the C-SPAN cable television program, American astronaut Buzz Aldrin said: "We should visit the moons of Mars. There's a monolith there -- a very unusual structure on this little potato shaped object that goes around Mars once every seven hours." Aldrin did not offer any further explanation of the mysterious structure. Aldrin added, "When people find out, they will say, 'who put that there? who put that there?' Well, the universe put it there. If you choose, God put it there." The moonlet in question is Phobos. As far as the secrets of the moonlet, well, Marina Popovich tried her best to get the world to pay attention, as did others, including Professor Burdakov. Apparently, Americans know quite a lot, too; as do others, which would explain why a new joint Russian-Chinese mission to Phobos was under discussion for years.

FAILED SEQUEL

China and Russia planned to launch a joint mission to Mars in 2009 to scoop up samples from the Red Planet and one of its moons. Russia would launch the spacecraft, while China would provide the survey equipment to carry out the unmanned exploration. The preparation for the joint mission was beset by a number of problems, and it was actually launched two years later than planned. After a very long break in its exploration of the solar system, Russia (with Chinese participation) did launch the risky mission to land on the mysterious Martian moon, Phobos, and to return samples of its soil back to Earth.

The mission, named Phobos-Grunt, failed almost immediately after its operational launch. By December 10, 2011, Roskosmos (Russian Federal Space Agency) and Russia's Ministry of Defence formed a joint operational group tasked to track the re-entry of the Phobos-Grunt spacecraft. The announcement about the creation of this task force essentially confirmed that the agency had exhausted all hopes for establishing control over the mission and the uncontrolled re-entry of the spacecraft had now been inevitable. The spacecraft did renter the Earth atmosphere on January 15, 2012.

The Roskosmos chief Vladimir Popovkin suggested Phobos-Grunt fell victim to foreign sabotage. A more plausible scenario for quick demise of Phobos-Grunt was leaked from industry sources to the online forum of the *Novosti Kosmonavtiki* magazine on January 17, 2012. The most likely culprit in the failure of the probe's propulsion unit to ignite soon after it had entered orbit (on November 9, 2011) was a programming error in the flight control system. The failure of Phobos-Grunt mission is a tragedy. Indeed, it was a tragedy not only for the Russian and Chinese space exploration programs. Since it was truly an international project, the failure impacted mankind's space exploration in general. Many scientists and leaders who pushed for the mission realize even now that the mysteries of Phobos are worth the risk. Does this mean that humanity will abandon its dream to reach Mars and its moons? Mars and its moons are most perplexing, without a doubt, and many of the answers we seek about Mars will only be answered when humans finally land on its surface. It could well be that there is more of a mystery here than just trying to explain Mars and its planetary formation. It would seem that our efforts to study the planet at close quarters are constantly dogged by either our own technical inadequacies or by circumstances that yet remain a complete mystery and quite rightly once again fall into the unexplained category. Thus, we remain haunted by the circumstances surrounding the Phobos 2 mission and the perplexing photograph it sent back to Earth shortly before it was lost in space.

CONCLUSION

Yuri Smirnov, a prominent Russian ufologist, once described the state of contemporary Russian ufology. He said that gone are the days when Soviet UFO research, as other aspects of Soviet life, was largely sheltered from Western influences. There was some, quite scant, one-way information exchange with foreign UFO research groups, limited basically to delivery of occasional Western publications. Thus, Soviet ufology remained "pure" and free from the influences of yellow and tabloid press. Scientific and military research conducted in the USSR was a forbidden subject, and only after the Gorbachev's *perestroika* did Soviet UFO researchers and those in the West interested in their research begin truly working together.

Moscow in 1987

The KGB, too, had its own programs and data collection, partially revealed in the early 1990s. Occasionally we see and hear sensational bits of information about other KGB UFO research aspects, and while such information may be true, we simply do not have the evidence in our hands to support it. In this book we have made every attempt to describe as fully as possible Soviet and Russian UFO cases, research areas, prominent personalities involved in such research (military, intelligence agencies, and civilian), the opinions and viewpoints of those who were and are serious in their approach to study of anomalous phenomena. Obviously, we will not give forum to dubious contactees; spinners of tall tales; sociopaths who deny Westerners the right to write about Russian ufology and who denigrate esteemed Russian and Ukrainian researchers that happen to have different views; UFO cultists, and other similar types. We thank those who have helped us in our endeavour, including Russian, Ukrainian,

Central Asian and other UFO researchers. They are all kind, intelligent, open-hearted people dedicated to the pursuit of knowledge. Our book is not meant be definitive, as that would be impossible, but it is meant to show the UFO research has been and still is very active in contemporary Russia, Ukraine, and other countries that once comprised the Soviet Union. We hope that by publishing this book we will enable greater cooperation between East and West in what some have called "The Greatest Mystery Known to Mankind." Only time will tell if we have been successful or not.

Please look for our companion book, RUSSIAS'S USO SECRETS .
Paul Stonehill and Philip Mantle.

MORE FROM FLYING DISK PRESS

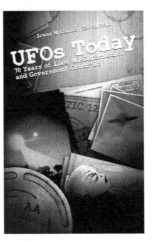

FOLLOW US ON FACEBOOK

https://www.facebook.com/flyingdiskpress

Printed in Great Britain
by Amazon